T0223530

Communications
in Computer and Information Science   333

Ming Zhou   Guodong Zhou   Dongyan Zhao
Qun Liu   Lei Zou (Eds.)

Natural Language Processing and Chinese Computing

First CCF Conference, NLPCC 2012
Beijing, China, October 31-November 5, 2012
Proceedings

 Springer

Volume Editors

Ming Zhou
Microsoft Research Asia
Beijing, China
E-mail: mingzhou@microsoft.com

Guodong Zhou
Soochow University
Suzhou, China
E-mail: gdzhou@suda.edu.cn

Dongyan Zhao
Peking University
Beijing, China
E-mail: zhaody@pku.edu.cn

Qun Liu
Institute of Computing Technology
Chinese Academy of Sciences
Beijing, China
E-mail: liuqun@ict.ac.cn

Lei Zou
Peking University
Beijing, China
E-mail: zoulei@pku.edu.cn

ISSN 1865-0929   e-ISSN 1865-0937
ISBN 978-3-642-34455-8   e-ISBN 978-3-642-34456-5
DOI 10.1007/978-3-642-34456-5
Springer Heidelberg Dordrecht London New York

Library of Congress Control Number: 2012949755

CR Subject Classification (1998): I.2.7, H.3.1, H.1.2, H.3.3, H.3.5, H.5.2, I.2.1

Typesetting: Camera-ready by author, data conversion by Scientific Publishing Services, Chennai, India

Printed on acid-free paper

Springer is part of Springer Science+Business Media (www.springer.com)

Preface

NLP&CC (CCF Conference on Natural Language Processing & Chinese Computing) is the annual conference of the CCF TCCI (Technical Committee of Chinese Information). As a leading conference in the field of NLP and Chinese computing of CCF, NLP&CC is the premier forum for NLP researchers and practitioners from academia, industry, and government in China and Asia Pacific area to share their ideas, research results and experiences, which will highly promote the research and technical innovation in these fields domestically and internationally. The papers contained in these proceedings address challenging issues in Web mining, search and ads, social networks, multi-lingual access, question answering as well as the fundamentals and applications in Chinese computing.

This year, NLP&CC received 151 submissions. After a thorough reviewing process, 27 English papers and 16 Chinese papers were selected for presentation as full papers. The acceptance rate is 28%. Furthermore, this year's NLP&CC also included nine posters. The Chinese full papers together with posters are published by ACTA Scientiarum Naturalium Universitatis Pekinensis, and are not included in this volume. This volume contains the 27 English full papers presented at NLP&CC 2012.

The high-quality program would not have been possible without the authors who chose NLP&CC 2012 as a venue for their publications. We are very grateful to the Program Committee members and Organizing Committee members, who put a tremendous amount of effort into soliciting and selecting research papers with a balance of high quality and new ideas and new applications.

We hope that you enjoy reading the proceedings of NLP&CC 2012.

October 2012

Ming Zhou
Guodong Zhou

Organization

NLP&CC 2012 was organized by the Technical Committee of Chinese Information of CCF, Peking University, and Microsoft Research Asia.

Organizing Committee

Conference Co-chairs
JianGuo Xiao — Peking University, China
Bo Zhang — Tsinghua University, China

Program Co-chairs
Ming Zhou — Microsoft Research Asia, China
Guodong Zhou — Soochow University, China

Area Chairs
Fundamentals on CIT
Houfeng Wang — Peking University, China

Applications on CIT
Zhi Tang — Peking University, China

Web Mining
Jun Zhao — Harbin Institute of Technology, China

Search and Ads
Shaoping Ma — Tsinghua University, China

NLP for Social Networks
Juanzi Li — Tsinghua University, China

Machine Translation
Qun Liu — Chinese Academy of Sciences, China

Question Answering
Xuanjing Huang — Fudan University, China

Demo Co-chairs

Haifeng Wang   Baidu corporation, China
Yi Guan   Harbin Institute of Technology, China

Organization Chair

Dongyan Zhao   Peking University, China

Publication Co-chairs

Qun Liu   Chinese Academy of Sciences, China
Lei Zou   Peking University, China

ADL/Tutorial Chair

Chengqing Zong   Chinese Academy of Sciences, China

Evaluation Chair

Xiaojun Wan   Peking University, China

Financial Chair

Zhengyu Zhu   China Computer Federation, China

Sponsor Chair

Dongyan Zhao   Peking University, China

Website Chair

Aixia Jia   Peking University, China

Program Committee

Yuki Arase   Microsoft Research Asia
Jiajun Chen   Nanjing University
Hsin-Hsi Chen   National Taiwan University
Xiaoqing Ding   Tsinghua University
Lei Duan   Microsoft Bing
Yang Feng   Sheffield University
Jianfeng Gao   Microsoft Research Redmond
Tingting He   Central China Normal University
Hongxu Hou   Inner Mongolia University
Yunhua Hu   Microsoft Research Asia
Degen Huang   Dalian University of Technology
Xuanqing Huang   Fudan University

Long Jiang	Alibaba Corp.
Wenbin Jiang	Chinese Academy of Sciences
Sadao Hurohash	Kyoto University
Wai Lam	The Chinese University of Hong Kong
Mu Li	Microsoft Research Asia
Baoli Li	Henan University of Technology
Juanzi Li	Tsing University
Wenjie Li	The Hong Kong Polytechnic University
Henry Li	Microsoft Research Asia
Ning Li	University of Science and Technology Beijing
Qingsheng Li	Anyang Normal University
Shoushan Li	Soochow University
Dekag Lin	Google
Hongfei Lin	Dalian University of Technology
Bingquan Liu	Harbin Institute of Technology
Changsong Liu	Tsinghua University
Qun Liu	Chinese Academy of Sciences
Ting Liu	Harbin Institute of Technology
Xiaohua Liu	Microsoft Research Asia
Yang Liu	Tsinghua University
Yajuan Lv	Chinese Academy of Sciences
Xueqiang Lv	TRS
Qing Ma	RyuKoku University
Yanjun Ma	Baidu
Jun Ma	Shandong University
Shaoping Ma	Tsinghua University
Yuji Matsumoto	Nara Institute of Science and Technology
Massaki Nagata	NIT
Jianyun Nie	University of Montreal
Cheng Niu	Microsoft Bing
Tao Qin	Microsoft Research Asia
Liyun Ru	Sohu
Xiaodong Shi	Xiameng University
Shumin Shi	Beijing Institute of Technology
Shuming Shi	Microsoft Research Asia
Rou Song	Beijing Language and Culture University
Jinsong Su	Xiameng University
Zhi Tang	Peking University
Jie Tang	Tsinghua University
Junichi Tsujii	Microsoft Research Asia
Xiaojun Wan	Peking University
Bin Wang	Chinese Academy of Sciences
Haifeng Wang	Baidu
Houfeng Wang	Peking University

Mingwen Wang	Jiangxi Normal University
Xiaojie Wang	Beijing University of Posts and
	Telecommunications
Wenjun Wang	Tianjin University
Bo Wang	Tianjin University
Furu Wei	Microsoft Research Asia
Yunqing Xia	Tsinghua University
Jianguo Xiao	Peking University
Deyi Xiong	Singapore I2R
Jinan Xu	Beijing Jiaotong University
Jun Xu	Microsoft Research Asia
Endong Xun	Beijing Language and Culture University
Muyun Yang	Harbin Institute of Technology
Zhengtao Yu	Kunming University of Science and Technology
Chengxiang Zhai	University of Illinois at Urbana-Champaign
Jiajun Zhang	Chinese Academy of Sciences
Ruiqiang Zhang	Yahoo
Min Zhang	Tsinghua University
Min Zhang	Singapore I2R
Yangsen Zhang	Beijing Information Science and Technology
	University
Dongdong Zhang	Microsoft Research Asia
Yujie Zhang	Beijing Jiaotong University
Shiqi Zhao	Baidu
Dongyan Zhao	Peking University
Jun Zhao	Chinese Academy of Sciences
Tiejun Zhao	Harbin Institute of Technology
Hai Zhao	Shanghai Jiaotong University
Guodong Zhou	Soochow University
Ming Zhou	Microsoft Research Asia
Jingbo Zhu	Northeastern University
Qiaoming Zhu	Soochow University
Qing Zhu	Renming University
Chengqing Zong	Chinese Academy of Sciences
Ngodrup	Tibet University
Turgun Ibrahim	Xinjing University
Nasun-Urt	Inner Mongolia University
Tse ring rgyal	Qinghai Normal University

Organizers

Organized by

China Computer Federation, China

Hosted by

Peking University   Microsoft Research Asia

In Cooperation with:

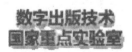 

State Key Laboratory   ACTA Scientiarum   Springer
of Digital Publishing,   Naturalium Universitatis
Beijing, China   Pekinensis

Sponsoring Institutions

Sina Weibo   Tencent Weibo   Mingbo Education Technology

Table of Contents

Applications on Language Computing

Fundamentals on Language Computing

Machine Translation and Multi-lingual Information Access

NLP for Search, Ads and Social Networks

Question Answering and Web Mining

Personalized Paper Recommendation Based on User Historical Behavior

Yuan Wang[1], Jie Liu[1,*], XingLiang Dong[1], Tianbi Liu[2], and YaLou Huang[1,2]

[1] College of Information Technology Science, Nankai University, Tianjin, China
[2] College of Software, Nankai University, Tianjin, China
{yayaniuzi23,dongxingliang,liutianbi}@mail.nankai.edu.cn,
{jliu,huangyl}@nankai.edu.cn

Abstract. With the increasing of the amount of the scientific papers, it is very important and difficult for paper-sharing platforms to recommend related papers accurately for users. This paper tackles the problem by proposing a method that models user historical behavior. Through collecting the operations on scientific papers of online users and carrying on the detailed analysis, we build preference model for each user. The personalized recommendation model is constructed based on content-based filtering model and statistical language model.. Experimental results show that users' historical behavior plays an important role in user preference modeling and the proposed method improves the final predication performance in the field of technical papers recommendation.

Keywords: Personalized Recommendation, User Historical behavior, Similarity, Recommendation Model.

1 Introduction

With the rapid development of the Internet, researchers tend to share and search for papers in Digital Libraries (DLs). Most latest papers first appear on the Internet for researchers to search for and to read, which means DLs are stepping into a golden age. Nowadays there are some famous platform providing researchers rapidly sharing academic achievements, such as arXiv.org, sponsored by Cornell University and Science Paper Online(www.paper.edu.cn),sponsored by the Ministry of Education of China. However, the number of papers on the Internet grows exponentially, bringing the problems of information overload, which makes it difficult for researchers to find useful information efficiently. Faced up with these problems, recommendation technique is one of the most effective means. So far, Elsevier, PubMed and SpringLink have offered recommendation service for their users. These sites offer paper recommendation that meets users' personal interests by sending them emails or through RSS subscription. But all the recommendation requires users to state their interests explicitly, either to provide information about their interested categories initiatively.

---

* Corresponding author.

M. Zhou et al. (Eds.): NLPCC 2012, CCIS 333, pp. 1–12, 2012.
© Springer-Verlag Berlin Heidelberg 2012

In this paper, we proposed a personalized recommendation model based on researchers' expressions of interest through analysis of their historical behavior in which users do not need to specify their preference explicitly. In a paper sharing system, the users are usually researchers from different areas, and they have specific preference for certain areas. Therefore, we hypothesize that the users' interests can be excavated from their behaviors on the site that are accumulated spontaneously when they browse the pages, which does not need extra provision. By collecting and analyzing users' behavioral information bearing users' interests, we built a personalized recommendation model and choose candidate papers for recommendation. The experiment shows that our recommendation model based on users' behaviors improves the accuracy of paper recommendation.

For newly registered and inactive users whose behavioral information is scarce and easy to be noisy, we cannot get thorough knowledge about their preference, so it's hard to provide service for them well. Meanwhile, such as user A and user B share same preference, user B and user C have close preference, but A and C share a little same content or papers. So it is hard for us to find some correlation between A and C ,which ignoring potential association between the two . To solve this problem, we further optimize our model, which will be showed in detail in Section 3. In the experiment section, we discussed the optimization of our model.

The paper is organized as follows. Section 1 introduces related work. Section 2 discusses how to build personalized recommendation model based on users' behaviors. Section 3 makes an analysis on relationship of user preference transmission and we go further into how to optimize the model for new and inactive users. Section 4 verifies the accuracy of our personalized recommendation model to recommend through experiments. The last section briefly comes to some conclusions and proposes future work.

2   Related Work

Personalized Recommendation is an active service technique, in which servers collect and analyze user information to learn about their behaviors and interests to build a model, and provide services that meet their personal needs based on the personalized interest model. Nowadays, many personalization systems have been built to achieve personalized service in different ways, among which information filtering is a relatively successful one. There are two mainly approaches in filtering: collaborative filtering and content-based filtering.

Collaborative filtering approach[1] is to filter information based on the similarity of users. AT&T Lab built PHOAKS[2] and REFERRAL Web[3] recommendation system in 1997. Kurt[4] introduced personalized recommendation based on collaborative filtering approach to CiteSeer search engine in 2000. Being able to filter some complex concepts such as information quality and taste, which are hard to express, this approach is mainly used in commercial recommendation systems like Amazon[1] , eBay[2] and Douban[3] . However, because of large resource sets and the sparseness of rating data, collaborative filtering fails to solve the problems of cold start and others. Recently researches focus on creating virtual users to augment grading for items[5], explain new products with fuzzy natural language processing[6], or cluster users and apply collaborative filtering to clustered groups[7].

Content-based filtering approach has a simple and effective structure, which is mainly used in text recommendation system[8] and hybrid collaborative filtering recommendation[9]. The earliest recommendation system was based on content-based filtering including Web Watcher[10], LIRA[11], Leticia[12] and et al. All of them recommended resources by evaluating the similarity between resource content and user interest.

Personalized recommendation for scientific papers draws the attention of providing service for researchers. McNee[13] realized recommendation by building paper reference graph with collaborative filtering. Torres[14] combined collaborative filtering with content-based filtering. Since Torres accepted recommendation results from other systems before filtering, it was difficult to implement such input, thus preventing it from being applied to practical applications. Yang [15]proposed a sort-oriented collaborative filtering approach, which extracted users' behavioral preference from users' web log and coped with the cold start problem in collaborative filtering. But noises we mentioned above in web log reduced the credibility of web data and affected the results of recommendation.

Notice that scientific papers consist of text and text can imply rich information. Taking into account the issues of sparse data and cold start in collaborative filtering, we believe that content-based filtering is more effective. Up to now, recommendation by extracting text reflecting users' preference from the log and building preference model for users has proved to be effective. Based on statistical principles, Chu and Park[16]built users' personalized model with metadata, which means treat papers users read as a unit. Kim[17] et al. designed user frequency model according to terms' weight through users' web log to recommend based on content.

The methods mentioned above mainly based on inter-citation by the historical papers[13][18], or based on use of user's browse log [16][17][14]. While modeling based on references between papers didn't take each researcher's interest into all-sided consideration. When considering web log, they treat user as a center, but overlook the noise problem inside. The method we propose in this paper utilizes users' structured behavioral information on the scientific paper sharing site with content-based filtering to provide personalized recommendation for registered users.

---

[1] http://www.amazon.com/

[2] http://www.ebay.com/

[3] http://www.douban.com/

3   Personalized Recommendation Model

To implement user-centered personalized recommendation, we first need to track users' behavior to collect sufficient information and figure out what can reflect users' features. The selection of behaviors has a great influence on modeling user preference. By analyzing the structure of the site and its records as well as existing data, we chose the following behaviors to represent users' preference: publishing a paper, marking a paper as favorite, rating a paper, making a comment, and tagging a paper. All above are users' active operations on papers. For each user, we extract the title, abstract and keywords of papers that they operate on to form a text file as their configuration file. The personalize recommendation model we propose in this paper is to use users' profile, according to which the paper sets are filtered by content and then recommendation sets are formed.

We define recommendation task as a triple relationship: (D_i, D_x, U), in which U refers to the current user, D_x is the document set the user is viewing, and D_i is the document set to be recommended to the user. We adopt probability model to calculate the probability that we recommend D_i, given the current user U and the document set D_x being viewed. We define the similarity between our recommended resource and user as:

$$P(d_i|u_k, d_x) = \frac{P(u_k, d_x|d_i) \cdot P(d_i)}{P(u_k, d_x)} \tag{1}$$

To make it easier to calculate $P(d_i|u_k, d_x)$, we suppose that users and documents draw from independent identical distribution. Then,

$$P(d_i|u_k, d_x) = \frac{P(u_k|d_i) \cdot P(d_x|d_i) \cdot P(d_i)}{P(u_k, d_x)} \tag{2}$$

Given that the current user is viewing the current paper, $P(u_k, d_x)$ is constant. Therefore the similarity between user and paper is proportion to the numerator:

$$P(d_i|u_k, d_x) \propto P(u_k|d_i) \cdot P(d_x|d_i) \cdot P(d_i) \tag{3}$$

Then the solution to the model can be achieved by calculating $P(u_k|d_i)$, $P(d_x|d_i)$, $P(d_i)$, in the condition of current user u_k and the paper d_x being viewed now. In Equation (3), $P(u_k|d_i)$ denotes users' preference. Without $P(u_k|d_i)$, it will become statistical language model which acts as a baseline. We define the above three as similarity between the user and the paper, similarity between papers and the priori probability of a document respectively. We discuss details about them in the following part.

3.1   Priori Probability of Paper

The priori probability of paper here means to evaluate the probability that a document will be selected. It is evaluated by users' historical behaviors to grading papers throughout the global website. We make a reasonable assumption that a document is more valuable when global users operate more on it. First, we define users' behavior set: A= {down, keep, visit, tag, score, comment, collect,···} which refers to downloading, marking as favorite, viewing, tagging, scoring, commenting and so on. D is the set of all documents in the corpus. Then we have:

$$P(d_i) = \prod_{a \in A} P(d_i|a) = \prod_{a \in A} \frac{C(d_i|a)}{\sum_{d_j \in D} C(d_j|a)} \qquad (4)$$

In the equation, a iterates all behaviors in A, and $C(d_i|a)$ is the number of operations users had on document d_i. We assume that all behaviors are independent because of the randomness of users' behaviors. The normalized probability of behaviors is used as an overall evaluation for documents.

Considering that records for user-registered users are sparse, or that bad-quality documents might have few users' behavior records, the value of Eigen function $C(d_i|a)$ is 0. To avoid this situation, we adopted a technology named absolute discount smoothing[19]. It is to subtract a constant value from events in the model, and distribute the subtracted values evenly into events that do not appear. In this paper, the value of Eigen function is term frequency and we do not have to add up the probabilities to 1 when discounting. We assign a small value (0.1 in this paper) to those whose Eigen function values are 0 to achieve absolute discount smoothing, so that they can get a lower score.

$$C(d_i|a) = \begin{cases} C(d_i|a) & , C(d_i|a) \neq 0 \\ 0.1 & , C(d_i|a) = 0 \end{cases} \qquad (5)$$

3.2 Similarity between Papers

We mention $P(d_x|d_i)$ as the similarity between paper d_x and paper d_i. We can easily apply statistical language model on it. The title, abstract, keywords can give a graphic description of the document, while the domain of area of it is decided by users who was submitters. So we use the title, abstract, keywords and domain of area as documents' feature, and calculate the similarity through word segmentation:

$$P(d_x|d_i) = \sum_{w \in d_x} P(w|d_i) = \sum_{w \in d_x} ((1-a) \cdot \frac{tf(w, d_i)}{tf(d_i)} + a \cdot \frac{tf(w, D)}{tf(D)}) \qquad (6)$$

where w refers to any word in the document d_x. $tf(w, d_i)$ is the frequency in which w appears in d_i. $tf(d_i)$ means the frequency of all words in d_i. $tf(w, D)$ is the frequency that w appears in all documents, and $tf(D)$ is the total frequency that all words appear in all documents. a is a parameter used for smoothing (we use 0.1 here).

3.3 Similarity between User and Paper

The similarity between the user and the document is represented $P(u_k|d_i)$, where users' preference information becomes fully integrated into personalized recommendation model. According to VSM (Vector Space Model), we discompose user information and document information into terms, to calculate the similarity based on probability statistics language model. The representation of document is the same as discussed in 3.2. Users are represented, as mentioned above, through the characteristic of preference model built according to users' behaviors. We can get the similarity between the two:

$$P(u_k|d_i) = \sum_{w \in W_k} P(w, u_k|d_i) = \sum_{w \in W_k} P(u_k|w, d_i) \cdot P(w|d_i), \qquad (7)$$

where W_k refers to the entry set in user k's Eigen space. Since the one-dimensional characteristic of user and document is independent, we have:

$$P(u_k|w, d_i) \approx P(u_k|w), \qquad (8)$$

Under our assumption, the final equation is:

$$P(u_k|d_i) = \sum_{w \in W_k} P(w, u_k|d_i) \approx \sum_{w \in W_k} P(u_k|w) \cdot P(w|d_i), \qquad (9)$$

where $P(u_k|w)$ refers to the ratio of w appears in user u_k and in all users.

$$P(u_k|w) = \frac{tf(w, u_k)}{tf(u_k)} \qquad (10)$$

The measurement of $P(w|d_i)$ is the same as what is mentioned in 3.2.

4   The Optimization of the Model

In practical applications, the amount of terms in documents and the number of users are quite huge-larger than a hundred thousand. Despite the enormous total amount, the term vectors for each user are usually rather sparse. For one user: Firstly, a user has a specific area of interest, and he does not care about other areas. Therefore, terms in other areas are meaningless for the user, making the user-word matrix global sparse, local dense. Secondly, if a user has just registered or has little information, almost all values of his terms are 0. The above two points both will lead to data sparse. With sparse data, content-based recommendation will not get a good performance. For example, we suppose three users:A,B and C, where B focuses on interdisciplinary. When A and B have high relevance to each other, while B and C share same interests. But because A and C have a few common preference, we directly consider A and C don't have any relevance, which ignores potential associations between them [20]paper21. When recommendation papers for A, it will male recommendation results confined to a certain field without C's field blind to A. This problem is also recommendation technical difficult problem. Under this circumstance, we need to get relevant information from other users as global information to make up complement users with less information. To cope with the problem of insufficient information, we have to increase the density of the third part of our model.[20] predicted the missing items by diffusion and iterative optimization method to smooth the original matrix, so as to increase the density of matrix. Here we redefine user-word matrix based on random walk. In Equation (9), $P(u_k|w)$ needs to be calculated from the whole domain. We built a UW matrix, i.e., user-word matrix as follows:

$$C(U,W) = \begin{pmatrix} C_{u_1w_1} & \cdots & C_{u_1w_m} \\ \vdots & \ddots & \vdots \\ C_{u_kw_1} & \cdots & C_{u_kw_m} \end{pmatrix} \tag{11}$$

In Matrix (11), $C_{u_iw_j}$ refers to the frequency in which w_j appears in u_i. Normalize the matrix by column, and we can get

$$P(U,W) = \begin{pmatrix} P_{u_1w_1} & \cdots & P_{u_1w_m} \\ \vdots & \ddots & \vdots \\ P_{u_kw_1} & \cdots & P_{u_kw_m} \end{pmatrix} \tag{12}$$

In Matrix (12), $P_{u_iw_j}$ is the percentage of the number of occurrence of w_j in u_i to that of w_j in all user configuration files, i.e., the value of $P(u_k|w_j)$.

We normalize $C(U,W)$ by row, and get a new matrix:

$$P(W,U) = \begin{pmatrix} P_{w_1u_1} & \cdots & P_{w_1u_k} \\ \vdots & \ddots & \vdots \\ P_{w_mu_1} & \cdots & P_{w_mu_k} \end{pmatrix} \tag{13}$$

where $P_{w_iu_j}$ is a ratio of the number of occurrence of w_j in u_i to the number of that of all words in u_i.

In order to reduce the number of 0 in the matrix, we randomly walk on UW matrix which means multiply $P(W,U)$ and $P(U,W)$ to get a new $C^n(U,W)$, it's defined as follows:

$$C^n(U,W) = C(U,W) \cdot [P(W,U) \cdot P(U,W)]^{n-1} \tag{14}$$

where $C^1(U,W) = C(U,W)$, as the number of iteration increases, the matrix will become denser and denser. But on the other side, the deviation with the original term frequency matrix becomes larger, and comes to a constant number in the end. Therefore, the number of tighten is determined by the equation (15):

$$n = \arg\min_n |C^{n+1}(U,W) - C^n(U,W)| \tag{15}$$

If the change exceeds a given threshold, it stops. Maintain each tighten matrix and we mix the primitive matrix with it. As equation (16) shows, a is influence factor, which measures the original matrix and iterative matrix how effect the description in the user preferences.

$$C^{final}(U, W) = (1 - a) \cdot C(U, W) + a \cdot C^n(U, W) \tag{16}$$

In this section, we optimize the original user preference modeling based on random walk model, where the potential association between users is taken into account. After optimization, the content for new or inactive users can be complemented, so that we can provide better content-based recommendation. Meanwhile we take advantage of delivery relationship among users' content, which improve the performance in predicting users' potential preference. Beyond that, we filter more interesting things to recommend to users.

5   Experiments

In this section, we will examine the performance of our content-based method personalized recommendation model based on users' behaviors. Here we carry on three groups of experiments. The first experiment compared the recommendation results of considering users' preference and without considering. Beyond that, we analysis the optimal model based on random walk with different iteration times. Finally, combining preference information after optimal iteration and original preference, we get a fusion model to find the better solution for select better technique papers to recommend. The results show that the optimized model has a good performance for recommendation as well as good robustness.

5.1   Dataset

Our dataset is provided by Science Paper Online (www.paper.edu.cn), which is a well-known scientific paper sharing system. On this platform, researchers can fast share their papers, do some reviewing, tagging, etc. Especially, the section of "the First Publications " shares the first published scientific research from users. Users in the website can publish, keep, download, visit, tag, score and make comments about papers. In the experiments , we choose five actions to represent users' preference: publishing, keeping, tagging, commenting and scoring. The data we use include users' behavioral information and first publish of papers from October 1, 2010 to March 1, 2011.

According to the practical situation of the website, we got test data as (U, D_x, D_i, L) after processing the original data. U refers to user id. D_x is the paper the user is currently reading, while D_i is the paper to be recommended and L refers to a label. In this paper, we assign L the value 1 when users are interested in the recommended paper with clicking and the value 0 when they are not interested. There are 638 data samples, 339 labeled with 1 and 299 with 0. Involved are 26 users and 93 papers. We divide them into 108 groups.

In our personalized recommendation model, papers with a higher probability mean more confidence to recommend, while papers with a lower probability are not recommended to users.

5.2   Quantitative Evaluation

In recommendation, it is necessary as IR to evaluation the top recommendation results. We utilize the MAP and $NDCG$ in information retrieval to evaluate our recommendation model. MAP is short for Mean Average Precision:

$$MAP = \frac{\sum\limits_{k} avgP_k}{N_d}, \qquad (17)$$

where N_d is the total number of papers currently viewed , $avgP_k$ is the average accuracy of recommended papers when paper k is viewed. It is defined as:

$$avgP_k = \sum_{j=1}^{M} \frac{p(j) \cdot l(j)}{C(d_i)}, \qquad (18)$$

where M is size of recommended paper set, $p(j)$ is the accuracy of first j recommended papers, $l(j)$ is label information, which is 1 if the recommended paper is relevant and 0 if not.$C(d_i)$ is the total number of related papers to the viewed one d_i.MAP reflects the accuracy of recommendation and evaluates the global effectiveness of personalized model.

The second criterion is $NDCG$ (Normalized Discounted Cumulative Gain), which is sort-oriented.$NDCG$ is applied to evaluate the accuracy of top results in recommendation set.

Given a sorted paper sequence, the $NDCG$ of the nth paper $NDCG@n$ is:

$$NDCG@n = Z_n \sum_{i=1}^{n} \frac{(2^{r(i)-1})}{\log(1+i)}, \qquad (19)$$

where $r(i)$ refers to the relevant grade of ith paper and Z_n is a normalized parameter, which assures and the values $NDCG@n$ of top results add up to 1. If the number of result set is less than r, the value of $NDCG@n$ is re-calculated. In this paper, we experiment with the evaluation from $NDCG@1$ to $NDCG@6$.

5.3   Experiment Results

Three groups of experiments have been designed. The first experiment compared the recommendation results of considering users' preference and without considering. In this group experiment, we use original user-word matrix to represent users' preference. The following is the comparison:

The result of comparison shows that the MAP of personalized recommendation model is improved from 86% to 91%, increased by nearly five percent . Figure 1(b) shows the recommendation accuracy evaluated using $NDCG@1$ to $NDCG@6$, and the average improvement of $NDCG$ is 10.2%. It verifies the effectiveness of our recommendation model with users' preference based on their behavior .

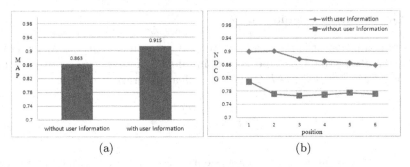

Fig. 1. Comparision on MAP (a) and NDCG (b)

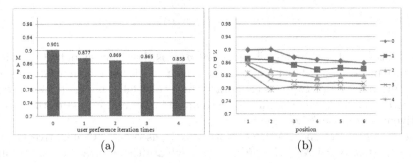

Fig. 2. Comparision between different iterations on MAP (a) and NDCG (b)

For the optimized part of the model, we test different setting of parameter
n of dense matrix with experiment, and results are shown in Fig. 2(different
graphic symbol means different iteration times). Fig. 2 reveal that the performance of the model declines as the number of interations increases. When the
number of iterations are 0, 1, 2, 3, the degrees of decrease are similar to each
other. The more iterations, the sharper MAP declines. This is because that the
original information is lost as the number of iterations increases. Users' personalized information will be lost when we random walk on the user-word matrix.So
we adopt the method of weighting to evaluate the model. Having compare original user preference to fusion model with weighted iteration information, as per
equation(16). The generalized cross-validation leads to a good selection of reg-
ularization parameters a (In equation (16), here is set 0.35). we get Fig. 3(a)
and Fig. 3(b)(represent as $ori + n$, where ori means original model, n means the
iteration times): Figure 3(a) shows that when we take the original information
into account and iterate the user-word matrix once, the effect is better than
that without iteration information. When iterating more than twice (such as
twice and third), fusion model get increasement compared with original model,
approximately 0.1%. But iterating more than three times result in performance
degradation(see in Fig. 3(a) column 5). It's concluded that fusion model with
one time iteration has got a best performance under our algorithm.

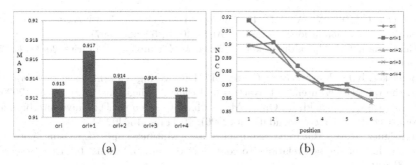

Fig. 3. Comparision between fusion model on MAP (a) and NDCG (b)

This section conducted experiments to evaluate the personalized recommendation model based on users' behavior and got relatively good results, which verified the effectiveness of the model. It can be concluded from the experiment results that analyzing users' behaviors is useful to recommendation model, because it makes the recommendation more personalized and can satisfying to users' different needs.

6   Conclusion

In this paper we proposed a personalized recommendation model based on users' historical behavior, which can effectively represent researchers' interests. With users' preference profile extracted from historical behavior, this paper generates recommendation with the help of content from user model and paper information. Try to avoid recommending one-sided due to modeling only based on single user himself and ignore the relationship between them, we introduce random walk model in original model to helping correlation transformation between users. Therefore new users and inactive users both benefit from it. Experimental results verified the effectiveness of our model in the field of technique papers recommendation. But as the amount of data increases, it is unnecessary to conduct global recommendation for users within specific areas. Clustering before analysis can help to reduce the recommendation set. In the future we will think about clustering based on content and filtering preference-deviating information to improve the performance further.

Acknowledgments. Thanks to the anonymous reviewers, especially regarding writing and experiments. This research is supported by the National Natural Science Foundation of China under Grant No. 61105049.

References

1. Liu, R.-R., Jia, C.-X., Zhou, T., Sun, D., Wang, B.-H.: Personal recommendation via modified collaborative filtering. Physica A: Statistical Mechanics and its Applications 388(4), 462–468 (2009)

2. Terveen, L., Hill, W., Amento, B., McDonald, D., Creter, J.: Phoaks: a system for sharing recommendations. Commun. ACM 40(3), 59–62 (1997)
3. McKiernan, G.: The hidden web. Science & Technology Libraries 20(4), 65–74 (2001)
4. Bollacker, K.D., Lawrence, S., Giles, C.L.: Discovering relevant scientific literature on the web. IEEE Intelligent Systems and their Applications 15(2), 42–47 (2000)
5. Seung-Taek, P., David, P., Omid, M., Nathan, G., Dennis, D.: Naive filterbots for robust cold-start recommendations (2006), 10.1145/1150402.1150490
6. Rodriguez, R.M., Macarena Espinilla, P.J.S., Marínez-López, L.: Using linguistic incomplete preference relations to cold start recommendations. Internet Research 20(3) (2010)
7. Zhenhuan, H.: The study of personalized recommendation based on web data mining. In: 2011 IEEE 3rd International Conference on Communication Software and Networks (ICCSN), pp. 386–390 (2011)
8. Adomavicius, G., Tuzhilin, A.: Context-Aware Recommender Systems Recommender Systems Handbook, pp. 217–253. Springer, US (2011)
9. Yize, L., Jiazhong, N., Yi, Z., Bingqing, W., Baoshi, Y., Fuliang, W.: Contextual recommendation based on text mining (2010)
10. Armstrong, R., Dayne Freitag, T.J., Mitchell, T.: Webwatcher: A learning apprentice for the world wide web (1995)
11. Balabanovic, M., Shoham, Y.: Learning Information Retrieval Agents: Experiments with Automated Web Browsing. In: AAAI Spring Symposium on Information Gathering from Heterogenous, Distributed Resources, Stanford, CA, pp. 13–18 (1995)
12. Lieberman, H.: Letizia: An agent that assists web browsing. In: International Joint Conference on Aritificial Intelligence, pp. 924–929
13. McNee, S.M., Albert, I., Cosley, D., Gopalkrishnan, P., Lam, S.K., Rashid, A.M., Konstan, J.A., Riedl, J.: On the recommending of citations for research papers. In: Proceedings of the 2002 ACM Conference on Computer Supported Cooperative Work, CSCW 2002, pp. 116–125. ACM, New York (2002)
14. Torres, R., McNee, S.M., Abel, M., Konstan, J.A., Riedl, J.: Enhancing digital libraries with techlens+ (2004)
15. Yang, C., Wei, B., Wu, J., Zhang, Y., Zhang, L.: Cares: a ranking-oriented cadal recommender system. In: Proceedings of the 9th ACM/IEEE-CS Joint Conference on Digital Libraries, JCDL 2009, pp. 203–212. ACM, New York (2009)
16. Chu, W., Park, S.T.: Personalized recommendation on dynamic content using predictive bilinear models (2009)
17. Kim, H.-N., Ha, I., Lee, S.-H., Jo, G.-S.: A Collaborative Approach to User Modeling for Personalized Content Recommendations. In: Buchanan, G., Masoodian, M., Cunningham, S.J. (eds.) ICADL 2008. LNCS, vol. 5362, pp. 215–224. Springer, Heidelberg (2008)
18. Kautz, H., Selman, B., Shah, M.: Referral web: combining social networks and collaborative filtering. Communication of ACM 40(3), 63–65 (1997)
19. Martin, S.C., Ney, H., Zaplo, J.: Smoothing methods in maximum entropy language modeling. In: IEEE International Conference on Acoustics, Speech, and Signal Processing, vol. 1, pp. 545–548 (1999)
20. Huang, Z., Chen, H., Zeng, D.: Applying associative retrieval techniques to alleviate the sparsity problem in collaborative filtering. ACM Transactions on Information Systems 22(1), 116–142 (2004)

Integration of Text Information and Graphic Composite for PDF Document Analysis

Canhui Xu[1,2,3], Zhi Tang[1,3], Xin Tao[1,3], and Cao Shi[1]

[1] Institute of Computer Science and Technology, Peking University, Beijing, China
[2] Postdoctoral Workstation of the Zhongguancun Haidian Science Park and Peking University Founder Group Co. Ltd, Beijing, China
[3] State Key Laboratory of Digital Publishing Technology, Beijing, China
{ccxu09,caoshi}@yeah.net, tommie@founder.com.cn,
jolly.tao@pku.edu.cn

Abstract. The trend of large scale digitization has greatly motivated the research on the processing of the PDF documents with little structure information. Challenging problems like graphic segmentation integrating with texts remain unsolved for successful practical application of PDF layout analysis. To cope with PDF documents, a hybrid method incorporating text information and graphic composite is proposed to segment the pages that are difficult to handle by traditional methods. Specifically, the text information is derived accurately from born-digital documents embedded with low-level structure elements in explicit form. Then page text elements are clustered by applying graph based method according to proximity and feature similarity. Meanwhile, the graphic components are extracted by means of texture and morphological analysis. By integrating the clustered text elements with image based graphic components, the graphics are segmented for layout analysis. The experimental results on pages of PDF books have shown satisfactory performance.

Keywords: PDF document, graphic segmentation, graph based method, text clustering.

1 Introduction

Large-scale digitization projects undergoing at public and commercial digital libraries, such as the Million Book Project and the Google Book Search database, have indicated the significance and necessity of large scale processing of electronic documents. Different from scanned documents, the born-digital documents are generated by document processing software such as Microsoft Word, PowerPoint and LaTex. In addition, it has reliable typesetting information, such as embedded style and font information for textual content. However, current digitalization and OCRed format like Portable Document Format (PDF) documents contain no logical structure at any high level, such as explicitly delimited paragraphs, captions, or figures. By using formatting and font features embedded within the document, identifying logical structure of the document has attracted much attention both in academic and practical fields.

M. Zhou et al. (Eds.): NLPCC 2012, CCIS 333, pp. 13–22, 2012.

As the premise of robustness of logical layout understanding, various researches on layout analysis of PDF format documents were launched [1-2]. ICDAR (International Conference on Document Analysis and Recognition) has already held two competitions on Book Structure Extraction Competition focusing on structure recognition and extraction for digitized books [3-4]. It is well known that text only documents like novels are relatively easy to handle for PDF converters [1]. In applications of converting PDF to re-flowable formats like ePub or CEBX (Common e-Document of Blending XML), reliable layout analysis is highly desired to enrich the reading experience of e-book on small portable screens of handheld devices, such as mobile phone and PDA. Due to the large variety of the documents categories, open problems remain challenging for reliable layout analysis of PDF converters, including graph recognition integrating with text segmentation [1], tables and equation identification, etc..

Current page segmentation methods participating in ICDAR Page Segmentation Competitions perform better in separating text than non-text regions [5]. However, it is claimed that the leading text segmentation algorithms still have limitations for contemporary consumer magazine [2]. Illustrative graphic segmentation receives little attention. A complete layout understanding system requires that the full reconstruction of the document in scale of both high semantic and low-level [6]. For this purpose, the graphics in documents need to be segmented and identified accurately.

2   Related Work

Image-based document analysis and understanding has been discussed for decades. Most of the existing research concentrates on inputs objects like scanned images or camera documents. Image-based document layout analysis segments the document image into homogenous geometric regions by using features like proximity, texture or whitespace. Most of the research has been done on connect components (CCs) of page images. The "docstrum" method [7] exploited the k nearest-neighbor pairs between connect component centers by features like distance and angle. Kise [8] pointed out that connected components of black pixels can be utilized as primitives so as to simplify the task of page segmentation by combining connected components appropriately. It performed page segmentation based on area Voronoi diagrams by using distance and area ratio of connected components for deleting superfluous edges. Simon [9] proposed a bottom-up method based on Kruskal algorithm to classify the text and graph. Xiao [10] utilized a Delaunay triangulation on the point set from the bounded connected components, and described the page structure by dividing the Delaunay triangles into text area and fragment regions. Ferilli [11] used the distance between connect component borders for bottom-up grouping method. Recently, Koo [12] developed a new approach to assign state estimation on CCs to perform text block identification and text line extraction. It claims that the limitation of this method suffers from non-text objects.

The methodologies in page segmentation can be extended for digital-born documents analysis such as PDF documents. A large number of documents are created or converted in PDF format. These documents represent characters and images in explicit form, which can be straightforwardly exploited for layout analysis. Graphic, also called as figure or illustration in certain context, is a powerful way of illustrating and presenting the key ideas or findings. It has various categories such as photograph from conventional cameras or microscopes, drawing, 2D or 3D plot, diagram and flow chart. In PDF, figures and tables usually need to be recognized through grouping page primitives such as lines, curves, images and even text elements. Current digital library metadata has little improvement in graphic identification covering all kinds of documents. There exist several attempts in graphic identification and understanding. Chao [13] proposed a method to identify and extract graphic illustrations for PDF documents, which is based on the proximity of page elements. Shao [14] focused the research on graphic recognition of figures in vector-based PDF documents by using machine learning to classify figures with various grapheme statistics, which aims at the application of diagram retrieval. However, the extraction of the figure content including graphics and the text inside the figures is accomplished by grouping the primitives near the end of the content stream in PDF articles published with a standard Adobe FrameMaker template, which is not the common case in most of PDF books or magazines. The Xed system [15] is proposed to convert PDF to XML, and it claimed that traditional document analysis will drastically improve PDF's content extraction.

It is reported that the detection of graphic components and their integration with text segmentation will greatly improve the layout analysis performance [1]. In this paper, the goal is to group text into visually homogeneous regions and recognize the graph object integrating with text elements. A hybrid method is proposed and its application on PDF documents is presented. The preprocessing step and the graph based method are presented in Section 3 and 4. Its application on PDF sources is presented at section 5. The conclusion is given in Section 6.

3   Preprocessing

It is assumed that the inherent meta-data structure information can be provided by born-digital documents like true PDFs, other than PDF files embedded with scanned document page image. The PDF documents are described by low-level structural objects like text elements, lines, curves and images etc., and associated style attributes such as font, color, etc.. All the basic low-level elements from a PDF document are extracted in preprocessing step. The PDF parser using in this work is provided by Founder Corporation to parser the low-level objects, which is introduced in [16]. Basic objects here imply the elements or primitives in each page, which cannot be subdivided into smaller objects, including text, image elements or operations. The composite object is constituted by basic objects with certain predefined similarity. A graphic object includes picture, geometric graphic or graphic character element. From another perspective, text elements can be categorize as body text from the article, text belonging to graph or picture (or image), text inside table, and text for footer, header or other decorations, etc..

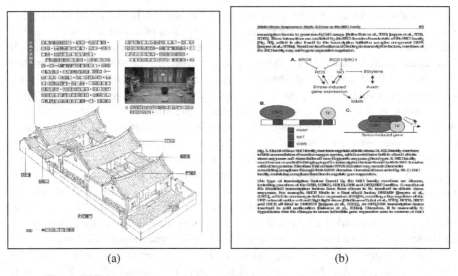

(a)   (b)

Fig. 1. PDF document pages with bounding boxes on the parsed text elements

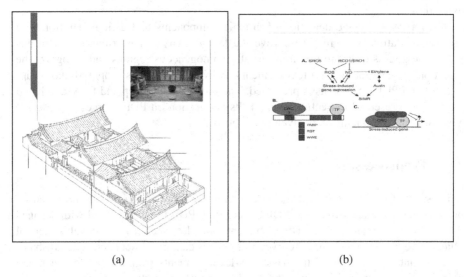

(a)   (b)

Fig. 2. Non-text objects in the "left-over" PDF document images

The complexity of graphic recognition has become a significant step to be handled in building a complete document understanding system. To extract the graphic and text primitives corresponding to figures, a hybrid method incorporating both low-level structural elements analysis and vision based image analysis is proposed. Firstly, the bounding boxes of the parsed text elements embedded by PDF are exported and then converted from the metric of logic units to pixels. As Fig.1 has demonstrated, by imposing the bounding boxes of text elements on the original document page image, the super-pixel representation of a page image has provided the layout analysis with great convenience. The text regions in a page image can be regarded as an array of bounding boxes in two dimensions. As is given in Fig.1 (a), a two-column page in Chinese from an electronic book is plotted with all the bounding boxes of the parsed text elements. It contains a composite graph combining a line graph component with surrounded text elements, a photo graph, horizontal body text and vertical marginal decoration, etc. Fig.1 (b) is an example page from an English e-book crawled from the web. These cases are challenging to segment the graphic components when either the graphic has been embedded with text or has touched text elements. For PDF documents, in fact, the graphic of line drawing in Fig.1 (a) is not parsed as a whole object but as numerous paths and sub-images, which is the same case for the flowchart graphic in Fig.1 (b).

To use the layer information provided by low-level structure elements embedded in PDF documents, the extracted text elements in each page are subtracted from the original input image before passing the cleaned image to graphic region analysis. As is shown in Fig.2, all the text elements in pages are covered with white pixels and the non-text page images only contains graphic parts, lines and decorations, etc..

4   Graphic Segmentation

After the preprocessing step, the text layer input is analyzed by applying the graph based analysis proposed in section 4.1, and the non-text graphic layer is processed by texture features and morphological analysis given in section 4.2.

4.1   Graph Based Analysis

As perceptual grouping works in human vision, graph-based method [17] developed can capture certain perceptually important non-local image characteristics for segmentation purposes. In [12], the connect component (CCs) are used as graph vertices. Unlike its application on image segmentation in pixel level or CC state, in this paper, page element or primitive corresponding to a vertex are constructed in the graph. All the text elements can be connected by establishing a neighbourhood system. Delaunay tessellation is applied in this regard. It is a convenient and powerful neighbourhood representation of 2D image.

An undirected graph can be defined as $G = (V, E)$ whose vertex set is V and $(v_i, v_j) \in E$ are the edges connecting two vertexes. The dissimilarity between adjacent elements v_i and v_j is measured as weights $w(v_i, v_j)$ for each edge $(v_i, v_j) \in E$ constructed. In this application, the elements in V are the centroids of the bounding boxes extracted from PDF parser.

$$w(v_i, v_j) = \sum_k \lambda_k f_k(v_i, v_j) \qquad (1)$$

where k is the dimension of feature dissimilarity $f_k(v_i, v_j)$ between adjacent elements v_i and v_j, and λ_k is the coefficient corresponding to each feature function. $w(v_i, v_j)$ is a linear combination of the selected feature functions. The undirected graph constructed can be called as page graph in the field of document analysis [9].

Two feature functions are defined based on the Euclidean distance function $f_E(v_i, v_j)$ and an angle dissimilarity function $f_A(v_i, v_j)$:

$$f_E(v_i, v_j) = \left[(v_i(x) - v_j(x))^2 + (v_i(y) - v_j(y))^2 \right]^{1/2} \tag{2}$$

$$f_A(v_i, v_j) = \left[\tan^{-1} \frac{\Delta y_{i,j}}{\Delta x_{i,j}} \right]_{180°} \tag{3}$$

where $\Delta x_{i,j} = \left| v_j(x) - v_i(x) \right|$, $\Delta y_{i,j} = \left| v_j(y) - v_i(y) \right|$, $[\cdot]_{180°}$ indicates $0 \le f_A(v_i, v_j) \le 180°$. The weight for each edge $(v_i, v_j) \in E$ is selected as:

$$w(v_i, v_j) = \lambda_E f_E(v_i, v_j) + \lambda_A f_A(v_i, v_j) \tag{4}$$

As are defined in [17], the internal difference $Int(C)$ within one composite component $C \subseteq V$ and the inter-component difference $Dif(C_1, C_2)$ between two components $C_1, C_2 \subseteq V$ play an important role in graph based segmentation, which are formulated as:

$$Int(C) = \max_{e \in MST(C,E)} w(e) \tag{5}$$

$$Dif(C_1, C_2) = \min_{v_i \in C_1, v_j \in C_2, (v_i, v_j) \in E} w((v_i, v_j)) \tag{6}$$

The measures indicate that when the edge weights are equal or smaller than $Int(C)$, the vertices connecting them are considered to be in one composite component. If two vertices are not in the same component, $Dif(C_1, C_2)$ is larger than the internal difference within at least one components, $Int(C_1)$ and $Int(C_2)$. The pairwise region comparison predicate is defined as:

$$D(C_1, C_2) = \begin{cases} true, & if \quad Dif(C_1, C_2) > MInt(C_1, C_2) \\ false, & otherwise \end{cases} \tag{7}$$

where the minimum internal difference $MInt(C_1, C_2)$ is defined as:

$$MInt(C_1, C_2) = \min(Int(C_1) + \tau(C_1), Int(C_2) + \tau(C_2)) \tag{8}$$

To identify an evidence for a partition, the difference between two components must be greater than the internal difference. The extreme case is that the size of component is 1, and $Int(C) = 0$. Therefore, a threshold function τ can solve this problem:

$$\tau(C) = 1/|C| \tag{9}$$

where $|C|$ is the size of C.

In the graph based method, the edge causing the grouping of two components is exactly the minimum weight edge between the components. That implies the edges causing merges are exactly the edges that would be selected by Kruskal's algorithm for constructing minimum spanning tree of each component [17]. The computational complexity is reduced by path-compression.

A spanning tree of a page graph is defined as a tree contains all the vertices of a graph, which indicates that when given n_V vertices or primitives in a page, the spanning tree of the page has $n_V - 1$ edges. In the undirected graph $G = (V, E)$, the goal is to find an acyclic subset $F \subseteq E$ connecting all the vertices. And the total weight is minimized:

$$w(F) = \sum_{(v_i, v_j) \in F} w(v_i, v_j) \tag{10}$$

Minimal spanning tree requires that the sum of the edge weights is minimal among all other possible spanning trees of the same graph. A minima spanning tree of page graph is built by the Kruskal algorithm.

4.2 Texture Entropy and Morphological Analysis

The co-occurrence matrix is generally defined over an image. It reflects the distribution of co-occurring values at a given offset. Mathematically, it is formulated as:

$$C_{\Delta x, \Delta y(i,j)} = \sum_{p=1}^{n} \sum_{q=1}^{m} \begin{cases} 1, & if \quad I(p,q) = i \quad and \quad I(p + \Delta x, q + \Delta y) = j \\ 0, & otherwise \end{cases} \tag{11}$$

where C is a co-occurrence matrix over image I with size $n \times m$, and $(\Delta x, \Delta y)$ is the offset. The texture entropy En is defined as:

$$En = \sum \sum p_{ij} \log p_{ij} \tag{12}$$

where i and j are the row and column, p_{ij} is the probability matrix.

The morphological filter consisting of opening followed by closing is applied to eliminate the noise, and region filling is performed on the preprocessed page image containing non-textual graphic objects. The outside bounding box of graphic object can be identified on the specific connected component.

5   Graphic Segmentation Results and Analysis

5.1   Delaunay Triangulation and Text Elements Clustering

To construct the neighborhood system of text elements, Delaunay triangulation is generated by conventional incremental method. The features from all the vertices of triangles are extracted, including font dissimilarity, Euclidean distance, orientation angle, which can be utilized for further segmentation. In these two cases, the text elements are clustered into the right graphic regions.

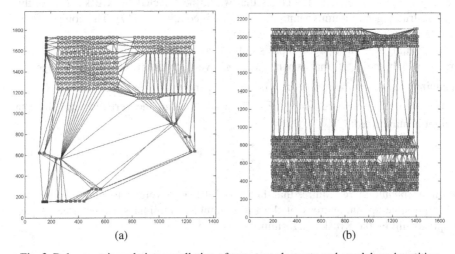

(a)   (b)

Fig. 3. Delaunay triangulation tessellation of page text elements and graph based partition

As can be seen, the super-pixel representation and Delaunay triangulation of Fig.1 (a) and (b) are illustrated in Fig.3 (a) and (b) respectively. The clustering of text elements is based on the algorithm proposed in Section 4.1 according to predefined threshold of feature dissimilarity, which is a combination of font similarity and Euclidean distance. The clusters of the elements are presented in different marker face color. The text elements belonging to the body text area, title, foots and notes, graphic components are clustered into separate classes. Similarly, the outside bounding boxes of each class can be identified on the page images for the purpose of integrating text elements and graphic object.

5.2   Segmentation of Graphics

The graphic segmentation results in Fig.4 are satisfactory. By region grouping technique, the line drawing in Fig.4 (a) of an architecture integrating with surrounded illustrative text elements is accurately detected, so are the photo graph, separating lines and marginal graph. The composite graph in Fig.4 (b) is identified as a whole component with all the pictorials texts.

The proposed hybrid segmentation algorithm was tested on two Chinese e-books, one English e-book and one consumer magazine. As is pointed out in [1], precise quantitative evaluation for books and magazines requires ground truth. Although the construction of evaluation set is very time-consuming, preliminary work has been already initiated, which will be further carried out in evaluation of both low-level and high-level page segmentation. However, we manually counted the integration of text and graph. It can achieve over 80% accuracy by means of counting the number of graphics.

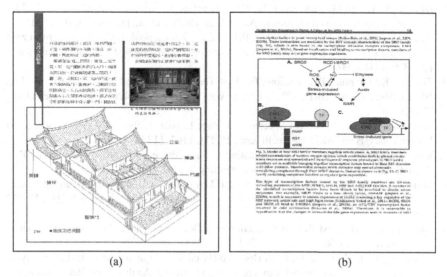

(a)   (b)

Fig. 4. Graphic segmentation results of PDF document pages in Fig.1

6   Conclusions

In this work, a hybrid segmentation scheme is proposed to segment the graphics in PDF documents. By utilizing inherent advantages of born-digital documents embedded with characters and images in explicit form, the provided structural information can benefit the layout analysis. Delaunay tessellation is applied on the centroids of the page elements to build the neighborhood system for parsed text elements. The proposed hybrid method uses graph based concept to group the text elements according to edge weights like the proximity and font information. Graphic segmentation integrating with texts is accomplished by text clustering and connected components segmentation. The experimental results on document pages of PDF books and magazines have shown satisfactory performance.

Acknowledgements. This work was supported by the National Basic Research Program of China (973 Program) (No. 2010CB735908).

References

1. Marinai, S., Marino, E., Soda, G.: Conversion of PDF Books in ePub Format. In: 11ᵗʰ International Conference on Document Analysis and Recognition, pp. 478–482 (2011)
2. Fan, J.: Text Segmentation of Consumer Magazines in PDF Format. In: 11ᵗʰ International Conference on Document Analysis and Recognition, pp. 794–798 (2011)
3. Doucet, A., Kazai, G., Dresevic, B., Uzelac, A., Radakovic, B., Todic, N.: Book Structure Extraction Competition. In: 10ᵗʰ International Conference on Document Analysis and Recognition, pp. 1408–1412 (2009)
4. Doucet, A., Kazai, G., Meunier, J.-L.: Book Structure Extraction Competition. In: 11ᵗʰ International Conference on Document Analysis and Recognition, pp. 1501–1505 (2011)
5. Antonacopoulos, A., Pletschacher, S., Bridson, D., Papadopoulos, C.: Page Segmentation Competition. In: 10ᵗʰ International Conference on Document Analysis and Recognition, pp. 1370–1374 (2009)
6. Tombre, K.: Graphics Recognition: The Last Ten Years and the Next Ten Years. In: Liu, W., Lladós, J. (eds.) GREC 2005. LNCS, vol. 3926, pp. 422–426. Springer, Heidelberg (2006)
7. O'Gorman, L.: The Document Spectrum for Page Layout Analysis. IEEE Transactions on Pattern Analysis and Machine Intelligence 15(11), 1162–1173 (1993)
8. Kise, K., Sato, A., Iwata, M.: Segmentation of Page Images Using the Area Voronoi Diagram. Computer Vision and Image Understanding 70, 370–382 (1998)
9. Simon, A., Pret, J.C., Johnson, A.P.: A Fast Algorithm for Bottom-up Document Layout Analysis. IEEE Transactions on Pattern Analysis and Machine Intelligence 19(3), 273–277 (1997)
10. Xiao, Y., Yan, H.: Text Region Extraction in a Document Image Based on the Delaunay Tessellation. Pattern Recognition 36, 799–809 (2003)
11. Ferilli, S., Biba, M., Esposito, F.: A Distance-Based Technique for Non-Manhattan Layout Analysis. In: 10ᵗʰ International Conference on Document Analysis and Recognition, pp. 231–235 (2009)
12. Koo, H.I., Cho, N.I.: State Estimation in a Document Image and Its Application in Text Block Identification and Text Line Extraction. In: Daniilidis, K., Maragos, P., Paragios, N. (eds.) ECCV 2010, Part II. LNCS, vol. 6312, pp. 421–434. Springer, Heidelberg (2010)
13. Chao, H.: Graphics Extraction in PDF Document. In: Document Recognition and Retrieval X, Santa Clara, CA, USA, vol. 5010, pp. 317–325 (2003)
14. Shao, M., Futrelle, R.P.: Recognition and Classification of Figures in PDF Documents. In: Liu, W., Lladós, J. (eds.) GREC 2005. LNCS, vol. 3926, pp. 231–242. Springer, Heidelberg (2006)
15. Hadjar, K., Rigamonti, M., Lalanne, D., Ingold, R.: Xed: A New Tool for Extracting Hidden Structures from Electronic Documents. In: International Workshop on Document Image Analysis for Libraries, pp. 212–224 (2004)
16. Fang, J., Tang, Z., Gao, L.: Reflowing-Driven Paragraph Recognition for Electronic Books in PDF. In: SPIE-IS&T International Conference of Document Recognition and Retrieval XVIII, vol. 7874, pp. 78740U-1–78740U-9 (2011)
17. Felzenszwalb, P.F., Huttenlocher, D.P.: Efficient Graph-Based Image Segmentation. International Journal of Computer Vision 59(2), 167–181 (2004)

Automatic Generation of Chinese Character Based on Human Vision and Prior Knowledge of Calligraphy

Cao Shi[1], Jianguo Xiao[1], Wenhua Jia[1], and Canhui Xu[1,2,3]

[1] Institute of Computer Science & Technology, Peking University, Beijing, China
[2] Postdoctoral Workstation of the Zhongguancun Haidian Science Park and Peking University Founder Group Co. Ltd, Beijing, China
[3] State Key Laboratory of Digital Publishing Technology, Beijing, China
{Caoshi,ccxu09}@yeah.net, {xiaojianguo,jwh}@pku.edu.cn

Abstract. Prior knowledge of Chinese calligraphy is modeled in this paper, and the hierarchical relationship of strokes and radicals is represented by a novel five layer framework. Calligraphist's unique calligraphy skill is analyzed and his particular strokes, radicals and layout patterns provide raw element for the proposed five layers. The criteria of visual aesthetics based on Marr's vision assumption are built for the proposed algorithm of automatic generation of Chinese character. The Bayesian statistics is introduced to characterize the character generation process as a Bayesian dynamic model, in which, parameters to translate, rotate and scale strokes, radicals are controlled by the state equation, as well as the proposed visual aesthetics is employed by the measurement equation. Experimental results show the automatically generated characters have almost the same visual acceptance compared to calligraphist's artwork.

Keywords: Chinese character, automatic generation, human vision, prior knowledge of calligraphy, Bayesian statistics.

1   Introduction

The automatic generation of Chinese character attracts researchers' attention[1-7]. It is significant to explore underlying principles on Chinese character glyph in various aspects. Chinese script, which has evolved along with change of society and culture, transmitted information in daily life and provided aesthetic perception in art. Its geometrical shape in particular historical period implied Calligraphic trend and distinctive civilization feature. Moreover, a calligraphist's unique handwriting skills infer his own emotion and experience. This paper employs visual aesthetics and prior knowledge of calligraphy to generate Chinese character.

Two types of organizations paid most attention on Chinese glyph: font companies[8-11] and Chinese character research groups. Font companies must supply sufficient new fonts to China media market in time. The new fonts need to match the commercial requirements as well as satisfy the Chinese government standard, such as GB2312, GBK and GB13000.1 etc. These companies employ a large amount of glyph designers and workers to manufacture elaborate Chinese font. The production process

M. Zhou et al. (Eds.): NLPCC 2012, CCIS 333, pp. 23–33, 2012.

of font is time-consuming and costly. During the whole process, firstly, basic strokes of originality are created by font designer to decide stroke style of the new font. Secondly, radicals are composed of the created strokes. Finally, radicals construct Chinese characters. The three steps are logical. In fact, the production process is dynamic and iterative, in other words, the design of stroke, the composition and the decomposition of radicals or characters are iterative so that the number of characters increases gradually and dynamically.

In order to speed up font manufacture and realize calligraphic manifestation using information technology, innovative models[1-6, 12] and systems[7, 13-15] were proposed to automatically generate Chinese character. In general, methodologies broadly exploit two categories of ideas: imitating handwriting procedure[1-3, 6, 13, 16] and composing new characters with samples[4, 5, 17, 18]. Being different from previous work, this paper considers automatic generation of Chinese character from a novel perspective on visual aesthetics and prior calligraphic knowledge. One research goal is to provide an effective and efficient way to build a prototype for a new style font. The prototype would assist font designer to make or adjust blueprint immediately avoiding failure of the whole production process. Another goal is to fast generate customized Chinese character for digital entertainment in cyberspace.

The remainder of this paper is organized as follows. In next section, previous work on automatic generation of Chinese character is reviewed. Prior knowledge of calligraphy is modeled in Section 3, which reveals unique individual handwriting pattern. In Section 4, visual aesthetics is investigated, which is applied with the proposed model of calligraphic prior knowledge for a novel algorithm to automatically generate Chinese character. The experiments and discussion are presented in Section 5, and Section 6 concludes this paper.

2   Previous Work

Classical Chinese character generation algorithms are reviewed in this section, as mentioned above, which can be generally classified into two categories: handwriting imitation and samples based character generation. The methodology of handwriting imitation extracts geometric and topological features, on which based strokes are drawn. As a topological feature, skeleton of glyph was extracted by Yu et al.[19], and Zhuang et al.[20] explored orientation of strokes using Gabor filter. On the other hand, contour of glyph is a critical geometric feature. Xu et al.[21] extracted contour feature using a weighted mask which slipped along contour of glyph. Moreover, a heuristic method using configured ellipses along skeleton to represent contour was proposed by Wong et al.[12]. After feature extraction, a natural methodology is to imitate handwriting process. Mi et al.[7, 14] designed a virtual brush to draw calligraphic artwork. Bai et al.[1, 2] proposed more complicated brush geometry and dynamic models to represent deformation of brush. Whereas, in order to reduce computational complexity, Yao et al.[16] applied B-Spline to generate Chinese calligraphy instead of sophisticated brush model. For the automatic generation of more elegant character, Xu et al.[15] presented a robust algorithm drawing calligraphy along stroke trajectories.

The other important methodology is to construct new characters using samples. This partly inherits the idea of font production process. Lai et al.[17, 18] utilized the hierarchical relationship of strokes and radicals to compose Chinese character. To further exploit contour feature of glyph, Xu et al.[4, 5] considered both topology between strokes and shape of stroke, etc.

The strategy of handwriting imitation emphasizes the reconstruction of handwriting progress according to extracted geometric and topological features, such as skeleton and contour. It partly considers prior knowledge of calligraphy: the stroke style and the structure of character, however, this paper considers more on calligraphy training process in which the unique individual handwriting pattern of calligraphist is formed. The sampled based character composition exploits correlation between characters depending on statistics. Nevertheless, the research on this paper exceeds statistical correlation, which takes an attempt that using visual aesthetics to generate Chinese character. A character generation algorithm based on calligraphic prior knowledge and visual aesthetics is proposed in the next two sections.

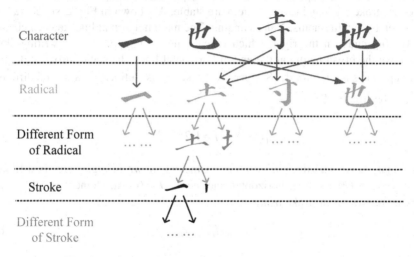

Fig. 1. Five layers framework to represent Chinese character

3   Modeling Prior Knowledge of Calligraphy

In the training process of Chinese calligraphy, a learner practices the sophisticated cooperation between mind and hand. It is always a very long period for a learner and even a whole life for a calligraphist. In this section, the prior knowledge of Chinese calligraphy includes two parts. The first part is the structure of Chinese character, which has been taught to every Chinese pupil for a few years. A five layers framework is proposed in this section to represent the structure of Chinese character, as shown in Fig. 1. The five layers are Character layer (C layer), Radical layer (R layer), Different Form of Radical layer (DFR layer), Stroke layer (S layer), and Different Form of Stroke layer (DFS layer). In the top layer, each element is a Chinese character, which belongs to a layout pattern. Characters "一" and "也" belong to Single-Component layout pattern, "寺" belongs to Top-Bottom layout pattern, and "地" belongs to Left-Right layout pattern. The character "寺" can be decomposed to a top radical "土" and a bottom radical "寸" in R layer. In fact, each radical is a meaning unit which can not be decomposed to smaller radical. However, each radical may have different forms in DFR layer, such as radical "土" has at least two different forms. The two lower layers are S layer and DFS layer. Each element in DFR layer can be decomposed to one or more strokes in S layer, and each stroke may have different forms in DFS layer. The second part of prior knowledge of calligraphy is concerned with calligraphist's unique handwriting skills, on which more details are given in next two sub-sections.

3.1 Modeling Stroke and DFS

Traditionally, a calligraphist practices his unique handwriting skills in whole life, hence the stroke style and layout pattern are stable. As shown in Fig. 2, six characters are written by a calligraphist Yan Zhenqing. The main horizontal lines in each character have big ends on the right, which reveals the calligraphist's handwriting skill: press down the brush hardly at the end of horizontal line. The stable stroke style provides superior samples for DFS layer. A stroke s_i is defined as a set of different forms of the stroke dfs_{ij}:

$$s_i = \left\{ dfs_{ij} \right\} \quad j = 1, 2, ..., J \quad (1)$$

All six main horizontal lines in different characters shown in Fig. 2 are six different forms strokes of the stroke: horizontal line, here, $J = 6$. An element in DFR layer can be composed from stroke using (2):

$$dfr_{mk} = RCom\left(rl_k, s_1, s_2, ..., s_n \right) \quad (2)$$

where different forms of strokes are chosen for strokes $s_1, s_2, ..., s_n$ according to radical layout rl_k, and $RCom(\cdot)$ composes the chosen different forms of strokes to dfr_{mk}, where m indicates the radical r_m.

Fig. 2. Six characters written by a famous calligraphist Yan Zhenqing (Tang Dynasty, A.D. 709-785). The right ends of main horizontal lines (red strokes), which are marked with dash circles, indicate the calligraphist's handwriting skill: press down the brush hardly at the end of horizontal line.

3.2 Modeling Radical and DFR

As mentioned in the above sub-section, the layout pattern of a calligraphist's character is stable. As shown in Fig. 3, the same character "感" has two kinds of layout patterns: partially surrounding pattern and top-bottom pattern. In Fig. 3(a)~(c), the radical "心" is partially surrounded by radical "咸", and in Fig. 3(d), the top radical "咸" is just above the bottom radical "心". The core is not concerned with which pattern is correct but which one is your pattern. Hence, the calligraphist's personal layout pattern, as shown in Fig. 3(a)~(b), provides unique layout style for C layer, and also determines rl_k in (2). A character c_p in C layer can be composed by radicals in R layer using (3):

$$c_p = CCom\left(cl_p, r_1, r_2, ..., r_m\right) \tag{3}$$

where different forms of radicals are chosen for radicals $r_1, r_2, ..., r_m$ according to character layout cl_p, and the character c_p can be composed with the chosen different forms of radicals using $CCom(\cdot)$.

In brief, the structure of Chinese character is modeled using the proposed five layers framework, and the calligraphist's unique handwriting skills provide effective composition strategies for (1)~(3). Two kinds of prior knowledge of calligraphy are made well used to compose Chinese character. An automatic generation algorithm of Chinese character based on visual aesthetics is proposed in next section.

| (a) | (b) | (c) | (d) |

Fig. 3. The same character with different layout pattern. (a) Yan Zhenqing's character "感"; (b) Yan Zhenqing's character "感" with the same layout pattern of (a); (c) a Kai Ti font "感" with the same layout pattern of (a); (d) another Kai Ti font "感" with a different layout pattern.

4 Automatic Generation Algorithm of Chinese Character

Chinese character can be composed based on prior knowledge of calligraphy using (1) ~ (3). Five layers framework illustrated in Fig. 1 gives a top-down strategy to guide stroke and radical composition. However, formula (2) and (3) only have conceptual solutions. In this section, numerical solutions for (2) and (3) are given using a bottom-top nonlinear and non-Gaussian algorithm based on Marr's vision assumptions[22].

4.1 Modeling Stroke and DFS

The spatial arrangement of objects in an image was investigated by Marr[22] according to a series of physical assumptions. The conclusion of the investigation can be summarized as six points: 1. Average local intensity; 2. Average size of similar objects; 3. Local density of the objects; 4. Local orientation of the objects; 5. Local distances associated with the spatial arrangement of similar objects; 6. Local orientation associated with the spatial arrangement of similar objects. It is inspired from Marr's investigation on spatial arrangement that visual aesthetics is proposed in this subsection.

According to Marr's points 1~3, average stroke intensity and stroke intensity are defined as:

$$\rho_{ij} = Area\left(dfs_{ij}\right) \tag{4}$$

$$\rho'_{mk} = \frac{Area\left(dfr_{mk}\right)}{RNum\left(dfr_{mk}\right)} \tag{5}$$

where $Area(\cdot)$ is the function to calculate area of stroke or radical, and $RNum(\cdot)$ returns the number of strokes in dfr_{mk}. ρ_{ij} is a constant which represents the area of each element in DFS layer. ρ'_{mk} is the ratio of the area of dfr_{mk} to the number of strokes.

The orientation of stroke θ_{ij} and the orientation of radical θ'_{mk} are proposed corresponding to Marr's points 4 and 6. Obviously, it's easy to calculate θ_{ij} of dfs_{ij}. θ'_{mk} is equal to the θ_{ij} of the main stoke in dfr_{mk}. Here, the main stroke of dfr_{mk} is the stroke which has the biggest area among all strokes. The orientation of layout rl_k and cl_p can be represented respectively by:

$$\sum \theta_{ij} - \theta_{i'j'} \tag{6}$$

$$\sum \theta'_{mk} - \theta'_{m'k'} \tag{7}$$

Moreover, the distance between strokes in radical or radicals in character are defined as:

$$\delta_{ij,i'j'} = center\left(dfs_{ij}\right) - center\left(dfs_{i'j'}\right) \tag{8}$$

$$\delta'_{mk,m'k'} = center\left(dfr_{mk}\right) - center\left(dfr_{m'k'}\right) \tag{9}$$

where $center(\cdot)$ calculates the center point of a stroke or a radical. And intersection between strokes and radicals are detected using $Area\left(dfs_{ij} \cap dfs_{i'j'}\right)$ and $Area\left(dfr_{mk} \cap dfr_{m'k'}\right)$. Formula (6)~(9) match Marr's point 5.

As discussed above, rl_k and cl_p are quantified through (4)~(9) inspired by Marr's vision assumption. A nonlinear Bayesian algorithm is proposed in next subsection to implement (2) and (3).

4.2   Nonlinear Bayesian Algorithm to Generate Character

In order to generate Chinese character satisfying the proposed visual aesthetics, three transformation operators are defined to adjust strokes and radicals described in Fig. 1. The three operators include scaling S, rotation R, and translation T:

$$SRT = \begin{bmatrix} sx & 0 & 0 \\ 0 & sy & 0 \\ 0 & 0 & 1 \end{bmatrix} \cdot \begin{bmatrix} \cos\varphi & -\sin\varphi & 0 \\ \sin\varphi & \cos\varphi & 0 \\ 0 & 0 & 1 \end{bmatrix} \cdot \begin{bmatrix} 1 & 0 & tx \\ 0 & 1 & ty \\ 0 & 0 & 1 \end{bmatrix} \quad (10)$$

The core of character generation is to figure out proper parameters sx, sy, φ, tx, ty, on which depending strokes and radicals are adjusted so that the group of coefficients on visual aesthetics: ρ_{ij}, ρ'_{mk}, $\sum \theta_{ij} - \theta_{i'j'}$, $\sum \theta'_{mk} - \theta'_{m'k'}$, $\delta_{ij,i'j'}$, $\delta'_{mk,m'k'}$, $Area\left(dfs_{ij} \cap dfs_{i'j'}\right)$, and $Area\left(dfr_{mk} \cap dfr_{m'k'}\right)$ etc, satisfy prior knowledge of calligraphy. Obviously, this is an optimal problem.

Firstly, consider the condition that character is composed with two radicals, as described in (3). The Bayesian dynamic models[23] is introduced to solve the optimal problem. The state vector $\mathbf{x}$, $\mathbf{x}'$ and the measurement $\mathbf{z}$ are defined as:

$$\mathbf{x} = \left[sx, sy, \varphi, tx, ty\right]^{T} \quad \mathbf{x}' = \left[sx', sy', \varphi', tx', ty'\right]^{T} \quad (11)$$

$$\mathbf{z} = \left[\rho'_{mk}, \sum \theta'_{mk} - \theta'_{m'k'}, \delta'_{mk,m'k'}, Area\left(dfr_{mk} \cap dfr_{m'k'}\right)\right]^{T} \quad (12)$$

The state equation and the observation equation are:

$$\left[\mathbf{x}_k, \mathbf{x}'_k\right] = f_k\left(\left[\mathbf{x}_{k-1}, \mathbf{x}'_{k-1}\right]\right) \quad (13)$$

$$\mathbf{z}_k = h_k\left(SRT\left(\mathbf{x}_k\right) \cdot HCdfr_{mk}, SRT\left(\mathbf{x}'_k\right) \cdot HCdfr_{m'k'}\right) \quad (14)$$

where $SRT\left(\mathbf{x}_k\right)$ is transformation matrix in (10), and $HCdfr_{mk}$ represents homogeneous coordinates of pixel in dfr_{mk}. Formulae (13) and (14) indicate the states vectors $\mathbf{x}_k$ and $\mathbf{x}'_k$ update along time k until the coefficients on visual aesthetics calculated from two radicals dfr_{mk} $dfr_{m'k'}$ match prior knowledge of calligraphy. The solutions to (13) and (14) are concerned with estimation of probability density function (pdf) using Bayesian theory. Generally, it is hard to figure out analytical solution. Instead, Particle Filter[24], Sequential Importance Sampling (SIS)[25] algorithm, Markov Chain Monte Carlo (MCMC)[26] method, and Sampling Importance Resampling (SIR)[27] filter etc are used to approximate the optimal solution.

The above automatic generation algorithm of Chinese character is concluded as follows:

Step 1: Input prior information of target character and absent radicals.

Step 2: If all radicals to compose the character exist, then turn to Step 4.

Step 3: Compose the absent radicals using the Bayesian dynamic models, similar to (11)~(14).

tep 4: Compose the target character with necessary radicals using the Bayesian dynamic models.

Step 5: Output the target character.

5   Experiments and Discussion

In order to evaluate the proposed algorithm, Yan Zhenqing's 130 calligraphy characters are collected to build a data set. These calligraphy characters are converted into vector graphics and decomposed to radicals and strokes for DFR layer and DFS layer, as illustrated in Fig. 1. The two processes of conversion and decomposition are both executed manually. As shown in Fig. 4, the first row contains ten samples from the calligraphy data set, the second row illustrates vector graphics corresponding to the ten samples in the first row, and the third row demonstrate two radicals and seven strokes of the character "判".

The 14 automatically generated Chinese characters are mixed with Yan Zhenqing's 14 calligraphy characters to quantify the visual acceptance of characters. And 17 persons are invited to pick characters with the worst visual acceptance. The number of picked characters is in the range from 0 to 28. The picking result is visualized in Fig. 5. The horizontal arrow and the vertical arrow indicate characters and invited persons respectively. The black grid represents the picked character as well as the person who picked it. Intuitively, the picked characters are sparse. In fact, the picked probability values of Yan Zhenqing's calligraphy and generated characters are 0.45 and 0.55 respectively. In other words, the proposed algorithm in this paper could generate Chinese characters with almost the same visual acceptance of Yan's calligraphy. To further explore the reason that characters were picked out, five characters are numbered including three calligraphy characters (No.1~3) and two generated characters (No.4~5). Actually, the No.1 character is Yan's calligraphy, and people always subconsciously believe Yan's calligraphy is elegant because of his reputation. The essential reason to pick out No.1 character is that the form of No.1 character in modern age is "琢", of which the right radical is different with Yan's. Hence, the lack of prior knowledge of calligraphy guides people to pick out the No.1 character. The bottom of the No.2 character isn't sealed so well that a hook is exposed. This phenomenon is caused by Yan's handwriting style, which directly lead to the No.4 and No.5 were picked out with the same reason: the exposed hook. As can be seen, the No.3 character and the No.5 character have the same layout pattern "top-bottom", and even the same bottom radical "心". It is a potential reason resulting in that the two characters were picked, whereas, it proves that the proposed algorithm successfully maintains Yan Zhenqing's handwriting style.

In brief, the characters generated by the proposed algorithm get almost the same visual acceptance relative to Yan Zhenqing's calligraphy. The lack of prior knowledge of calligraphy results in contrary visual aesthetics. And the handwriting style of calligraphist can be remained in the generated characters using the proposed algorithm.

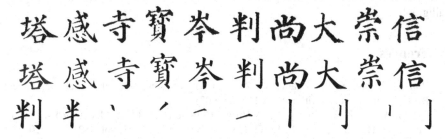

Fig. 4. Ten calligraphy samples, vector graphics and decomposition of character. The first row shows ten samples from the collected Yan Zhenqing's calligraphy data set. The second row illustrates vector graphics corresponding to the first row. And the third row demonstrates two radicals and seven strokes of the character "判".

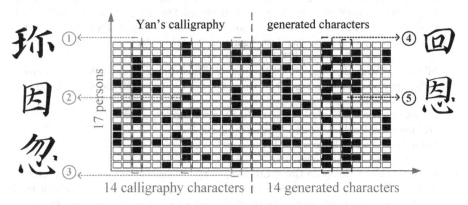

Fig. 5. Visualization of picking results. 17×(14×2) girds are employed to illustrate the visual acceptance of characters. The horizontal arrow and the vertical arrow indicate characters and invited persons respectively. The black grid represents the picked character as well as the person who picked it. The numbered five characters (three calligraphy characters and two generated characters) with high picked probability are showed at two sides.

6   Conclusions

In this paper, prior knowledge of Chinese calligraphy is modeled, and a five layers framework is presented to represent Chinese character. Considering a calligraphist's unique handwriting skills, strokes, radicals and layout pattern are modeled, which provides raw elements for each layer. Marr's vision assumption is deeply analyzed to propose the visual aesthetics for the proposed automatic generation algorithm of Chinese character. The whole generation process can be described as a Bayesian dynamic model, in which, the state equation control the update of parameters to adjust strokes, radicals and their layout, and the proposed visual aesthetics is employed by the measurement equation. Experimental results show the automatically generated characters have almost the same visual acceptance compared to Yan Zhenqing's calligraphy. One reason affecting visual acceptance is the extent of mastering prior knowledge of calligraphy.

References

1. Bai, B., Wong, K.-W., Zhang, Y.: An Efficient Physically-Based Model for Chinese Brush. Frontiers in Algorithmics, 261–270 (2007)
2. Bai, B., Wong, K.-W., Zhang, Y.: A Virtual Chinese Hairy Brush Model for E-Learning. In: Leung, H., Li, F., Lau, R., Li, Q. (eds.) ICWL 2007. LNCS, vol. 4823, pp. 320–330. Springer, Heidelberg (2008)
3. Yang, L., Li, X.: Animating the Brush-Writing Process of Chinese Calligraphy Characters. In: Eighth IEEE/ACIS International Conference on Computer and Information Science (ICIS 2009), pp. 683–688 (2009)
4. Xu, S., Jiang, H., Jin, T., Lau, F.C.M., Pan, Y.: Automatic Facsimile of Chinese Calligraphic Writings. Computer Graphics Forum 27(7), 1879–1886 (2008)
5. Xu, S., Jiang, H., Jin, T., Lau, F.C.M., Pan, Y.: Automatic Generation of Chinese Calligraphic Writings with Style Imitation. IEEE Intelligent Systems 24(2), 44–53 (2009)
6. Zhu, X., Jin, L.: Calligraphic Beautification of Handwritten Chinese Characters: A Patternized Approach to Handwriting Transfiguration. In: International Conference on Frontier on Handwriting Recognition, ICFHR 2008 (2008)
7. Mi, X.-F., Tang, M., Dong, J.-X.: Droplet: A Virtual Brush Model to Simulate Chinese Calligraphy and Painting. Journal of Computer Science and Technology 19(3), 393–404 (2004)
8. Founder Electronics Co. Ltd., http://www.foundertype.com/
9. Dynacomware Co. Ltd., http://www.dynacw.cn/
10. Beijing Hanyi Keyin Information Technology Co. Ltd., http://www.hanyi.com.cn/
11. China Great Wall Computer Group Co., Ltd., http://www.greatwall.com.cn/
12. Wong, S.T.S., Leung, H., Ip, H.H.S.: Brush Writing Style Classification from Individual Chinese Characters. In: 18th International Conference on Pattern Recognition (ICPR 2006), pp. 884–887 (2006)
13. Chang, W.-D., Shin, J.: Interactive Virtual Oriental Brush with Pen-Tablet System. Knowledge-Based Intelligent Information and Engineering Systems, 387–394 (2007)

14. Mi, X., Xu, J., Tang, M., Dong, J.: The Droplet Virtual Brush for Chinese Calligraphic Character Modeling. In: Sixth IEEE Workshop on Applications of Computer Vision (WACV 2002), pp. 330–334 (2002)
15. Xu, S., Jiang, H., Lau, F.C.M., Pan, Y.: An Intelligent System for Chinese Calligraphy. In: Proceedings of the 22nd National Conference on Artificial Intelligence, Vancouver, British Columbia, Canada, vol. 2, pp. 1578–1583 (2007)
16. Yao, F., Shao, G., Yi, J.: Extracting the Trajectory of Writing Brush in Chinese Character Calligraphy. Engineering Applications of Artificial Intelligence 17(6), 631–644 (2004)
17. Lai, P.-K., Pong, M.-C., Yeung, D.-Y.: Chinese Glyph Generation Using Character Composition and Beauty Evaluation Metrics. In: International Conference on Computer Processing of Oriental Languages (ICCPOL), Honolulu, Hawaii, pp. 92–99 (1995)
18. Lai, P.-K., Yeung, D.-Y., Pong, M.-C.: A Heuristic Search Approach to Chinese Glyph Generation Using Hierarchical Character Composition. Computer Processing of Oriental Languages 10(3), 281–297 (1997)
19. Yu, K., Wu, J., Zhuang, Y.: Skeleton-Based Recognition of Chinese Calligraphic Character Image. In: Huang, Y.-M.R., Xu, C., Cheng, K.-S., Yang, J.-F.K., Swamy, M.N.S., Li, S., Ding, J.-W. (eds.) PCM 2008. LNCS, vol. 5353, pp. 228–237. Springer, Heidelberg (2008)
20. Zhuang, Y., Lu, W., Wu, J.: Latent Style Model: Discovering Writing Styles for Calligraphy Works. Journal of Visual Communication and Image Representation 20(2), 84–96 (2009)
21. Xu, L., Ding, X., Peng, L., Li, X.: An Improved Method Based on Weighted Grid Micro-Structure Feature for Text-Independent Writer Recognition. In: 2011 International Conference on Document Analysis and Recognition (ICDAR 2011), pp. 638–642 (2011)
22. Marr, D.: Vision: A Computational Investigation into the Human Representation and Processing of Visual Information. W.H. Freeman and Company, New York (1982)
23. West, M., Harrison, J.: Bayesian Forecasting and Dynamic Models. Springer, New York (1997)
24. Carpenter, J., Clifford, P., Fearnhead, P.: Improved Particle Filter for Nonlinear Problems. IEE Proceedings on Radar, Sonar and Navigation 146(1), 2–7 (1999)
25. Doucet, A., Godsill, S., Andrieu, C.: On Sequential Monte Carlo Sampling Methods for Bayesian Filtering. Statistics and Computing 10(3), 197–208 (2000)
26. Carlin, B.P., Polson, N.G., Stoffer, D.S.: A Monte Carlo Approach to Nonnormal and Nonlinear Statespace Modelling. Journal of the American Statistical Association 87(418), 493–500 (1992)
27. Gordon, N.J., Salmond, D.J., Smith, A.F.M.: Novel Approach to Nonlinear/Non-Gaussian Bayesian State Estimation. IEE Proceedings-F, Radar and Signal Processing 140(2), 107–113 (1993)

A Spoken Dialogue System Based on FST and DBN

Lichun Fan[1,*,**], Dong Yu[2], Xingyuan Peng[1], Shixiang Lu[1], and Bo Xu[1]

[1] Interactive Digital Media Technology Research Center
Institute of Automation Chinese Academy of Sciences, Beijing, China
[2] International R&D Center for Chinese Education
College of Information Science, Beijing Language and Culture University, China

Abstract. Natural language understanding module and dialogue management module are important parts of the spoken dialogue system. They directly affect the performance of the whole system. This paper proposes a novel method named action-group finite state transducer (FST) model to cope with the problem of natural language understanding. This model can map user utterances to actions, and extract user's information according to the matched string. For dialogue management module, we propose dynamic Bayesian network (DBN) model. It can reduce the demands for the corpus compared with Markov decision process (MDP) model. The experiments on the action-group FST model and DBN model show that they significantly outperform the state-of-the-art approaches. A set of subjective tests on the whole system demonstrate that our approaches can satisfy most of the users.

Keywords: spoken dialogue system, natural language understanding, dialogue management, FST, DBN.

1 Introduction

Spoken dialogue systems abstract a great deal of concern from its appearance in the 1990s. In the past two decades, spoken dialogue systems developed rapidly. However, due to the difficulties of natural language understanding and dialogue management, most spoken dialogue systems still stay in the laboratory stage.

As the prior part of the dialogue management, natural language understanding plays an important role in spoken dialogue system. In previous studies [1,2], the user utterance is usually mapped to the system state vector, and the dialogue strategy depends only on the current system state. Natural language parsing is relatively simple keyword matching or form filling based on syntax network. These natural language understanding methods have a poor ability in describing language, and these mapping methods will lose a wealth of language information in user utterances.

---

* Contact author: lichun.fan@ia.ac.cn
** This work was supported by the National Natural Science Foundation of China (No. 90820303) and 863 program in China (No. 2011AA01A207).

M. Zhou et al. (Eds.): NLPCC 2012, CCIS 333, pp. 34–45, 2012.
© Springer-Verlag Berlin Heidelberg 2012

As the center of spoken dialogue system, dialogue management has been a hot academic research area for many years. Early spoken dialogue systems are entirely designed by experts. The systems usually employ a finite state machine model [3] including a large number of artificial designed rules. These artificial rules are written in a very good expression and they describe the specific applications correctly, but the preparation and improvement of the rules will become increasingly difficult when the dialogue task becomes complex. In recent years, data-driven based dialogue management model gradually attracts the researchers' attention. This kind of dialogue management model obtain knowledge through the annotated dialogue corpus automatically. Dialogue management mathematical model based on Markov decision process (MDP) is proposed in [4], and the reinforcement learning (RL) is proposed to learn the model parameters in the same study. Studies in [5] propose a partially observable MDP (POMDP) dialogue management model. These models have become hot topics of the dialogue management approaches since they are proposed.

However, there remain many problems when these models are used in the actual applications. Firstly, the system uses a reinforcement learning mechanism. Interaction with the actual users is very time-consuming, and is hard to achieve the goal. Many systems get the optimal parameters from the interaction with the virtual users, so there are some difference between the optimal strategy and the real dialogue. Secondly, the dialogue models obtained by this method lack of priori knowledge of dialogue, so they are difficult to be controlled.

In this paper we propose the finite state transducer (FST) model to solve the natural language understanding problem. The FST model maps the user utterances to user actions, and extracts the attribute-value information in user utterances. For dialogue management problem, we propose dynamic Bayesian network (DBN) model. It generates the dialogue strategy not only considering the system state, but also depending on the user actions.

The paper is organized as follows: the action-group FST model and the details of using action-group FST model to detect the user actions are presented in section 2. Section 3 describes the dynamic bayesian network and dialogue management based on DBN model. Section 4 presents our spoken dialogue system and the performance of the two modules. Finally, conclusions are presented in section 5.

2   User Action Detection Based on Action-Group FST

2.1   User Action-Group FST Model

Each utterance corresponds to a single action. We annotate the utterances by action labels, and mark out the information contained in the utterances. Then we collect the utterances which have the same action label together to generate an action-group. We use the "determinize" and "minimize" operation described in the openFST tools [6] to unite and optimize the action-group FST. Fig.1 shows the building process of an action-group FST for a particular action-group.

Fig. 1. The building process of action-group FST

It is unrealistic to establish a multiple action-group FST by many action-groups which are built through dividing all of the daily utterances into different action groups. In this paper, the proposed action-group FST is only used in the fields identified by the dialogue scenes. The utterances used for building the action-group FST are collected in these particular fields.

These utterances are labeled in two stages, the first stage only marks which action-group the utterances belong to, while the second stage needs to mark out the information contained in every utterance. We use attribute-value pairs [7] to describe the information contained in utterances, such as "currency=dollar". The purpose of the second-level label is to parse the user utterances automatically according to the string sequence in the FST model that matches the user utterance properly. If the action-group is labeled according to domain knowledge, the model will be too sparse, and the portability will be poor. However, it is unable to accomplish the dialogue management tasks if the action-group is labeled based on sentence structure. Therefore, we design the action-group according to [7]. Table 1 lists the major action-groups that we used in our system.

Table 1. Action-group list

Action	Description
hello(a=x,b=y)	open a dialog and give information a=x, b=y,...
inform(a=x,b=y)	give informationa=x, b=y,...
request(a,b=x,...)	request value for a given b=x ...
reqalts(a=x,...)	request alternative with a=x,...
confirm(a=y,b=y,...)	explicitly confirm a=x,b=y,...
confreq(a=x,...,d)	implicitly confirm a=x,.. and request d
select(a=x,b=y,...)	select either a=x or a=y
affirm(a=x,b=y,...)	affirm and give a=x, b=y,...
negate(a=x)	negate and give further info a=x
deny(a=x)	deny that a=x
bye()	close a dialogue

2.2 User Action Detection Based on Action-Group FST

We hope to find the most similar word sequence as the user utterance in the action-group FSTs. Then we consider the user utterance belongs to the action-group where the word sequence is in. In this paper, the edit distance is used to measure the degree of similarity between the two word sequences. The decoder's work is to find the optimal word sequences' path in action-group FST that can make the edit distant minimum.

The most common method used to calculate the edit distance is the Wagner-Fischer algorithm [8]. This is a string to string edit distance calculation method, and its core idea is dynamic programming. We improve the Wagner-Fischer algorithm to compute the edit distance between the string and the network. The algorithm is also based on the idea of dynamic programming. It calculates the edit distance between user word string and each node in the FST respectively. The pseudo-code for this dynamic programming process is shown in Table 2.

Table 2. Improved Wagner-Fischer algorithm

inputs: W is a word string
F is a FST model with M states
Initial:Compute $minEDcost(n_0, W)$
For each state n_i in F, $0 < i \leq$
Compute $cost(n_{i-1,n_i})$
$minEDcost(n_i, W) = min(minEDcost(n_{i-1}, W) + cost(n_{i-1}, n_i))$
Output: S is the road that has the least $EDcost$ with W in F

In table 2, $minEDcost(n_i, W)$ represents the accumulated minimum edit distance from state 0 to state i and $cost(n_{i-1}, n_i)$ represents the increased edit distance from state $i - 1$ to state i.

When the user utterance matches a string sequence which has the smallest edit distance with the utterance from an action-group FST, we assume the user utterance belongs to the action-group. At the same time we can automatically extract the attribute-value information in user utterance according to the matched string.

3   Dialogue Management Based on DBN

3.1   DBN

Dynamic Bayesian network (DBN) is a probabilistic graphical model that can deal with the data with timing characteristics. It is formed by adding time information in the conventional Bayesian network. In the DBN, the topology of the network in each time slice is the same. Time slices are connected through a number of arcs which represent the relationship between the random variables in different time slices. Fig.2 shows the topology of a DBN model.

Bayesian network learning consists of two categories: parameter learning and structure learning. Parameter learning is to estimate the conditional probability distribution of each node by the training data when the network structure is known. The structure learning, also known as model selection, is to establish the network topology through training data. Structure learning problem is very

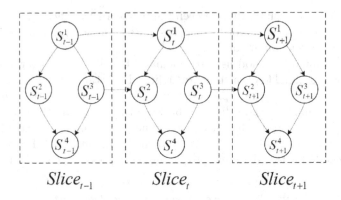

Fig. 2. The topology of DBN

complex, so we manually define the network structure and mainly consider the problem of parameter learning in this paper. Under the conditions of a given network structure, parameter learning can be divided into two categories according to the observability of nodes.

If all nodes can be observed, the model parameters can be obtained directly by a large number of data samples. However, in most cases the data we collected is not enough, then the Dirichlet distribution can be used as the prior distribution of parameters. We update the model through the "evidence" until we get the ultimate posterior probability parameters. We use the notation B^h to represent the Bayesian network topology, and $X = x_1, \ldots, x_n$ to represent a set of n discrete random variables in the network, where each x_i has r_i possible values $x_i^1, x_i^2, \ldots, x_i^{r_i}$. Then the joint probability distribution of X can be shown as the following equation:

$$P(X|\theta_s, B^h) = \prod_{i=1}^{n} P(x_i|parents(x_i), \theta_i, B^h) \tag{1}$$

where $p(x_i|parents(x_i), \theta_i, B^h)$ is the local probability distribution that corresponding with node x_i, and $\theta_s = (\theta_1, \ldots, \theta_n)$ is the parameters of the network model. We assume the training data set $D = \{d_1, \ldots, d_N\}$ has a total of N samples, and each sample includes all the observable nodes. Then the Bayesian network parameter learning problem can be summarized as follows: calculate the posterior probability distribution $P(\theta_s|D, B^h)$ when given the data set D. We get the following equation:

$$\theta_{ijk} = P(x_i^k|parents^j(x_i^k), \theta_i, B^h) \tag{2}$$

where $\theta_i = ((\theta_{ijk})_{k=2}^{r_i})_{j=1}^{q_i}$ and $q_i = \prod_{parents(x_i)} r_i$. We define $\theta_{ij} = (\theta_{ij1}, \ldots, \theta_{ijr_i})$ and assume that parameter vectors θ_{ij} are independent with each other, then the posterior probability of the model parameters is shown as the following equation:

$$P(\theta_s|D, B^h) = \prod_{i=1}^{n} \prod_{j=1}^{q_i} p(\theta_{ij}|D, B^h) \tag{3}$$

The prior distribution of Parameters θ_i is Dirichlet distribution, and then we get the follow equation:

$$P(\theta_{ij}|D, B^h) = Dir(\theta_{ij}|\alpha_{ij1} + N_{ij1}, \alpha_{ij2} + N_{ij2}, \ldots, \alpha_{ijr_i} + N_{ijr_i}) \tag{4}$$

where N_{ijk} is the number of occurrences of $x_i = x_i^k$, $parents(x_i) = parents^j(x_i)$ in the data set D, and α_{ijk} is the number of occurrences of the events in priori, and $\alpha_{ij} = \sum \alpha_{ijk}$, $N_{ij} = \sum_k N_{ijk}$. Finally, according to equation 3 and equation 4, we obtain the following equation[9]:

$$P(X|D, B^h) = \prod_{i=1}^{n} \frac{\alpha_{ijk} + N_{ijk}}{\alpha_{ij} + N_{ij}} \tag{5}$$

When there are hidden nodes in the network, the parameters of the model can be estimated via the EM algorithm. In the E-step the expectations of all nodes are calculated, while in the M-step these expectations can be seen as observed, and the system learns new parameters that maximize the likelihood based on this. After a number of iterations, the system will converge to a local minimum.

3.2 Dialogue Management Based on DBN

In this paper, we do not use the complex state space in the spoken dialogue system. We just put the user action into the dialogue management model to affect the dialogue action [10]. Similarly, we assume that the dialogue process has the Markov property, and then get the following equation:

$$P(a_t|S_1^t, A_1^{t-1}, U_1^t) = P(a_t|s_t, u_t) \tag{6}$$

where S_1^t, A_1^{t-1}, and U_1^t represent the system state, the system action, and the user action that from the initial moment to time t, respectively. s_t, a_t, and u_t represent the system state, the system action, and the user action at time t. The DBN model will take the system input at every time into account, so we add the user action into every time slice in order to make the model depend on the user action. The system action at time t depends on the system state s_t and the current user action u_t. Meanwhile, the current user action u_t as a system input also directly affects the system state s_t. We retain the transfer connection arc between the states in adjacent time slices. The DBN model structure described above is shown in Fig.3.

According to the above description, the DBN model consists of four parts: the system state space S, system dialogue action space A, the DBN network topology B and the user action space U. We collect a series of dialogue corpus as "evidence" to learn the model parameters and infer the optimal system action.

If the system state vector s_t is observable, we can update s_t according to the attribute-value information that extracted by the action-group FST model.

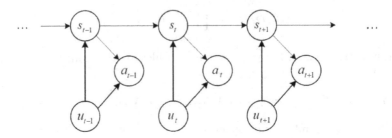

Fig. 3. The DBN Model with user action

Then we can estimate the model parameters directly from the data according to the parameter learning method described in section 3.1. To inference the system action, we directly calculate the joint conditional probability distribution of the system action under the conditions of the system state vector s and user action vector u, and take the maximum probability of action as the current system action. This idea is described by the following equation:

$$\hat{a}_t = \arg\max_{a_i \in A} P(a_i|s_t, u_t) \tag{7}$$

If the system state vector is unobservable, we have to use the EM algorithm to estimate model parameters from the "evidence". The current system action is calculated by the following equation:

$$\begin{aligned}\hat{a}_t &= \arg\max_{a_i \in A} P(a_i|u_t) \\ &= \arg\max_{a_i \in A} \sum_k P(a_i|u_t, S = s_k)P(S = s_k|u_t)\end{aligned} \tag{8}$$

4   System Structure and Experimental Results

The previous content describes the modeling method of natural language understanding module and the dialogue management module. This section presents the overall design of the spoken dialogue system, and provides several experiments to verify the performance of each module. Finally, the experimental results are analyzed.

4.1   Overall Structure of the Spoken Dialogue Systems

A typical spoken dialogue system not only includes the natural language understanding (NLU) module and the dialogue management (DM) module, but also contains the automatic speech recognition (ASR) module, the text to speech (TTS) module, and the natural language generation (NLG) module. For the spoken dialogue system in particular scene, it also contains a database or network database for inquiry. Our spoken dialogue system structure is shown in Fig.4.

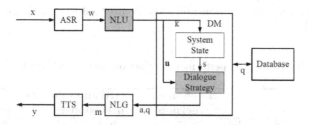

Fig. 4. The structure of our spoken dialogue system

The implementation of the ASR module and the TTS module in Fig.4 uses the open source HTK tools [11] while the NLG module uses template filling [3] method. We use mysql to bulid the database and use query to build communication between the database and DM module. The NLU module and dialogue strategy in the shaded blocks are the focus of our studies. This system receives the user voice x, and uses the ASR module to convert it to the text sequence w. Then the action-group FST model in the NLU module maps the word sequence w to the user action u and attribute-value information k. The dialogue management module has two functions: to maintain the system state and to give the dialogue strategy. We use form filling method to represent the system state [1]. The dialogue management module uses the attribute-value information k to update the system state s, and then uses the DBN model to calculate the dialogue strategy based on the system state s and the user action u. If a user requests for information, the dialogue management module needs to interact with the database to query information q. Then the dialogue management module sends the system action a and the information q to the NLG module where the information will be integrated into the response text m. Finally, the synthetical voice y generated by the TTS module is passed to the user.

4.2   Experimental Results

Experiments on Action-Group FST Model. In this section, we will present the action-group FST model built by openFST toolkit. The annotated data is divided into the training and testing set. The training set consists of 100 dialogues, with a total of 671 rounds data, while the attribute-value pairs in user words are 846. The testing set consists of 20 dialogues, with a total of 138 rounds data, while the attribute-value pairs in the user words are 185. In the annotating process, words that cannot be listed have an alternative, such as the amount of money in the currency exchange scene is replaced by "amount". We use the classification accuracy of user action and the precision, recall and F-measure of the attribute-value pairs in user utterance to evaluate the action-group FST model.

The experiments are divided into two groups. We test the effect of the action-group FST model and the traditional keyword matching respectively. The rules of keyword matching method are studied from the training set only, and they are used to identify user action and extract user information. The results are shown in Table 3.

Table 3. The performance of action-group FST Model

	classification	attribute-value pairs extraction		
	precision	precision	recall	F-measure
action-group FST model	92.75%	92.05%	87.57%	89.75%
keyword matching	90.58%	96.25%	83.24%	89.27%

The experimental results prove that the action-group FST model outperforms the keyword matching method. The keyword matching method has better precision, but its recall is worse than that of the action-group FST model. The overall effect of the action-group FST model has a slight improvement compared with the manual keyword matching method. However, the keyword matching method needs experts to spend much time to write the rules, and this work will become very difficult when the amount of data increases. The action-group FST model will perform better if the amount of data increases, and it has good portability. In summary, the action-group FST model has more advantages.

Experiments on DBN Model. This section presents the DBN model built by the BNT toolkit [12]. The annotated data is also divided into the training and testing set, and the data size is the same as described above.

In the training phase, 671 rounds of dialogue data are sent to the DBN model by sequence to estimate the model parameters. The priori parameters of the initial model are obtained by the Dirichlet distribution. In the testing phase, we send the user utterances to the DBN model by their sequence in the dialog. The difference between the system output action and real data is recoded. When the system generates a wrong action, we send the user utterance by sequence just as there is not any error. Finally, we use the precision of the system output to evaluate the performance of the DBN model.

In this section, we test the DBN model and the MDP model separately, and the experiments on the DBN model are divided into three groups. We assume all nodes in the DBN model are observable in the first experiment. Therefore, there are three variables in the training data. They are the user action, the system state and the system action. The testing data include only the user action and the system state, and the DBN model infers the most suitable system output action according to these two variables. In the second experiment, we set the system state in the previous time slice as evidence both for training and testing. Therefore, the DBN model infers the most suitable system output action based on three variables. We hide the system state in the third experiment. Therefore, there are only the user action and the system action in the training data. We use EM algorithm to estimate the parameters of the DBN model and the DBN model infers the most suitable system output action based only on the user action.

Table 4. The performance of DBN model

	DBN			MDP
	$P(a_t|s_t, u_t)$	$P(a_t|s_{t-1}, s_t, u_t)$	$P(a_t|u_t)$	$P(a_t|s_t, u_t)$
precision	90.58%	89.13%	88.41%	81.88%

Table 4 shows the results of these experiments. The last experimental result in Table 4 is obtained by the MDP model [4] on the same data set described above. In the training phase, the award value of each step is set to -1. If the dialogue ends with satisfaction, then the system rewards 20 for the whole dialogue. There are about 10 rounds in each dialogue, so the whole dialogue gets a positive award sum if the dialogue ends with satisfaction, otherwise it gets a negative award sum. The final jump probability is obtained according to the normalized award value.

From the results shown in Table 4, we can see that the DBN model in the first experiment outperforms the model in the second experiment. This proves that the simple DBN model performs better than the complex model in short dialogue. In the third experiment, the performance degrades significantly when the system state is hidden. This means the system state is very important for DBN model. In related work [7], more complex method is used to describe and maintain the system state, which is consistent with our experimental results. In addition, the performance of the MDP model is poor. This is probably because the MDP model is to get the global award maximum while the DBN model is to seek a single round of local optimal. In the case of limited training data, it is difficult to get the optimal solution for the MDP model. This conclusion is consistent with the related work in [4].

4.3   The Overall Performance of Our Spoken Dialogue System

Natural language understanding and dialogue management, as two of the most important modules in spoken dialogue systems, have good performance separately through the action-group FST model and the DBN model. However, a conclusion concerning the performance of the whole system cannot be drawn easily through these results. A subjective experiment on our overall system proves that the system can basically meet user's needs. A survey of the user of our system is shown in Table 5. The results show that the performance of the system is related to the users, and researchers' test results are much better than those of the other users. The main reasons for the errors are that the user utterances is beyond the training data, and ordinary users are more likely to say words outside the training set. Fig.5 is an instance of the spoken dialogue system interaction with human in a currency exchange scene.

5   Conclusion

This paper focuses on the natural language understanding and dialogue management in spoken dialogue system. To cope with these tow problems, we propose

Fig. 5. An instance of our spoken dialogue system

Table 5. A user survey of the spoken dialogue system

user types	total dialogues	dialogues end with satisfaction
researcher	30	27
ordinary user	30	22

the action-group FST model and the DBN model. The advantages of these two models include: (1) the model can work on a small-scale data set, while the model will perform better on a large-scale data set; (2) these two models have good portability because there is little artificial work in model designing.

Although the action-group FST model and DBN model show good performance in some specific fields of spoken dialogue systems, there remains much to improve. If the concept of word similarity is added into the action-group FST model, the edit distance calculation results of the synonyms will be a decimal. Then the action-group FST model can perform better when matching user utterances. In addition, the form filling method used for representing the system state cannot meet the system's needs when the system becomes complex. Furthermore, the DBN structure design and parameter learning will be more complex when the system state becomes a high-dimensional vector. These issues will be addressed in future work.

References

1. Seneff, S., Polifroni, J.: Dialogue Management in the Mercury Flight Reservation System. In: Proceeding ANLP/NAACL Workshop on Conversational Systems, pp. 11–16 (2000)

2. Pietquin, O.: A probabilistic framework for dialog simulation and optimal strategy learning. IEEE Transactions on Audio, Speech, and Language Processing, 589–599 (2004)
3. Pieraccini, R., Levin, E., Eckert, W.: AMICA: the AT&T mixed initiative conversational architecture. In: Proceedings of the European Conference on Speech, Communication and Technology, pp. 1875–1878 (1997)
4. Levin, E., Pieraccinin, R., Eckert, W.: A stochastic model of computer-human interaction for learning dialog strategies. IEEE Transactions on Speech and Audio Processing, 11–23 (2000)
5. Williams, J.D., Young, S.: Partially observable Markov decision processes for spoken dialog systems. Computer Speech and Language, 393–422 (2007)
6. Allauzen, C., Riley, M., Schalkwyk, J., et al.: OpenFst: A General And Efficient Weighted Finite-State Transducer Library. In: Proceedings of International Conference on Implementation and Application of Automate, pp. 11–23 (2007)
7. Young, S.: Still Talking to Machines (Cognitively Speaking). In: Interspeech, pp. 1–10 (2010)
8. Wagner, R.A., Fischer, M.J.: The String-to-String Correction Problem. Journal of the ACM, 168–173 (1974)
9. Heckerman, D.: A tutorial on learning with Bayesian networks. SCI (2008)
10. Yu, D.: Research on Error Detection and Human-Computer Dialogue for Error Correction in Cross-language Conversation, pp. 50–56. Institute of Automation, Chinese Academy of Sciences, Beijing (2011)
11. Young, S., Evermann, G., Gales, M., et al.: The HTK Book (for HTK Version 3.4). Cambridge University Engineering Department (2009)
12. Murphy, K.: The Bayes Net Toolbox for Matlab. In: Computing Science and Statistics: Proceedings of the Interlacel (2001)

Sentiment Analysis Based on Chinese Thinking Modes

Liang Yang, Hongfei Lin, and Yuan Lin

Department of Computer Science and Engineering,
Dalian University of Technology, Dalian 116023, China
{yangliang,yuanlin}@mail.dlut.edu.cn, hflin@dlut.edu.cn

Abstract. Sentiment analysis is an important research domain for NLP, and currently it mainly focuses on text context. While our research concentrates on the thinking modes, which influence the formation of language. "Spiral graphic mode", "concreteness" and "scattered view", are taken into consideration to assist sentiment analysis and classification in this paper. According to these explicit Chinese modes, a Chinese sentiment expression model (CSE) is proposed, which can effectively improve the accuracy of emotion classification. In order to solve the implicit Chinese sentiment expression, Latent Semantic Analysis (LSA) is applied when the CSE model could not classify the implicit emotions accurately. By comparing with two traditional sentiment analysis methods, experimental results show that the performance of sentiment analysis included the Chinese thinking mode factors is significantly better than which not included.

Keywords: Chinese thinking mode, Chinese sentiment expressing model, LSA.

1 Introduction

Sentiment analysis is a popular research topic in NLP in recent years. It aims to assist computers to recognize the human emotions, which is more widely used in industry and academia. For example, whenever we need to make a decision, we often seek out the opinions of others. Qiu et al [1] constructed the double propagation between opinion word and target aspect to get the sentiment orientation of the opinion to the target aspect. Wang et al [2] proposed a rating regression approach to analyze the rating text review data, which could generate summaries about aspects for consumers. Another example is the word-of-mouth on social media, such as Blog and Micro-Blog, and mining the tendency of a group of peoples' opinions is badly needed. There has been some work by researchers. Such as Wang et al [3] presented a graph-based hashtag sentiment classification approach to analyze the sentiment tendency in Twitter.

In China, researchers concentrate on phrase level and sentence level sentiment classification recently, such as COAE (Chinese Opinion Analysis Evaluation) [4]. Less work has been done on passage level comparing with the former two levels, for the structures and patterns of emotion expressions are more complex. Turney [5] proposed a lexicon based method to identify the passage's emotion by using the average score of emotion word and phrase. Tan et al [6] constructed a group of domain lexicons to guarantee the accuracy. Although the existing lexicon based method gets a

M. Zhou et al. (Eds.): NLPCC 2012, CCIS 333, pp. 46–57, 2012.

good result, its flexibility and human annotation accuracy are still a potential problem. Xu et al [7] proposed a method based on semantic resources, and Condition Random Field (CRF) is applied to label emotion sentence by sentence; after the emotion chain formed, the emotion of the passage is determined.

In this paper, we analyze relationships between thinking modes and language, and three Chinese thinking modes are taken into consideration to assist sentiment analysis and emotion classification. Then a Chinese sentiment expression model (CSE) is proposed based on the thinking modes, and DUTIR affective ontology [8] is also combined to identify the explicit emotions. Finally Latent Semantic Analysis (LSA) is applied when the CSE model could not classify the implicit emotions accurately.

The paper is organized as follows: Section 2 introduces the Chinese and Western Thinking Modes and their features. Then Section 3 describes the quantification of Chinese thinking modes and the Chinese sentiment expression model (CSE). In section 4, implicit emotion mining method based on Latent Semantic Analysis (LSA) is explained. Section 5 presents experiments and results. Finally, we conclude this work and point out some directions for future research in Section 6.

2   Thinking Modes

In Wikipedia, thought (or thinking) [9] generally refers to any mental or intellectual activity involving an individual's subjective consciousness. It can refer either to the act of thinking or the resulting ideas or arrangements of ideas. Different civilizations cradle different thinking mode, and thinking modes determine the expression way of languages. From the concept of thinking, we can find that thinking and language are inseparable. Language is the expression way of thinking, and it carries the abstraction of the reality. When we express our thinking, to a large degree, the features of thinking play a decisive role. Every nation has its own thinking mode, so researches on thinking mode are essential to sentiment analysis. Later, we will introduce Western and Chinese thinking modes respectively.

2.1   "Spiral Graphic Mode" and "Straight Line Mode"

"Spiral graphic mode" is one of Chinese thinking modes, and it commonly reflects in the passage organization aspect. Because of the implicit characteristic, Chinese normally introduces the topic in an indirect way like a spiral graphic, so the topic of the passage is discussed after examples. On the other hand, "Straight Line Mode" is the feature of English passage organization, for Western thinking is influenced by the Roman philosophy, so they focus on deduction and thinking in a straight line way. On passage organization aspect, they tend to state their views directly and frankly. Take these sentences below as examples:

(1) Chinese: "他被眼前的一幕震惊了。"
    English: "He was shocked by what he saw."
(2) Chinese: "经过反复的思考，我终于得到了完美的答案。"
    English: "I got a perfect answer after deeply thinking."

Form the above mentioned examples, we can find that the key emotion words "shocked" and "perfect" appear in the front part of the sentence, but the Chinese emotion word "震惊" and "完美" locate at the end part of the sentences.

2.2   "Concreteness" and "Abstractness"

The second Chinese thinking mode is called "concreteness", for Chinese is a hieroglyphic language, which means that quantities of specific words, shapes, sounds and description are used in Chinese to illustrate abstract things, and some character components can reflect this characteristic. But the English lay emphasize on "abstractness", which is another western thinking mode. They tend to implement general vocabularies and their variants to express abstract feelings or opinions, such as "-ion", "-ance" and "-ness", but concrete things are seldom applied to explain.

   (3) Chinese: "土崩瓦解。" English: "Disintegration."
   (4) Chinese: "有志者，事竟成。" English: "Where there is a will, there is a way."

From example (3), we found that concrete things, soil, tile, appeared in Chinese idiom, while only the variant of disintegrate is used to explain these meaning in English. And in example (4), we could get an overview that verb has advantages in Chinese, but noun is more frequent used flexibly in English.

2.3   "Scatter View" and "Focus View"

"Scatter view" [10] is the third Chinese thinking modes. From the angle of ontology, Chinese tend to emphasize unified whole, which means think from more to one. When Chinese express their feelings or comments, they are usually inclined to use various words to enhance their emotion. "Scatter View" is usually applied in the Chinese expression, for example, we can frequently find that more than one verb is used in one Chinese sentence, but the sentence is still fluent. While English pay more attention to logical reasoning or deduction, they tend to express their feelings or emotions briefly, and it is a kind of focusing thinking, which is called "Focus View". "Focus view" can be reflected by the only one verb, which normally is the core of one sentence. "Focus view" is widely adopted in English. Here are two examples about "Scatter view" and "Focus view" below:

   (5)Chinese: "他拿着课本走进了教室。"
       English: "He walked into the classroom with a textbook in hands."
   (6)Chinese: "他们俩青梅竹马，两小无猜。"
       English: "The boy and the girl were playmates in their childhood."

From the examples (5), we can clearly find that more than one word are implemented in Chinese sentence, but each English sentence only contain one word, and it is the core of the sentence. In example (6), "Scatter View" is embodied in Chinese expression, which is reflected by more words used to express the same meaning.

   To sum up the above mentioned Western and Chinese thinking modes [11], we find that "Scatter view" and "Focus View" is the feature of sentence structure;

"concreteness" and "abstractness" are the characteristic of vocabulary usage; "Spiral graphic mode" and "Straight line mode" are reflections on passage expression model. "Scatter view" and "Spiral graphic mode" are explicit in Chinese articles, such as vocabulary variants, while "concreteness" mostly appears in an implicit way. These thinking modes provide us a new angle to analyze text sentiment orientation.

3   Description of Chinese Sentiment Expression Model

3.1   External Resource

So far, there is no standard in emotional classification, the paper uses DUTIR Emotion Ontology [8] as the external resource. Because human emotion is complicated and changeable, and people have insufficient cognition about it, so the emotion is divided into 4, 6, 8, 10 and 20categories etc. While in DUTIR Emotion Ontology, the emotion is classified into 7 categories and 20 subcategories, and it can be applied widely in sentiment analysis and emotion classification.

To recognize the affective lexicon, we calculate mutual information between the lexicon and ontology in the resource, and then we combine some affective lexicon rules, such as part-of-speech rules, co-occurrence rules, and context rules at el. Machine learning method is also used to automatically expand the emotion ontology. Conditional Random Fields [12, 13] (CRFs) is adopted as the automatic acquisition method, the formula is defined as follows:

$$P_{\theta}(y \mid x) = \exp(\sum_{e \in E,k} \lambda_k f_k(e, y\mid_e, x) + \sum_{v \in V,k} u_k g_k(v, y\mid_v, x)$$

(1)

Where x is a data sequence and y a label sequence, $y\mid v$ is the set of components of y associated with the vertices in sub graph S. The features f_k and g_k are given and fixed.

While in Chinese Opinion Analysis Evaluation (COAE) [4], emotion is classified into 4 categories, which are "happy", "angry", "sad" and "fear", and opinion evaluation consists of positive and negative. So we made some adjustments on DUTIR Emotion Ontology to complement the standard of COAE.

3.2   Quantification of Similarities between Thinking Modes

Although there are differences between Western and Chinese thinking modes, there are still some similarities. For example, no matter what Chinese or English articles are, the negative words locate in front of emotion or opinion words to express contrary feelings or attitudes; adverb of degree is placed before adjective to enhance or decrease the its intensity; if an adversative occurs, the emotion of the sentence is determined by the part after the adversative.

Sentence is the foundation of constructing paragraph and passage, and it is the minimum level to meet sentiment phenomenon on the above mentioned part. So sentence level is chosen as minimum research object level. Modifier window strategy is adopted to analyze the emotion of a sentence and its score. In this strategy, negative words, adverb of degree and adversative are detected if they exist in the modifier window.

3.2.1   Quantification of "Spiral Graphic Mode"

"Spiral graphic mode" is a Chinese sentence or passage organization characteristic, the topic of article is introduced in an indirect way. Demonstration comes first, and the theme usually locates the tail of the sentence or passage. On the contrary to the above mentioned, the nearer emotion words locate the tail of the sentence, the more important they are to determine the emotion of the sentence. For example:

(7)Chinese: "这个酒店什么都好，就是服务让人失望。"
English: "Every aspect about the hotel is ok except the disappointing service."

Although the former part presents a positive opinion, the word "失望" (disappointing) in later part determines the emotion of the whole sentence. So the example sentence shows a negative opinion. Based on the statistic data of our corpus, we find that the emotion-determining words mostly locate the end part of Chinese sentences. And this conclusion is still useful to paragraphs and passages [14].

In order to simulate the "spiral graphic mode", equation (2) is applied:

$$score(A) = \sum_i \left(1 + position(a_i) / count(a \mid A)\right) \times score(a_i) \qquad (2)$$

Where A can be a passage, paragraph or sentence, a can be a paragraph, sentence or a word. $score(A)$ is the emotion score of A, and $position(a_i)$ is the position of the emotion unit a_i.

From the equation (2) we can find that if the closer a_i locates the tail, the larger the $score(a_i)$ will be. Take example (7), the word "失望" (disappointing) locates near the tail of the sentence, it can get a larger score than the word "好" (good) after computing by equation (2), so different emotion words regain new emotion weights, so this sentence tends to have a negative tendency.

3.2.2   Quantification of "Concreteness"

Based on the analysis of the differences between "abstractness" and "concreteness", we find that the characteristic or property of a certain word is helpful to sentiment analysis. In all nations, adjective tends to have a better performance to express feeling or emotion than the other part of speech word. While in Chinese sentiment expression, verb also plays an important role, such as "溃败" (be defeated) and "脸红" (blush). The former tries to express a "fear" feeling and the latter means shy or embarrassed. In order to simulate this thinking and language characteristic, different part of speech word and sentence structure are adopted different tactics. The details can be seen as follows in equation (3).

$$score(a) = \sum_i^n W_i^{adj} + \sum_j^m W_j^{verb} + \sum_k^l W_k$$

(3)

Where a is a sentence, and $score(a)$ is the score of sentence a. W_i^{adj} is the i th adjective, W_j^{verb} is the j th adjective, and W_k is other part of speech word in sentence a.

In equation (3), it does not simply add all these part of speech words' weights together, but give the highest priority to adjective, then the higher priority is given to the verb, finally other words are processed. "Concreteness" is implemented by the priority to the verb, and which meets the Chinese thinking explicitly.

3.2.3   Quantification of "Scatter View"

In Chinese writing, authors are likely to use a number of similar expressions to express the same sentiment or emotion. And a great number of nouns or adjectives are used as predicate and this has been discussed above. In order to simulate the Chinese thinking mode "scatter view", view-window is adopted, which means that in specific position different sizes of windows are applied to reflect this characteristic. Based on our experiment, when the size of window is fixed at 6, we can get the best result. If the size of view-window is too small, it cannot capture the words which significantly assist the sentiment analysis; on the contrary, too much noise will be introduced, which will also mislead the analysis.

3.3   Chinese Sentiment Expression Model

After analyzing the features of Western and Chinese thinking modes and their specific quantification methods, in this part, we will introduce a Chinese sentiment expression model, which is the combination of Chinese thinking modes. When we try to get the sentiment or emotion tendency of the text content, all of the Chinese thinking modes are taken into consideration.

"Scatter view" and "Spiral graphic mode" are conclusions on Chinese expression, and they are both explicit features of Chinese thinking modes. "Scatter view" is the feature of sentence structure, and "Spiral graphic mode" is a characteristic of passage organization. While in English expression, only one verb is contained in one sentence, so the emotion of this sentence is easy to determine after analyzing the key verb. But due to the "Scatter view" thinking mode, Chinese tend to use more verb and their variants to express emotions.

In order to enrich the vocabulary, DUTIR Emotion Ontology [8] is adopted. In Chinese Opinion Analysis Evaluation (COAE) [4], the emotions are classified into four group, which are "happy", "angry", "sad", and "fear", and opinion-bearing words are classified into "positive" and "negative". For this coarse granularity partition can avoid the intersection among different emotions, which can significantly reduce the classification error rate and improve the accuracy. 22773 emotion words and 6 groups are chosen manually to testify the influence of "Scatter view" on sentiment analysis. Therefore the number of emotion words can explain the characteristic "Scatter", but the emotion groups can maintain that every passage has an explicit topic.

Due to the complexity of the sentence structure, sometimes sentiment analysis or emotion classification would be misled by negative words and degree words. For example, the negative words can change the emotion tendency, and the degree words can enlarge or lessen the emotion intensity. So in this article, degree words, negative words and adversative are all taken into consideration.

After integrating the two Chinese thinking modes, "Scatter view" and "Spiral graphic mode", the Chinese sentiment expression model is proposed. DUTIR Ontology [8] and classification principle are applied to implement the characteristic of "Scatter view", and "spiral graphic mode" is simulated based on the position-influenced strategy.

4   Implicit Chinese Sentiment Expression Mining Based on LSA

The above mentioned Chinese sentiment expressions are extracted based on the explicit Chinese thinking mode "Scatter view" and "spiral graphic mode". But the Chinese thinking mode "concreteness" mostly appears in an indirect way. If the emotion of the sentence cannot be analyzed by using explicit features, the thinking mode "concreteness" is helpful. Chinese express their emotions or feelings influenced by "concreteness" thinking mode, and they tend to make use of familiar and similar object. So it is an implicit feature for implicit emotion mining. In this paper LSA is used to determine the emotion of the implicit emotions, and it has been widely applied to calculate the similarity between word and word, word and passage, or passage and passage. In section 4.1, we discuss what kind of texts is labeled as implicit emotion text. Then we introduce the method to determine the emotion of implicit emotion text.

4.1   The Criterion of Implicit Emotion Sample

When people express their emotions or feelings, some articles can be identified just by analyzing the tendency of emotion words, but others are not. The articles, which cannot be determined by emotion words, are implicit emotion articles. Because the implicit emotion articles mostly have low scores comparing with the explicit ones, so the threshold is needed to classify the explicit emotion sample and the implicit ones.

In this paper, a group of samples are chosen to determine the threshold, and we call them threshold sample. The threshold samples are the sentences which only contain one explicit emotion word, and its intensity is 9 in DUTIR Emotion Ontology [8]. The strong intensity of the emotion ontology is applied to guarantee the explicitness of sentiment expression. The scores are implemented to determine the threshold.

4.2   Implicit Emotion Classification Based on LSA

LSA (Latent Semantic Analysis) is proposed by Dumais et al in the year 1988, which is used in statistic method to analyze mass texts, and get the latent semantic relationships among words. The main object of LSA is to map the higher dimension Vector Space Model (VSM) to lower dimension latent semantic space.

The main reason why the implicit samples exist is that the no emotion words are indexed in emotion lexicon. For the implicit emotion samples express emotion in an indirect way, so we need to further analysis, and the samples which scores are larger than the threshold are chosen as seed samples [15]. Then LSA is implemented to mine the latent semantic relationships between the implicit samples and the seed samples.

After the above steps, we can obtain the emotion tendency of the implicit samples. Equation (4) is used to compute the score of the implicit sample, and then identify the emotion of the sample:

$$score_j \left(A_i \right) = \sum_k sim \left(A_i, s_{jk} \right) \times score \left(s_{jk} \right)$$

(4)

Where *Score(A$_i$)* denotes the score of implicit sample A_i in Emotion *j*; S_{jk} is the *k* th sample in Emotion *j*; sim(*A$_i$*, *S$_{jk}$*) denotes the similarity of implicit sample A_i and sample S_{jk}; *score(s$_{jk}$)* is the score of sample S_{jk} in Chinese sentiment expression model.

5   Experiment Setting and Evaluation

5.1   Experiments of Chinese Thinking Modes in Different Domains

In order to test and verify whether the Chinese thinking modes can assist sentiment analysis, three group experiments have been done on Evaluation data set provided by Tan [16]. The data set contains three domains, which are 4000 hotel reviews, 1608 electronics reviews and 1047 stock reviews, and each domain has its positive and negative subset. The reviews in the data set cover sentence level, paragraph level, and passage level, and this can avoid the particularity of sentence structure. The baseline is the method proposed by Turney [5], and three thinking modes are integrated to see whether they are helpful to assist sentiment analysis. The results of thinking modes method and method proposed by Turney are shown in figure 1, and the columns in it from 1 to 6 respectively represent the subsets: elec-neg, elec-pos, hotel-neg, hotel-pos, stock-neg and stock-pos.

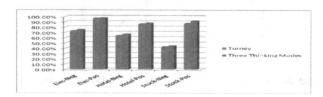

Fig. 1. Precision Results between Turney and Chinese thinking modes

From the results in figure 1, we can get a conclusion that no matter positive or negative review subset are, there is still an increase in all domains. It proves that the Chinese thinking modes can assist the sentiment analysis indeed, and they have independence to different fields. Other three groups of experiments have been done to analyze the three Chinese thinking modes in different domains.

The first group experiments are adopted on electronics negative and positive reviews. The reviews in elec-neg data set are relatively longer and rich in verbs. From figure 2, we can find that after adding each Chinese thinking mode the precision has increased. The precision of elec-pos reviews is not increasing obviously. That is because too much nouns are in the text context and less emotion words are used to express the only one emotion.

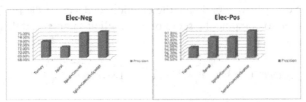

Fig. 2. Precisions on Elec-Neg data set and Elec-Pos data set

The second group experiments are implemented on negative and positive hotel reviews. Adding the "spiral graphic mode", the results on hotel-neg and hotel-positive data sets are basically remained the same level. But after the "concreteness" is taken into consideration, the results are much higher than before. It verifies that "concreteness" is much helpful in Chinese sentiment analysis. The size of view-window is decided by the specific data set to get the best result. The experiment results of hotel reviews are shown in figure 3 as follows.

Stock reviews are used to do the third group of experiments results. The result of stock-neg data set is not good in figure 4. After we analyze the errors, we find the reason that a great number of specialized words exist and part of them does not appear in DUTIR emotion ontology [8]. That is also the limitation of lexicon based method. From figure 4, there is an improvement after adding these three Chinese thinking modes. Due to most stock reviews are passage-level passages, the length of the review is relatively long than the former two electronic and hotel data sets. And it can explicitly reflect the Chinese thinking modes – spiral graphic mode and its advantage.

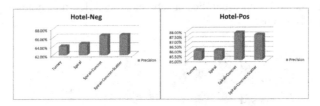

Fig. 3. Precisions on Hotel-Neg data set and Hotel-Pos data set

5.2   Experiment of Chinese sentiment Expression Model and LSA

In this experiment part, the experiment data set is ChnSentiCorp [17], and it is about hotel evaluation, which consists of hotel service quality, food quality, surrounding

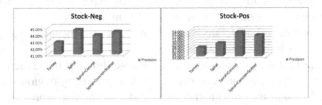

Fig. 4. Precisions on Stock-Neg data set and Stock-Pos data set

and so on. There are 2000 positive passages and 2000 negative passages in it. After checking the label result, the noisy texts are removed and parts of the passages are relabeled. Then we get 1828 positive passages and 2163 negative passages.

For comparison, we implement two baseline methods: one is lexicon based method proposed by Turney [5], which decides the passage polarity only by its emotion words. If they are positive-orientated, then the passage is positive-orientated. The same goes for a negative-orientated passage; the other method is based on semantic resource proposed by Xu [7], which takes semantic resource into consideration, such as negation and transition. The result is listed in table 1.

From the results in table 1, we find that the precision of lexicon based method is close to that of CSE. After we analyze the error list, the main reason is the implicit emotion samples. Due to the emotions of implicit samples are unclear, the method applied in experiments have a higher probability to be misclassified by them, and that will decrease the precision in the long run. Some statistic jobs on implicit emotion samples have also been done. Later we will illustrate them.

Semantic method focuses on the sentence level, and we can see that there is a precision increase of our proposed method - CSE from the comparing results. In order to identify the opinion tendency of the whole passage, the semantic method proposed by Xu [7] has to count the numbers of positive sentences and negative ones, and the larger number determines the opinion orientation of the passage. So we can see that the CSE model has a better performance in binary opinion classification than Xu [7].

Table 1. Experiment results on ChnSentiCorp

	Lexicon	Semantic	CSE
Pos	1575/1828(86.16%)	1502/1828(82.17%)	1575/1828(86.16%)
Neg	1727/2163(79.84%)	1811/2163(83.73%)	1827/2163(84.47%)
Total	3302/3991(82.74%)	3313/3991(83.01%)	3402/3991(85.24%)

Implicit emotion sample classification is a difficult problem in sentiment analysis. Based on the classification results of the former experiment in 5.2, and we can find that although the precisions are close, the correct classification number of implicit emotion sample is not good comparing with lexicon based method. So the implicit emotion classification based on LSA is necessary. Some statistic jobs have been done by us, and the details are listed in table 2.

Table 2. Statistic data of implicit samples

	Lexicon	CSE
Pos-Implicit	751/1575(47.68%)	640/1575(40.63%)
Neg-Implicit	836/1827(45.76%)	624/1827(34.15%)
Total	1587/3402(46.65%)	1264/3402(37.15%)

In order to solve the implicit emotion problem, LSA is implemented. Each implicit emotion sample is used as a query to index the relevant seed sample in latent semantic space. Based on the opinion orientation of seed sample, the emotion of the implicit sample is determined. To capture the higher similarities between implicit emotion sample and seed sample, the similarity threshold value is given 0.8 empirically. Figure 5 is the results after secondary classification in positive and negative data sets in ChnSentiCorp [17]. Figure 6 is macro-average precision of the former two data sets.

From figure 5 to 6, we can find that after secondary classification by implementing LSA, there is a significant increase. And the precision of the whole data set reaches higher than 90%.

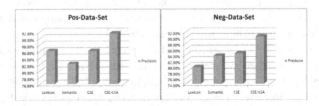

Fig. 5. Precisions on ChnSentiCorp Pos-Data-Set and Neg-Data-Set

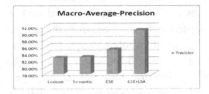

Fig. 6. Macro-Average-Precision of different methods in ChnSentiCorp

Chinese sentiment expression model is applied to get the emotion tendency of the explicit emotion sample from Chinese thinking modes, "spiral graphic mode" and "scatter view", and the results show that it cannot only guarantee the precision, but also make sure the credibility of emotion classification. LSA is adopted in secondary classification to do the mining work between seed sample and implicit sample in latent semantic space based on the "concreteness" thinking mode.

After analyzing the error samples, we find that classification errors in this paper mainly focus on the following two aspects: First, some of the seed samples are misclassified. There are 8 misclassified seed samples in positive data set and 15 of that in negative data set; second, due to the variety of implicit emotion samples, some of the implicit emotion samples cannot index the samples with higher similarities.

6   Conclusion

The contribution of this paper is to propose the Chinese sentiment expression model, which focuses on the thinking modes. Three Chinese thinking modes, "spiral graphic mode", "concreteness" and "scattered view", are applied to assist sentiment analysis and emotion classification. According to these explicit Chinese modes, a Chinese sentiment expression model (CSE) is proposed. From the experiment results, it can effectively improve the accuracy of emotion classification. Thinking mode "concreteness" mostly exists in implicit emotion expressions. In order to solve this, Latent Semantic Analysis (LSA) is applied to implement "concreteness" when CSE model could not classify the implicit emotions accurately. Two traditional sentiment analysis methods are used to verify the effectiveness of proposed method, CSE and LSA. Experimental results show that the performance of sentiment analysis included the Chinese Thinking mode factors and LSA mining is better than that not included.

References

1. Guang, Q., Bing, L., Jiajun, B., et al.: Opinion word expansion and target extraction through double propagation. Computational Linguistics 37(1), 9–27 (2011)
2. Hongning, W., Yue, L., Chengxiang, Z.: Latent aspect rating analysis without aspect keyword supervision. In: Proceedings of the 17th ACM SIGKDD International Conference on Knowledge Discovery and Data Mining, USA, NY, pp. 618–626 (2011)
3. Xiaolong, W., Furu, W., Xiaohua, L., et al.: Topic sentiment analysis in twitter: A graph-based hashtag sentiment classification approach. In: Proceedings of the 20th ACM Conference on Information and Knowledge Management, USA, NY, pp. 1031–1040 (2011)
4. Hongbo, X., Tianfang, Y., Xuanjing, H., et al.: Overview of Chinese opinion analysis evaluation (EB/OL) (2009), http://ir-china.org.cn/coae2009.html
5. Turney, P.D., Littman, M.L.: Measuring praise and criticism: Inference of semantic orientation from association. ACM Transactions on Information Systems 21(4), 315–346 (2003)
6. Weifu, D., Songbo, T.: Building domain-oriented sentiment lexicon by improved information bottleneck. In: Proceedings of the 18th ACM Conference on Information and Knowledge Management, pp. 1749–1752. ACM Press, New York (2009)
7. Linhong, X., Hongfei, L.: Discourse affective computing based on semantic features and ontology. Journal of Computer Research and Development 44(z2), 356–360 (2007)
8. Linhong, X., Hongfei, L., Yu, P.: Constructing the affective lexicon ontology. Journal of the China Society for Scientific and Technical Information 27(2), 180–185 (2008)
9. Wikipedia. Thought (EB/OL), http://en.wikipedia.org/wiki/Thinking
10. Shuneng, L.: Mdes of thinking: Chinese and western. Foreign Languages and Their Teaching 2, 40–48 (2002)
11. Yan, C.: Thinking difference and modes of English and Chinese expressions. The Northern Forum 5, 111–113 (2001)
12. Jianmei, C., Hongfei, L., Zhihao, Y.: Automatic acquisition of emotional vocabulary based on syntax. Caai Transactions on Intelligent Systems 4(2), 100–106 (2009)
13. Lafferty, J., McCallum, A., Pereira, F.: Conditional random fields: Probabilistic models for segmenting and labeling sequence data. In: Proceedings of the18th International Conference on Machine Learning, Waltham, Massachusetts, pp. 282–289 (2001)
14. Ku, L.W., Liu, I.C., et al.: Sentence-level opinion analysis by CopeOpi in NTCIR-7 (EB/OL),
http://research.nii.ac.jp/ntcir/workshop/OnlineProceedings7/index.html
15. Qiong, W., Songbo, T., Gang, Z., et al.: Research on cross-domain opinion analysis. Journal of Chinese Information Processing 1, 77–83 (2010)
16. Qiong, W., Songbo, T., Haijun, Z., et al.: SentiRank: Cross-domain graph ranking for sentiment classification. In: Proceedings of the 2009 IEEE/WIC/ACM International Joint Conference on Web Intelligence and Intelligent Agent Technology, pp. 309–314. IEEE Computer Society, Washington, DC (2009)
17. ChnSentiCorp (EB/OL),
http://www.searchforum.org.cn/tansongbo/corpus-senti.htm

Ontology-Based Event Modeling for Semantic Understanding of Chinese News Story

Wei Wang[1,2] and Dongyan Zhao[1]

[1] Institute of Computer Science & Technology, Peking University, Beijing, China
[2] Department of Electronic Technology, Engineering University of CAPF, Xi'an, China
{wjwangwei,zhaodongyan}@pku.edu.cn

Abstract. Describing and extracting event semantic information is essential to build an event knowledge base and applications in event and semantic level. However, most existing work deals with documents so they fail to provide sufficient semantic information about events in news articles. In this paper, considering *What, Who, When, Where, Why* and *How*, the 5W1H elements of a piece of news, we propose a News Ontology Event Model (NOEM) which can describe 5W1H semantic elements of an event. The model defines concepts of entities (time, person, location, organization etc.), events and relationships to capture temporal, spatial, information, experiential, structural and causal aspect of events. A comparison to existing event models and an empirical case study show that NOEM can effectively model the semantic elements of news events and their relationship; and has a strong ability to represent knowledge facts and easily adapt to new domains.

Keywords: Ontology, 5W1H, Event Model, Ontology Population.

1 Introduction

In the past decade, event has emerged as a promising research field in Natural Language Processing (NLP), Information Retrieval (IR) and Information Extraction (IE). In online news services domain, event-based techniques which can extract entities, such as time, person, location, organization etc. from news stories and find relationship among them to represent structural events, have been paid wildly attention. Based on the identification and extraction of these valuable event facts, more convenient and intelligent services can be implemented to facilitate online news browsing in event and semantic level.

However, the definition and representation of event are different in various research areas. In the literature, there are a number of event models nowadays. For example, event templates used in Message Understanding Conference (MUC) [1], a structural event representation in Automatic Content Extraction (ACE) [2], a generic event model E [3] [4] in event-centric multimedia data management, and ontology-based event models, such as ABC [5], PROTON [6] and Event-Model-F [7] in knowledge management. But these models are not suitable for semantic

M. Zhou et al. (Eds.): NLPCC 2012, CCIS 333, pp. 58–68, 2012.
© Springer-Verlag Berlin Heidelberg 2012

understanding of news events. In order to support semantic applications, for example, event information extraction and semantic relation navigation, we propose a News Ontology Event Model (NOEM) to describe entities and relations among them in news events.

As we know, 5W1H (including What, Who, When, Where, Why, How), a concept in news style is regarded as basics in information gathering. The rule of the 5W1H originally states that a news story should be considered as complete if it answers a checklist of 5W1H. The factual answers to these six questions, each of which comprises an interrogative word: what, who, when, where, why and how, are considered to be elaborate enough for people to understand the whole story [8].

In NOEM, in order to address the whole list of 5W1H, we define concepts of entities (time, person, location, organization etc.), events and relationships to capture temporal, spatial, information, experiential, structural and causal aspect of events. The comparison of NOEM with existed event models shows that it has a better knowledge representation ability, feasibility and applicability. By automatically extracting structural 5W1H semantic information of events and populating these information to NOEM, an event knowledge base can be built to support event and semantic level applications in news domain.

The rest of the paper is organized as follows. We first review related work in Sec. 2 by discussing event definitions and event modelings. The proposed ontology event model NOEM is introduced in Sec. 3. In Sec. 4, we evaluate the representative ability of NOEM by comparing it with existing event models and demonstrate its feasibility and applicability by means of case study. In Sec. 5, we conclude this paper.

2   Related Work

2.1   Event Definitions

The notion of an *event* has been widely used in many research fields related to in natural language processing, although with significant variance in what exactly an event is. A general definition of *event* is "something that happens at a given place and time", according to WordNet [9]. Cognitive psychologists look events as "happenings in the outside world", and they believe people observe and understand the world through event because it is a suitable unit in accordance with aspect of human cognition. Linguists have worked on the underlying semantic structure of events, for example, Chung and Timberlake (1985) stated that "an event can be defined in terms of three components: a predicate; an interval of time on which the predicate occurs and a situation or set of conditions under which the predicate occurs." In [10], Timberlake further supplements it as "events occur in places, under certain conditions, and one can identify some participants as agents and some as patients."

In recent years, some empirical research have been developed on the cognitive linguistics theoretical basis. TimeML [11] is a rich specification language for event and temporal expressions in natural language text. Event is described as "a cover term for situations that happen or occur. Events can be punctual or last for a period of time". In event-based summarization, Filatova et.al. [13] define a concept of *atomic event*. Atomic events link major constituent parts (participants, locations, times) of events through verbs or action nouns labeling the event itself. In IE community, an event represents a relationship between participants, times, and places. The MUC extracts prespecified event information and relates the event information to particular organization, person, or artifact entities involved in the event. The ACE describes event as "an event involving zero or more ACE entities, values and time expressions".

The event extraction task in ACE requires that certain specified types of events that are mentioned in the source language data be detected and that selected information about these events be recognized and merged into a unified representation for each detected event. According to the requirements of semantic understanding of news and the characteristics of news story, we define event as "an event is a specific occurrence which involves in some participants". It has three components: a predicate; core participants, i.e., agents and patients; auxiliary participants, i.e., time and place of the event. These participants are usually named entities which correspond to the *what, who, whom, when, where* elements of an event. The relationships among entities and events are also concerned. By analyzing the connections between the predicates, we can get the *why* and *how* elements which are cause and effect of the event.

2.2 Event Modeling

Event modeling involves event definition, event information representing and storing. There have been several event models in different application domains.

Probabilistic Event Model. In [12], a news event probabilistic model is proposed for Retrospective news Event Detection (RED) task in Topic Detection and Tracking (TDT). In the model, news articles are represented by four kinds of information: *who* (persons), *when* (time), *where* (locations) and *what* (keywords). Because news reports are always aroused by news events, a news event is modeled by mixture of three unigram models for persons, locations and keywords and one Gaussian Mixture Model (GMM) model for timestamps.

Atomic Event Model. In event-based summarization, Filatova et.al. [13] denote atomic events as triple patterns $<n_m, t_i, n_n>$. The triples consist of an event term t_i and two named entities n_m, n_n. This event model was adopted by a number of work in event-based summarization [14] [15].

Structural Event Model. In IE domain, event model is a structural template or frameset in MUC and ACE respectively. In MUC, the event extraction task is a slots filling task for given event templates. That is, extracting pre-specified event information and relating the event information to particular organization, person, or artifact entities involved in the event. In ACE, the event is a complex event structure involving zero or more ACE entities, values and time expressions.

Generic Event Model. Jain and Westermann propose a generic event model E for event-centric multimedia data management applications [3]. The model is able to capture temporal aspect, spatial aspect, information aspect, experiential aspect, structural aspect and causal aspect of events [4].

Ontology Event Model. Ontology is an explicit and formal specification of a shared conceptualization [16]. It is an important strategy in describing semantic models. ABC ontology [5] developed in Harmony Project[1] is able to describe event-related concepts such as event, situation, action, agent, and their relationships. PROTON, a base upper-level ontology developed from KIMO Ontology in Knowledge and Information Management (KIM) [6] platform, has the ability to describe events which cover event annotation types in ACE. In [7], a formal model of events Event-Model-F is proposed. The model can represent arbitrary occurrences in the real world and formally describe the different relations and interpretations of events. It actually blends the six aspects defined for the event model E and interrogatives of the Eventory system [17] to provide comprehensive support to represent time and space, objects and persons, as well as mereological, causal, and correlative relationships between events.

We mainly concern about ontology-based event models in this paper.

3 News Ontology Event Model

On the basis of analyzing existing event models, we build NOEM for semantic modeling news event in this work. The main advantages of ontology-based modeling lie in two aspects: 1) It is able to provide common comprehension of domain knowledge, determine commonly recognized terminologies, and implement properties, restrictions and axioms in a formulated way at different levels within certain domains. 2) Implicit knowledge can be acquired from known facts (events, entities and relations) by using inference engine of ontology.

3.1 The Design of NOEM

Our goal of designing NOEM is to provide a basic vocabulary for semantic annotation of event 5W1Hs in news stories. So classes and properties are carefully selected to guarantee NOEM's compactedness as well as to supply abundant semantics. In accordance with Jain's generic event model, our model also tries to capture temporal, spatial, information, experiential, structural and causal aspect of events. The proposed event model is able to cover information of events in three levels.

- *Event information:* Based on existing event models, we select general concepts such as 'space', 'time', 'events', 'objects', 'agents', etc. to represent an event and its *5W* elements. The ACE event hierarchy is imported to identify event's types by trigger words. We only capture actions which can

---

[1] The Harmony Project, http://metadata.net/harmony

uniquely identify an event. Since events are spatial and temporal constructs, the event information component necessarily contains the time period of the activity and its spatial characteristics. Additionally, entities like people or objects that participate in an event are described. Concepts defined in NOEM is shown in Table 1.

- **Event relations:** Events (and the activities underlying them) may be related to other events (activities) that occur in the system. Examples of such relations can be temporal and spatial co-occurrences, temporal sequencing, cause-effect relations, and aggregations of events. By defining new concepts, for example, 'situation' and 'constellation', and properties such as 'precedes' and 'follows', the model achieves the ability of describing an event in a fine-grained manner, and of relating and grouping events. Relations defined in NOEM is shown in Table 2.

- **Event media:** Events can be described in various media, e.g. audio, video, text. Since we only care about news stories, we define concepts of 'document' and 'topic' to capture the characteristics of the news articles. Information such as news types, resource locators, or indexes corresponding to specific document that support the given event are modeled. CNML (Chinese News Markup Language) is imported to represent a news article's topic so that we can connect an event to its category in document-level.

Table 1. Concepts in NOEM

| Thing | Entity | Happening | Time | Place| Document | Topic | Phisical | Abstracts| Event | Situation | Action | Constellation | Agent | LogicalTime | PhysicalTime | RelativeTime | Logical Place | Physical Place | Relative Place |

Table 2. Relations in NOEM

| hasSubject | hasObject | hasCause | hasResult | isSubeventOf | involvesIn | atTime| inPlace | predeces | follows | hasAction | describedIn | hasTopic | hasClass | hasType |

3.2   Main Concepts and Properties in NOEM

In this section, we discuss main concepts, properties of NOEM and how they are used to represent 5W1H semantic elements of an event in detail. The designed News Ontology Event Model is shown in Fig. 1, for the sake of clarity, only main concepts and properties are included.

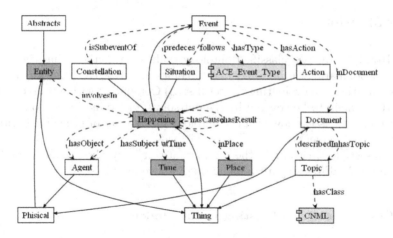

Fig. 1. News Ontology Event Model

- **Happening** is the superclass of all types of eventuality. It has four sub-classes: 'Event' denotes dynamic event, 'Situation' denotes static status, 'Action' denotes an activity and 'Constellation' denotes an event set. Properties 'hasCause' and 'hasEffect' of 'Happening' represent cause-effect connections between events. This is helpful for future work of analyzing *why* among events.
- **Event** is a concept denotes dynamic 'Happening'. An event always has a type which can be used to specify *what*. We import all types of ACE event, 'Business', 'Conflict', 'Contact', 'Justice', 'Life', 'Movement', 'Personnel' and 'Transaction'. They appear as a component in Figure 1.
- **Situation** describes static status preceding or following an event. Properties 'precedes' and 'follows' can be used to represent *how*.
- **Constellation** is a set of happenings with some relations among them, e.g., cause-effect and core-peripheral. It describes a complete happening caused by a key event and developed by sub-events.
- **Agent** is a concept to represent *who* and *whom*. It is the superclass of 'Group' and 'Person'.
- **Time** apparently represents *when*. Its subclasses 'logicalTime', 'physical-Time' and 'relativeTime' are reserved for our future work of time normalization and inference.
- **Place** represents *where*. Its subclasses 'logicalPlace', 'physicalPlace' and 'relativePlace' are reserved for our future work of location normalization.
- **Document** is the media aspect of an event. It has an URI (Universal Resource Identifier) refers to a news article.
- **Topic** is a concept in document level. It is related to category of a news story, for example, 'Sports', 'Law', 'Politics' and so on. We import 2082 subclasses from CNML taxonomy for topic classification.

4   Evaluation

Janez Brank et. al. [18] classified ontology evaluation methods into four categories: (1) Comparing the ontology to a "golden standard"; (2) Using an ontology in an application and evaluating the results; (3) Comparing with a source of data about the domain to be covered by the ontology; (4) Evaluation is done by humans who try to assess how well the ontology meets a set of predefined criteria, standards, requirements.

In this section, we evaluate the representative ability, the feasibility and applicability of NOEM using a combination of above methods.

4.1   Comparison with Existing Event Models

When designing the NOEM, we analyzed existing event-based systems and event models with respect to the functional requirements. These models are motivated from different domains such as the Eventory system for journalism, the structural representation of event in MUC and ACE, the event model E for event-based multimedia applications and Ontology-based models, such as the Event Ontology as part of a music ontology framework, ABC, PROTON for knowledge management and Event-Model-F for distributed event-based systems. All models are domain-dependant and they are too simple or too complicated for news event understanding task in this paper.

By analyzing the representative ability of existing Event models, we obtain six factors: action, entity, time, space, relations (here we concern structural, causal and correlation among events) and event media. An overview of the analysis results and comparison to the features of NOEM along the representative ability is listed in Table 3. It shows that NOEM has a better representative ability than structural event models, i.e., probabilistic, atomic and MUC/ACE models. In addition, NOEM's representative ability is as good as PROTON and Event-Model-F, two classic ontologies. At the same time, NOEM has a more compact design with only a few classes and relations, and is suitable to modeling Chinese News.

4.2   Manually Evaluation

To evaluate NOEM in a practical environment, four postgraduate students are invited to manually analyze 6000 online news stories from XinHua and People news agency. These news stories cover 22 topics of CNML such as politics, economy, military, information technology, sports and so on. With the help of headline of each news item, one topic sentence that contains the key event is identified. Then 5W1H elements of the key event are labeled from the headline and the topic sentence according to the NOEM definition. The annotation result shows that 85 percent of online news story can be described by NOEM appropriately.

Table 3. Comparison of Event Models

Event Model	Domain	Representative Ability							
		Action	Entity	Time	Space	Relation			Media
						Str.	Cau.	Cor.	
Probabilistic	TDT/RED	Y	Y	Y	Y	N	N	N	N
Atomic	Event-based Sum.	Y	Y	N	N	N	N	N	N
MUC/ACE	IE	Y	Y	Y	Y	Y	N	N	N
Eventory	Journalism	Y	Y	Y	Y	Y	Y	N	N
E	Multimedia Mana.	Y	Y	Y	Y	Y	Y	Y	Y
Event Ontology	Music Mana.	Y	Y	Y	Y	Y	Y	Y	N
ABC	Knowledge Mana.	Y	Y	Y	Y	Y	Y	Y	N
PROTON	IR	Y	Y	Y	Y	Y	Y	Y	Y
F	Event-based Sys.	Y	Y	Y	Y	Y	Y	Y	Y
NOEM	EE	Y	Y	Y	Y	Y	Y	Y	Y

Abbreviations: Str.=Structural, Cau.=Causal, Cor.=Correlation,
Mana.=Management, Sum.=Summarization, Sys.= System

4.3 A Case Study

Here we take a story from Xinhua news agency September 9, 2005 as an example to extract and describe the key event elements. The snippet of the news is shown in the left part of Fig. 2. We first use a machine learning method in our previous work [19] to identify the topic sentence about the key event of this story. And then we use a verb-driven method, along with Name Entity identification and semantic role labeling method proposed in work [20] to get the key event's 5W1H information from the story.

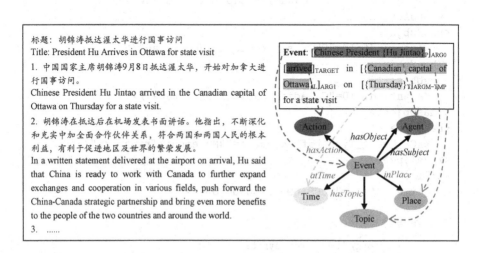

Fig. 2. Snippet of a news story, the identified key event and its 5W1H elements

From the key event of the news, "Chinese President Hu Jintao arrived in the Canadian capital of Ottawa on Thursday for a state visit.", we get an ACE *"Movement"* event and its 5W1H elements (right part of Fig. 2). The extracted 5W1H semantic event information, their types and semantic relations are denoted in RDF (Resource Description Framework)[2] triples. For the example event, we get triples < *Chinese President Hu Jintao, arrive, Canadian capital of Ottawa*>, < *arrive, isTypeof, Movement/Transport*>, < *Chinese President Hu Jintao, isTypeof, Person*>, < *2005-09-08T00:00:00, isTypeof, Time*> (*Thursday* is normalized as 2005-09-08) and < *Ottawa, isTypeof, Place*>.

4.4   Population of NOEM

The proposed NOEM is built on Protégé[3]. By using a predefined template, an OWL (Web Ontology Language)[4] file is automatically generated in which triples are mapped to the concepts and relations according to NOEM. By this means, the event 5W1H elements can be populated into Protégé as instances.

A snippet of automatic generated OWL file of the example story is listed below.

```
<Event rdf:ID="NewsEvent_588">
   <rdfs:comment>
      Hu Arrives in Ottawa.
   </rdfs:comment>
   <inDocument>
      <Document rdf:resource="#588"/>
   </inDocument>
   <hasAction>
      <Action rdf:ID="<Chinese President Hu Jintao,arrive,
                       Canadian capital of Ottawa>"/>
   </hasAction>
   <hasSubject>
      <Agent rdf:ID="Chinese President Hu Jintao"/>
   </hasSubject>
   <hasObject>
      <Agent rdf:ID="Canadian capital of Ottawa"/>
   </hasObject>
   <hasType>
      <ACE_Event_Type rdf:resource="#Movement/Transport"/>
   </hasType>
   <atTime>
      <Time rdf:ID="2005-09-08T00:00:00"/>
   </atTime>
   <inPlace>
```

---
[2] http://www.w3.org/TR/REC-rdf-syntax/
[3] http://protege.stanford.edu/
[4] http://www.w3.org/TR/owl-ref/

```
    <Place rdf:ID="Ottawa"/>
    <Place rdf:ID="Canada"/>
  </inPlace>
</Event>
```

Besides the key event, < *Chinese President Hu Jintao, deliver, a written statement* > is also identified as a subevent and associated to the key event by relationship "follows". The automatically mapping and populating the 5W elements and relations into Ontology shows the feasibility and applicability of NOEM.

5   Conclusions and Future work

In this paper, NOEM, an event Ontology which describes concepts of 5W1H event semantic elements and relationships of events is proposed. NOEM is able to capture temporal, spatial, information, experiential, structural and causal aspect of an item of news. By taking advantage of logical reasoning ability of the NOEM ontology, the output of *why* and *how* elements together with relationships among *who*, *what*, *whom*, *when* and *where* of events can be used to build a multidimensional news event network. This will largely facilitate online news browsing in event and semantic level.

Our future work is to build a news events knowledge base and a semantic retrieval engine on NOEM. This will strongly support semantic information retrieval on event level and other event level semantic applications.

Acknowledgment. This work is supported by the National High-Tech Project of China (Grant No. 2012AA011101).

References

1. Chinchor, N., Marsh, E.: MUC-7 Information Extraction Task Definition (version 5. 1). In: MUC-7 (1998)
2. ACE (Automatic Content Extraction).: Chinese Annotation Guidelines for Events. National Institute of Standards and Technology (2005)
3. Westermann, U., Jain, R.: E - A generic event model for event-centric multimedia data management in eChronicle applications. In: The 2006 IEEE International Workshop on Electronic Chronicles, Atlanta, GA (2006)
4. Westermann, U., Jain, R.: Towards a Common Event Model for Multimedia Applications. IEEE MultiMedia 14(1) (2007)
5. Lagoze, C., Hunter, J.: The ABC Ontology and Model. J. Digit. Inf. (2001)
6. Kiryakov, A., Popov, B., Kirilov, A., Manov, D., Ognyanoff, D., Goranov, M.: Semantic Annotation, Indexing, and Retrieval. In: 2nd International Semantic Web Conference, Florida, USA (2003)
7. Scherp, A., Franz, T., Saathoff, C., Staab, S.: F-a model of events based on the foundational ontology dolce+DnS ultralight. In: 5th International Conference on Knowledge Capture (K-CAP), California, USA (2009)

8. Carmagnola, F.: The five ws in user model interoperability. In: 5th International Workshop on Ubiquitous User Modeling, Gran Canaria, Spain (2008)

9. Miller, G., Beckwith, R., Fellbaum, C., Gross, D., Miller, K.: Introduction to Word-Net: An online lexical database. International Journal of Lexicography 3(4), 235–312 (1990)

10. Timberlake, A.: Aspect, tense, mood. In: Shopen, T. (ed.) Language Typology and Syntactic Description 3, Grammatical Categories and the Lexicon (Language Typology and Syntactic Description), pp. 280–333. Cambridge University Press, Cambridge (2007)

11. Pustejovsky, J., Castano, J., Ingria, R., Sauri, R., Gaizauskas, R., Setzer, A., et al.: TimeML: Robust Specification of Event and Temporal Expressions in Text. In: AAAI Spring Symposium on New Directions in Question Answering, Tilburg, Netherlands (2003)

12. Li, Z., Wang, B., Li, M., Ma, W.: A probabilistic model for retrospective news event detection. In: SIGIR, pp. 106–113 (2005)

13. Filatova, E., Hatzivassiloglou, V.: Event-based Extractive summarization. In: ACL, pp. 104–111 (2004)

14. Li, W., Wu, M., Lu, Q., Xu, W., Yuan, C.: Extractive Summarization using Inter- and Intra- Event Relevance. In: ACL (2006)

15. Liu, M., Li, W., Wu, M., Lu, Q.: Extractive Summarization Based on Event Term Clustering. In: ACL (2007)

16. Gruber, T.R.: Toward principles for the design of ontologies used for knowledge sharing? Int. J. Hum.-Comput. Stud. 907–928 (1995)

17. Wang, X., Mamadgi, S., Thekdi, A., Kelliher, A., Sundaram, H.: Eventory – An Event Based Media Repository. In: ICSC, pp. 95–104 (2007)

18. Brank, J., Grobelnik, M., Mladenic, D.: A survey of ontology evaluation techniques. In: 8th International Multi-Conference Information Society (IS 2005), pp. 166–170 (2005)

19. Wang, W., Zhao, D., Zhao, W.: Identification of topic sentence about key event in Chinese News. Acta Scientiarum Naturalium Universitatis Pekinensis 47(5), 789–796 (2011)

20. Wang, W., Zhao, D., Zou, L., Wang, D., Zheng, W.: Extracting 5W1H Event Semantic Elements from Chinese Online News. In: Chen, L., Tang, C., Yang, J., Gao, Y. (eds.) WAIM 2010. LNCS, vol. 6184, pp. 644–655. Springer, Heidelberg (2010)

Dependency Forest for Sentiment Analysis

Zhaopeng Tu*, Wenbin Jiang, Qun Liu, and Shouxun Lin

Key Laboratory of Intelligent Information Processing,
Institute of Computing Technology, CAS, Beijing, China
{tuzhaopeng,jiangwenbin,liuqun,sxlin}@ict.ac.cn

Abstract. Dependency Grammars prove to be effective in improving sentiment analysis, because they can directly capture syntactic relations between words. However, most dependency-based systems suffer from a major drawback: they only use 1-best dependency trees for feature extraction, which adversely affects the performance due to parsing errors. Therefore, we propose an approach that applies dependency forest to sentiment analysis. A dependency forest compactly represents multiple dependency trees. We develop new algorithms for extracting features from dependency forest. Experiments show that our forest-based system obtains 5.4 point absolute improvement in accuracy over a bag-of-words system, and 1.3 point improvement over a tree-based system on a widely used sentiment dataset. Our forest-based system also achieves state-of-the-art performance on the sentiment dataset.

Keywords: dependency forest, sentiment analysis.

1 Introduction

Dependency grammars have received a lot of attention in sentiment analysis (SA). One important advantage of dependency grammars is that they can directly capture syntactic relations between words, which are key to resolving most parsing ambiguities. As a result, employing dependency trees produces substantial improvements in sentiment analysis [12,6,10].

However, most dependency-based systems suffer from a major drawback: they only use 1-best dependency trees for feature extraction, which adversely affects the performance due to parsing errors(93% [8] and 88% [3] accuracies for English and Chinese on standard corpora respectively). To make things worse, sentiment corpora usually consist of noisy texts from web, which will lead to a much lower parsing quality. As we will show, the tree-based systems still commits to using features extracted from noisy 1-best trees. Due to parsing error propagation, many useful features are left out of the feature set.

To alleviate this problem, an obvious solution is to offer more alternatives. Recent studies have shown that many tasks in natural language processing can benefit from widening the annotation pipeline: using packed forests [13] or dependency forests [20] instead of 1-best trees for statistical machine translation,

---

* Corresponding author.

M. Zhou et al. (Eds.): NLPCC 2012, CCIS 333, pp. 69–77, 2012.

packed forests for semantic role labeling [22], forest reranking for parsing [2], and word lattices reranking for Chinese word segmentation [4].

Along the same direction, we propose an approach that applies dependency forest, which encodes exponentially many dependency trees compactly, for tree-based sentiment classification systems. In this paper, we develop a new algorithm for extracting features from dependency forest. Experiments show that our forest-based system obtains 5.4 point absolute improvement in accuracy over a bag-of-words system, and 1.3 point improvement over a tree-based system on a widely used sentiment dataset [18].

2 Related Work

Our research builds on previous work in the field of sentiment classification and forest-based algorithms. For sentiment classification, the design of lexical and syntactic features is a fundamental step. There has been an increasing amount of work on feature-based algorithms for this problem. Pang and Lee [18] and Dave et al. [9] represent a document as a bag-of-words; Matsumoto et al. [12] extract frequently occurring connected subtrees from dependency parsing; Joshi and Penstein-Ros'e [6] use a transformation of dependency relation triples; Liu and Seneff [10] extract adverb-adjective-noun relations from dependency parser output while Wu et al. [21] extract features from phrase dependency parser.

Previous research has convincingly demonstrated forests ability to offer more alternatives, which is useful to solving parsing error propagation problem, and has led to improvements in various NLP tasks, including statistical machine translation [13,20], semantic role labeling [22], and parsing [2].

3 Background

In this section, we present the baseline system that extracts features from 1-best dependency trees.

Figure 1(a) shows a dependency tree of the English sentence *the film is sick, slick fun*. The dependency tree expresses relation between words by head-dependents relationships of nodes. The arrow points from the dependent to its head. For example, in Figure 1(a), *fun* is the head of *slick*.

Inspired by the previous work [12], we extract connected subtrees from dependency trees. A connected subtree is a more general form obtained by removing zero or more nodes from the original dependency tree. Figure 1(b) shows some examples. The top left subtree is obtained by removing the node *slick*, and the bottom left subtree is obtained by further removing the node *the*.

Recent studies show that this kind of partial subtrees could capture the syntactic information between words quite well [12,14,5]. For example, in Figure 1(b), to express the relation between the words *film* and *fun*, a subtree *t* does not only show the co-occurrence of *film* and *fun*, but also make sure that they are syntactically connected by the word *is*.

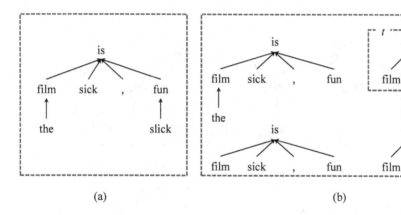

Fig. 1. A dependency tree of the sentence the film is sick, slick fun and examples of corresponding dependency substructures

Since the number of dependency features tends to be very large, we only remain the features that occur frequently in the corpus.

4 Dependency Forest

As the tree-based system relies on 1-best trees, the quality of features might be affected by parsing errors and therefore ultimately results in classification mistakes. We propose to encode multiple dependency trees in a compact representation called dependency forest, which provides an elegant solution to the problem of parsing error propagation.

Figure 2(a) and 2(b) show two dependency trees for the example English sentence in Figure 1. The word sick can either be an adjective as an attribute of the film, or be a modificatory word like slick for the word fun. The two dependency trees can be represented as a single dependency forest by sharing common nodes and edges, as shown in Figure 2(c).

Each **node** in a dependency forest is a word. We assign a span to each node to distinguish among nodes. For example, the span of the word *sick* is (3,4) because it is the fourth word in the sentence. Since the seventh word *fun* dominates the word *slick*, the span is (5,7). Note that the position of *fun* itself is taken into consideration.

The nodes in a dependency forest are connected by **hyperedges**. While a edge in a dependency tree points from a dependent to its head, a hyperedge groups all dependents of their common head. For example, the hyperedge e_2:

$$e_2: \langle is_{0,7}, (film_{0,2}, fun_{3,7}) \rangle$$

denotes that both $film_{0,2}$ and $fun_{3,7}$ are dependents of the head $is_{0,7}$.

Formally, a *dependency forest* is a pair $\langle V, E \rangle$, where V is a set of nodes, and E is a set of hyperedges. For a given sentence $w_{1:n} = w_1 \ldots w_n$, each node

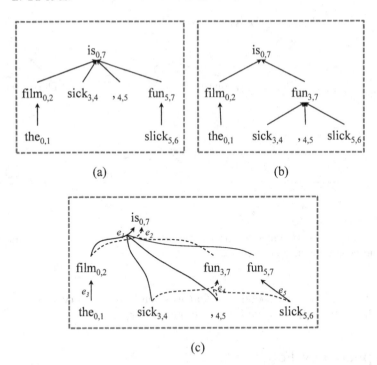

Fig. 2. (a) the dependency tree in Figure 1, (b) another dependency tree for the same sentence, and (c) a dependency forest compactly represents the two trees.

$v \in V$ is represented as $w_{i,j}$, denoting that the word w dominates the substring $w_{i+1} \ldots w_j$. Each hyperedge $e \in E$ is a pair $\langle head(e), tails(e) \rangle$, where $head(e) \in V$ is the head of the hyperedge and $tails(e) \in V$ are its dependents.

We followed the work [20] to construct dependency forest from k-best parsing results, and transform a dependency forest into a hypergraph.

5   Forest-Based Subtree Extraction

In tree-based systems, we can extract dependency subtrees by simply enumerating all nodes in the tree and combining the subtrees of their dependents with the heads. However, this algorithm fails to work in the forest scenario because there are usually exponentially many subtrees of a node.

To solve this problem, we develop a new bottom-up algorithm to extract dependency subtrees. Our approach often extracts a large amount of dependency subtrees as each node has many hyperedges. To maintain a reasonable feature set size, we discard any subtrees that dont satisfy two constraints:

1. appear in at least f distinct sentences in the dataset [12];
2. the *fractional count* should not be lower than a pruning threshold p;

Here the fractional count of a subtree is calculated like in the previous work [13,20]. Given a tree fragment t, we use the inside-outside algorithm to compute its posterior probability:

$$\alpha\beta(t) = \alpha(root(t)) \times \prod_{e \in t} p(e) \times \prod_{v \in leaves(t)} \beta(v) \tag{1}$$

where $root(t)$ is the root of the subtree, e is an edge, $leaves(t)$ is a set of leaves of the subtree, $\alpha(\cdot)$ and $\beta(\cdot)$ are outside and inside probabilities, respectively. For example, the subtree rooted at $fun_{3,7}$ in Figure 2(c) has the following posterior probability:

$$\alpha(fun_{3,7}) \times p(e_4) \times \beta(sick_{3,4}) \times \beta(._{,4,5}) \times \beta(slick_{5,6})$$

Now the fractional count of the subtree t is

$$c(t) = \frac{\alpha\beta(t)}{\alpha\beta(TOP)} \tag{2}$$

where TOP is the root node of the forest. As a partial connected subtree might be non-constituent, we approximate the fractional count by taking that of the minimal constituent tree fragment that contains the connected subtree.

We observed that if a subtree appears in at least f distinct sentences, then each edge in the subtree should also occurs at least f times. According to this observation, we can first enumerate all edges that appear in at least f distinct sentences, then we can check whether the edge in this set when dealing with a head and a dependent. Take the edge $\langle sick, fun \rangle$ in Figure 2(c) for example, if the occurrence of the edge is lower than f, then any subtree that contain this edge could not be possible appear in at least f times.

Algorithm 1 shows the bottom-up algorithm for extracting subtrees from a dependency forest. This algorithm maintains all available subtrees for each node (line 12). The subtrees of a head can be constructed from those of its dependents. For instance, in Figure 2(c), as the subtree rooted at $fun_{3,7}$ is

$$(slick) \; fun$$

we can obtain another subtree for the node $is_{0,7}$ by attaching the subtree of its dependent to the node ($EnumerateSubtrees$ in line 8)

$$is \; ((slick) \; fun)$$

Note that we only keep the subtrees that appear in at least f distinct sentences (line 6), and have a fractional count not lower than p (line 10).

6   Experiments

We carried out experiments on the movie review dataset [18], which consists of 1000 positive reviews and 1000 negative reviews. To obtain dependency trees,

Algorithm 1. Algorithm of extracting subtrees from a dependency forest. All subtrees should appear in at least f distinct sentences and have a fractional count not lower than p.

Input: a forest F, and f and p
Output: minimal subtree set $\mathcal{T}$
1: $avail\_edges \leftarrow$ [edges that appear in at least f distinct sentences]
2: **for** each node $v \in V$ in a bottom-up order **do**
3:      **for** each hyperedge $e \in E$ and $head(e) = v$ **do**
4:          $avail\_nodes \leftarrow \emptyset$
5:          **for** each node $w \in tails(e)$ **do**
6:              **if** edge $\langle v, w \rangle \in avail\_edges$ **then**
7:                  $avail\_nodes$.append(w)
8:          $S \leftarrow EnumerateSubtrees$ (v, $avail\_nodes$)
9:          **for** each subtree $t \in S$ **do**
10:             **if** $c(t) \geqslant p$ **then**
11:                 $\mathcal{T}$.append(t)
12:     keep subtrees for v

---

we parsed the document using the Stanford Parser [7] to output constituency trees and then passed the Stanford constituency trees through the Stanford constituency-to-dependency converter [11].

We consider two baselines:

1 **Unigrams**: using unigrams that occur at least 4 times [18]
2 **Unigrams+Subtree$_{1-best}$**: Unigrams features plus partial connected subtrees extracted from 1-best dependency trees

We construct dependency forest from 100-best parsing list.[1] We set the parameter $f = 10$ for both dependency trees and forests, and pruning threshold $p = 0.01$ for dependency forests.[2] All experiments are carried out using the MaxEnt toolkit[3] with default parameter settings. All results reported are based on 10-fold cross validation.

Table 1 shows the result on the movie review dataset. The first column Features indicates where the features are extracted from: 1-best dependency trees, 100-best list or dependency forests. The second column denotes the averaged number of extracted features, while the last column is the averaged time of subtree extraction. We compare our method to previously published results on the same dataset (rows 9-11), showing that our approach is very competitive. We find that using subtrees from 100-best list or forests achieve significant improve-

---

[1] The speed of construction is approximately dozens of milliseconds per sentence. Most of the time cost is attributed to the calculation of inside and outside probabilities.
[2] We only use fractional count pruning for dependency forest, because the inside-outside algorithm for computing fractional count is only available for hypergraphs. As we extract features from the trees in k-best list individually, we cannot use it for k-best list scenario.
[3] http://homepages.inf.ed.ac.uk/lzhang10/maxent_toolkit.html

Table 1. Result on the movie review dataset. Here "Number" (column 2) indicates the averaged number of features used and "Time" (column 4) denotes the averaged subtree extraction time (second/document). "Subtree$_{structure}$" denotes that the subtrees are extracted from 1-best tree, 100-best list or forest. The baseline system (row 2) used the unigrams that occur at least 4 times, and another baseline system (row 4) furthermore incorporates dependency subtrees extracted from 1-best trees. We use "†" to denote a result is better than baseline "Unigram" significantly, and "‡" denote better than both "Unigram" and "Unigram + Subtree$_{1-best}$" significantly, at p < 0.01 (sign test).

Features	Number	Accuracy	Time
Unigram	17,704	86.2	–
Subtree$_{1-best}$	12,282	74.2	0.33
Unigram + Subtree$_{1-best}$	29,986	90.3†	–
Subtree$_{100-best}$	24,006	81.9	35.47
Unigram + Subtree$_{100-best}$	41,710	90.2†	–
Subtree$_{forest}$	18,968	81.2	6.93
Unigram + Subtree$_{forest}$	36,674	**91.6‡**	–
Pang et al. [18]	–	87.1	–
Ng et al. [17]	–	90.5	–
Yessenalina et al. [23]	–	91.8	–

ment over 1-best trees, validating our belief that offering more alternatives could produce substantial improvements. Using 100-best list produce only double subtrees in over 100 times longer than using 1-best trees, indicating that a k-best list has too few variations and too many redundancies [2]. When incorporating unigrams features, forest-based system obtains significant improvement of 5.4 point in accuracy over the bag-of-words system, and 1.3 point improvement over the tree-based system. An interesting finding is that combining subtrees from 100-best list and unigrams features doesnt achieve any improvement over 1-best tree. We conjecture that: (1) as most syntactic information is already captured by 1-best trees, using 100-best list can introduce little new information, (2) more noisy information would be introduced when extracting features from 100-best list, because there would be some low-quality parsing trees in the 100-best list (e.g. the trees at the foot of 100-best list). In contrast, we can extract new subtrees from dependency forests, which could not be extracted from any single tree in 100-best list (e.g. a subtree that consists of two parts from two different dependency trees). On the other hand, with the help of fractional count pruning, we would discard most low-quality subtrees.

7 Conclusion and Future Work

In this paper, we have proposed to extract features represented as partial connected subtrees from dependency forests, and reduced the complexity of the extraction algorithm by discard subtrees that have low fractional count and occurrence. We show that using dependency forest leads to significant improvements over that of using 1-best trees on a widely used movie review corpus.

In this work, we still select features manually. As convolution kernels could exploit a huge amount of features without an explicit feature representation [14,5,1,16,15,19], we will combine dependency forest and convolution kernels in the future.

Acknowledgments. The authors were supported by 863 State Key Project No. 2011AA01A207. We thank the anonymous reviewers for their insightful comments.

References

1. Bunescu, R., Mooney, R.: A Shortest Path Dependency Kernel for Relation Extraction. In: Proceedings of Human Language Technology Conference and Conference on Empirical Methods in Natural Language Processing, pp. 724–731. Association for Computational Linguistics, Vancouver (2005)
2. Huang, L.: Forest reranking: discriminative parsing with non-local features. In: Proceedings of ACL 2008: HLT, Columbus, Ohio, pp. 586–594 (May 2008)
3. Jiang, W., Liu, Q.: Dependency parsing and projection based on word-pair classification. In: Proceedings of the 48th Annual Meeting of the Association for Computational Linguistics, pp. 12–20. Association for Computational Linguistics, Uppsala (2010)
4. Jiang, W., Mi, H., Liu, Q.: Word lattice reranking for chinese word segmentation and part-of-speech tagging. In: Proceedings of the 22nd International Conference on Computational Linguistics (Coling 2008), pp. 385–392. Coling 2008 Organizing Committee, Manchester (2008)
5. Johansson, R., Moschitti, A.: Syntactic and semantic structure for opinion expression detection. In: Proceedings of the Fourteenth Conference on Computational Natural Language Learning, Uppsala, Sweden, pp. 67–76 (July 2010)
6. Joshi, M., Penstein-Rosé, C.: Generalizing dependency features for opinion mining. In: Proceedings of the ACL-IJCNLP 2009 Conference Short Papers, pp. 313–316. Association for Computational Linguistics, Suntec (2009)
7. Klein, D., Manning, C.D.: Accurate Unlexicalized Parsing. In: Proceedings of the 41st Annual Meeting of the Association for Computational Linguistics, pp. 423–430. Association for Computational Linguistics, Sapporo (2003)
8. Koo, T., Collins, M.: Efficient third-order dependency parsers. In: Proceedings of the 48th Annual Meeting of the Association for Computational Linguistics, pp. 1–11. Association for Computational Linguistics, Uppsala (2010)
9. Kushal Dave, S.L., Pennock, D.: Mining the peanut gallery: Opinion extraction and semantic classification of product reviews. In: Proceedings of the 12th International Conference on World Wide Web, pp. 519–528. ACM (2003)
10. Liu, J., Seneff, S.: Review Sentiment Scoring via a Parse-and-Paraphrase Paradigm. In: Proceedings of the 2009 Conference on Empirical Methods in Natural Language Processing, Singapore, pp. 161–169 (August 2009)
11. de Marneffe, M.C., Manning, C.D.: The stanford typed dependencies representation. In: Proceedings of the COLING Workshop on Cross-Framework and Cross-Domain Parser Evaluation, Manchester (August 2008)
12. Matsumoto, S., Takamura, H., Okumura, M.: Sentiment Classification Using Word Sub-sequences and Dependency Sub-trees. In: Ho, T.-B., Cheung, D., Liu, H. (eds.) PAKDD 2005. LNCS (LNAI), vol. 3518, pp. 301–311. Springer, Heidelberg (2005)

13. Mi, H., Huang, L.: Forest-based translation rule extraction. In: Proceedings of the 2008 Conference on Empirical Methods in Natural Language Processing, Honolulu, Hawaii, pp. 206–214 (September 2008)
14. Moschitti, A.: Efficient Convolution Kernels for Dependency and Constituent Syntactic Trees. In: Fürnkranz, J., Scheffer, T., Spiliopoulou, M. (eds.) ECML 2006. LNCS (LNAI), vol. 4212, pp. 318–329. Springer, Heidelberg (2006)
15. Moschitti, A., Pighin, D., Basili, R.: Tree kernels for semantic role labeling. Computational Linguistics 34(2), 193–224 (2008)
16. Moschitti, A., Quarteroni, S.: Kernels on Linguistic Structures for Answer Extraction. In: Proceedings of ACL 2008: HLT, Short Papers, pp. 113–116. Association for Computational Linguistics, Columbus (2008)
17. Ng, V., Dasgupta, S., Arifin, S.M.N.: Examining the Role of Linguistic Knowledge Sources in the Automatic Identification and Classification of Reviews. In: Proceedings of the COLING/ACL 2006 Main Conference Poster Sessions, Sydney, Australia, pp. 611–618 (July 2006)
18. Pang, B., Lee, L.: A Sentimental Education: Sentiment Analysis Using Subjectivity Summarization Based on Minimum Cuts. In: Proceedings of the 42nd Annual Meeting of the Association for Computational Linguistics, Barcelona, Spain, pp. 271–278 (June 2004)
19. Tu, Z., He, Y., Foster, J., van Genabith, J., Liu, Q., Lin, S.: Identifying high-impact sub-structures for convolution kernels in document-level sentiment classification. In: Proceedings of the 50th Annual Meeting of the Association for Computational Linguistics (Volume 2: Short Papers), pp. 338–343. Association for Computational Linguistics, Jeju Island (2012)
20. Tu, Z., Liu, Y., Hwang, Y.S., Liu, Q., Lin, S.: Dependency Forest for Statistical Machine Translation. In: Proceedings of the 23rd International Conference on Computational Linguistics (Coling 2010), Beijing, China, pp. 1092–1100 (July 2010)
21. Wu, Y., Zhang, Q., Huang, X., Wu, L.: Phrase Dependency Parsing for Opinion Mining. In: Proceedings of the 2009 Conference on Empirical Methods in Natural Language Processing, Singapore, pp. 1533–1541 (August 2009)
22. Xiong, H., Mi, H., Liu, Y., Liu, Q.: Forest-based semantic role labeling. In: Twenty-Fourth AAAI Conference on Artificial Intelligence, pp. 1039–1044 (2010)
23. Yessenalina, A., Choi, Y., Cardie, C.: Automatically generating annotator rationales to improve sentiment classification. In: Proceedings of the ACL 2010 Conference Short Papers, pp. 336–341. Association for Computational Linguistics, Uppsala (2010)

Collation of Transliterating Tibetan Characters

Heming Huang[1,2,*] and Feipeng Da[1]

[1] School of Automation, Southeast University, Nanjing, Jiangsu 210096, China
[2] School of computer Science, Qinghai Normal University, Xining, Qinghai 810008, China
huang-heming@sohu.com, dafp@seu.edu.cn

Abstract. The transliterating Tibetan characters used specially to transliterate foreign scripts have two collations: collation with the rules of native Tibetan dictionary and with that of transliterating Tibetan dictionary. This paper proposes two general structures for transliterating characters. Based on these general structures, a collation scheme is developed so that all transliterating characters can be collated correctly and effectively.

Keywords: Tibetan, character, collation, structure.

1 Introduction

The Tibetan script is an alphasyllabary, a segmental writing system in which consonant-vowel sequences are written as a unit. Tibetan has two alphabets: the native Tibetan alphabet used in daily life of Tibetan people and the transliterating Tibetan alphabet used specially to transliterate foreigner scripts especially the Sanskrit.

The native Tibetan has 30 consonants and four vowels. The 30 consonants are ཀ, ཁ, ག, ང, ཅ, ཆ, ཇ, ཉ, ཏ, ཐ, ད, ན, པ, ཕ, བ, མ, ཙ, ཚ, ཛ, ཝ, ཞ, ཟ, འ, ཡ, ར, ལ, ཤ, ས, ཧ, and ཨ while the four vowels are ཨི, ཨུ, ཨེ, and ཨོ. In addition to native Tibetan alphabet, a special alphabet was invented so as to transliterate the Buddhist scripture written in Sanskrit. Because of the exact one-to-one correspondence between this special invented alphabet and the Sanskrit alphabet, any Sanskrit sentence can be converted into the Tibetan sentence exactly and vice versa. This transliterating alphabet has 34 consonants and 16 vowels. The 34 consonants are ཀ, ཁ, ག, གྷ, ང, ཅ, ཆ, ཇ, ཇྷ, ཉ, ཊ, ཋ, ཌ, ཌྷ, ཎ, ཏ, ཐ, ད, དྷ, ན, པ, ཕ, བ, བྷ, མ, ཙ, ཚ, ཛ, ཛྷ, ཝ, ཞ, ཟ, འ, ཡ, ར, ལ, ཤ, ཥ, ས, ཧ, and ཀྵ, and the 16 vowels are ཨ, ཨཱ, ཨི, ཨཱི, ཨུ, ཨཱུ, ཨྲྀ, ཨྲཱྀ, ཨླྀ, ཨླཱྀ, ཨེ, ཨཻ, ཨོ, ཨཽ, ཨཾ, and ཨཿ. As shown in Fig. 1, the two alphabets are different but they share 28 letters ཀ, ཁ, ག, ང, ཅ, ཆ, ཇ, ཉ, ཏ, ཐ, ད, ན, པ, ཕ, བ, མ, ཙ, ཚ, ཛ, ཝ, ཞ, ཟ, འ, ཡ, ར, ལ, ཤ, ས, ཧ, and ཨ in common.

The transliterating Tibetan is different from the native Tibetan in many ways. One difference is that the transliterating Tibetan has two kinds of collation. The first kind is that all the characters need to be collated are just the transliterating characters and

---

* Corresponding author.

M. Zhou et al. (Eds.): NLPCC 2012, CCIS 333, pp. 78–84, 2012.

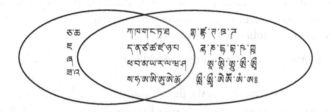

Fig. 1. The native Tibetan alphabet (left) and the transliterating Tibetan alphabet (right)

the collation of these characters follows the sorting rules of the transliterating Tibetan dictionary [1]. The second kind involves the collation of both the transliterating characters and the native Tibetan syllables, and the collation follows the sorting rules of the native Tibetan dictionary [2].

Di Jiang et al. have proposed a sorting algorithm of Tibetan script [3]. Heming Huang et al. have evaluated each Tibetan letter or symbol with the Unicode collation element and proposed a general structure for collation of Tibetan syllables [4-5]. As a matter of fact, they just collate both the transliterating characters and the native Tibetan syllables with the sorting rules of the native Tibetan dictionary. Although, not used so frequently, the transliterating characters are great in number: there are more than 6600 transliterating Tibetan characters [6-7]. By far, it is still an open problem to collate the transliterating Tibetan characters with the sort rules of the transliterating Tibetan dictionary.

2   The Judgment of the Transliterating Tibetan Characters

To realize the second kind collation accurately, it is necessary to distinguish the transliterating characters from the native Tibetan syllables correctly.

It is easy to distinguish a transliterated sentence from a native Tibetan sentence. As shown in Fig. 2, there is an inter-syllable separator '·' between every two syllables of a native Tibetan sentence while there is no such separator in a transliterated sentence.

ས་བོད་རྒྱ་གསུམ་ཁན་སྐྱར་གྱི་ཚིག་མཛོད།

སྐྱིད་སྡོང་སྩོན་ཏི་པུ་ཧྲུ་ཏཱ་ཐཱ༔

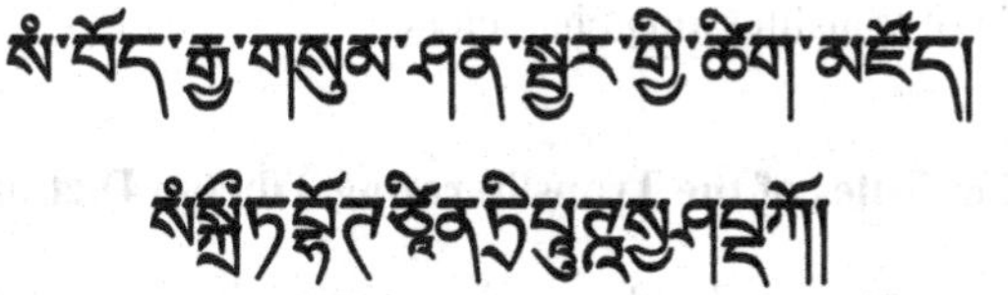

Fig. 2. A native Tibetan sentence (row 1) versus a transliterated sentence (row 2)

Some transliterated characters or phrases are used as a common syllable in a native Tibetan sentence. For example, the first syllable "ས" in the first row of Fig. 2 is a transliterating character; however, it is separated by "·" from others as if it is a native syllable. Therefore, it is not easy to distinguish a transliterating character from the native Tibetan syllables under this circumstance. It should be judged with the native Tibetan orthography. Generally, a pre-composed character is a transliterating character if it meets one of the following conditions.

1) A pre-composed character has the transliterating vowel ཨ, ཨི, ཨུ, ཨེ, ཨཻ, ཨོ, ཨཽ, ཨཾ, ཨཿ, ཨྃ, or ༁ྃ.

2) A pre-composed character has the diacritic sigh ༵, ༷, ༹, ༾, ༿, ཱ, ཱཱ, or ༑.

3) A pre-composed character has the transliterating consonants ཀྵ, ཥ, ཊ, ཋ, ཌ, ཎ, ཌ, ཥ, ཥ, ཊ, or ཀྵ.

4) A pre-composed character has two consonants, but the first consonant is none of ར, ལ, and ས while the second consonant is none of ཝ, ཡ, ར, and ལ. Examples of such characters are ཀྱ, ཊ, ཟ, and ཀ.

5) A pre-composed character has three consonants, but the first one is none of ར, ལ, and ས while the third one is none of ཝ, ཡ, ར, and ལ. Examples of such characters are ཀྱ, ཀྲ, ཀྵ, and ཀྱ.

6) A pre-composed character has more than three consonants. Examples of such characters are ཀྵ, ཀྵ, and ཀྵ.

7) A horizontal combination of several consonants, but there is no prefix consonant or suffix consonant according to the restriction rules of native Tibetan Standard orthography to these positions. Examples of such combinations are ཀཀཀ, ཀཌ, ཀཔཔ, and ཁརས.

8) A horizontal combination of a consonant and a pre-composed character, but the consonant is neither the prefix consonant nor the suffix consonant. Examples of such combinations are ཀཔི, ཀཐ, ཀཊ, ཀཕ, and ངར.

9) A horizontal combination of several pre-composed characters, but the last one is none of ཨ, ཨ, and ཨ. Examples of such combinations are ཀཀ, ཀཋ, and ཀཔ.

3   The General Structure of Transliterating Characters

The collation of a transliterating character is not decided by its component letters directly. A transliterating character may be decomposed into several syllables firstly and then its collation is decided by those syllable series. Therefore, it is necessary to describe the syllable of transliterating characters.

3.1   The Collation Rules of the Transliterating Tibetan Dictionary

A transliterating character may be the vertical composition of basic consonant, foot consonant, and vowel and there are no concepts of prefix consonant, suffix consonant, and superscript consonant. Therefore, the phrases ཀཐི, ཤཧར, and པཙ belong to the chapters ཀ, ཤ, and པ respectively; and the phrases ཀཐ, ཤཕ, and ཀཐ belong to the chapters ར, ལ, and ས respectively. Furthermore, a transliterating syllable may have two foot consonants and two vowels. For example, the syllable ཀༀ has two vowels. The first one is ཨ

and the second one is ०ঃ. The diacritics ৎ, ঀ, ঙ, ঙ, ౙ, ᠃, ᠃, and ~ should be treated as the first vowel either.

Before collation, a transliterating character or phrase should be decomposed into syllable series. For example, to collate the phrase སྐད, it should first be decomposed into syllable series ས་ཀ་ད and then the collation of the phrase སྐད is decided by the corresponding syllable series ས་ཀ་ད.

The collation of the single transliterating syllable is as follows.

1) The syllables with ཀ as the basic consonant are sorted as

ཀ་ཀི་ཀྀ ཀི་ཀི་ཀྀ ཀི་ཀི་ཀྀ ཀུ་ཀུ་ཀུ ཀུ་ཀུ་ཀུ ཀྀ་ཀྀ་ཀྀ ཀྀ་ཀྀ་ཀྀ ཀྀ་ཀྀ་ཀྀ ཀ་ཀི་ཀྀ ཀ་ཀི་ཀྀ ཀ་ཀི་ཀྀ ཀ་ཀི་ཀྀ (followed with those syllables that are the vertical combination of ৈ, ৈ, and ཀ with the vowels respectively).

2) The syllables with ཁ as the basic consonant are sorted as 1).

     ......

3) The syllables with ག as the basic consonant are sorted as 1).

3.2   The General structure of All Transliterating Characters

As mentioned above, a transliterating syllable is a pre-composition of a basic conso-nant with no more than two foot consonants and no more than two vowels. So, it has a general structure as shown in Fig. 3.

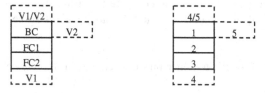

Fig. 3. The general structure of a transliterating syllable (left) and its sort order (right). Where V stands for the vowel, BC stands for the basic consonant, and FC stands for the foot consonant.

If a transliterating character cannot be represented by the general structure, it should be further decomposed into several syllables so that each of them can be represented by the general structure. For example, the character ཿ cannot be represented by the general structure directly but it can be decomposed into syllable series ད་ཿ, and both the syllables ད and ཿ can be represented by the general structure.

4   Collation of Transliterating Characters

The transliterating characters have two kinds collation: 1) collated with the rules of the native Tibetan dictionary and 2) collated with the rules of the transliterating cha-racter dictionary.

4.1   Collated with the Rules of the Transliterating Character Dictionary

When two transliterating characters are collated with the rules of the transliterating character dictionary, the scheme of the transliterating character collation consists of the following five steps as shown in Fig. 4.

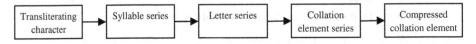

Fig. 4. The scheme of the transliterating character collation

Step 1: Decompose each transliterating character into syllable series first.

Step 2: Expand each syllable further into the letter series according to the sort order shown in Fig. 3. If there is no letter in a certain position, a space '□' is used instead.

Step 3: Replace each letter in the letter series with the corresponding collation element.

Step 4: Compress the collation element series.

Step 5: Compare the two compressed collation element series and we have got the collation result of two transliterating characters.

However, this paper just focuses on the first three steps.

To collate the two characters ཀྱུ and ཀྲུ, for example, they should firstly be expanded into syllable series 'ཀྱུ' and 'ཀྲུ' respectively; and then each syllable is further expanded into letter series, thus we have got 'ཀ□□□□ཀྱ□□□' and 'ཀ□□□□ཀྲ□□'; Finally, compare the two letter series as we compare two English strings and we have got the collation result of two characters ཀྱུ and ཀྲུ. Table 1 gives some more examples of this kind collation.

Table 1. The collation of the transliterating characters with the rules of the transliterating character dictionary

Characters	Syllable series	Letter series
ཀྱུ	ཀྱུ	ཀ□□□□ཀྱ◌□□□
ཀྲུ	ཀྲུ	ཀ□□□□ཀྲ◌ ◌□□
ཀཙ	ཀཙ	ཀ□□□□ཙ□□□□
ཀསྲ	ཀསྲ	ཀ□□□□ས◌□□◌
གུ	གུ	ག◌◌□◌
ཅུ	ཅུ	ཅ□□□□ག◌◌□◌
ཀྵ	ཀྵ	ཀ□□□□ས□□◌◌

4.2   Collated with the Rules of Native Tibetan Syllable Dictionary

A typical Tibetan syllable, such as བསྒགས, is a two-dimensional combination of its letters. To syllable བསྒགས, the letter ག at the center is the base consonant, the letter ས above the base consonant is the head consonant, the letter བ in the prefix position is the prescript consonant, the letter ཟ, a variant of the letter ར, is the foot consonant, the sign ི is a representation of the vowel ཻ, and the two letters ག and ས after the base consonant are the postscript consonant and the post-postscript consonant respectively. The Tibetan orthography has strict restrictions to the letters in each position, for example, only the letters ག, ད, བ, མ, and འ can appear in the prescript position.

A few native Tibetan syllables have two foot consonants. For example, the syllable ཪ has two foot consonants ཟ and ཱ and the syllable ཥ has two foot consonants ཾ and ཱ. Furthermore, many transliterating characters, collected in the national standards of P. R. China on Tibetan Character Set, have two foot consonants.

When a transliterating character is collated with the rules of the native Tibetan syllable dictionary, a generalized structure should be constructed so that it can represent both the transliterating syllables and the native Tibetan syllables. The left part of Fig. 5 is such general structure.

	V1/V2				6/7		
PC	HC	PC/V2	PPC	2	3	7	8
	BC				1		
	FC1				4		
	FC2				5		
	V1				6		

Fig. 5. The generalized syllable structure (left) and the sort order of the component letters (right). Where PC stands for the prefix consonant, HC stands for the head consonant, BC stands for the basic consonant, FC stands for the foot consonant, V stands for the vowel, PC stands fort the postscript consonant, and PPC stands for the post-postscript consonant.

When a transliterating character compares with a native Tibetan character or another transliterating character with the rules of the native Tibetan dictionary, it firstly should be decomposed into a serial of transliterating syllables as shown in the middle column of Table 2; and then each syllable is decomposed into a letter series by following the sort order shown in the right part of Fig. 5. If there is no letter in a certain position, a space 'ཌ' is used instead; Finally, compare the two letter series shown in the right column of Table 2.

Table 2. The collation of the transliterating characters and the native Tibetan characters

Characters or syllables	Syllable series	Letter series
ཀྵ	ཀྵ	ཀཌཌཌཌཌཌཌཀཌཌཥཌཌ
ཀྵ	ཀྵ	ཀཌཌཌཌཌཌཌཀཌཌཟཌཥཌ
ཀྵ	ཀྵ	ཀཌཌཌཌཌཌཥཌཌཌཌཌ
ཀྵ	ཀྵ	ཀཌཌཌཌཌཌཌཥཌཌཱཌཌི
ཀྵ	ཀྵ	ཀཌཌཟཱཌིཌཌ
ཀྵགས	ཀྵགས	ཀཟཥཟཱཌཱགཥ
ཀྵ	ཀྵ	ཱཌཌཌཌཌཌཌཱཌཌཱ
ཀྵ	ཀྵ	ཱཌཌཌཌཌཌཌཥཌཌཌཌཱ

5   Conclusion

Compared with the native Tibetan characters, the transliterating characters are used not so popularly; however, there are more than six thousands of them. Therefore, it is necessary to study the collation of these transliterating characters. The paper proposes two structures that can deal with the two kinds of collation of transliterating characters: collated with rules of native Tibetan dictionaries and with the rules of transliterating dictionaries. Based on the proposed structures, all transliterating characters can be collated successfully and effectively with the rules of two different dictionaries.

Acknowledgment. This work is partially supported by NSFC under Grant No.60963016 and Key laboratory of Tibetan Information Processing, Ministry of Education of the People's Republic of China. The authors also thank the anonymous reviewers for their invaluable comments and suggestions.

References

1. An, S.: Sanskrit-Tibetan-Chinese dictionary. Nationalities Publishing House, Beijing (1991)
2. Zhang, Y.: Tibetan-Chinese Dictionary. Nationalities Publishing House, Beijing (1985)
3. Jiang, D., Kang, C.: The sorting mathematical model and algorithm of written Tibetan language. Chinese Journal of Computers 27(4), 524–529 (2004)
4. Huang, H., Da, F.: General Structure Based Collation of Tibetan Syllables. J. Inf. Comput. 6(5), 1693–1703 (2010)
5. Huang, H., Da, F.: Discussion on Collation of Tibetan Syllables. In: IALP 2010, pp. 35–38 (December 2010)
6. National Standard of PRC, Information Technology-Tibetan Coded Character Sets for Information Interchange-Extension A (GB/T 20542-2006). Standards Press of China, Beijing (May 2007)
7. National Standard of PRC, Information Technology-Tibetan Coded Character Sets for Information Interchange-Extension B (GB/T 22238-2008). Standards Press of China, Beijing (January 2009)

Topic Structure Identification of PClause Sequence Based on Generalized Topic Theory[*]

Yuru Jiang[1,3] and Rou Song[1,2]

[1] Computer School, Beijing University of Technology, Beijing, China
jiangyuru@bistu.edu.cn, songrou@blcu.edu.cn
[2] Information Science School, Beijing Language and Culture University, Beijing, China
[3] Computer School, Beijing Information and Science Technology University, Beijing, China

Abstract. To solve the problem of topic absence at the beginning of Chinese Punctuation Clause(abbreviated as PClause), this study, with due regard to the characteristics of topic structure and the stack model having been clearly explained by Generalized Topic Theory, proposes a scheme for identifying the topic structure of PClause sequence. The accuracy rate for open test is 15 percent higher than the baseline, which proves the effectiveness of employing Generalized Topic Theory in identifying the topic structure of PClause sequence.

Keywords: PClause sequence, generalized topic, topic structure, topic clause.

1 Introduction

The study of discourse structure plays a crucial role in language engineering, including but not limited to summarization, information extraction, essay analysis and scoring, sentiment analysis and opinion mining, text quality assessment, as well as machine translation[1]. A common practice adopted by present studies is to decompose the text into small units such as sentences, phrases and words, which are selected as features in statistical methods or machine learning approaches. However, the characteristics of the discourse structure are rarely exploited.

Chinese discourses are characterized with a high frequency of anaphora, especially zero anaphora[2], so that when a Chinese discourse is decomposed into sentences, some anaphoric components will be missing. This has been a big problem affecting the discourse-related NLP applications. Chinese linguists have done a lot of theoretical researches on the zero anaphora in Chinese from four aspects, namely, syntax, pragmatics, discourse analysis and cognitive linguistics. But the characteristics and distribution rules of zero anaphora having been found are hard to formalize and hence inapplicable in computerization. On the other hand, many insightful statistics-based and rule-based studies on anaphora resolution in Chinese by the NLP researchers

---

[*] This study is supported by National Natural Science Foundation of China, subject No. 60872121, 61171129 and 61070119.

M. Zhou et al. (Eds.): NLPCC 2012, CCIS 333, pp. 85–96, 2012.

exploiting linguistics knowledge are largely focused on the resolution of pronouns and nouns, with quite little research on the resolution of zero anaphora[3].

With regard to the characteristics of Chinese discourses, Generalized Topic Theory[4] sets punctuation clauses (PClauses hereafter), which have clear boundaries, as basic units of Chinese discourse, and proposes the concepts of generalized topic and topic clause, so that such characteristics as the discourse structure and topic clauses are explicitly described. Within this framework, a stack model of the dynamic generation of topic clauses is devised, providing theoretical basis and formal approach for Chinese discourse analysis.

Based on the Generalized Topic Theory, a study on identifying the topic clause of individual PClause has been done[5]. In that work, a topic clause corpus has been constructed and a scheme for constructing a candidate topic clause(CTC) set has been devised. Then semantic generalization and editing distance are employed to select the correct topic clause. Experiments yield an accuracy rate of 73.36% for open test, which has great significance for discourse related Chinese processing. On the basis of this work, this paper presents a study on identifying the topic structure of PClause sequences.

In the rest of the paper, section 2 briefly introduces the Generalized Topic Theory and its concepts relevant to this study; section 3 describes the scheme for identifying the topic structure of a PClause sequence; section 4 presents the corpus, baseline and evaluation criteria of the identification experiment; section 5 shows the experiment result and the analysis on it; and the last section provides a summary and future work.

2   Generalized Topic Theory

2.1   PClause Sequence

The basic unit of Chinese discourse is PClause, which is a string of words separated by punctuation marks of comma, semicolon, period, exclamation mark or question mark or direct quotation marks. [6]

E.g.1. (Fortress Besieged by Ch'ien Chung-shu)
这几个警察并不懂德文，居然传情达意，引得犹太女人格格地笑，比他们的外交官强多了。
(These policemen knew no German, but were trying to flirt, made the Jews women giggle, were much better than their diplomats.)[1]

In E.g.1, the discourse fragment consists of four PClauses, and its PClause sequence can be represented as below:

c_1. 这几个警察并不懂德文，   (These policemen knew no German,)
c_2. 居然传情达意，   (but were trying to flirt,)

---

[1]   Since word order differs significantly in Chinese from in English, which directly affects the topic clause recognition, the translation of examples in this paper will be direct, keeping as much syntactic information in Chinese as possible.

c_3.　引得犹太女人格格地笑,　　　　　(made the Jews women giggle,)
c_4.　比他们的外交官强多了。　　　　　(were much better than their diplomats.)

Some PClauses can stand alone as a sentence, having a complete structure of topic-comment. For example, in c_1, the topic is "这几个警察 (these policemen)", the comment is "并不懂德文 (knew no German)". But some PClauses, which may miss sentence components, cannot stand alone. c_2, for example, is just a comment. Its topic "这几个警察 (these policemen)" is in c_1.

2.2　Topic Structure

The topic structure of Chinese is the syntactic structure of PClause sequence, which is composed of a generalized topic and one or more comments. A comment itself can be a topic structure too, so that one topic structure can be nested in another topic structure. Such a structure can be represented by indented new-line representation[6]. For instance, E.g.1 can be represented as below.

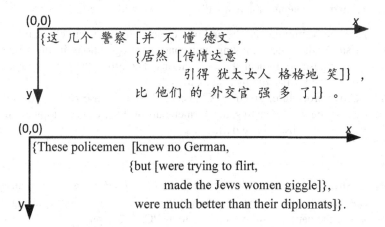

In the above graph, what is quoted by the "[]"marks is comment, the left of which is the topic. And what is quoted by the "{}"marks is the topic structure. The left part of c_1 is at $x=0$, and the other PClauses are indented to the right edge of its topic.

In the indented new-line representation, if the x value of the topic of a topic clause is 0, then it is the outmost topic of the topic structure.

2.3　Topic Clause

If all the missing topic information, including the outmost topic, of each PClause is filled up, then the complete structure is termed as a topic clause.

Given a PClause c_i and its topic clause t_i, each PClause and its respective topic clause are:

c_1.这几个警察并不懂德文， t_1.这几个警察并不懂德文，
          (These policemen knew no German,)
c_2.居然传情达意， t_2.这几个警察居然传情达意，
          (These policemen but were trying to flirt,)
c_3.引得犹太女人格格地笑， t_3.这几个警察居然引得犹太女人格格地笑，
          (These policemen but made the Jews women giggle,)
c_4.比他们的外交官强多了。 t_4.这几个警察比他们的外交官强多了。
          (These policemen were much better than their diplomats.)

Below is the generating process of the above topic clauses.

$t_1=c_1$;

The topic of c_2 is "这几个警察(these policemen)" in t_1. Remove the right side of this topic in t_1 and concatenate the rest with c_2, and we will have t_2;

The topic of c_3 is "居然(but)" in t_2. Remove the right side of this topic in t_2 and concatenate the rest with c_3, and we will have t_3;

The topic of c_4 is "这几个警察(these policemen)" in t_3. Remove the right side of this topic in t_3 and concatenate the rest with c_4, and we will have t_4.

If we regard the beginning and the end of a topic clause respectively as the bottom and top of a stack, then the removing and concatenating actions in the generating process of topic clause are typical stack operations. Therefore, the generating process of topic clause can be formalized by a stack model.

From the above procedure, given a PClause c, its topic clause t can be c itself, but it can also be a string concatenating the former part of the preceding topic clause t_{pre} with c. Hence a topic clause can be defined as

$$t = tw_l^i \frown c \tag{1}$$

Here tw_l^i is a string of i words in the former part of t_{pre}, $i \in [0,n]$, and $\frown$ is an operator that concatenates the two strings together. When $i=0$, tw_l^i is an empty string. In the following part of the paper, i will be referred to as PClause depth.

3   Identification Scheme

Strategies employed in identifying the topic clause of individual PClause[5] include the following strategies: using stack model to generate CTCs, using Edit Distance to calculate similarity, using semantic generalization to solve the problem of data sparse, and using completeness of topic clause restriction to select the optimum CTC. This will be the basis for our work to devise the topic clause identification scheme of PClause sequence.

3.1   Identification Objective

For a PClause sequence, if its topic clause sequence can be identified, then the topic structure of the PClause sequence can be obtained. Therefore, the objective of this paper is to identify the topic clause sequence for a given PClause sequence, viz., given a PClause sequence $c_1,...,c_n$, where the topic clause of c_1 is c_1 itself, then the objective is to identify the topic clause of each PClause $t_1,...,t_n$.

3.2   Identification Process

The process of identifying the topic clauses of a PClause sequence can be stored and represented as a tree. E.g.2 is the first four PClauses (in word-segmented form) from an article about "raja kenojei". The identification process of this PClause sequence is shown in Fig.1.

E.g.2. raja kenojei (from China Encyclopedia)
c_1. 斑鳐 是 鳐形目 鳐科 鳐属 的 1 种 。
c_2. 吻 中长 ，
c_3. 尖 突 。
c_4. 尾 细长 ，
(c_1. raja kenojei is rajiformes   rajidae raja de one species,
c_2.   snout medium-sized,
c_3.   tip projecting.
c_4.   tail slim and long.)

The topic clause of c_1 is t_1, same as c_1, which is the root node in Fig.1.

According to formula (1), for the given t_1 and c_2, since there are eight words in t_1, the value range of i in $tw_1{}^i$ that generates t_2 is [0,8], and the following strings can be generated as the CTCs of c_2.

[1].吻 中长 ，
[2].斑鳐 吻 中长 ，
[3].斑鳐 是 吻 中长 ，
[4].斑鳐 是 鳐形目 吻 中长 ，
[5].斑鳐 是 鳐形目 鳐科 的 吻 中长 ，
[6].斑鳐 是 鳐形目 鳐科 鳐属 吻 中长 ，
[7].斑鳐 是 鳐形目 鳐科 鳐属 的 吻 中长 ，
[8].斑鳐 是 鳐形目 鳐科 鳐属 的 1 吻 中长 ，
[9].斑鳐 是 鳐形目 鳐科 鳐属 的 1 种 吻 中长 ，
([1].snout medium-sized,
[2].raja kenojei snout medium-sized,
[3].raja kenojei is snout medium-sized,
[4].raja kenojei is rajiformes snout medium-sized,
[5].raja kenojei is rajiformes rajidae snout medium-sized,
[6].raja kenojei is rajiformes rajidae raja snout medium-sized,
[7].raja kenojei is rajiformes rajidae raja de snout medium-sized,
[8].raja kenojei is rajiformes rajidae raja de one snout medium-sized,
[9].raja kenojei is rajiformes rajidae raja de one species nout medium-sized,)

They form the nodes on the second level in the tree shown in Fig.1. (For convenience, only 3 nodes are displayed.)

Similarly, the CTCs of c_3 can be generated by using c_3 and the CTC of c_2 (although t_2 still uncertain yet, it must be a node on the second level in the tree). For instance, given a CTC on the second level in the tree, such as "斑鱝 是 鱝形目 吻 中长 (raja kenojei is rajiformes snout medium-sized)", and c_3, we can have the CTCs shown in Fig.1 A part; given "斑鱝 是 吻 中长 (raja kenojei is snout medium-sized)", and c_3, we can have the CTCs shown in Fig.1 B part; given "斑鱝 吻 中长 (raja kenojei snout medium-sized)", and c_3, we can have the CTCs shown in Fig.1 C part. They form the nodes on the third level in the tree shown in Fig.1. By the same token, a tree of CTCs can be generated for the text 斑鱝(raja kenojei).

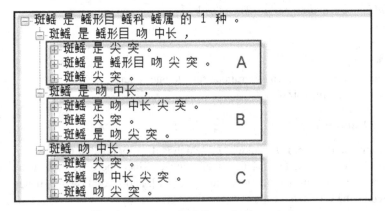

Fig. 1. Part of the CTC Tree of   Example 2

Adopting proper strategies to calculate the value of each node in the CTC tree, we can then calculate the path value of each leaf node to the root node. The path with the largest path value can be found and the nodes on it from the root node to the leaf node are the topic clause sequence to be found.

In this way, the task of identifying the topic clause of a PClause sequence is converted to searching the maximum path in the tree.

3.3   Recognition Algorithm

Input: PClause Sequence $c_1,...,c_n$
Output: topic clause sequence $t_1,...,t_n$
1. Generate CTC tree of a PClause Sequence

As section 3.2 describes, given a PClause sequence $c_1,...,c_n$, a CTC tree can be constructed correspondingly, which has n levels. On each level, there will be a number of nodes, and each node can be described with the 5-tuple $<k,ct,v,n_1,n_2>$, which corresponds to one CTC of c_k, where k is the level id, with $1 \leq k \leq n$, ct is the string sequence of the CTC, v is the path value from the root node to the current node, n_1 is the sequence number of the node in level k, and n_2 is the sequence number of the father node in level k-1.

Level 1: $[<1,ct_1,0,1,0>]$, $ct_1=c_1$.

Given level k-1 is $[<k$-$1,ct_1,v_1,1,n_1>, <k$-$1,ct_2,v_2,2,n_2>,\ldots, <k$-$1,ct_m,v_m,m,n_m>]$, the kth level will be generated by three steps.

Step 1: Crude Generation – to construct all possible CTC nodes from every node on level k-1 and c_k. Supposing p nodes have been generated on level k from the i-1 nodes on level k-1, and the word sequence ct_i, of the CTC on the ith node on level k-1 is $[tw_1,\ldots,tw_s]$, then the jth node on level k generated from node $<k$-$1,ct_i,v_i,i,n_i>$ is

$<k,tw_j^{j-1} \frown c_k,v_i+score(tw_j^{j-1} \frown c_k),p+j,i>$

where $1 \leq j \leq s+1$, tw_1^0=nil, $tw_i^j=[tw_1,\ldots,tw_j]$, and score is a scoring function for CTC, the definition of which please refer to section 3.4.

Step 2: Pruning – to delete the nodes of low score by some strategies.

Two pruning strategies are adopted.

a. single-node-based pruning: For all the CTC nodes constructed from a node on level k-1 and c_k, if the number of nodes is greater than 3, only the top 3 nodes with the largest node value are kept, the rest being pruned. If two CTCs have the same value, then the shorter one is given priority.

b. level-based pruning: If the number of nodes on level k-1 is greater than 50, then the top 50 nodes with largest path value are kept and the rest are deleted.

Step 3: Sorting – After the above steps, the nodes on level k are sorted in descending order by v value. The sorted nodes on this level are then numbered starting from one.

2. Generating CTC Sequence

Given that the set of CTC nodes on level i in the tree is marked as $tcs(i)$, then $t_n=ct_i$, where $<n,ct_j,v_j,j,n_j> \in tcs(n)$, and $v_j=max\{v_p|<n,ct_p,v_p,p,n_p> \in tcs(n)\}$.

For a known t_k $(2 \leq k \leq n)$, then $t_{k-1}=ct_r$, where $<k,t_k,v,j,n_j> \in tcs(k)$, $<k$-$1,ct_r,v_r,r,n_r> \in tcs(k$-$1)$, $r=n_j$.

So that $t_1=c_1$.

3.4   CTCs Scoring Function

In the previous work[5], a Topic Clause Corpus (Tcorpus) is used and two approaches of similarity calculation and semantic generalization are adopted to select the optimum topic clause from the CTCs.

Given a CTC d of PClause c, a topic clause most similar to d is found from the corpus, whose similarity is marked as $sim\_CT(d)$. For any two strings x and y, given that their similarity is $sim(x,y)$. $sim\_CT(d)$ is defined as

$$sim\_CT(d) = \max_{t \in Tcorpus} sim(d,t)$$

(2)

From the CTC generating process it can be seen that the topic clause of a PClause is related to the PClause itself and the topic clause of precedent PClause which are the context of the topic clause. Therefore, when identifying the topic clause of a PClause, the context in which the topic clause is generated must be taken into account.

Given a CTC d, the PClause d_c from which d is generated, and the topic clause of the PClause preceding d_c is d_t_{pre}, the context similarity of d is defined as

$$ctxSim\_CT(d) = \max_{t \in Tcorpus} (\lambda_1 sim(d,t) + \lambda_2 sim(d\_c,t\_c) + \lambda_3 sim(d\_tc_{pre},t\_tc_{pre})) \quad (3)$$

where t is the topic clause in Tcorpus, t_c is the PClause from which t is generated, and t_t_{pre} is the topic clause of the PClause preceding t_c. (Please note that in Tcorpus, for the sake of calculating the context similarity of d, t_c and t_t_{pre} are kept as well as the information of topic clause t.)

Experiments have been done which separately adopted $sim\_CT(d)$ and $ctxSim\_CT(d)$ as the scoring functions, and the result shows that the accuracy rate using the latter is 11.3% higher (see section 4). For E.g.3:

E.g.3.

d_tc_{pre} :　　A 一般均具 H 或 H C ,
　　　　　　　(A usually is equipped with both H or H C ,)

d_c :　　　　用以 引诱 食饵。 (for baiting.)

t_1 :　　　　A 一般均具 H 用以 引诱 食饵。
　　　　　　　(A usually all is equipped with H for baiting.)

st_1 :　　　　A C 一般具 H , (usually   A C is equipped with H,)

t_2 :　　　　A 一般均具 H 或 H C 用以 引诱 食饵。

　　　　　　　(A is usually be equipped with H or H C for baiting.)

The above is the generalized form of some sentences, which is used in similarity calculation. Alphabet symbols are the generalized mark for words, e.g. A stands for fish terms, H for appearance and C for body parts. The none-alphabetical words are not generalized in current stage. t_1 is the topic clause of d_c identified by sim_CT, but is not the correct one. The topic clause most similar to t_1 is st_1 in Tcorpus, but the similar parts of them (the shaded words) has nothing to do with d_c.

The correct topic clause is t_2, which is identified by $ctxSim\_CT$. The topic clause in Tcorpus most similar to t_2 in E.g.3 and its context are as below:

t_tc_{pre} :　　　A 有些 B C 具 C , (A has some B C is equipped with C,)

t_c :　　　　以 引诱 食饵 , (for baiting.)

t :　　　　　A 有些 B C 具 C 以 引诱 食饵 ,

　　　　　　　(A has some B C is equipped with C for baiting,)

It can be seen that d_c is very close to t_c, t_2 and t share many similar components, and that d_t_{pre} and t_t_{pre} also have some components in common (similar components are underlined). Therefore the topic clauses in Tcorpus identified by $ctxSim\_CT$ can more objectively test whether the CTC is the right one for the PClause at hand. In other words, $ctxSim\_CT$ is better than sim_CT in CTC evaluation.

4   The Experiment Process

4.1   Corpus

This study exploits 202 texts about fish in the Biology volume of China Encyclopedia, which consists of 9508 PClauses whose topic clauses are manually tagged. A modern Chinese general-purpose word segmentation system[7] developed by Beijing Language University is used for word segmentation and generalization. To ensure the accuracy rate for word segmentation, the original GPWS vocabulary bank, ambiguous word bank and the semantic tag bank are extended.

15 texts are used for test in the experiment. When identifying the topic structure of one text, the topic clauses in the rest 201 texts constitute the training corpus Tcorpus. There are 717 PClauses and 46 topic structures in these 15 texts. On average, each topic structure consists of 15.59 PClauses. In the 717 PClauses, 452 share the component of fish names, a proportion of 63.04%.

4.2   Baseline

In the texts about fish in the encyclopedia, the topic clause of a PClause is mostly obtained by simply concatenating the fish name (the title of the text) to the beginning of the clause. Therefore, the baseline is defined as

baseline=number of PClauses whose topic is the text title/total number of PClauses (4)

According to the statistics on the topic clauses of the 9508 PClauses in the 202 texts about fish, the number of PClauses whose topic clause is the PClause concatenated with the text title is 5786. Therefore, the baseline is 5786/9508=0.6085.

4.3   Evaluation Criteria

For N PClauses, if the number of PClauses whose topic clauses are correctly identified is hitN, then the identification accuracy rate is hitN/N.

5   Experiment Result and Analysis

5.1   Experiment Result

The result of open test on 15 texts is shown in Fig.2. If $sim\_CT(d)$ is used as the scoring function, the accuracy rate is 64.99%, 4.14 percent points higher than the baseline. But if $ctxSim\_CT(d)$ is used as the scoring function, when λ_1=0.5, λ_2=0.4, λ_3=0.1, the accuracy rate reaches 76.25%, 15.44 percent points higher than the baseline.

5.2   Analysis

(1) The reason for the low accuracy rate for texts about barbinae

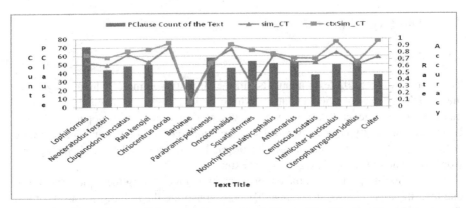

Fig. 2. PClause Count and Accuracy Rate for Topic Clause Identification about 15 texts

Most PClauses have only one topic clause, so that in the experiment there is only one correct answer for each PClause. However, some PClauses may have more than one CTCs that can be regarded as the correct answer. For example:

E.g.4.

$tc_{pre.}$ 本亚科 鱼类 通称 鲃。

(Fish of this subfamily are generally called barbels.)

c.   体 近 纺锤形，(have a spindle-shaped body,)

$ctc_1.$ 本亚科 体 近 纺锤形，(this subfamily have a spindle-shaped body,)

$ctc_2.$ 本亚科 鱼类 体 近 纺锤形，

(Fish of this subfamily have a spindle-shaped body,)

In E.g.4, ctc_1 and ctc_2 are two correct answers. However, ctc_2 is the specified right answer while ctc_1 is the one selected by program. In text about barbinae, there are 23 such "mistakes" have taken place. Taking this into consideration, the number of correctly identified topic clauses should be 25, reaching an accuracy rate of 78.13%. Other texts also have similar issues.

(2) On some levels in the CTC tree, there may be nodes with the same CTC string. In extreme cases, all the nodes in one level have the same CTC string.

For example, on the 3rd level in Fig.1, the node "斑鰶 尖 突 (raja kenojei tip projecting)" appears three times. In some texts for testing, there are cases that in the CTC tree, some levels may have nodes that contain identical CTC information. If the CTC is not the correct one, and the topic information for the subsequent PClauses is absent, a chain of errors will be caused.

Therefore, to ensure the heterogeneity of the nodes on each level is an issue to be considered in future work. A plausible approach could be that when constructing the nodes on each level in the CTC tree, same brother nodes, if any, will be merged into one node while keeping the total number of nodes on each level unchanged. The CTC tree will thus be transformed into a CTC graph, which preserves more path information with the space complexity unchanged.

(3) The relation between accuracy rate and the PClause position(Sequence number of the PClause in the text).

From the PClause identification process, esp. the construction process of CTC tree, it can be seen that the accuracy rate on an upper level may affect that on the lower levels. It appears that the farther a PClause is from the beginning, the lower the accuracy rate for its topic clause identification. But as a matter of fact, there is no positive correlation between the PClause position and the accuracy rate for topic clause identification.

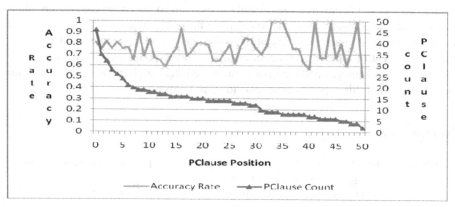

Fig. 3. PClause Position, PClause Count and the Accuracy Rate for Topic Clause Identification

(4) The relation between the accuracy rate and the PClause depth

Fig. 4 shows that the PClause depth may contribute to the decline of accuracy rate. There are as many as 139 PClauses with depth of 2, the accuracy rate for their topic clause identification being as low as 53.96%.

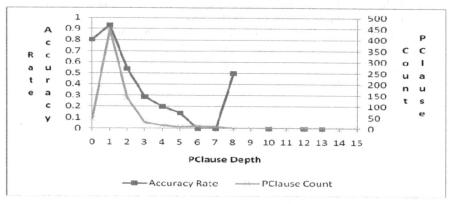

Fig. 4. PClause Depth, PClause Count and the Accuracy Rate for Topic Clause Identification

6   Summary and Future Work

This paper briefly describes Generalized Topic Theory, on the basis of which it proposes a research scheme for identifying the topic structure of PClause sequence. Correspondingly, experiments are devised and completed. In the study, tree structure is adopted to store the CTC sequence generation process. Edit Distance and semantic generalization are employed as the basis for context-based similarity calculation to evaluate the CTC nodes in the tree. Finally, by building the scoring function for the nodes and with proper pruning strategies, the topic structure of PClause sequence is identified with satisfying experiment results.

However, there are some aspects where this work needs to be improved. First, the values of λ_1, λ_2 and λ_3 are given empirically in the context similarity calculation. More scientific methods should be found to calculate the values reasonably. Second, it is a question how to keep heterogeneity of the nodes on each level in the tree. In addition, the achievement of topic clause identification in encyclopedia texts about fish can be extended to other encyclopedia corpora. Further efforts should be made to probe into the application of this experiment scheme to more fields.

References

1. Webber, B., Egg, M., Kordoni, V.: Discourse Structures and Language Technology. Journal of Natural Language Engineering 1, 1–40 (2012)
2. Chen, P.: Discourse Analysis of Zero Anaphora in Chinese. Zhongguo Yuwen 5, 363–378 (1987)
3. Huang, X., Zhang, K.: Zero Anaphora in Chinese—the State of Art. Journal of Chinese Information Processing 23(4), 10–15 (2009)
4. Song, R., Jiang, Y., Wang, J.: On Generalized-Topic-Based Chinese Discourse Structure. In: 1st CIPS-SIGHAN Joint Conference on Chinese Language Processing, pp. 23–33. Tsinghua University Press, Beijing (2010)
5. Jiang, Y., Song, R.: Topic Clause Identification Based On Generalized Topic Theory. Journal of Chinese Information Processing 26(5) (2012)
6. Song, R.: Research on Properties of Syntactic Relation Between PClauses in Modern Chinese. Chinese Teaching in the World 2, 26–44 (2008)
7. A modern Chinese general-purpose word segmentation system v3.5,
   http://democlip.blcu.edu.cn:8081/gpws/

Chinese Semantic Role Labeling with Dependency-Driven Constituent Parse Tree Structure

Hongling Wang, Bukang Wang, and Guodong Zhou

NLP Lab, School of Computer Science & Technology, Soochow University, Suzhou, China
{hlwang,20094227014,gdzhou}@suda.edu.cn

Abstract. This paper explores a tree kernel-based method for nominal semantic role labeling (SRL). In particular, a new dependency-driven constituent parse tree (D-CPT) structure is proposed to better represent the dependency relations in a CPT-style structure, which employs dependency relation types instead of phrase labels in CPT. In this way, D-CPT not only keeps the dependency relationship information in the dependency parse tree (DPT) structure but also retains the basic structure of CPT. Moreover, several schemes are designed to extract various kinds of necessary information, such as the shortest path between the nominal predicate and the argument candidate, the support verb of the nominal predicate and the head argument modified by the argument candidate, from D-CPT . Evaluation on Chinese NomBank shows that our tree kernel-based method on D-CPT achieves comparable performance with the state-of-art feature-based ones. This indicates the effectiveness of the novel D-CPT structure for better representation of dependency relations in tree kernel-based methods. To our knowledge, this is the first research of tree kernel-based SRL on effectively exploring dependency relationship information, which achieves comparable performance with the state-of-the-art feature-based ones.

Keywords: Semantic Role Labeling, Dependency Parse Tree, Tree Kernel.

1 Introduction

Semantic role labeling (SRL) has been drawing more and more attention in recent years due to its fundamental role in deep NLP applications, such as information extraction [1], question answering [2], co-reference resolution [3] and document categorization [4]. Given a sentence and a predicate (either a verb or a noun) in a sentence, SRL recognizes and maps the constituents in the sentence into their corresponding semantic arguments (roles) of the predicate. According to predicate type, SRL can be divided into SRL for verbal predicates (verbal SRL) and SRL for nominal predicates (nominal SRL).

Usually, there are two kinds of methods for SRL. One is feature-based methods, which map a predicate-argument structure to a flat feature vector. The other is tree kernel-based methods, which represent a predicate-argument structure as a parse tree and directly measure the similarity between two predicate-argument parse trees instead of the feature vector representations. Although feature-based methods have been

M. Zhou et al. (Eds.): NLPCC 2012, CCIS 333, pp. 97–109, 2012.

consistently performing much better than kernel-based methods and represent the state-of-the-art in SRL, tree kernel-based methods have the potential in better capturing structured knowledge in the parse tree structure, which is critical for the success of SRL, than feature-based methods. In the literature, however, there are only a few studies [5-8] employing tree kernel-based methods for SRL and most of them focus on the constituent parse tree (CPT) structure.

Although some feature-based methods [9-10] have attempted to explore structured information in the dependency parse tree (DPT) structure, few tree kernel-based methods directly employ DPT due to its sparseness in that DPT only captures the dependency relationship between two words. While both DPT and CPT are widely used to represent the linguistic structure of a sentence, however, there still exist some important differences between them. For example, DPT mainly concerns with the dependency relationship between individual words, instead of the phrase structure in a sentence as done in CPT. Therefore, these two kinds of syntactic parse tree structures may behave quite differently in capturing different aspects of syntactic phenomena.

In this paper, we explore a tree kernel-based method for Chinese nominal SRL using a new syntactic parse tree structure, called dependency-driven constituent parse tree (D-CPT). This is done by transforming DPT to a new CPT-style structure, using dependency relation types instead of phrase labels in the traditional CPT structure. In this way, our tree kernel-based method can benefit from the advantages of both DPT and CPT since D-CPT not only keeps the dependency relationship information in DPT but also retains the basic structure of CPT. Evaluation of Chinese nominal SRL on Chinese NomBank shows that our tree kernel-based method achieves comparable performance with the state-of-the-art feature-based methods.

The rest of this paper is organized as follows: Section 2 briefly reviews the related work on SRL. Section 3 introduces our tree kernel-based method over the novel D-CPT structure. Section 4 presents the experimental results. Finally, Sections 5 draws the conclusion.

2   Related Work

Since this paper focuses on tree kernel-based methods for SRL, this section only overviews the related work on tree kernel-based methods for SRL. For an overview on feature-based methods for SRL, please refer to Xue [11] and Li et al [12].

- **Tree Kernel-Based Methods for SRL**

Moschitti [5] pioneers the research of tree kernel-based methods for English verbal SRL. In his work, a Predicate Argument Feature (PAF) structure is extracted from CPT to include salient substructures in the predicate-argument structure. Then, the similarity between two PAFs is computed using a convolution tree kernel, proposed by Collins and Duffy [13]. Motivated by this work, more and more tree kernel-based methods are proposed and explored in SRL since then [7,8,14].

Moschitti et al [7] improves the PAF structure by simply differentiating the node which exactly covers the argument to denote its boundary property. Che et al [14] further separates the PAF structure into a path portion and a constituent structure portion. Then, a composite kernel is proposed to combine two convolution tree kernels over these two portions. Zhang et al [8] proposes a grammar-driven convolution tree kernel to better explore grammatical substructures by considering the similarity between those non-identical substructures with similar syntactic properties.

To our knowledge, there are no reported studies on tree kernel-based methods for SRL from the DPT structure perspective. However, there are a few related studies in other NLP tasks, such as semantic relation extraction between named entities [15] and co-reference resolution [16], which employ DPT in tree kernel-based methods and achieve comparable performance to the ones on CPT. For example, Nguyen et al [15] explore three schemes to extract structured information from DPT: dependency words (DW) tree, grammatical relation (GR) tree, and grammatical relation and words (GRW) tree.

- **SRL on Chinese**

With recent release of Chinese PropBank and Chinese NomBank for verbal and nominal predicates of Chinese, respectively, Xue and his colleagues [11,17,18] systematically explore Chinese verbal and nominal SRLs using feature-based methods, given golden predicates. Among them, Xue and Palmer [17] study Chinese verbal SRL on Chinese PropBank and achieve the performance of 91.3 and 61.3 in F1-measure on golden and automatic CPT structures, respectively. Xue [18] extends their study on Chinese nominal SRL and attempts to improve the performance of nominal SRL by simply including the Chinese PropBank training instances into the training data for nominal SRL. Xue [11] further improves the performance on both verbal and nominal SRLs with a better constituent parser and more features.

Since then, Li et al [12] improve Chinese nominal SRL by integrating various features derived from Chinese verbal SRL via a feature-based method on CPT, and achieve the state-of-art performance of 72.67 in F1-measure on Chinese NormBank. Li et al [19] further present a feature-based SRL for verbal predicates of Chinese from the views of both CPT and DPT.

To our knowledge, there are no reported studies on tree kernel-based methods for Chinese SRL from either CPT or DPT perspectives.

3   Tree Kernel-Based Nominal SRL on D-CPT

Syntactic parsing aims at identifying the grammatical structure in a sentence. There are two main paradigms for representing the structured information: constituent and dependency parsing, which produces different parse tree structures. In particular, the DPT structure encodes grammatical relations between words in a sentence, with the words as nodes and corresponding dependency types as edges. An edge from a word to another word represents a grammatical relation between these two words. Every word in a dependency tree has exactly one parent except the root.

Fig. 1 shows an example of the DPT structure for sentence (中国 进出口 银行 与 企业 加强 合作/*The Import & Export Bank of China and the enterprise strengthen*

the cooperation). It also shows a nominal predicate and its respective arguments annotated. Specifically, the nominal predicate " 合作/cooperation" with " 加强
/strengthen" as the support verb has a argument, "中国 进出口 银行 与 企业/the
Import & Export Bank and the enterprise ", as Arg0. In addition, W, R and G denote
the word itself, its dependency relation with the head argument, and its part-of-speech
(POS), respectively. In this section, we first describe how to construct the D-CPT
structure. Then, we explore different ways to extract necessary structured information
from this new parse tree structure. Finally, we briefly present the convolution tree
kernel for computing the similarity between two parse trees and its combination with
a feature-based linear kernel via a composite kernel for further performance
improvement.

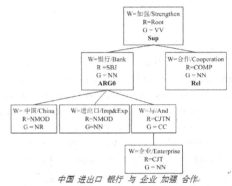

中国 进出口 银行 与 企业 加强 合作.

The Import & Export Bank of China and the enterprise strengthen the cooperation.

Fig. 1. Example of DPT structure with nominal predicate and its related arguments annotated

3.1   D-CPT

Just as described in the introduction, both DPT and CPT have their own advantages.
The new D-CPT structure benefits from the advantages of both DPT and CPT since

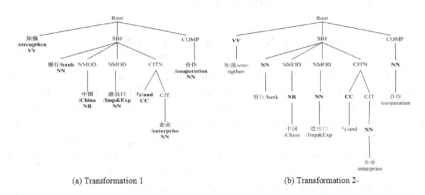

(a) Transformation 1   (b) Transformation 2

Fig. 2. Example of achieving D-CPT structure from DPT structure

D-CPT not only keeps the dependency relationship information in DPT but also retains the basic structure of CPT. This is done by transforming the DPT structure to a new CPT-style structure, using dependency types instead of phrase labels in the traditional CPT structure. In particular, two transformations are done to achieve the D-CPT structure from the DPT structure:

1. For each node in DPT, create a new node by moving its contained word W and part-of-speech G as its left-most child while only keeping its contained dependency relation type R. Fig. 2(a) illustrates an example of the resulted parse tree, corresponding to Fig. 1.
2. For each terminal node, create a new node by moving its contained word W as its (only) child while only keeping its contained part-of-speech. Fig. 2(b) illustrates an example of the resulted parse tree, corresponding to Fig. 2(a).

3.2   Extraction Schemes

Given a predicate and an argument candidate, the key is to extract an appropriate portion of the D-CPT structure in covering necessary information to determine their semantic relationship. Generally, the more substructures of the tree are included, the more structured information would be provided at the risk of more noisy information.

In our study, we examine three schemes for this purpose, considering the specific characteristics of nominal SRL. Since D-CPT takes the advantages of both CPT and DPT, these schemes can directly encodes the argument structure of lexical units populated at their nodes through corresponding dependency relations.

1) Shortest path tree (SPT)

This extraction scheme only includes the nodes occurring in the shortest path connecting the predicate and the argument candidate, via the nearest commonly-governing node. Fig. 3(a) shows an example of SPT for nominal predicate "合作/cooperation" and argument candidate "企业/enterprise".

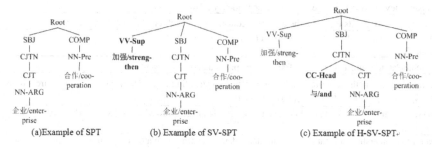

Fig. 3. Extraction schemes

2) SV-SPT

(Chinese) NomBank adopts the same predicate-specific approach in representing the core arguments of a predicate as (Chinese) PropBank, with special treatment for nominal predicate-specific phenomena, such as support verbs, which cover much useful information in determining the semantic relationship between the nominal predicate and the argument candidate. Specifically, there is a specific label, Sup, to indicate the support verb of the nominal predicate. Fig. 1 includes an example support verb "加强/strengthen", in helping introduce the arguments of the nominal predicate "合作/cooperation". Normally, a verb is marked as a support verb only when it shares some arguments with the nominal predicate. Statistics on NomBank and Chinese NomBank shows that about 20% and 22% of arguments are introduced via a support verb, respectively. This indicates the importance of support verb in nominal SRL. Since the support verb of a nominal predicate normally pivots outside the nominal predicate and its arguments in the D-CPT structure, e.g. the one as shown in Fig. 2(b), it is necessary to include the support verb information in nominal SRL. Fig. 3(b) shows an example of SPT after retaining the support verb information. We call the new structure as SV-SPT.

3) H-SV-SPT

It is well proven that the head argument of the argument candidate plays a critical role in verbal SRL. In our study, we also consider the head argument information in nominal SRL. Fig. 3(c) illustrates an example after attaching the head argument information to SV-SPT. We call the new structure as H-SV-SPT.

3.3   Kernels

Given a parse tree structure, this paper employs the well-known convolution tree kernel [13] to compute the similarity between two parse trees. In principle, the convolution tree kernel works by counting the number of common sub-trees as the syntactic

Table 1. Features explored in the feature-based linear kernel

Feature   Remarks (Feature instance with regard to Fig. 1)
Dependent word and its POS tag: the modifying word and its POS tag in the dependency relation. (企业/enterprise,   NN)
Dependency relation type: the type of the dependency relation. (CJT)
Predicate word and its POS tag: the current predicate and its POS tag. (合作/ cooperation, NN)
Head word and its POS tag: the modified (head) word and its POS tag in the dependency relation. (与/and, CC)
DepSubCat: the subcategorization frame of the predicate. (COMP->)
DeprelPath: the path from predicate to argument concatenating dependency labels with the direction of the edge. (CJT ↑ CJTN ↑ SBJ ↑ ROOT ↓ COMP)
POSPath: same as DeprelPath, but dependency labels are exchanged for POS tags. (NN ↑ CC ↑ NN ↑ VV ↓ NN)
Family membership: indicating how the dependency relation is related to the predicate in the family. (siblings' grandchildren)
ChildDepSet: the set of dependency labels of the children of the predicate. (None)
ChildPOSSet: the set of POS tags of the children of the predicate. (None)
SiblingDepSet: the set of dependency labels of the siblings of the predicate. (SBJ)
SiblingPOSSet: the set of POS tags of the siblings of the predicate. (NN)
Position: the position of the argument with respect to the predicate. (before)

similarity between two parse trees. Thus, this tree kernel implicitly defines a large feature space.

Besides, in order to capture the complementary nature between feature-based methods and tree kernel-based methods, we combine them via a composite kernel, which has been proven effective in the literature [8]. In particular, our composite kernel is combined by linearly interpolating a convolution tree kernel KT over a parse tree structure and a feature-based linear kernel KL as follow:

$$CK = \alpha \cdot K_L + (1-\alpha) \cdot K_T \qquad \text{where } \alpha \text{ is a coefficient for } K_L$$

Table 1 shows a list of features in the feature-based linear kernel extracted from the DPT structure. Here, we only select those features widely used in CoNLL-2008 and CoNLL-2009 shared tasks, which aim at performing and evaluating SRL using a dependency-based representation for both syntactic and semantic dependencies on English and other languages.

4 Experimentation

4.1 Experimental Setting

Following the experimental setting in Xue [11] and Li et al [12], 648 files (chtb_081 to 899.fid) are selected as the training data, 72 files (chtb_001 to 040.fid and chtb_900 to 931.fid) are held out as the test data, and 40 files (chtb_041 to 080.fid) as the development data, with 8642, 1124, and 731 propositions, respectively.

To save training time, we use a simple pruning strategy to filter out the dependency nodes that are less likely to be semantic arguments to the predicate according to the specific characteristics of Chinese NomBank. In particular, given the nominal predicate as the current node, we only keep its father, grandfather, grandfather's siblings, grandfather's children, siblings, siblings' children, siblings' grandchildren, children, grandchildren with respect to the DPT structure. As a result, our pruning strategy effectively reduces the number of instances for semantic role labeling by approximately 2-3 folds at the risk of 2% loss of semantic arguments. After pruning, we first do argument identification for those remaining candidates, and then classify the positive ones into their corresponding semantic roles.

We use the SVM-light toolkit with the convolution tree kernel function SVMlight–TK as the classifier. In particular, the training parameters C (SVM) and λ (tree kernel) are fine-tuned to 4.0 and 0.5 respectively. For the composite kernel, the coefficient α is fine-tuned to 0.5. Since SVM is a binary classifier, we apply the one vs. others strategy to implement multi-class classification, which builds multiple classifiers so as to separate one class from all others. The final decision of an instance in the multiple binary classifications is determined by the class which has the maximal SVM output.

To have a fair comparison of our system with the state-of-the-art ones, we use the widely-used segment-based evaluation algorithm, proposed by Johansson and Nugues [10]. To see whether an improvement in F1-measure is statistically significant, we also conduct significance tests using a type of stratified shuffling which in turn is a type of computation-intensive randomized tests. In this paper, '>>>', '>>', and '>'

denote p-values less than or equal to 0.01, in-between (0.01, 0.05], and bigger than 0.05, respectively.

4.2   Experimental Results on Golden Parse Trees

Table 2 shows the performance of our tree-kernel-based method using different extraction schemes on the D-CPT structure. Here, the golden CPT structure is converted into the DPT structure using the same conversion toolkit as adopted by the CoNLL-2009 shared task.

Table 2. Performance of our tree-kernel-based method using different extraction schemes on the D-CPT structure of golden parse trees

Scheme	P(%)	R(%)	F1
SPT	76.07	58.26	65.98
SV-SPT	79.64	62.27	69.89
H-SV-SPT	79.79	62.86	**70.32**

Table 2 shows that:

1) SPT achieves the performance of 65.98 in F1-measure with a much lower recall of only 58.26%, compared to 76.07% in precision. This indicates the necessity of incorporating more structured information into SPT.
2) SV-SPT achieves the performance of 69.89 in F1-mesure. This means that SV-SPT performs significantly better than SPT by 3.91 (>>>) in F1-measure, much due to the gain in both precision and recall. This indicates the discriminative ability of the support verb in determining the semantic relationship between the nominal predicate and the argument candidate.
3) H-SV-SPT further slightly improves the performance by 0.43 (>) in F1-measure, due to considering the head argument information, which has been proven useful in feature-based methods.

Table 3. Comparison of different kernels on golden parse trees

Kernel	P(%)	R(%)	F1
Linear kernel	79.96	60.02	68.57
Tree kernel	79.79	62.86	70.32
Composite Kernel	80.85	67.03	**73.29**

Table 3 illustrates the performance comparison with different kernel setups on golden parse trees. It shows that:

1) Our tree kernel on the new D-CPT structure using the extraction scheme of H-SV-SPT performs much better than a popular feature-based linear kernel by 1.75 (>>). This denotes the effectiveness of our D-CPT structure in representing the

dependency relations in a tree kernel-based method, which may perform well without complicated feature engineering.

2) The tree kernel and the feature-based linear kernel is quite complementary that the combination of them via a simple composite kernel improves the performance by 4.72 (>>>) and 2.97(>>>) in F1-measure over the feature-based linear kernel and the tree kernel.

4.3 Experimental Results on Automatic Parse Trees

In previous subsection, we assume the availability of golden parse trees during the testing process. In this subsection, we evaluate the performance using automatic parse trees. In this paper, we firstly get the CPT structure using the word-based Berkeley parser and then convert it to the DPT structure using the same conversion toolkit as adopted by the CoNLL-2009 shared task. Table 4 and Table 5 present the performance on automatic parse trees.

Table 4. Performance of our tree-kernel-based method using different extraction schemes on the D-CPT structure of automatic parse trees

Scheme	P(%)	R(%)	F1
SPT	63.17	46.30	53.44
SV-SPT	66.06	50.17	57.03
H-SV-SPT	67.51	50.91	58.04

Table 5. Comparison of different kernels on automatic parse trees

Kernel	P(%)	R(%)	F1
Linear kernel	66.89	48.90	56.50
Tree kernel	67.51	50.91	58.04
Composite Kernel	66.59	55.07	60.28

Table 4 and Table 5 show that:

1) For each extraction scheme on D-CPT of automatic parse trees, our tree kernel-based method shows the performance tendency similar to golden parse trees. For example, our tree kernel-based method achieves the best performance of 58.04 in F1-measure when including the support verb and the head argument into SPT.

2) For each kernel, the performance on automatic parse trees drops by about 12 in F1-measure, compared with that on golden parse trees. This indicates the dependency of Chinese nominal SRL on the performance of syntactic parsing.

4.4 Comparison with Other Tree Kernel-Based Methods on DPT Structure

Nguyen et al [15] propose a dependency words (DW) tree, a grammatical relation (GR) tree, and a grammatical relation and words (GRW) tree, extracted from the DPT structure, to a similar task of semantic relation extraction between named entities. In their work, the DW tree is simply constituted by keeping the words in the DPT structure. The GR tree is generated by replacing the words in the DW tree with their dependency relations. The GRW tree is formed by combining the DW and GR trees, where the latter is inserted as a father node of the former.

Table 6. Comparison with other tree kernel-based on DPT structure

structure	P(%)	R(%)	F1
GR	79.42	28.17	41.59
DW	77.80	52.72	62.85
GRW	77.47	54.22	63.79
D-CPT (SPT)	76.07	58.26	65.98

Table 6 compares our D-CPT structure with the DW, GR and GRW trees on Chinese nominal SRL, using the same convolution tree kernel on golden parse trees. Table 6 shows that even SPT, extracted from the D-CPT using the simplest scheme, significantly outperforms the GR (>>>), DW (>>>) and GRW (>>>) trees. This indicates the effectiveness of our D-CPT structure in that D-CPT not only keeps the dependency information of the DPT structure but also retains the CPT structure.

4.5   Comparison with Other Systems

Finally, Table 7 compares our proposed method with the state-of-the-art ones on Chinese NomBank, Xue [11] and Li et al [12]. Both of them are feature-based ones with various features derived from the CPT structure via extensive feature engineering.

Table 7 shows that our tree kernel-based method achieves comparable performance with the state-of-the-art feature-based ones on either golden parse trees or auto parse trees. One advantage of our proposed tree kernel-based method on the novel D-CPT structure lies in its simplicity and effectiveness. Another advantage is its flexibility for further performance improvement. In this paper, we propose three simple extraction schemes to extract necessary information from D-CPT. It will be easy to incorporate other useful information, such as competitive information from other argument candidates.

Table 7. Comparison to the state-of-the-art systems

System	Golden (F1)	Auto (F1)
Linear kernel (Ours):feature-based	68.57	56.50
Tree kernel (Ours):D-CPT	70.32	58.04
Composite Kernel (Ours)	**73.29**	60.28
Xue[11]:feature-based	69.6	57.60
Li et al [12]:feature-based	70.63	58.66

4.6   Experimentation on the CoNLL-2009 Chinese Corpus

To further illustrate the effectiveness of the novel DR-CPT structure for better representation of dependency relations in tree kernel-based methods, we also do the experimentation on the CoNLL-2009 Chinese corpus.

Table 8. Performance of our tree-kernel-based on the CoNLL-2009 Chinese corpus

System	F1
Tree kernel (Ours):SPT	76.88
Tree kernel (Ours):H-SPT	77.43
Composite Kernel (Ours)	**78.47**
Bjorkelund et al[20]:feature-based	78.60
Meza-Ruiz and Riedel[21]:feature-based	77.73

Since most predicates in the CoNLL-2009 Chinese corpus are verbal and do not have the support verbs, here we only apply the SPT and H-SPT extraction schemes. Furthermore, we only select those simple features widely used in CoNLL-2008 and CoNLL-2009 shared tasks in the composite Kernel.

Predicate disambiguation is a sub-task of the CoNLL-2009 shared task. In order to better compare the results of SRL-only, we simply employ the predicate disambiguation module as proposed by Bjorkelund et al [20], who obtained the best F1 score on the Chinese corpus.

Table 8 compares the performance of different kernel setups on the CoNLL-2009 Chinese corpus. It shows that:

1) Our tree-kernel method achieves comparable performance with Meza-Ruiz and Riedel [21], who obtained the second best performance on the Chinese Corpus. It further denotes the effectiveness of our DR-CPT structure in a tree kernel-based method on SRL of verbal predicates.
2) Our composite kernel (without global re-ranking) achieves comparable performance with Bjorkelund et al [20], who employed a global re-ranking strategy and obtained the best performance on the Chinese Corpus.

5   Conclusion and Future Work

This paper systematically explores a tree kernel-based method on a novel D-CPT structure, which employs dependency types instead of phrase labels in the traditional CPT structure for nominal SRL. In particular, we propose a simple strategy, which transforms the DPT structure into a CPT-style structure. Generally, D-CPT takes the advantages of both DPT and CPT by not only keeping the dependency relationship information in DPT but also retaining the basic structure of CPT. Furthermore, several extraction schemes are designed to extract various kinds of necessary information for nominal SRL and verbal SRL (CoNLL-2009 corpus). Evaluation shows the effectiveness of D-CPT both on Chinese NomBank and CoNLL-2009 corpus.

To our knowledge, this is the first research on tree kernel-based SRL on effectively exploring dependency relationship information, which achieves comparable performance with the state-of-the-art feature-based ones.

In future, we will explore more necessary structured information in the novel D-CPT structure. Besides, we will explore this structure to similar tasks, such as semantic relation extraction between named entities and co-reference resolution.

Acknowledgements. This research is supported by Project BK2011282 under the Natural Science Foundation of Jiangsu Province, Project 10KJB520016 and key Project 11KJA520003 under the Natural Science Foundation of Jiangsu Provincial Department of Education.

Reference

1. Surdeanu, M., Harabagiu, S., Williams, J., Aarseth, P.: Using Predicate-argument Structures for Information Extraction. In: Proceedings of NAACL 2004, pp. 8–15 (2004)
2. Narayanan, S., Harabagiu, S.: Question Answering based on Semantic Structures. In: Proceedings of COLING 2004, Article No. 693 (2004)
3. Ponzetto, S.P., Strube, M.: Semantic Role labeling for Coreference Resolution. In: Proceedings of EACL 2006, pp. 143–146 (2006)
4. Persson, J., Johansson, R., Nugues, P.: Text Categorization Using Predicate-Argument Structures. In: Proceedings of NODALIDA 2009, pp. 142–149 (2009)
5. Moschitti, A., Bejan, C.A.: A Semantic Kernel for Predicate Argument Classification. In: Proceedings of CoNLL 2004, pp. 17–24 (2004)
6. Moschitti, A.: A Study on Convolution Kernels for Shallow Semantic Parsing. In: Proceedings of ACL 2004, Article No. 335 (2004)
7. Moschitti, A., Pighin, D., Basili, R.: Tree Kernel Engineering in Semantic Role Labeling Systems. In: Proceedings of EACL 2006, pp. 49–56 (2006)
8. Zhang, M., Che, W.X., Aw, A., Tan, C.L., Zhou, G.D., Liu, T., Li, S.: A Grammar-driven Convolution Tree Kernel for Semantic Role Classification. In: Proceedings of ACL 2007, pp. 200–207 (2007)
9. Hacioglu, K.: Semantic Role Labeling Using Dependency Trees. In: Proceedings of COLING 2004, Article No. 1273 (2004)
10. Johansson, R., Nugues, P.: Dependency-based Semantic Role Labeling of PropBank. In: Proceedings of EMNLP 2008, pp. 69–78 (2008)
11. Xue, N.W.: Labeling Chinese Predicates with Semantic Roles. Computational Linguistics 34(2), 225–255
12. Li, J.H., Zhou, G.D., Zhao, H., Zhu, Q.M., Qian, P.D.: Improving Nominal SRL in Chinese Language with Verbal SRL Information and Automatic Predicate Recognition. In: Proceedings of EMNLP 2009, pp. 1280–1288 (2009)
13. Collins, M., Duffy, N.: Convolution Kernels for Natural Language. In: Proceedings of NIPS 2001 (2001)
14. Che, W.X., Zhang, M., Liu, T., Li, S.: A Hybrid Convolution Tree Kernel for Semantic Role Labeling. In: Proceedings of ACL 2006, pp. 73–80 (2006)

15. Nguyen, T.T., Moschitti, A., Riccardi, G.: Convolution Kernels on Constituent, Dependency and Sequential Structures for Relation Extraction. In: Proceedings of ACL 2009, pp. 1378–1387 (2009)
16. Kong, F., Zhou, G.D., Qian, L.H., Zhu, Q.M.: Dependency-driven Anaphoricity Determination for Coreference Resolution. In: Proceedings of COLING 2010, pp. 599–607 (2010)
17. Xue, N.W., Palmer, M.: Automatic Semantic Role Labeling for Chinese verbs. In: Proceedings of IJCAI 2005, pp. 1160–1165 (2005)
18. Xue, N.W.: Semantic Role Labeling of Nominalized Predicates in Chinese. In: Proceedings of HLT-NAACL, pp. 431–438 (2006)
19. Li, S.Q., Lu, Q., Zhao, T.J., Liu, P.Y., Li, H.J.: Combing Constituent and Dependency Syntactic Views for Chinese Semantic Role Labeling. In: Proceedings of COLING 2010, pp. 665–673 (2010)
20. Bjorkelund, A., Hafdell, L., Nugues, P.: Multilingual Semantic Role Labeling. In: Proceedings of CoNLL 2009, pp. 43–48 (2009)
21. Meza-Ruiz, I., Riedel, S.: Multilingual Semantic Role Labeling with Markov Logic. In: Proceedings of CoNLL 2009, pp. 85–90 (2009)

Contextual-and-Semantic-Information-Based Domain-Adaptive Chinese Word Segmentation

Jing Zhang, Degen Huang, and Deqin Tong

School of Computer Science and Technology, Dalian University of Technology,
Dalian 116023, P.R. China
huangdg@dlut.edu.cn,
zhangjingqf@mail.dlut.edu.cn,
tongdeqin@gmail.com

Abstract. This paper presents a new domain-adaptive Chinese Word Segmentation (CWS) method. Considering the characteristics of the territorial Out-of – Vocabularies (OOVs), both the contextual information table and the semantic information are utilized based on Conditional Random Fields (CRFs) model to recall more OOVs and promote the performance of the CWS. This method is evaluated by the simplified domain-adaptive Chinese testing data from SIGHAN Bakeoff 2010. The experimental results show that the F-value and the recall of OOVs of the testing data in Computer, Medicine and Finance domain are higher than the best performance of SIGHAN Bakeoff 2010 participants, with the recall of OOVs of 84.3%, 79.0% and 86.2%, respectively.

Keywords: domain-adaptive CWS, Conditional Random Fields (CRFs), contextual variable table, semantic resources.

1   Introduction

CWS (Chinese Word Segmentation) is a fundamental task in Chinese Language processing. In recent years, widespread attention has been paid to CWS. Researchers in this field have made significant breakthrough with the rise of machine learning methods. Meanwhile, the Chinese word segmentation evaluations organized by SIGHAN (Special Internet Group of the Association for Computational Linguistics) play a prominent role in promoting the development of CWS, providing researchers with uniform training and testing data to compare their different methods of CWS in the same test platform. In previous SIGHAN Bakeoff, most of the systems with high-performance are based on machine learning methods to implement sequence labeling [1-2]. Among those methods, the character-based labeling machine learning methods [3-5] has got more and more attention and become the mainstream technology of CWS. However, Refs. [6-8] employed another sequence tagging based machine learn-ing methods, namely, a word-based segmentation strategy, which is also based on the character-base sequence annotation.

With the development of the Internet, an increasing number of non-standard text, containing lots of new words, has been generated, which has brought many challenges

M. Zhou et al. (Eds.): NLPCC 2012, CCIS 333, pp. 110–120, 2012.

to the CWS. Although many methods have shown impressive results in some segmentation evaluation tasks, they are limited to corpus on specific area. Their accuracy will obviously decrease when used in a different domain. In practical applications, it is impossible for a CWS system to train all types of text beforehand. Additionally, the vast majority of the texts, which need to be segmented, do not have feature tags, such as Source, Subject, Part-of-speech, and so on. It is when it deals with the corpus which is different from the training data, or has a large number of OOVs that the CWS system can contribute the maximum value [9]. Therefore, SIGHAN-CIPS has set up to examine the ability of the cross-domain word segmentation since 2010. In that task, participants are demanded to test the corpus from four different domains, including computer, medical, financial and literary. The CWS systems need to be adaptive to different domains by training on only one domain corpus, namely, the so-called cross-domain CWS. One important thing the Cross-domain CWS should take into account is that there are many common-used words and terminologies in a specific area, and those words, a big inevitable challenge for CWS systems, are usually regarded as OOVs in other areas. Different from common OOVs, most of those territoriality OOVs belong to a specific area, and usually appear several times in the context of their respective areas. No matter how large the vocabulary of the segmentation system is, it is unable to include all the new words, thus a good cross-domain CWS should have a great ability to identify OOVs. Ref. [6] proposed a new cross-domain segmentation method based on a joint decoding approach which combined the character-based and word-based CRF models, made good use of the chapter information and fragments of the words, and achieved an impressive result. In the evaluation of SIGHAN Bakeoff 2010, some other excellent cross-domain word segmentation systems emerged. Among those systems, Ref. [10] introduced a multi-layer CWS system based on CRFs, integrating the outputs of the multi-layer CWS system and the conditional probability of all possible tags as the features by SVM-hmm. This system achieved the best performance in the opening tests, while it is a little bit complicated. In Ref. [11], the hidden Markov model HMM (Hidden Markov Models) was used to revise substrings whose marginal probability was low, and achieved high performance in both closed and open tasks, but its recall of OOV was not outstanding. Ref. [12] proposed a new CWS approach using the cluster of Self-Organizing Map networks and the entropy of N-gram as features, training on a large scale of unlabeled corpus, and it obtained an excellent performance. However, most of the participating systems are dealing with the OOVs, which have their own distinct territorial characteristics, as the general ones instead of the cross-domain ones on the basis of ensuring the overall performance of the CWS. However, most of the participating systems are dealing with the OOVs, which have their own distinct territorial characteristics, as the general ones instead of the cross-domain ones on the basis of ensuring the overall performance of the CWS.

According to the characteristics of the territoriality OOVs, we propose a new statistic variable, the Contextual Variable table, which records the contextual information of a candidate word and can affect the cost factor of the candidate words. Those candidate words are selected by the character-based CRFs. At the same time, we utilize the information of the synonym in the system dictionary instead of the information of the OOVs in the candidate words, because of the similarity of syntax and context in the sentence environment. Moreover, we put all the candidate words into a set, which is called the word-lattice, and then we complete the word-lattice taking full advantage of the contextual information and the synonym information mentioned above. At last, we use the word-based CRFs to label the words in the word-lattice and select the best path as the final segmentation results.

The rest of this paper is organized as follows. Section 2 presents the machine learning models that we utilize in our experiments. In Section 3, we describe the Cross-Domain CWS algorithm. Section 4 shows the experimental results. Finally, some conclusions are given in Section 5.

2   Machine Learning Models

Conditional random fields (CRFs), a statistical model for sequence labeling, was first introduced by Lafferty et al in Ref. [2]. It is the undirected graph theory that CRFs mainly use to achieve global optimum sequence labeling. It is good enough to avoid label bias problem by using a global normalization.

2.1   Character-Based and Word-Based CRFs

In previous labeling task of character-based CRFs, the number of the characters in the observed sequence is as same as the one in the annotation sequence. However, for CWS task, the input of n-character will generate the output of m-word sequence on such a condition that m is not larger than n. But this problem can be well solved by word-lattice based CRFs, because the conditional probability of the output sequence depends no longer on the number of the observed sequence, but the words in the output path. For a given input sentence, its possible paths may be various and the word-lattice can well represent this phenomenon. A word-lattice can not only express all possible segmentation paths, but also reflect the different attributes of all possible words in the path. Refs. [13-14] have successfully used the word lattice in Japanese lexical analysis.

Our paper adopt the word-lattice based CRFs that combines the character-based CRFs and the word-based CRFs, and specifically, we put the candidate words selected by the character-based CRFs into a word-lattice, and then label all the candidate words in the word-lattice using word-based CRFs model. When training the word-lattice based CRFs model, the maximum likelihood estimation is used in order to avoid overloading. In the end, Viterbi algorithm is utilized in the decoding process which is similar with Ref. [6].

2.2   Feature Templates

The character-based CRFs in our method adopt a 6-tag set in Ref. [15] and its feature template comes from Ref. [11], including C_{-1}, C_0, C_1, $C_{-1}C_0$, C_0C_1, $C_{-1}C_1$ and $T_{-1}T_0T_1$, in which C stands for a character and T stands for the type of characters, and the subscripts -1, 0 and 1 stand for the previous, current and next character, respectively. Four categories of character sets are predefined as: Numbers, Letters, Punctuation and Chinese characters. Furthermore, the Accessor Variety in Ref. [16] (AV) is applied as global feature.

Two kinds of features are selected for the word-based CRFs, like Ref. [6]: unigram features and bigram features. The unigram ones only consider the attributes information of current word, and bigram ones are also called compound features, which utilize contextual information of multiple words. Theoretically, the current word's context sliding window can be infinitely large, but due to efficiency factors, we define the sliding window as 2. The specific features are W_0, T_0, W_0T_0, W_0T_1, T_0T_1, W_0W_1, where W stands for the morphology of the word, T stands for the part-of-speech of the words, and subscript 0 and subscript 1, respectively, stand for the former and the latter of two adjacent words.

3   Cross-Domain CWS algorithm

The recognition of the OOVs will be limited, because the construction of the word-lattice depends on the dictionary. That can be solved by adding all the candidate words selected by the N-Best paths of the character-based CRFs into the word-lattice, so there could exit more OOVs in the word-lattice. What is more, the words in the dictionary and the OOVs can be treated equally by the character-based CRFs, which is of great help to recall OOVs. In our experiment, we finally choose 3-Best paths, because too many incorrect candidate words will be added into the word-lattice if we chose more than 3-Best paths, which not only put bad impact on the performance of the segmentation, but also affect the efficiency. When we choose less than 3-Best paths, the segmentation system does not work well on recalling the OOVs.

In the process of building the word-lattice, if the POS and the Cost of the words can not get from the system dictionary, then it will be treated as one of four different categories: Chinese characters, letters , numbers and punctuation, whose POS is, respectively, conferred as a noun, strings, numbers, punctuation. Additionally, the cost of the words equals the average of the costs of the words with the same POS in the dictionary.

Taking the characteristics of the territorial OOVs into account, we apply the contextual information and semantic information to improve the recall of the cross-domain OOVs.

3.1   Contextual Information

The territorial OOVs may repeatedly emerge in the specific domain, but it is hard to segment them correctly every time. As a result, we propose the contextual information to record the some useful information about the out-of-vocabulary candidate words. This approach is mainly based on the following assumptions:

Assumption 1: The occurrence of a word will increase the possibility of emerging of the word in the same chapter.

In other words, if a string of characters is regarded as a candidate word in multiple contexts, then it is probably a word, in that case, the Contextual Variable is proposed to quantify this assumption. The Contextual Variable consists of the morphology of the word (w), part of speech (t), the difficulty of the emerging of a candidate word (*Cost*), the frequency of being a candidate word (*Frequency*), the frequency of being the node in the final segmentation path (*rNum*).

The acquisition of the contextual information is throughout the entire segmentation algorithm, and the specific process is as follows:

Firstly, put all the candidate words w included by 3-Best paths into the set S (w_1 , w_2 , ..., w_n). Secondly, search for each word w in set S from the system dictionary, if exists, then the information in the dictionary, such as the POS, the cost and so on, of the word w will be copied into the contextual information table. Otherwise, the contextual information table will be searched, and if there exits the candidate word w, then the *Frequency* in the table of the word increases by 1, and if not neither, then we will deal with the word as one of the four classification of the OOVs mentioned above. At last, repeat these steps until the last word w_n in set S has been searched.

It can be seen from the above process that the higher the frequency of the candidate word is, the more likely it tends to be a word. Considering that the *Frequency* and the *rNum* can affect the *Cost*, we adjust the *Cost* of the word w, according to Eq. (1), where $cost_0 (w)$ stands for the original cost of the words.

$$cost'(w) = \begin{cases} \dfrac{1.0}{rNum+1} \times cost_0(w) & rNum>0 \\ \left(\dfrac{0.2}{\log(frequency+2)} + 0.8\right) \times cost_0(w) & rNum=0 \end{cases} \qquad (1)$$

3.2 Semantic Information

The number of Chinese words is tens of millions, while the types of semantic relations are limited, so we utilize the synonym relations, one kind of semantic information, to identify the OOVs, considering the similarity in syntax and grammar in the sentence environment. When building the word-lattice, we propose the synonym information to obtain the property and cost of the candidate words selected by the character-based CRFs via selecting the 3-Best paths, because the property and the cost of OOVs can not be found in the system dictionary, but can be substituted by the information of their synonyms.

To illustrate, the word fragment "劳模", an Out-of-vocabulary, is in the word-lattice, but not in the system dictionary. So we can not get the information of the candidate word such as the POS, the cost and so on. In this case, the synonym forest is very useful if it includes a synonym which is also in the system dictionary. For this example, the information of the word "模范", a synonym of the candidate word "劳模", can take the place of the information of "劳模".

Al 05A 01= 模范标兵表率榜样师表轨范楷范英模典型丰碑
Al 05A 02= 劳模劳动模范

The semantic resources we used in this paper is synonym forest (extended version), containing a total of 77,343 items, which have been organized into tree-like hierarchical structure and divided into three categories. In the expanded version of the synonym forest with five-level coding, for each word information, there is a eight bit semantic encoding, which can represent each single word in the synonym forest. From left to right, the encoding is expressed like this: the first level with capital letters, the second level with lowercase letters, the third level with two bytes of decimal integer, the fourth level with capital letters, and the fifth level with two bytes of decimal coding, the end with the sign of "=", "#" and "@". The specific coding rules are shown in Table 1:

Table 1. The Rule of Word Coding

Code Bit	1	2	3	4	5	6	7	8
Example	D	a	1	5	B	0	2	=\#\@
Signification	General class	Middle class	Sub-class	Word group	Atomic Word group			
Level	1	2	3	4	5			

Except for the synonym and the classification information, the synonym forest also includes some self-governed words, which do not have any synonyms. In order to enhance the search efficiency, we delete those self-governed words. Because the closer the distance of two synonym sets are, the more similar their meanings are, we follow the principle of proximity when search for the synonym of the candidate words.

The search process is as follows: first, find the synonym set of the candidate word, and then look up each synonym of that synonym set into the system dictionary to find if the synonym exists. If there it is, then we will replace the candidate word with the synonym and the information of it, and if not, then the fifth level of the synonym sets will be searched, and if not neither, then the fourth level. If the fourth level does not contain the synonym of the candidate, then we would like to stop looking up rather than search further. There are two reasons, one is the efficiency factor, the other one is that if the set of the word is too far away, the meaning of the words in two different sets will be much different, so we would rather giving it up than using it and bringing a negative impact.

3.3   Word Segmentation Process

With the contextual information and synonyms information added, the cross-domain word segmentation process is as follows:

Step1. Put all the candidate words in 3-Best paths selected by the character-based CRFs model into the word-lattice.

Step2. To build the word-lattice, in other word, give properties and costs to each node, the candidate words selected by character-based CRFs in Step1, in the word-lattice, which is divided into four cases to deal with: ①If the candidate words are in the system dictionary, then assign the properties and cost of the words in the system dictionary directly to the candidate words in the word-lattice. ②If the candidate words are not in the system dictionary, but in the dictionary of contextual information, then the properties of the words in the contextual information dictionary will be assiged to the candidate words, and a weight value, calculated by Eq. (1), will be added to the cost of the candidate words. ③If the candidate words is not in the system dictionary, neither in the contextual information dictionary, then we will search the synonyms forest to find a synonym of the candidate words. If the synonym exits in the system dictionary, we'd like to replace the candidate word with it. ④If the above cases are not suitable for the candidate words, then the candidate words will be classified according to the classification mentioned above.

Step3. To find the optimal path, the least costly path of word segmentation, in the word-lattice using the Viterbi algorithm according to Eq. (4), and the values of $TransCost(t_i, t_{i+1})$ and $Cost(w_i)$ can be calculated by Eq. (2) and Eq. (3), respectively. Since all feature functions are binary ones, the cost of the word is equal to the sum of all the weight of the unigram features about the word, and the transition cost is equal to the sum of all bigram features about the two parts of speech.

$$Cost(w) = -factor * \sum_{f_k \in U(w)} \lambda_{f_k} \tag{2}$$

$$TransCost(t_1, t_2) = -factor * \sum_{f_k \in B(t_1, t_2)} \lambda_{f_k} \tag{3}$$

Where $U(w)$ is the unigram feature set of the current word, $B(t_1, t_2)$ is the bigram feature set of the adjacent words t_1 and t_2. λ_{f_k} is the weight of the corresponding feature f_k and factor is the amplification coefficient.

$$Score(Y) = \sum_{i=0}^{Y^{\#}} \left(TransCost(t_i, t_{i+1}) + Cost(w_i) \right) \tag{4}$$

It can be seen from the above process that the factors of recognizing the territorial words are considered in Step2. Contextual information as well as synonym information is used to adjust the cost and the properties of the candidate words in the path, which can contribute to the follow-up Step3 to select the best path.

4   Experimental Results and Analysis

4.1   Data Set

Our method is tested on the simplified Chinese domain-adaptive testing data from SIGHAN Bakeoff 2010. And it accords with the rules of the open test, since only a system dictionary and synonym forest is used in our method, without using any other manually annotated corpus resources. Thus, the experiment results are evaluated by P (Precise), R (Recall) and F-value. The system dictionary we used is extracted from the

People's Daily from January to June, in 2000, containing 85000 words, with the POS being the Peking University POS system. The word-based CRFs model is trained by the corpus with POS tag provided by the evaluation, which is from the People's Daily of January, in 1998).

4.2 Experimental Results

In order to prove the effect of the contextual information and semantic information described above, we have conducted four groups of experiments. Experiment 1 is the base experiment that does not include these two types of information. Experiment 2 is the +CV experiment with only contextual information added. Experiment 3 is the +CiLin experiment that add only synonyms information. Experiment 4 is the experiment with both two types of information added.

Table 2~5 give the segmentation results of four groups of experiments, respectively, in four different fields, including computer, medicine, finance and literary. It can be clearly seen from Table 2 to Table 5 that the performance in F-value and R_{oov} improves after the introduction of context and synonyms information, separately. And the improvement is more considerable when adding both of the two information simultaneously, with R_{oov} increasing by 1.6 to 5.6 percentage.

The following sentence fragments can help us analyze the impact of contextual information on the CWS:

"日本金融特任大臣①龟井静香 (Shizuka Kamei) 周五 (3月19日) 发表讲话……②龟井静香此前就一直呼吁推出新一轮的大规模经济刺激计划……③龟井静香表示，昨日发布的土地价格调查报告显示……④龟井静香还呼吁日本央行直接买入国债来为政府赤字提供融资……金融市场对⑤龟井静香的评论应该不会有太大反应……".

In the above five sentence fragments, the word "龟井静香"(name) appears five times totally in the context. If not bring the contextual information in the segmentation system, only three times that the word "龟井静香" is segmented correctly, while it is cut correctly all five times after adding the contextual information. Therefore, the contextual information is very helpful to identify such candidate words that repeat in a chapter, because its probability will be affected by the impact of the frequency of occurrence in the previous paragraph.

Table 2. The P, R and F value of computer

Computer	F	R	P	Roov
Base	0.9507	0.9562	0.9452	0.8233
+CV	0.9530	0.958	0.9481	0.8342
+CiLin	0.9515	0.9568	0.9462	0.83
++Both	0.9553	0.9591	0.9516	0.8428

Table 3. The P, R and F value of medicine

Medicine	F	R	P	Roov
Base	0.9424	0.946	0.9388	0.7563
+CV	0.9437	0.947	0.9404	0.7693
+CiLin	0.944	0.9473	0.9408	0.7788
++Both	0.9463	0.9492	0.9435	0.79

Table 4. The P, R and F value of finance

Finance	F	R	P	Roov
Base	0.9605	0.9585	0.9626	0.8458
+CV	0.962	0.9608	0.9631	0.852
+CiLin	0.9608	0.9592	0.9623	0.8517
++Both	0.9625	0.9609	0.9641	0.8618

Table 5. The P, R and F value of literature

Literature	F	R	P	Roov
Base	0.9421	0.9385	0.9458	0.6504
+CV	0.9433	0.9393	0.9473	0.6649
+CiLin	0.9437	0.9394	0.948	0.6839
++Both	0.946	0.9418	0.9506	0.7073

Table 6. Comparison with the open test results of Bakeoff

Corpora	Participants	F	R_{OOV}
Computer	1[10]	0.95	0.82
	2[12]	0.947	0.812
	3[11]	0.939	0.735
	ours	**0.955**	**0.843**
Medicine	1[12]	0.938	0.787
	2[10]	0.938	0.768
	3[11]	0.935	0.67
	ours	**0.946**	**0.790**
Finance	1[10]	0.96	0.847
	2[11]	0.957	0.763
	3[12]	0.951	0.853
	ours	**0.963**	**0.862**
Literature	1[11]	0.955	0.655
	2[17]	0.952	0.814
	3[12]	0.942	0.702
	ours	**0.946**	**0.707**

Table 6 shows the results of our method compared with the top three outstanding systems of the SIGHAN Bakeoff 2010 evaluation in F-value and R_{oov}. The experimental results show that the performance of our system in both F-value and R_{oov} is better than the best results of the SIGHAN Bakeoff 2010 evaluation in the three areas of the computer, medicine and finance.

5   Conclusions

In this paper, a new cross-domain CWS method is proposed. Due to the recurrences of the territorial OOVs in their specific areas, we bring up the contextual variable table to record the contextual information of the candidate words which are selected by the character-based CRFs, including the morphology of the word, the part-of-speech, the difficulty degree of appearing, the frequency as a candidate, and the frequency as the word node in the final segmentation path. Additionally, in order to approximate the cost of the candidate word in the entire path, we replace the property information and the cost of OOVs with their synonyms. As we know, the closer the sets of two synonyms are, the more similar their meanings are. Therefore, when we search for the synonym of a candidate word in the synonym forest, we follow the principle of proximity. At first, we get the 3-best paths with the help of character-based CRFs, and add all the words included by the 3-best paths into the word-lattice. And then, we make use of the contextual and semantic information to construct the word-lattice to recall more OOVs. At last, the word-based CRFs are utilized to select the least costly path from the word-lattice as the final segmentation results.

Our method not only take full advantage of character-based CRFs model to generate more OOVs, but also make good use of the lexical information of the territorial words. Our method is evaluated by the simplified Chinese domain-adaptive testing data from SIGHAN Bakeoff 2010. The experimental results show that the F-value and the recall of OOVs of the testing data in Computer, Medicine and Finance domain are higher than the best performance of SIGHAN Bakeoff 2010 participants, with the recall of OOVs of 84.3%, 79.0% and 86.2%, respectively.

Acknowledgements. This work has been supported by the National Natural Science Foundation of China (No.61173100, No.61173101), Fundamental Research Funds for the Central Universities (DUT10RW202). The authors wish to thank Jiang Zhenchao, Xu Huifang and Zhang Jing for their useful suggestions, comments and help during the design and editing of the manuscript.

References

1. Xue, N.: Chinese word segmentation as character tagging. J. Computational Linguistics 8(1), 29–48 (2003)
2. Lafferty, J., McCallum, A., Pereira, F.: Conditional Random Fields: probabilistic models for segmenting and labeling sequence data. In: Proceedings of ICML 2001, pp. 282–289. Morgan Kaufmann, San Francisco (2001)

3. Tseng, H., Chang, P., Andrew, G., Jurafsky, D., Manning, C.: A conditional random field word segmenter for SIGHAN bakeoff 2005. In: Proc. of the 4th SIGHAN Workshop on Chinese Language Processing, pp. 168–171. ACL, Jeju Island (2005)

4. Peng, F., Feng, F., McCallum, A.: Chinese segmentation and new word detection using conditional random fields. In: Proc. of COLING 2004, pp. 562–568. Morgan Kaufmann, San Francisco (2004)

5. Low, J.K., Ng, H.T., Guo, W.: A maximum entropy approach to Chinese word segmentation. In: Proc. of the 4th SIGHAN Workshop on Chinese Language Processing, pp. 161–164. ACL, Jeju Island (2005)

6. Huang, D., Tong, D.: Context Information and Fragments Based Cross-Domain Word Segmentation. J. China Communications 9(3), 49–57 (2012)

7. Zhang, R., Kikui, G., Sumita, E.: Subword-based tagging by conditional random fields for Chinese word segmentation. In: Proc. of HLT-NAACL 2006, pp. 193–196. ACL, Morristown (2006)

8. Huang, D., Jiao, S., Zhou, H.: Dual-Layer CRFs Baesed on Subword for Chinese Word Segmentation. Journal of Computer Research and Development 47(5), 962–968 (2010); 黄德根, 焦世斗, 周惠巍. 基于子词的双层CRFs中文分词. J. 计算机研究与发展 47(5), 962–968 (2010)

9. Huang, C.-R.: Bottleneck _ challenges _ turn for the better _new ideas of the Chinese word segmentation. In: Computational Linguistics Research Frontier 2007-2009, pp. 14–19. Chinese Information Processing Society, Beijing (2009); 黄居仁.黄居仁. 瓶颈_挑战_与转机_中文分词研究的新思维. 中国计算机语言学研究前沿进展(2007-2009), 14–19. 中国中文信息学会, 北京 (2009)

10. Gao, Q., Vogel, S.: A Multi-layer Chinese Word Segmentation System Optimized for Out-of-domain Tasks. In: Proc. of CIPS-SIGHAN Joint Conference on Chinese Processing, pp. 210–215. ACL, Beijing (2010)

11. Huang, D., Tong, D., Luo, Y.: HMM Revises Low Marginal Probability by CRF for Chinese Word Segmentation. In: Proc. of CIPS-SIGHAN Joint Conference on Chinese Processing, pp. 216–220. ACL, Beijing (2010)

12. Zhang, H., Gao, J., Mo, Q., et al.: Incporating New Words Detection with Chinese Word Segmentation. In: Proc. of CIPS-SIGHAN Joint Conference on Chinese Processing, pp. 249–251. ACL, Beijing (2010)

13. Zhang, C., Chen, Z., Hu, G.: A Chinese Word Segmentation System Based on Structured Support Vector Machine Utilization of Unlabeled Text Corpus. In: Proc. of CIPS-SIGHAN Joint Conference on Chinese Processing, pp. 221–227. ACL, Beijing (2010)

14. Nakagawa, T.: Chinese and Japanese word segmentation using word-level and character-level information. In: Proc. of COLING 2004, pp. 466–472. ACL, Geneva (2004)

15. Kudo, T., Yamamoto, K., Matsumoto, Y.: Applying conditional random fields to Japanese morphological analysis. In: Proc. of EMNLP 2004, pp. 230–237. ACL, Barcelona (2004)

16. Zhao, H., Huang, C., Li, M., et al.: Effective tag set selection in Chinese word segmentation via Conditional Random Field modeling. In: PACLIC 2006, pp. 87–94. ACL, Wuhan (2006)

17. Feng, H., Chen, K., Deng, X., Zheng, W.: Accessor variety criteria for Chinese word extraction. J. Computational Linguistics 30(1), 75–93 (2004)

Exploration of N-gram Features for the Domain Adaptation of Chinese Word Segmentation

Zhen Guo, Yujie Zhang, Chen Su, and Jinan Xu

School of Computer and Information Technology,
Beijing Jiaotong University, Beijing 100044, China
{08281153,yjzhang,08281138,jaxu}@bjtu.edu.cn

Abstract. A key problem in Chinese Word Segmentation is that the performance of a system will decrease when applied to a different domain. We propose an approach in which n-gram features from large raw corpus are explored to realize domain adaptation for Chinese Word Segmentation. The n-gram features include n-gram frequency feature and AV feature. We used the CRF model and a raw corpus consisting of 1 million patent description sentences to verify the proposed method. For test data, 300 patent description sentences are randomly selected and manually annotated. The results show that the improvement of Chinese Word Segmentation on the test data achieved at 2.53%.

Keywords: Chinese Word Segmentation, CRF, domain adaptation, n-gram feature.

1   Introduction

Chinese Word Segmentation (CWS) methods can be roughly classified into three types: dictionary-based methods, rule-based methods and statistical methods. Due to the large number of new words appearing constantly and the complicated phenomena in Chinese language, the expansion of dictionaries and rules encounter a bottleneck. The first two methods are therefore difficult to deal with the changes in language usages. Since the statistical method can easily learn new words from corpora, Chinese Word Segmentation systems based on such methods can achieve high performance. For this reason, the statistical method is strongly dependent on annotated corpora. Theoretically, the larger amount of the training data with higher quality annotation will bring about the better performance for Chinese Word Segmentation systems.

Texts to be processed may come from different domains of the real world, such as news domain, patent domain, and medical domain, etc. When switching from one domain to another, both vocabulary and its frequency distribution in texts usually vary because the ways of constructing words from characters are different. This fact brings great challenges to Chinese Word Segmentation. The accuracy of a developed system trained on one domain will decrease obviously when it is applied to the texts from other different domains.

M. Zhou et al. (Eds.): NLPCC 2012, CCIS 333, pp. 121–131, 2012.

A solution is to develop domain-specific system for each domain by using corresponding annotated data. In application, the target domain of a text to be processed is recognized first and then the corresponding system is applied. In this way, the best results can be expected. However, manual annotation is a time-consuming and hard work. At present, a large amount of annotated data with high quality is not available for each domain and therefore it is not practical to develop domain-specific system in this way.

In order to solve the problem of the domain adaptation for Chinese Word Segmentation, many methods have been proposed, such as data weighting algorithm and semi-supervised learning algorithm. (Meishan Zhang et al., 2012) propose an approach that can incorporate different external dictionaries into the statistical model to realize domain adaptation for Chinese Word Segmentation. However, these methods have limitations because the annotated corpora and domain-specific dictionaries are not resources readily available.

This paper proposes an approach in which n-gram features from large raw corpus are explored to realize domain adaptation for Chinese Word Segmentation. Compared with annotated corpus and domain-specific dictionary, a raw corpus is more easily to obtain. Our experimental results show that the proposed approach can effectively improve the ability of the Chinese Word Segmentation system for domain adaptation.

2   Chinese Word Segmentation Based on Conditional Random Fields

Conditional random fields (CRF) is a probabilistic framework for labeling and segmenting sequential data, which is first proposed by (John Lafferty et al.,2011) on the basis of the maximum entropy models and hidden Markov models. CRF are undirected graphical models in which the parameters are estimated by maximizing the joint probability over observation and label sequences given an observation sequence. Linear-chain CRF is most widely used in machine learning tasks.

2.1   Conditional Random Fields

A linear-chain CRF with parameters $\Lambda = (\lambda_1, \lambda_2, \ldots, \lambda_n)$ defines a conditional probability for a label sequence $Y = (y_1, y_2, \ldots, y_n)$ given an input sequence $X = (x_1, x_2, \ldots, x_n)$ to be:

$$P_\Lambda(Y \mid X) = \frac{1}{Z_X} \exp\{\sum_{t=1}^{T} \sum_k \lambda_k f_k(y_{t-1}, y_t, X, t)\} \qquad (1)$$

Where $f_k(y_{t-1}, y_t, X, t)$ is a feature function which is often binary-valued, λ_k is a learned weight associated with feature f and Z_X is the normalization factor over all state sequences.

$$Z_X = \sum_y \exp\{\sum_{t=1}^{T}\sum_k \lambda_k f_k(y_{t-1}, y_t, X, t)\} \qquad (2)$$

The most probable label sequence for an input X can be efficiently determined using the Viterbi algorithm.

$$Y^* = \arg\max_Y P_\Lambda(Y \mid X) \qquad (3)$$

For the sequence labeling task like Chinese Word Segmentation, CRF and ME performed better than HMM. In addition to the advantages of the discriminative models, CRF optimizes parameters and decodes globally by taking state transition probabilities into account and consequently can avoid label bias problem. CRF is one of the most effective machine learning models for sequence labeling task.

We use CRF++ (version 0.55)[1] in this paper.

Table 1. Description of 6-tag tagset

Tags	Tag sequences for words of different lengths
S; B; B_2; B_3; M; E.	S; BE; BB_2E; B B_2 B_3E; B B_2 B_3ME; B B_2 B_3M...ME.

Table 2. Feature templates

Type	Feature	Description
Unigram	C_{-2}, C_{-1}, C_0, C_1, C_2	C_0 denotes the current character; $C_n(C_{-n})$ denotes the character n positions to the right (left) of the current character.
Bigram	$C_{-2}C_{-1}$, $C_{-1}C_0$, C_0C_1, C_1C_2, $C_{-1}C_1$	ditto
Punctuation	$IsPu(C_0)$	Current character is punctuation
Character Type	$K(C_{-2})K(C_{-1})K(C_0)K(C_1)K(C_2)$	Types of character: date, numeral, alphabet, others

2.2   Tag Set and Feature Template

We apply CRF to Chinese Word Segmentation by regarding it as a sequence labeling task. This is implemented by labeling the position of each Chinese character in word that the character belongs to. (Zhao et al., 2006) reported that a 6-tag set can achieve the best performance among the tag sets for Chinese Word Segmentation. Therefore we also use the same 6-tag set, whose definition is descripted in Table 1 in detail.

---

[1] http://crfpp.sourceforge.net/

Following the work of (Low et al., 2005), we adopt feature templates and a context of five characters for feature generation. The feature templates used in our model are shown in Table 2. Character Type in the bottom of Table 2 is the types of Chinese characters. Four types are defined in Table 3.We call the information as basic features.

3   N-gram Features

In this paper, n-gram refers to a sequence of n consecutive Chinese characters. A word can be considered as a stable sequence of characters. In a large enough corpus, words with some meanings will occur here and there repeatedly. This implies corresponding sequences of characters will be repeated in the corpus. Reversely, the sequences re-peated in a large number of texts are more likely to be words. This is the basis on which n-gram features are used for word segmentation. In different domain, the ways of constructing words from characters are some different. When a target domain is

Table 3. Four types of Chinese characters

Type	Character set
date	年、月、日
numeral	1,2,3,4,5,6,7,8,9,0,一, 二, 三, 四, 五, 六, 七, 八, 九, 零
alphabet	a,b,c,d,e,f,g,h,i,j,k,l,m,n,o,p,q,r,s,t,u,v,w,x,y,z,A,B,C,D,E,F,G,H,I,J,K,L,M,N,O,P,Q,R,S,T,U,V,W,X,Y,Z
others	Other characters

shortage of large annotated corpus, an approach proposed in this paper can be applied for automatic domain adaptation by exploiting the n-gram features from the raw corpus of the target domain.

In this work, we examined two kinds of n-gram features: n-gram frequency feature and AV feature. Our experimental results show that these simple statistical features are indeed effective in improving the ability of CWS system for domain adaptation.

3.1   N-gram Frequency Feature

We define n-gram frequency as the number of occurrences of n-gram in a corpus. The reason for considering this information is that the higher the frequency of n-gram, the greater the possibility of it being a word.

N-gram frequencies are extracted from raw corpus of target domain for ($2=<n<=5$) in this paper. In fact,we also tried n=6,but the results were not satisfied.Considering efficiency in computing, n-grams whose frequency values are less than five are filtered out. In order to alleviate the sparse data problem, we group all the frequency values into three sets: high-frequency (H), middle-frequency (M), and low-frequency (L) (Yiou Wang et al, 2011). The grouping way are defined as follows: if the frequency value of a n-gram is one of the top 5% of all the frequency values, the frequency value of this n-gram is represented as H; if it is between top 5% and 20%, it is represented as M, otherwise it is represented as L. In this way, n-gram frequency lists are produced. We regard the n-gram as words in the following processing.

For CRF training and decoding, the features of current character are generate as follows. We retrieve the n-gram lists for candidate words that contain the current character. From a candidate word, a feature is generated in the form of "A-B", where A is the position of the current character in the candidate word and B is the frequecy of this candidate word. Then, the feature generated from each candidate word is conca-tenated with each other by "|" as one n-gram frequency feature. Note that the conca-tenating order follows the position orders of the current character in candidate words, i.e. B、 B_2、 B_3、 M、 E, for standardization.

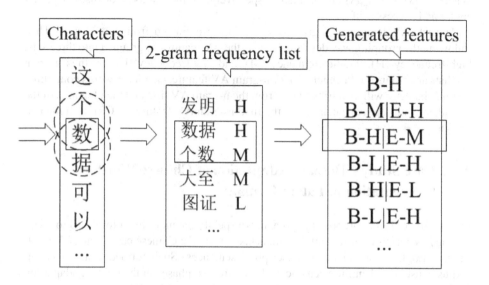

Fig. 1. Generation of 2-gram frequency feature

Fig.1 shows the generation process of 2-gram frequency feature for the sentence " 这个数据可以..." (The data can ...). The feature for the current character "数" (numeral), displayed in a square frame, is generated as follows. First, candidate words " 个数" (number) and "数据" (data) are retrieved from the 2-gram frequency list. From the candidate word "个数" a feature "E-M" is generated because its frequency is "M" and "数" is the last character of the word. After that, another feature from the candidate word "数据" is generated as "B-H" because the frequency is "H" and "数" is the first character of the word. Finally, the 2-gram frequency feature is represented as "B-H|E-M".

3.2   N-gram AV Feature

AV (Accessor Variety) is a statistical standard used in (Feng et al., 2004) to determine whether a character sequence is a word when extracting words from Chinese raw texts.

(Hai Zhao and Chuyu Kit, 2007; Hai Zhao and Chuyu Kit, 2008) has explored an approach to extract AV global features from raw corpus for CRF learning. Following the work of (Luo and Huang, 2009), we focus on improving the way of generating features for CRF learning and on avoiding data sparseness at the same time.

Different from the n-gram frequency, the n-gram AV has a selection for frequency. The main idea of the AV is that if a character sequence appear in a variety of context, then the sequence is likely to be a word. The AV of a sequence s is defined as:

$$AV(s) = \min\{L_{av}(s), R_{av}(s)\} \tag{4}$$

Where $L_{av}(s)$ and $R_{av}(s)$ are defined, respectively, as the numbers of distinct predecessor and successor of s.

At first, AV feature of n-gram ($2 =< n <= 5$) are extracted from raw corpus. Then following the grouping way described in 2.1, the AV feature are grouped into three sets, high-frequency (H), middle-frequency (M), and low-frequency (L) and thus n-gram AV lists are produced. In generation of n-gram AV feature, candidate words containing current character will be retrieved out from the n-gram AV lists and then features of the candidate words are concatenated as the final n-gram AV feature for CRF training and decoding.

4   Case Study—Domain Adaptation of Chinese Word Segmentation to Patent Domain

In order to verify the proposed approach, we specify patent domain for CWS to adapt to. The raw corpus of the patent domain is taken from the Chinese part of the NTCIR-9[1] Chinese-English parallel patent description sentences. Such formed Chinese patent corpus consists of 1 million sentences. There are two phases in the domain adaptation implementation, construction of n-grim statistical information base and generating of n-gram features. In the first phase, n-gram frequency features and n-gram AV features are extracted from the corpus and n-gram statistical information base including n-gram frequency lists and n-gram AV lists is produced.In the second phase, n-gram features are generated for the sentences.

4.1   Construction of N-gram Statistical Information Base

According to the definitions of n-gram frequency feature and the n-gram AV feature described in section 2, we extracted character sequences of n-gram ($2 =< n <= 5$) from the Chinese patent corpus for construction of n-gram statistical information base. The overview of the construction of n-gram statistical information base is shown in Fig.2.

---

[1] http://research.nii.ac.jp/ntcir/ntcir-9/

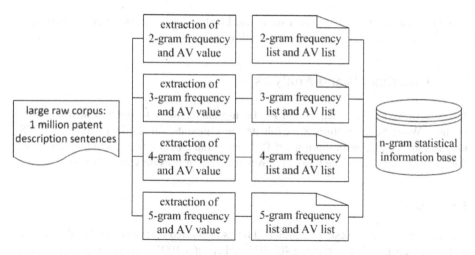

Fig. 2. Construction of n-gram statistical information base

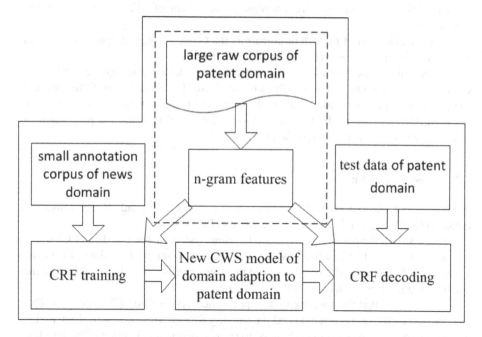

Fig. 3. Framework of domain adaptation of CWS system to patent domain

4.2   Generation of N-gram Features

In CRF training and decoding, n-gram features are generated for each character of sentences. The method of generating n-gram features has been described in 2.1 and 2.2, respectively. The framework of domain adaptation of CWS system to the patent domain is shown in Fig.3. The part surrounded by the dotted line is the core component for the CWS system to adapt to the patent domain.

5   Experiments and Analyses

In order to verify the contribution of the n-gram features to domain adaptation of Chinese Word Segmentation, we evaluate the segmentation results of the new CWS system incorporated with the n-gram features of the patent domain and then compare the results with those of the baseline CWS system that uses only basic features.

5.1   Data

We used the Penn Chinese Treebank (CTB) as annotated corpus and defined data sets as follows: chapter 1-270, chapter 400-931 and chapter 1001-1151 for training data set; chapter 270-300 for test data sets. The proportion of unknown words is 3.47%. Since the data of the corpus is mainly from newswire, the domain of CTB may be regarded as news domain.

The unlabeled data of the patent domain is the Chinese patent corpus. The n-gram statistical information base is built from this raw corpus.

For test data of the patent domain, we randomly selected 300 sentences from the Chinese patent corpus and manually annotated word segmentations following the specification of Penn Chinese Treebank Project. As a result, 10636 Chinese words are obtained. By referring to the training data of CTB, we found that the proportion of unknown words in this patent test data is 22.4%.

5.2   Results and Analyses

We used recall (R), precision (P), and F_1 as evaluation metrics and also measured the recall on OOV (R_{OOV}) tokens and in-vocabulary (R_{IV}) tokens.

Table 4 shows the performances of the baseline system on the test data of CTB and the patent domain. The baseline system is developed on the training data of CTB by using the basic features. The proportions of unknown words in test data of CTB and the patent domain are respectively 3.47% and 22.4%.

Table 4 shows that the baseline system performed very well on CTB test data. This can be explained that the test data and the training data are from the same domain, i.e. the news domain. When test data changed to the patent domain, F_1 value of the baseline

Table 4. Performances of baseline CWS system on test data from different domains

CWS System	Source of test data	R	P	F_1	R_{OOV}	R_{IV}
Baseline	CTB(news domain)	98.02%	97.21%	97.62%	75.18%	98.85%
	NTCIR(patent domain)	86.05%	81.83%	83.89%	63.70%	92.51%

Table 5. Performances of different CWS systems on test data from the patent domain

CWS System	R	P	F_1	R_{OOV}	R_{IV}
Baseline	86.05%	81.83%	83.89%	63.70%	92.51%
+(a)n-gram frequency feature	87.95%	84.32%	86.09%	69.15%	93.37%
+(b)n-gram AV feature	88.29%	84.28%	86.24%	69.15%	93.82%
+(a)+(b)	88.31%	84.61%	86.42%	69.91%	93.63%

system greatly decreased to 83.89% from 97.62%. For a more detailed investigation, R_{OOV} decreased to 63.70% by 11.48% and R_{IV} decreased to 92.15% by 6.34%. The degree of decline on OOV is about twice that on in-vocabulary. These investigation results demonstrated the serious impacts brought to the performance of Chinese Word Segmentation by the changes of domain. The task of domain adaptation is therefore very important for Chinese Word Segmentation.

The performances of the CWS systems developed by using the proposed approach are shown in Table 5, where "a" refers to using n-gram frequency feature and "b" refers to using n-gram AV feature. The test data is the 300 sentences of the patent domain. For comparison, the result of the baseline system on the same test data is also shown in Table 5. The results show that both n-gram frequency feature and n-gram AV feature contributed to the improvement in performance from the view of each metric, and that the combination of (a) and (b) achieved further improvements.

Through the observation of Table 4 and Table 5, we may conclude as follows.

- The impact of interdisciplinary on Chinese Word Segmentation is very obvious, and the introduction of a large number of OOV will cause a serious decline in the performance of CWS system.
- The n-gram features including n-gram frequency feature and n-gram AV feature are very effective in each evaluation metric and the combination of them can achieve further improvement.
- In terms of F_1 measure, the improvement contributed by n-gram AV feature is greater than that contributed by n-gram frequency feature. In terms of recall, n-gram AV feature is more effective than n-gram frequency feature, while n-gram frequency feature is more effective than n-gram AV feature in terms of precision.
- N-gram features can effectively increase the recall of OOV in CWS system.

It is further observed that some scientific and technical terms were successfully recalled after n-gram features of the raw corpus have been added into the system. For instance, one manually annotated sentence "它/可用于/驱动/电光层/到/显示/数据…" (…which may be used to drive the electro-optic layer to a state in which display datum…) was segmented as "…/电光/层到/…" by the baseline system, while the new system obtained the correct result. For another manually annotated sentence: "而/不/使用/压电/元件/或/楔板/换能器" (…without piezoelectric element or wedge transducer...), the baseline system segmented the word "换能器" into two parts, "换" and "能器" , while the new system avoided this erroneous segmentation. The word " 电光层" and "换能器" are both physics terms which seldom occur in the news domain. The original intention of the paper is to explore n-gram features of the target domain corpus for a CWS system to be able to recognize the new words and the CWS system on the patent domain performed as we expected.

Through the above experimental results and analyses, we observed that n-gram features are effective for the CWS system to adapt to the patent domain from the news domain.

6   Conclusion

This paper proposes an approach in which n-gram features from large raw corpus are explored to realize domain adaptation for Chinese Word Segmentation. The n-gram features include n-gram frequency feature and AV feature. Our experiments on the patent domain show that the n-gram features are effective in domain adaptation of Chinese Word Segmentation. This approach can be easily implemented because the n-gram features can be extracted from a raw corpus of the target domain. Compared with an annotated corpus and a domain-specific dictionary, a raw corpus of the target domain is easily obtained with low cost.

In the future, we will conduct further study on how to explore more effective features from large raw corpus and how to incorporate them into statistical learning model for domain adaptation of Chinese Word Segmentation.

References

1. Zhang, M., Deng, Z., Che, W.: Combining Ststistical Model and Dictionary for Domain Adaptation of Chinese Word Segmentation. Journal of Chinese Information Processing (2012)
2. Lafferty, J., McCallum, A., Pereira, F.: Conditional Random Fields: Probabilistic Models for Segmenting and Labeling Sequence Data. In: ICML (2001)
3. Zhao, H., Huang, C., Li, M., Lu, B.: Effective tag set selection in Chinese Word Segmentation via conditional random field modeling. In: PACLIC 2006, Wuhan, China, pp. 87–94 (2006)
4. Low, J.K., Ng, H.T., Guo, W.: A Maximum Entropy Approach to Chinese Word Segmentation. In: Proceedings of the 4th SIGHAN Workshop on Chinese Language Processing (SIGHAN 2005), pp. 161–164 (2005)
5. Wang, Y., Kazama, J., Tsuruoka, Y., Chen, W., Zhang, Y., Torisawa, K.: Improving Chinese Word Segmentation and POS Tagging with Semi-supervised Methods Using Large Auto-Analyzed Data. In: Proceedings of the 5th IJCNLP, pp. 309–317 (2011)
6. Feng, H., Chen, K., Deng, X., Zheng, W.: Accessor variety criteria for Chinese word extraction. J. Computational Linguistics 30, 75–93 (2004)
7. Zhao, H., Kit, C.: Incorporating global information into supervised learning for Chinese Word Segmentation. In: PACLING 2007, Melbourne, Australia, pp. 66–74 (2007)

8. Zhao, H., Kit, C.: Unsupervised Segmentation Helps Supervised Learning of Character Tagging for Word Segmentation and Named Entity Recognition. In: Proceedings of the Six SIGHAN Workshop on Chinese Language Processing, Hyderabad, India, pp. 106–111 (2008)
9. Luo, Y., Huang, D.: Chinese Word Segmentation Based on the Marginal Probabilities Generated by CRFs. Journal of Chinese Information Processing 23, 3–8 (2009)
10. Xia, F.: The Segmentation Guidelines for the Penn Chinese Treebank (3.0) (2000)

Fusion of Long Distance Dependency Features for Chinese Named Entity Recognition Based on Markov Logic Networks

Zejian Wu[1], Zhengtao Yu[1,2,*], Jianyi Guo[1,2], Cunli Mao[1,2], and Youmin Zhang[1]

[1] The School of Information Engineering and Automation, Kunming University of Science and Technology, Kunming 650051, China
[2] The Institute of Intelligent Information Processing,Computer Technology Application Key Laboratory of Yunnan Province, Kunming 650051, China
{liipwujian,ztyu,gjade86}@hotmail.com,Maocunli@163.com,316935430@qq.com
http://www.liip.cn

Abstract. For the issue that existing methods for Chinese Named Entity Recognition(NER) fail to consider the long-distance dependencies, which is common in the document. This paper, Fusion of long distance dependency, proposes a method for Chinese Named Entity Recognition(NER) based on Markov Logic Networks(MLNs), which comprehensively utilizes local, short distance dependency and long distance dependency features by taking advantage of first order logic to represent knowledge, and then integrates all the features into Markov Network for Chinese named entity recognition with the help of MLNs. Validity of proposed method is verified both in open domain and restricted domain, experimental result shows that proposed method has better effect.

Keywords: Chinese Named Entity Recognition; Markov Logic Networks; Long distance dependency; Statistic Rational Learning; Natural Language Processing

1 Introduction

Named Entity Recognition (NER) is one of the key techniques in the fields of Information Extraction, Question Answering, Parsing, Metadata Tagging in Semantic Web, etc. NER task is to identify the three categories (entity, time and digital), seven subclasses (person, organization, place, time, date, currency and percentage) of named entities in the text [1-2]. Because of word flexibility of person, organization and place, their recognition is very difficult, while, composition of time, date, currency and percentage tends to have more obvious rules. Therefore, NER generally refers to the recognition of person, organization and place. As early as in 1995, MUC-6 established the special evaluation of NER, greatly promoted the development of English NER technology. MUC-6 and MUC-7 also

---

* Corresponding author.

M. Zhou et al. (Eds.): NLPCC 2012, CCIS 333, pp. 132–142, 2012.
© Springer-Verlag Berlin Heidelberg 2012

established a multi-language entity recognition evaluation task MET (Multilingual Entity Task), including Japanese, Spanish, Chinese and other languages. BAKEOFF-3 and BAKEOFF-4, Held in 2006 and 2008, established a special evaluation task for Chinese NER. In 2003 and 2004, "Chinese information processing and intelligent human-machine interface technology evaluation" task, held by "863 Program", established Chinese Named Entity Recognition evaluation task. These evaluation tasks had played a very important role in promoting the development of Chinese Named Entity Recognition. Compared to English NER, Chinese NER is more difficult [2]. The main differences between Chinese NER and English NER lie in: (1) Unlike English, Chinese lacks the capitalization information which can play very important roles in identifying named entities. (2) There is no space between words in Chinese, so we have to segment the text before NER. Consequently, the errors in word segmentation will affect the result of NER. In this paper, we propose a Chinese NER model based on Markov Logic Networks with emphasizes on (1) Combining local feature, short distance dependency feature and long distance dependency feature into a unified statistical relational learning model; (2) Integrating probabilistic learning and relational learning for Chinese NER by MLNs. In order to deduce the complexity of the model and the searching space, we divide the recognition process into two steps: (1) word segmentation and POS tagging; (2) named entity recognition based on the first step. Proposed method is tested on the open domain and restricted domain corpus. The Precision, Recall and F1 in open domain and restricted domain are respectively (78.39%, 85.89%, 81.97%) and (85.39%, 88.89%, 87.10%). Experimental result shows that proposed model is better than Condition Random Fields when only use local and short distance dependency features, and long distance dependency features can effectively improve the recognition effect.

2   Related Work

Early approaches to Named Entity Recognition involve a lot of human effort, require researchers to write a series of complex regular expressions to match candidate entity, and need to develop a large dictionary of common entities. Moreover, these approaches could only be engineered to suit a specific domain [1]. These limitations motivate the development of machine learning systems in natural language processing. Bikel, et al first proposed a named entity recognition method based on Hidden Markov Models (HMM) [3]. While, because HMM is a generative model, theres only one feature variable with each state. However, we may want to incorporate more output features in our model to improve the accuracy of the tagger. For example, for a given token, we do not only want to consider the identity of the word. We would also want to take more output features into account such as the previous token, the next token, whether the token includes any digits or symbols etc. To maintain tractability of computation, HMM have to assume that observation features are independent of each other. In real life, most observations do have complex dependencies, and assuming independence between the features can severely impair the performance of the model. To handle the limitation of HMM, Liao, et al proposed many methods for NER based on linear-chain Conditional Random Fields (CRF) [4]. Even though linear chain CRF has many advantages over some of the more traditional models, it also has weaknesses. In a linear chain CRF, we assume that the only dependencies are between the labels of adjacent words. Thus, linear chain CRF is not able to use information from longer distance dependencies to assist label. While in real life, there are many long distance dependencies in a document. For example, if a word is tagged as a category, when the subsequent sections in the document again or repeatedly involved this word, it always appears in the same or similar form and its labeling is often the same. J Liu, et al, integrated long distance dependencies, proposed a method for biomedical named entities recognition based on skip-chain CRF [5]. Skip-chain CRF can handle relatively simple long distance dependencies, while, in real life, there are many complex long distance dependencies, skip-chain CRF is also unable to handle them.

As a result, researchers have turned to using a variety of statistical relational learning methods to increase the accuracy of English NER, while, related researches for Chinese NER is still rare. Statistical Relational Learning (SRL) is a combination of probabilistic learning and relational learning [6]. The strength of probabilistic models is that they can handle uncertainty in learning and reasoning. Meanwhile, first order logic or relational databases can effectively represent a wide range of knowledge. SRL techniques attempt to combine the strength of the two approaches. This combined strength of probabilistic learning and relational learning gives SRLs more power in learning and inferences. Recently, there have been some studies in the application of SRL techniques to information extraction. Bunescu and Mooney have used Relational Markov Networks to identify protein names in biomedical text [7]. Domingos and Poon have applied Markov Logic Networks for the segmentation and entity resolution of bibliographic citations [8].

Here, we propose to use the power of Markov Logic Networks to model long distance dependencies for Chinese NER. To the best of our knowledge, this is the first research work that, integrated long distance dependencies, applies Markov logic Networks to Chinese NER. This paper is organized as follows. In section 3 we will review the related definitions of MLNs. In section 4 we will introduce our method for Chinese NER, followed by the experiment in section 5. The conclusions are given in section 6.

3   Markov Logic Review

Among many statistical relational learning methods, Markov Logic Networks (MLNs) is a powerful, direct approach. It is a first-order knowledge base with a weight attached to each formula which can be viewed as templates for features of Markov networks. It is defined as follows [9-10]:

A Markov Logic Network L is a set of pairs $\{(F_i, w_i)\}_{i=1}^{m}$, where F_i is a formula in first-order logic and w_i is a real number. Together with a finite set of constants

$C = \{C_1, C_2, C_3, ..., C_{|c|}\}$, it defines a Markov network $M_{L,C} = < X, E, \{\varphi_k\} >$ as follows:

1. $M_{L,C}$ contains one binary node for each possible grounding of each predicate appearing in L. The value of the node is 1 if the ground atom is true and 0 otherwise.

2. $M_{L,C}$ contains one feature for each possible grounding of each formula F_i in L. The value of this feature is 1 if the ground formula is true and 0 otherwise. The weight of the feature is w_i associated with F_i in L.

For simplicity, a Markov logic network $M_{L,C}$ is a set of weighted first-order clauses. Together with a set of constants, it defines a Markov network with one node per ground atom and one feature per ground clause. The weight of a feature is the weight of the first-order clause that originated it. The probability of a state x in such a network is given by the log-linear model:

$$P(X = x) = \frac{1}{Z} \prod_{k=1}^{nc} \phi_k(x_k) = \frac{1}{Z} \prod_{i=1}^{m} (e^{w_i})^{n_i(x)} = \frac{1}{Z} \exp\{\sum_{i=1}^{m} [w_i \cdot n_i(x)]\} \quad (1)$$

Where Z is normalization constant, w_i is the weight of the i-th formula, and $n_i(x)$ is the number of satisfied groundings.

4   Chinese Name Entity Recognition Based on MLNs

4.1   Feature Selection and Their First Order Logic Representation

Local Features. Word itself, part of speech, word context and some specific dictionaries can be taken into consideration when select local features. However, for the reason that dictionary and some others external resources are the common entity resources by manual sorting, they have very small contribution to verity the effectiveness of proposed approach. Therefore, in order to better verify the validity of the method, we only select the inherent features of the document. Basic features we selected as follows:

1) Independent Feature: Represent information in the words of candidate entity. It includes word itself and its POS tag and it aims to inspect the internal information in candidate entity. For example, if a candidate entity includes word " 公司(Corporation)", the probability that it is labeled as organization will be increased. First-order logic formula that represents this feature as follows:

$$Word(+x) \wedge Tag(x, t) \Rightarrow Label(x, +l)$$

Denote that the labels of words in the text rely on the word itself and its POS tag information. "+" means separate weight is learned for different grounding formulas.

2) Local Context Feature: Represent information between current word and its adjacent words. For example, "机器学习领域著名学者周志华教授(Well-known scholar in the field of machine learning, "Zhou Zhihua" Professor)", suppose the word we want to tag is "周志华(Zhou Zhihua)". It is very difficult to directly label

the word, however, if we consider its previous adjacent word "学者(scholar)" and its next adjacent word "教授(professor)", the probability that the word " 周志华(Zhou Zhihua)" tagged as person will be increased. First order logic formula that represents this feature as follows:

$$Neighbour(x, y) \land Word(+x) \Rightarrow Label(y, +l)$$

$$Neighbour(x, y) \land Word(+y) \Rightarrow Label(x, +l)$$

$Neighbour(x, y)$ denotes that x is the previous adjacent word of y. The formulas denote that candidate entities'adjacent words have impact on its label.

Short Distance Dependency Features. Local features are the information that can be extracted directly from the corpus, while it does not take into account the dependencies between the labels of candidate entities. However, there is a wealth of relationship between the labels in a document. Such as, the label of an entity's previous word always is non-entity label, etc. For example, In the sentence "来自北京大学、清华大学等200所院校现场接受考生及家长的咨询. (200 person in charge from Peking University, Tsinghua University and other institutions to the scene to accept the students and parents consulting.)", "北京大学(Peking University)" and "清华大学(Tsinghua University)" are organizations, labels of their previous words (" 来自"("from") and ", ") are all non-entity label. Therefore, dependencies of the labels of candidate entities should be used effectively. CRF is able to handle these short distance dependent features, and achieves fairly good result in the entity recognition task [12]. So we follow the idea of CRF, assume that the label of current word only relies on the label of its previous adjacent word and its next adjacent word. First order logic formula that represents this feature as follows:

$$Neighbour(x, y) \land label(x, +l) \Rightarrow Label(y, +label)$$

$$Neighbour(x, y) \land label(y, +l) \Rightarrow Label(x, +label)$$

The two formulas denote that the label of current word depend on the label of its previous adjacent word and its next adjacent word.

Long Distance Dependency Features. If a candidate entity is tagged as a category in a document, when the entity again or repeatedly involved in the subsequent sections of the document, it usually appears in the same or similar form. And some of the candidate words themselves has ambiguity, if there is no prior knowledge, it is very difficult to recognize. For instance:

1). " 云南大学、昆明理工大学，云南师范大学等省内重点高校研招计划于昨日公布(Yunnan University, Kunming University of Science and Technology, Yunnan Normal University and other provincial key universities graduate enrollment plan announced yesterday)"

2). "云南大学、昆明理工大学仍是我省招生规模最大的两所大学(Yunnan University, Kunming University of Science and Technology are still the two universities whose enrollment is the largest in our province)"

3). "我省有包括云大、昆工、天文台等共17所招收研究生的高校及科研机构(In our province, there are 17 universities and research institutions, including , that including Yunnan University, Kunming University of Science and Technology and the Observatory, that recruit graduate students)"

The three sentences above are extracted from one news report in accordance with the original order. In sentence 1), " 云南大学(Yunnan University)" and "昆明理工大学(Kunming University of Science and Technology)" can be judged as organization. The two entities are repeated in 2), we can obtain the correct category by the result of 1). "云大(YunDa)" and "昆工(KunGong)" are the abbreviation of "云南大学(Yunnan University)" and "昆明理工大学(Kunming University of Science and Technology)", and it is very difficult to label them only based on the local features as well as short distance features. While, once taking advantage of long distance features, they can be labeled straightforward by the correct category by the result of 1) and 2). Therefore, long distance features are very useful in the identification of candidate entities. This paper takes two types of long distance dependencies into consideration: 1) Homomorphism Repetition. Donate that if a candidate entity appears in different locations of the same document, the label of these entities should be labeled as the same. Regular expression is used to match homomorphism repetition to get the entity repetition information. 2) Abbreviation Repetition. Donate that if an entity appears in a document, and in the follow-up portion of the document, the abbreviation of the entity appears, the two candidate entities should be labeled as the same category. However, identification of the abbreviation of a name entity also is a difficult problem in NER task. In order to ensure the system's recognition accuracy, accuracy of extracting abbreviation repetition should be guaranteed, while recall rate of abbreviation repetition should be relatively relaxed. Abbreviation repetition can be identified by matching candidate word with the key words of entity's full name. In both cases, first order logic formulas can be uniformly represented as follows:

$$SameToken(x, y) \land label(x, +l) \Rightarrow Label(y, +l)$$

4.2   Weight Learning

Weight Learning in MLNs is to estimate the weights of formulas utilizing the training data [8-10]. We adopt Discriminative Weight Learning (DWL) to learn formulas'weights. The prerequisite of DWL is that it must be known priori that which predicates will be evidence and which ones will be queried. For the problem of Chinese NER, this is known. DWL divides grounding atoms in the domain into two sets: a set of evidence atoms X and a set of query atoms Y. In our approach, Y is all the grounding atoms of $Label(y, +l)$; others all belong to X.

The conditional likelihood (CLL) of Y given X is:

$$P(y|x) = \frac{1}{Z_x} \exp(\sum_{i \in F_y} w_i n_i(x, y)) = \frac{1}{Z_x} \exp(\sum_{j \in G_y} w_j g_j(x, y)) \qquad (2)$$

Where Z_x is the partition function given X, F_y is the set of all MLNs clauses with at least one grounding involving a query atom, $n_i(x, y)$ is the number of true groundings of the $i-th$ clause involving query atoms, G_y is the set of ground clauses in $M_{L,C}$ involving query atoms, and $g_j(x, y) = 1$ if the $j-th$ ground clause is true in the data and 0 otherwise. By taking partial derivation of log-likelihood function of the formula above, we can obtain:

$$\frac{\partial}{\partial w_i} \log p_w(y|x) = n_i(x, y) - E_w[n_i(x, y)] \qquad (3)$$

The time complexity of calculating $E_w[n_i(x, y)]$ accurately is enormous. Its approximate value can be calculated by calculating $n_i(x, y_w^*)$, y_w^* represents predicates in its Markov Blanket. Therefore, it translates into counting $n_i(x, y_w^*)$ in the maximum posteriori hypothesis state $y_w^*(x)$. Then, we can obtain the weight of the formulas.

4.3   Inference

Inference in Markov Logic Networks includes maximum likelihood inference, calculating marginal probabilities and calculating conditional probability [8-11]. This paper only needs the maximum possible explanation (MPE) which involves only the maximum likelihood inference. The following is a brief introduction to the method of maximum likelihood inference we used in Markov Logic Network. The maximum likelihood inference process can be stated as: given evidence set of X, seek the most probable state of the world Y. That is:

$$\max_y p(y|x) \qquad (4)$$

According to Markov logic network's joint probability distribution, the equation above can be transformed into:

$$\max_y \sum_i w_i n_i(x, y) \qquad (5)$$

Therefore, the MPE problem in Markov logic reduces to finding the truth assignment that maximizes the sum of weights of satisfied clauses. The most commonly used approximate solver is MaxWalkSAT, a weighted variant of the WalkSAT local-search satisfiability solver, which can solve hard problems with hundreds of thousands of variables in minutes. While, One problem with MaxWalkSAT is that they require propositionalizing the domain (i.e., grounding all atoms and clauses in all possible ways), which consumes memory exponential in the arity of the clauses. By taking advantage of the sparseness of relational domains, where most atoms are false and most clauses are trivially satisfied, MPE inference can be conducted by LazySAT algorithm which only ground atoms and clauses that is needed and can save memory exponentially. Therefore, we adopt LazeSAT for inference in proposed method.

5 Experiment

To objectively evaluate the effect of proposed method, we organize two set of experiments in open and restricted domain. Open domain experiment is based on People's Daily's open corpus in January 1998. For the reason that there are more repetitions of attractions, places and other entities in the fields of tourism which could reflect the effect of proposed method better, restricted domain experiments are based on the corpus in tourism field of Yunnan by manual collection.

5.1 Data

In open domain experiment, effectiveness of proposed method is tested on People's Daily's open corpus in January 1998, in which the average repetition of entities in each document is about three times. we select three types of entities (person, place and organization), and then process the corpus in specific way: First, each word in the corpus is divided into a separate row, then, tag the label behind the corresponding word and its POS tag, which each entity tag is labeled in the form of beginning, intermediate and end label, each non-entity is labeled by non-entity label. Example of corpus after pre-processing is as follows:
Original corpus:

> [黔南州(Qian Nan Zhou) /ns民族(nationality) /n 干部(cadre) /n 学
> 校(school) /n]nt

Processed corpus:

> 黔南州(Qian Nan Zhou) /ns ntb
> 民族(nationality) /n ntm
> 干部(cadre) /n ntm
> 学校(school) /n nte

Experiment in restricted domain is based on artificially collected 2000 documents in the field of Yunnan tourism. Firstly, pre-process the corpus utilizing word segmentation and POS tagging tools. Then, manually tag the corpus into eight categories: Attraction (jd), Number (Numbers in Chinese, e.g. "五十三(Fifty-three)")(m), Person (pn), Snack(xc), Place(dd), Specialty(tc), Festival(jr),Time(Time in Chinese, e.g. " 二十一世纪(Twenty-first century)")(t). Example of the corpus after pre-processing is as follows:

> 也许(Maybe) /d o
> 你(You) /r o
> 逛(visit) /v o

了/u o
束河白(Shu He Bai) /nr jdB
沙(Sha)/nr jdE
雪嵩(Xue Song) /nr jdB
石鼓(Shi Gu) /n jdE

The first column is the segmentation result of original text, the second column is corresponding POS tag, and the third column is corresponding entity label tagged by manual where "o" indicates a non-entity label. The average repetition of entities in each document is about fifteen times. Detailed statistics of data collections are shown in Table 1.

Table 1. Table1 statistic of corpus

Number of Documents	Train Corpus	Open Test Corpus	Closed Test Corpus
2000	800	1200	400
Attractions(jd)	Number(m)	Person name(pn)	Snack(xc)
76	130	306	51
Place name(dd)	Specialty(tc)	Festival(jr)	Time(t)
128	31	79	61

5.2   Experimental Analysis

Three comparative experiments are organized for each of the two experiments: the first experiment is based on Conditional Random Fields; the second experiment is based on Markov Logic Networks which only use local features and short distance features; the third experiment is also based on Markov Logic Networks with comprehensive utilizing local, short distance dependency and long distance dependency features. Closed and open comparative experiments both are organized for each of the three types of experiments. Evaluation of the two sets of experiments is based on the following three indicators:

$$Precision = \frac{NumberCorrect}{TotalTagged}$$

$$Recall = \frac{NumberCorrect}{ExpectedLabels}$$

$$F1 = \frac{2*(Precision*Recall)}{Precision+Recall}$$

Table 2 gives detailed statistics of the comparative experimental result.

The experimental result shows that the Precision, Recall and F1 of proposed method in open domain and restricted domain are respectively (78.39%, 85.89%, 81.97%) and (85.39%, 88.89%, 87.10%). The reason why the accuracy of the experimental result is not very prominent is that, in order to verify the

Table 2. Table 2: Detailed comparative experimental result

	Open /Closed	Open Domain			Restricted Domain		
		Precision/%	Recall/%	F1/%	Precision/%	Recall/%	F1/%
CRF	Closed	70.30%	82.22%	75.79%	84.30%	87.22%	85.74%
	Open	66.33%	79.75%	72.42%	81.33%	78.75%	80.02%
MLNs(Local + Short)	Closed	85.19%	87.47%	86.31%	86.19%	87.47%	86.83%
	Open	73.28%	81.62%	77.23%	81.28%	82.62%	81.94%
MLNs(Local+ Short+ Long)	Closed	88.27%	93.46%	90.79%	90.27%	92.46%	91.35%
	Open	78.39%	85.89%	81.97%	85.39%	88.89%	87.10%

validity of the proposed method, we only select some inherent basic features in the document regardless of any excessive rules and more contexts (e.g. 2 or more gram model). Experimental result shows that using only local and short distance dependences features, experiment result of MLNs is better than CRF. When long distances dependency features are integrated into MLNs, experiments result both in open domain and restricted domain are all improved and more obvious in restricted domain. Increase of precision, Recall and F1 in open domain and restricted domain are respectively (5.11%, 4.27%, 4.66%) and (4.11%, 6.27%, 5.16%). This is because entities have more repetitions in restricted domain and then, long distances dependence features contribute more to improve the experimental result in restricted domain.

Acknowledgement. This paper is supported by National Nature Science Foundation (No.60863011, 61175068), and the Key Project of Yunnan Nature Science Foundation (No. 2008CC023), and the National Innovation Fund for Technology based Firms (No.11C26215305905), and the Open Fund of Software Engineering Key Laboratory of Yunnan Province (No.2011SE14), and the Ministry of Education of Returned Overseas Students to Start Research and Fund Projects.

References

1. Grishman, R.: Information Extraction. The Oxford Handbook of Computational Linguistics (2003)
2. Zhao, J.: A Survey on Named Entity Recognition, Disambiguation and Cross-Lingual Co-reference Resolution. Journal of Chinese Information Processing 23(2) (2009)
3. Bidel, D.M., Schwarta, R., Weischedel, R.M.: An Algorithm that learns what's in a Name. Machine Learning Journal Special Issue on Natural Language Learning 34(1-3), 211–231 (1999)

4. Liao, W., Veeramachanei, S.: A Simple Semi-supervised Algorithm for Name Entity Recognition. In: Proceedings of the NAACL HLT 2009 Workshop on Semi-Supervised Learning for Natural Language Processing, pp. 58–65 (2009)
5. Liu, J., Huang, M., Zhu, X.: Recognizing biomedical named entities using skip-chain conditional random fields. In: Proceedings of the 2010 Workshop on Biomedical Natural Language Processing, BioNLP 2010, pp. 10–18 (2010)
6. Xu, C.-F., Hao, C.-L., Su, B.-J., Lou, J.-J.: Research on Markov Logic Networks. Journal of Software 22(8), 1699–1713 (2011)
7. Bunescu, Mooney: Statistical Relational Learning for Natural Language Information Extraction. Introduction to Statistical Relational Learning, pp. 535–552. MIT Press, Cambridge (2007)
8. Poon, Domingos: Joint Inference in Information Extraction. In: Proceedings of the Twenty-Second National Conference on Artificial Intelligence, pp. 913–918. AAAI Press, Vancouver (2007)
9. Domingos, Richardson: Markov Logic: A Unifying Framework for Statistical Relational Learning. Introduction to Statistical Relational Learning, pp. 339–371. MIT Press, Cambridge (2007)
10. Domingos, P., Lowd, D.: Markov Logic: An Interface Layer for Artificial Intelligence. Morgan and Claypool, San Rafael (2009)
11. Poon, Domingos: Sound and Efficient Inference with Probabilistic and Deterministic Dependencies. In: Proceedings of the Twenty-First National Conference on Artificial Intelligence, pp. 458–463. AAAI Press, Boston (2006)
12. Sutton, McCallum: An Introduction to Conditional Random Fields for Relational Learning. Introduction to Statistical Relational Learning. MIT Press, Cambridge (2007)

Learning Latent Topic Information for Language Model Adaptation

Shixiang Lu[*,**], Wei Wei, Xiaoyin Fu, Lichun Fan, and Bo Xu

Interactive Digital Media Technology Research Center
Institute of Automation, Chinese Academy of Sciences
95 Zhongguancun East Road, Haidian District, Beijing 100190, China
shixiang.lu@ia.ac.cn

Abstract. This paper is concerned with data selection for adapting language model (LM) in statistical machine translation (SMT), and aims to find the LM training sentences that are topic similar to the translation task. Although the traditional methods have gained significant performance, they ignore the topic information and the distribution of words in calculating the sentence similarity. In this paper, the authors propose a topic model to discover the latent topics in the content of sentences, and combine the latent topic based similarity with TF-IDF into a unified framework for data selection. Furthermore, the authors combine a cross-lingual projecting method with the topic model, which makes the data selection depend on the source input directly. Large-scale experimental results demonstrate that the proposed approach significantly outperforms the traditional approaches on both LM perplexity and SMT performance.

Keywords: topic information, cross-lingual projection, data selection, language model adaptation, statistical machine translation.

1 Introduction

Over the past few years, selecting training data which are similar to the translation task from the large corpus has become an important approach to improve the performance of language model (LM) in statistical machine translation (SMT) [1-5]. This would empirically provide more accurate lexical probabilities, and thus better match the translation task at hand[5].

The major challenge for data selection is how to measure the similarity between the queried sentence and the LM training corpus. To solve this problem, many researchers proposed various kinds of similarity measures to select similar sentences for LM adaptation, such as TF-IDF[1-3, 6], centroid similarity[4], cross-entropy difference[5], cross-lingual information retrieval[7], and cross-lingual similarity (CLS)[8]. Unfortunately, they all take the similarity measure without considering the topic information and the distribution of words in the whole LM

---

* Contact author.
** This work was supported by 863 program in China (No. 2011AA01A207).

M. Zhou et al. (Eds.): NLPCC 2012, CCIS 333, pp. 143–153, 2012.

training corpus. These information have been successfully used for LM adaptation in SMT[9, 10] and been proved very useful. This approach infers the topic posterior distribution of the source text, and then applies the inferred distribution to the target language LM via marginal adaptation. However, it focus on modify the LM itself, which is different from data selection method for LM adaptation.

To address this problem, we propose a more principled latent topic based data selection model for LM adaptation in SMT. To the best of our knowledge, this is the first extensive and empirical study of learning the latent topic information for data selection to adapt LM. We employ the topic model (e.g., Latent Dirichlet Allocation) to discover the latent topics in the whole content of LM training corpus. Then we calculate the topic-similarity between the first pass translation hypotheses[1] and the sentences in the LM training corpus based on the latent topic information. Moreover, we propose a cross-lingual projecting method, which projects the source input sentences in the translation task to the target language representation, and then we combine it with the topic model. Therefore, when given the source input sentence, we can select the topic-similar sentences directly without the first pass translation hypotheses. TF-IDF and latent topic information are based on different knowledge, we assume they are complementary to each other, and the performance can be further improved by combining them, as we will show in the experiments.

The remainder of this paper is organized as follows. The next section introduces some related work of LM adaptation. Section 2 describes our proposed latent topic based data selection model for LM adaptation. Section 3 presents large-scale experiments and analyses, and followed by conclusions and future work in section 4.

2   Related Work

A variety of latent topic models have been used for LM adaptation in speech recognition (SR)[11-19], which show the latent topic information are very useful for LM adaptation. The previous works have primarily focused on customizing a fixed n-gram LM for each lecture by combining n-gram statistics from general conversational speech, other lectures, textbooks, and other resources related to the target lecture[11-14]. Moreover, they focus on in-domain adaptation using large amounts of matched training data[19]. However, most, if not all, of the data available to train an LM in SMT are cross-topic and cross-style. Therefore, these previous latent topic based LM adapting methods in SR are not suitable for SMT, and we will illustrate a novel latent topic based data selection model for LM adaptation in this paper.

To the best of our knowledge, none of the existing studies have addressed data selection for LM adaptation in SMT by learning the latent topics. In the next

---

[1] Following [2, 4], we call the initial translations hypotheses which are generated by the baseline SMT system as the firs pass translation hypotheses.

section, we explore a new approach to discover the latent topic information into the similar data selection for LM adaptation.

3   Latent Topic Based Data Selection for LM Adaptation

For the first pass translation hypotheses or the source input sentences in the translation task, we estimate the bias LM, from the corresponding similar LM training sentences. Since this size of selected sentences is small, the corresponding bias LM is specific and more effective, giving high probabilities to those phrases that occur in the selected sentences.

The generic LM $P_g(w_i|h)$ and the bias LM $P_b(w_i|h)$ is combined using linear interpolation as adapted LM $P_a(w_i|h)$ [2,7], which is shown to improve performance over the individual models:

$$P_a(w_i|h) = \gamma P_g(w_i|h) + (1 - \gamma)P_b(w_i|h) \tag{1}$$

where the interpolation factor γ can be simply estimated using the Powell Search algorithm[20] via cross-validation, and the bias LM is of the same order and smoothing algorithm as the generic LM.

The resulting adapted LM is then used in place of the generic LM in the translation process, would empirically provides more accurate lexical probabilities, and thus better matches the translation task at hand. Our work focuses on latent topic based data selection model, and the quality of this model is crucial to the performance of adapted LM.

3.1   Latent Topic Based Data Selection Model

Before introducing our proposed method, we first briefly describe the LDA model[21]. LDA models the generation of document content as two independent stochastic processes by introducing latent topic space. For an arbitrary word w in document d, (1) a topic z is first sampled from the multinomial distribution θ_d, which is generated from the Dirichlet prior parameterized by α; (2) and then the word w is generated from multinomial distribution ϕ_z, which is generated from the Dirichlet prior parameterized by β. The two Dirichlet priors for documents-topic distribution θ_d and topic-word distribution ϕ_z reduce the probability of overfitting training documents and enhance the ability of inferring topic distribution for new documents.

In latent topic based data selection model (LT), the first pass translation hypotheses and the sentences in the LM training corpus can be considered as documents. In this paper, we employ state-of-the-art topic model - LDA to discover the latent topics information and the distribution of words in them. We consider the first pass translation hypotheses as a question sentence s, and assume that s and the LM training sentence S are represented by a distribution over topics. $|s|$ represents the length of s, and we obtain the topic distribution of s by merging the topic distributions of words:

$$P_{LT}(z|s) = \frac{1}{|s|} \sum_{w \in s} P(z|w) \tag{2}$$

Then, we assume that s and S have the same prior probability, K represents the number of topics, N represents the numbers of s, so the score function can be written as:

$$P_{LT}(s|S) = \sum_z P_{LT}(s|z)P_{LT}(z|S)$$

$$= \sum_{z \in K} \frac{P_{LT}(z|s)P(s)}{P(z)} P_{LT}(z|S)$$

$$= \frac{K}{N} \sum_{z \in K} P_{LT}(z|s)P_{LT}(z|S) \quad (3)$$

3.2   Parameter Estimation

After introducing our proposed LT method, we will describe how to estimate the parameter used in the model. In LT, we introduce the new parameters, which lead to the inference not be done exactly. Expectation-Maximum (EM) algorithm is a possible choice for estimating the parameters of models with latent variables. However, EM suffers from the possibility of running into local maxima and the high computational burden. Therefore, we employ an alternative approach - Gibbs sampling[22], which is gaining popularity in recent work on latent topic analysis.

After training the model, we can get the following parameter estimations as:

$$\hat{\theta}_{sz} = \frac{n_{sz} + \alpha_z - 1}{\sum_{z'=1}^{K}(n_{sz'} + \alpha_{z'}) - 1} \quad (4)$$

$$\hat{\phi}_{zw} = \frac{n_{zw} + \beta_w - 1}{\sum_{v=1}^{V}(n_{zv} + \beta_v) - 1} \quad (5)$$

where n_{sz} and n_{zw} are the number of times of sentence s and word w which are assigned to the topic z, and V represents the number of unique words.

Next, we concentrate on how to select proper topic number to obtain our model with best performance and enough iteration to prevent the overfitting problem. We calculate the perplexity on LM training corpus C to estimate the performance of our model, which is a sequence of tuples $(s, w) \in C$:

$$Perplexity(C) = exp\{-\frac{\sum_{(s,w) \in C} lnP(w|s)}{|C|}\} \quad (6)$$

where, the probability $P(w|s)$ is calculated as follow:

$$P(w|s) = \sum_{z=1}^{K} P(w|z)P(z|s) \quad (7)$$

3.3 Combining Latent Topic with TF-IDF for Data Selection

Since the LT model and TF-IDF use different strategies for data selection, we assume that this two models are complementary to each other, it is interesting to explore how to combine their strength. In this section, we propose an approach to linearly combine the LT model with the TF-IDF model for data selection. In this paper, we choose TF-IDF as the foundation of our solution since TF-IDF has gained significant performance for LM adaptation in SMT[1-3, 6]. Formally, we have

$$P_{LT\_TF-IDF}(s|S) = \mu P_{LT}(s|S) + (1 - \mu)P_{TF-IDF}(s|S) \tag{8}$$

where, the relative importance of LT and TF-IDF is adjusted through the interpolation parameter μ.

3.4 Latent Topic Based Cross-Lingual Data Selection Model

Inspired by the work of CLS[8], we assume the following processing. The source sentence u and the target sentence v lie in two different vector space, we need to find a projection of u in the target vocabulary vector space before similarity can be evaluated. We estimate the bilingual word co-occurrence matrix Σ from an unsupervised, automatic word alignment induced over the SMT parallel training corpus. We use the GIZA++ toolkit to estimate the parameters of IBM Model 4, and combine the forward and backward viterbi alignments. Then, the projection of the source sentence u in the target vector space can be calculated by the vector-matrix product, as show:

$$\hat{v} = u\Sigma \tag{9}$$

The target term in $\hat{v}$ will be emphasized that most frequently co-occur with the source term in u. $\hat{v}$ can be interpreted as a "bag of words" translation of u. Next, we extend $\hat{v}$ into latent topic based cross-lingual data selection model (CLLT) for LM adaptation. We consider $\hat{v}$ as the first pass translation hypotheses $\hat{s}$, so CLLT can be written as follows:

$$P_{CLLT}(\hat{s}|S) = \frac{K}{N} \sum_{z \in K} P_{CLLT}(z|\hat{s})P_{CLLT}(z|S) \tag{10}$$

We use CLS to calculate the source sentence u to each target sentence S. However, due to the lack of optimization measures for sparse vector representation, the similarity is not accurate. In our model, we add the optimization measures (TF-IDF), called CLS_s, which improves the performance, as we will show in the experiment. What is more, we apply this criterion for the first time to the task of cross-lingual data selection for LM adaptation in SMT. This model can be written as follow:

$$P_{CLS_s}(\hat{s}|S) = \frac{S^T \cdot \hat{s}}{\|S\|\|\hat{s}\|}$$

$$= \frac{S^T \cdot u\Sigma}{\|S\|\|u\Sigma\|} \tag{11}$$

Lastly, we combine CLLT and CLSs into a cross-lingual data selection framework by the linear interpolation parameter, as follows:

$$P_{CLLT\_CLS_s}(\hat{s}|S) = \lambda P_{CLLT}(\hat{s}|S) + (1 - \lambda)P_{CLS_s}(\hat{s}|S) \tag{12}$$

where, the relative importance of CLLT and CLS_s is adjusted through the interpolation parameter λ.

4   Experiments and Results

We measure the utility of the proposed LM adaptation approach and the traditional approaches in two ways: (a) comparing the reference translations based perplexity of adapted LMs with the generic LM, and (b) comparing SMT performance of adapted LMs with the generic LM.

4.1   Corpus

We conduct experiments on two Chinese-to-English translation tasks: IWSLT-07 (dialogue domain) and NIST-06 (news domain).

IWSLT-07. The bilingual corpus comes from BTEC and CJK corpus, which contains 3.82K sentence pairs. The LM training corpus is from the English side of the parallel data (BTEC, CJK and CWMT2008), which consists of 1.34M sentences. IWSLT-07 test set consists of 489 sentences with 4 English reference translations each, and development set is the IWSLT-05 test set with 506 sentences.

NIST-06. The bilingual corpus comes from LDC[2], which consists of 3.4M sentence pairs. The LM training corpus is from the English side of the English Gigaword corpus[3], which consists of 11.3M sentences. NIST-06 MT Evaluation test set consists of 1664 sentences with 4 English reference translations each, and development set is NIST-05 MT Evaluation test set with 1084 sentences.

4.2   Iteration and Topic Number Selection

Fig. 1(a) shows the influence of iteration number of Gibbs sampling on the topic model generalization ability. Empirically, we set the topic number as 96 on IWSLT-07 and 168 on NIST-06, respectively, and change the iteration number in the experiments. Note that the lower perplexity value indicates better generalization ability on the holdout LM training corpus. We see that the perplexity values decreases when the iteration times are below 1000 on IWSLT-06 and 1400 on NIST-06, respectively. Fig. 1(b) shows the perplexity values for different settings of the topic number. We see that the perplexity decreases when the number

---

[2] LDC2002E18,   LDC2002T01,   LDC2003E07,   LDC2003E14,   LDC2003T17,
    LDC2004T07,   LDC2004T08,   LDC2005T06,   LDC2005T10,   LDC2005T34,
    LDC2006T04, LDC2007T09
[3] LDC2007T07

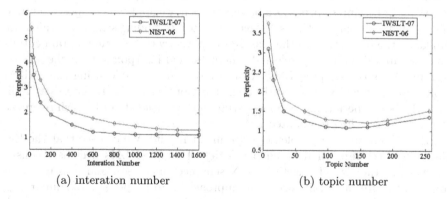

(a) interation number   (b) topic number

Fig. 1. Perplexity vs. the number of different iterations and topics on two LM training corpus

of topics starts to increase. However, after a certain point, the perplexity values start to increase. Based on the above experiments, we train our latent topic model using (a) 96 topics and 1000 iterations on IWSLT-07 and (b) 168 topics and 1400 iterations on NIST-06, respectively.

4.3 Perplexity Analysis

We randomly divide the development set into five subsets and conduct 5-fold cross-validation experiments. In each trial, we tune the parameter γ in Equation (1) with four of five subsets and then apply it to one remaining subset. The experiments reported below are those averaged over the five trials.

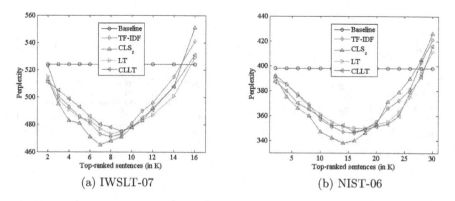

(a) IWSLT-07   (b) NIST-06

Fig. 2. English reference translation based perplexity of adapted LMs vs. the size of selected data on two test sets

For both IWSLT-07 and NIST-06, we estimate the generic 4-gram LM with the entire LM training corpus as a baseline. Then, we apply the proposed method and other traditional methods to select the top-N similar sentences which are similar to the test set, train the bias 4-gram LMs (with the same n-gram cutoffs tuned as above) with these selected sentences, and interpolate with the generic 4-gram LM as the adapted LMs. All the LMs are estimated using the SRILM toolkit[23]. Perplexity is a metric of LM performance, the lower values indicates the better performance. So we estimate the perplexity of English reference translation according to adapted LMs.

Fig. 2 shows the LM perplexity experiment results. We can see that the English reference translation based perplexity of adapted LMs decreases consistently when the size of selected top-N sentences increases, and also increases consistently after a certain size in all approaches. So proper size of similar sentences with the translation task make the LM perform well, but if too much noisy data take into the selected sentences, the performance become worse. Similar observations have been done by the previous work[1, 5]. The experiment results indicate that adapted LMs are significantly better predictors of the corresponding translation task at hand than the generic baseline LM.

4.4   Translation Experiments

To show the detailed performance of selected training data for LM adaptation in SMT, we carry out the later translation experiments with the lowest perplexity situation according to the above perplexity experiment, top 8K sentences on IWSLT-07 and top 16K sentences on NIST-06. We conduct translation experiments by HPB SMT[24] system, as to demonstrate the utility of LM adaptation in improving SMT performance by the BLEU[25] score, and use minimum error rate training[26] to tune the feature weights for maximum BLEU on the development set.

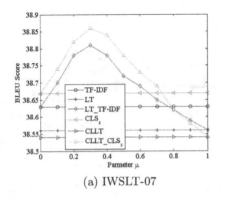

(a) IWSLT-07

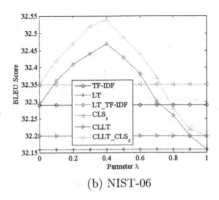

(b) NIST-06

Fig. 3. The impact of parameters μ and λ to SMT performance on two development sets

Fig. 3 illustrates the impact results of parameters μ and λ to SMT performance on two development sets. TF-IDF, CLSs, LT and CLLT are used for reference. We see that the combined model LT_TF-IDF and CLLT_CLS$_s$ perform better than each other alone when they are between 0 and 0.6, the best performance gains when they are 0.3 on IWSLT-07 and 0.4 on NIST-06, and we use these parameters on two test sets.

Table 1. SMT performance with different data selection models for LM adaptation on two test sets

Method	#	BLEU	
		IWSLT-07	NIST-06
Baseline	1	33.60	29.15
TF-IDF	2	34.14	29.78
CLS	3	34.08	29.73
CLS$_s$	4	34.18	29.84
LT	5	34.07	29.65
CLLT	6	34.05	29.69
LT_TF-IDF	7	**34.32**	**29.96**
CLLT_CLS$_s$	8	**34.37**	**30.03**

Table 1 shows the main SMT performance of LM adaptation. The improvements are statistically significant at the 95% confidence interval, and we see some clear trends:

(1) Our proposed CLS$_s$ performs better than CLS (row 4 vs. row 3), because of the added smoothing measure which makes similarity computation more accurate.

(2) Our proposed LT and CLLT do not outperform the baseline method TF-IDF (row 5 and row 6 vs. row 2). This demonstrates that the knowledge extracted from LT is not as effective as that extracted from TF-IDF. However, LT models word-topic information and word-distribution information from the whole LM training corpus. The knowledge extracted from LT is much noisier than that of TF-IDF. We suspect the above reason leads to the poor performance of LT and CLLT.

(3) Our proposed LT_TF-IDF significantly outperforms LT and TF-IDF (row 7 vs. row 2 and row 5), and CLLT_CLSs significantly outperforms CLLT and CLSs (row 8 vs. row 4 and row 6). This demonstrates that the latent word-topic and word-distribution information extracted from LT is complementary to the knowledge extracted from TF-IDF on data selection for LM adaptation.

(4) Our proposed CLLT_CLSs outperforms LT_TF-IDF (row 8 vs. row 7), and CLSs outperforms TF-IDF (row 4 vs. row 2). This demonstrates that the first pass translation hypotheses have lots of noisy data[27, 28], which mislead the selected similar sentences[9, 16, 27, 28], and take noisy data into the selected sentences. However, cross-lingual data selection model can avoid this problem,

and makes the sentence selection depend on the source input translation task directly.

5   Conclusions and Future Work

In this paper, we propose a novel latent topic based data selection model for LM adaptation in SMT. Furthermore, we expand it into cross-lingual data selection by a cross-lingual projection. Compared to the traditional approaches, our approach is more effective because it takes the distribution of words and the latent topic information into the similarity measure. Large-scale experiments conducted on LM perplexity and SMT performance demonstrate that our approach significantly outperforms the traditional methods.

There are some extensions of this work in the future. We will utilize our approach to mine large-scale corpora by distribute infrastructure system, and investigate the use of our approach for other domains, such as speech translation systems.

References

1. Eck, M., Vogel, S., Waibel, A.: Language model adaptation for statistical machine translation based on information retrieval. In: Proceedings of LREC, pp. 327–330 (2004)
2. Zhao, B., Eck, M., Vogel, S.: Language model adaptation for statistical machine translation with structured query models. In: Proceedings of COLING, pp. 411–417 (2004)
3. Kim, W.: Language model adaptation for automatic speech recognition and statistical machine translation. Ph.D. thesis, The Johns Hopkins University (2005)
4. Masskey, S., Sethy, A.: Resampling auxiliary data for language model adaptation in machine translation for speech. In: Proceedings of ICASSP, pp. 4817–4820 (2010)
5. Axelrod, A., He, X., Gao, J.: Domain adaptation via pseudo in-domain data selection. In: Proceedings of EMNLP, pp. 355–362 (2011)
6. Foster, G., Kuhn, R.: Mixture-model adaptation for SMT. In: Proceedings of ACL, pp. 128–135 (2007)
7. Snover, M., Dorr, B., Marcu, R.: Language and translation model adaptation using comparable corpora. In: Proceedings of EMNLP, pp. 857–866 (2008)
8. Ananthakrishnan, S., Prasad, R., Natarajan, P.: On-line language model biasing for statistical machine translation. In: Proceedings of ACL, pp. 445–449 (2011)
9. Tam, Y.-C., Lane, I., Schultz, T.: Bilingual-LSA based LM adaptation for spoken language translation. In: Proceedings of ACL, pp. 520–527 (2007)
10. Tam, Y.-C., Lane, I., Schultz, T.: Bilingual-LSA based adaptation for statistical machine translation. Machine Translation 21, 187–207 (2008)
11. Nanjo, H., Kawahara, T.: Unsupervised language model adaptation for lecture speech recognition. In: Proceedings of ICSLP (2002)
12. Nanjo, H., Kawahara, T.: Language model and speaking rate adaptation for spontaneous presentation speech recognition. IEEE Tran. SAP 12(4), 301–400 (2004)
13. Leeuwis, E., Federico, M., Cettolo, M.: Language modeling and transcription of the TED corpus lectures. In: Proceedings of ICASSP (2003)

14. Park, A., Hazen, T., Glass, J.: Automatic processing of audio lectures for information retrieval: vocabulary selection and language modeling. In: Proceedings of ICASSP (2005)
15. Tam, Y.-C., Schultz, T.: Dynamic language model adaptation using variational bayes inference. In: Proceedings of INTEERSPEECH, pp. 5–8 (2005)
16. Tam, Y.-C., Schultz, T.: Unsupervised language model adaptation using latent semantic marginals. In: Proceedings of ICSLP, pp. 2206–2209 (2006)
17. Heidel, A., Chang, H.-A., Lee, L.-S.: Language model adaptation using latent dirichlet allocation and an efficient topic inference algorithm. In: Proceedings of INTERSPEECH (2007)
18. Chen, K.-Y., Chiu, H.-S., Chen, B.: Latent topic modeling of word vicinity information for speech recognition. In: Proceedings of ICASSP, pp. 5394–5397 (2010)
19. (Paul) Hsu, B.-J., Glass, J.: Style & topic language model adaptation using HMM-LDA. In: Proceedings of EMNLP, pp. 373–381 (2006)
20. Press, W.H., Teukolsky, S.A., Vetterling, W.T., Flannery, B.P.: Numerical Recipes in C. Cambridge Univ. Press (1992)
21. Blei, D.M., Ng, A.Y., Jordan, M.I.: Latent dirichlet allocation. Journal of Machine Learning Research 3, 993–1022 (2003)
22. Gtiffiths, T.L.: Gibbs sampling in the generative model of latent dirichlet allocation (2002), http://wwwpsych.stanford.edu/gruffydd/cogsci02/lda.ps
23. Stolcke, A.: SRILM - An extensible language modeling toolkit. In: Proceedings of ICSLP, pp. 901–904 (2002)
24. Chiang, D.: A hierarchical phrase-based model for statistical machine translation. In: Proceedings of ACL (2005)
25. Papineni, K., Roukos, S., Ward, T., Zhu, W.: BLEU: A method for automatic evaluation of machine translation. In: Proceedings of ACL, pp. 311–318 (2002)
26. Och, F.J.: Minimum error rate training in statistical machine translation. In: Proceedings of ACL, pp. 160–167 (2003)
27. Wei, B., Pal, C.: Cross lingual adaptation: an experiment on sentiment classifications. In: Proceedings of ACL, pp. 258–262 (2010)
28. Lu, S., Wei, W., Fu, X., Xu, B.: Translation model based cross-lingual language model adaptation: from word models to phrase models. In: Proceedings of EMNLP-CoNLL, pp. 512–522 (2012)

Compact WFSA Based Language Model and Its Application in Statistical Machine Translation*

Xiaoyin Fu, Wei Wei, Shixiang Lu, Dengfeng Ke, and Bo Xu

Interactive Digital Media Technology Research Center
Institute of Automation, Chinese Academy of Sciences, Beijing, China
{xiaoyin.fu,wei.wei.media,shixiang.lu,dengfeng.ke,xubo}@ia.ac.cn

Abstract. The authors explore the fast query techniques for n-gram language model (LM) in statistical machine translation (SMT), and then propose a compact WFSA (weighted finite-state automaton) based LM motivated by the contextual features in process of model queries. It is demonstrated that the query based on WFSA can effectively avoid the redundant queries and accelerate the query speed. Furthermore, it is revealed that investigating a simple caching techni que can further speed up the query. The experiment results show that this method can finally speed up the LM query by 75% in relative. With the LM order increasing, the performance benefits by WFSA will be much more significant.

Keywords: N-gram Language Model, WFSA, Fast Query, SMT.

1 Introduction

N-gram language model is one of the important components in modern statistical machine translation systems. It helps to generate the reasonable translations which are corresponding to grammar and common usage of natural language. Using higher order LM models and more training data can significantly improve the translation performances [1]. However, decoding a single sentence can trigger hundreds of thousands of queries to the LM. Therefore, the LM must be fast for the actual SMT systems. Previous proposed techniques [2,3,4] employed the LM with trade-offs among time, space and accuracy. In this paper, we try to deal with this case by a compact WFSA based LM.

The weighted finite-state automaton has been introduced successfully in many natural language processing applications, as many of them have been possible to break down, both conceptually and literally, into cascades of simpler probabilistic finite-state transition [5]. We consider the LM query process as a sequence of state transitions in WFSA, which draws a uniform framework [6] for LM without almost any redundant operations and speeds up the queries substantially. Our WFSA based LM is organized with a *trie* structure which makes the LM stored in a compact way. We also introduce a simple LM cache by hash table to further

---

* This work was supported by 863 program in China (No. 2011AA01A207).

M. Zhou et al. (Eds.): NLPCC 2012, CCIS 333, pp. 154–163, 2012.

speed up the queries. The results show that our method can finally improve the query speed by about 75%.

2 Related Work

The current research efforts to speed up the query typically follow the context features of query process in n-gram LM [7,8,9]. Pauls [7] presented several language model implementations that were highly compact and fast to query. They introduced a language model that took a word-and-context encoding for the suffix of the original query to accelerate the scrolling queries. They also exploited the scrolling nature of queries in the *n*-grams encoded *tries* with last-rest instead of the reverse direction, although they found the speed improvement from switching to a first-rest encoding was modest. This has also been exploited by Li [8], who proposed equivalent language model states to explore the back-off property of *n*-gram language model. Heafield [9] presented a KenLM that implemented two data structures, the PROBING data structure and TRIE data structure, for efficient language model queries.

Mathias [10] and Kolak [11] captured the nature language model with a WFSA in speech translation. They used the concept of WFSA to represent the knowledge in a uniform, and broke the complex problems into a cascade of simple WFSA. Nasr [12] introduced the WFSA to construct a new kind of LM by several local models and a general model using a greedy finite state partial parser. Chiang [6] investigated Bayesian inference for WFSA and demonstrated the genericity of this framework which improved performance over EM. Most of current studies reduced the WFSA by a standard operation as minimization. Our WFSA based LM is designed with *trie* structure, which has already stored the LM in a compact way.

The rest of this paper is organized as follows: Sect. 3 introduces the motivation for our approach with the basic concept of LM and WFSA; Sect. 4 describes the system implementation, including the data structure of WFSA based LM and query method. Sect. 5 reports and analyzes the experimental results; and the conclusions are given in Sect. 6.

3 Motivation

3.1 N-gram Language Model

Generally, statistical language model are used to assign probabilities to string of words or tokens. Let w_1^L denote a string of L tokens over a fixed vocabulary. The n-gram language model assigns a probability to w_1^L according to

$$P(w_1^L) = \prod_{i=1}^{L} P(w_i|w_1^{i-1}) \approx \prod_{i=1}^{L} \hat{P}(w_i|w_{i-n+1}^{i-1}) \tag{1}$$

where the approximation reflects a Markov assumption that only the most recent $n-1$ tokens will be considered when predicting the next word.

The smoothing techniques [13,14] are usually introduced with back-off to avoid the sparse data problem in modeling the LM. The context-dependent back-off is used as follows

$$P(w_i|w_{i-n+1}^{i-1}) = \begin{cases} \pi(w_{i-n+1}^i) & w_{i-n+1}^i \in LM \\ \lambda(w_{i-n+1}^{i-1}) \cdot P(w_{i-n+2}^i) & \text{others} \end{cases} \quad (2)$$

where $\pi(\cdot)$ are pre-computed and stored probabilities, and $\lambda(\cdot)$ are back-off weights of the history. The LM file contains the parameter $\pi(\cdot)$ for each listed n-gram, and the parameters $\pi(\cdot)$ and $\lambda(\cdot)$ for each listed m-gram, $1 \leq m < n$; for unlisted m-grams, $\lambda(\cdot) = 1.0$ by definition.

3.2   Query Problems in N-gram LM

The state-of-art language model toolkit SRILM [15] uses *trie* to organize the n-grams. Querying in *trie* can be usually composed by two types: forward query and back-off query. However, both of the two query types will be a waste of time as: 1) if the forward query reaches the leaf node of *trie*, it has to do the forward query from the beginning of *trie* when the next word comes in. 2) if the n-gram is not involved in the LM, it has to do the back-off query still from the beginning of *trie*. Thus many nodes in *trie* are traversed with out any use.

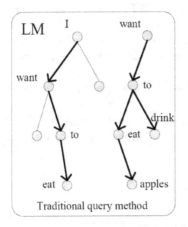 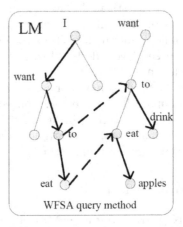

Traditional query method   WFSA query method

Fig. 1. The comparison of 4-gram LM query methods for "I want to eat apples" and "I want to drink"

A sample of traditional LM query is shown on the left side in Fig.1. The arrows in *trie* represent the query tracks. Although we only need the probability of want to eat apples when calculating the 4-gram LM of "I want to eat apples", the nodes such as "want", "want to" and "want to eat" are traversed completely useless. Moreover, because of the fragment "I want to drink does not involved in LM, it has to query the sub fragment "want to drink" according to (2). Thus the nodes "want" and "want to" still traversed uselessly.

We do not consider the query in LM as a random procedure but a continuous process. Still take the case in Fig.1 as an example. If we use a roll-back pointer to guide the query directly to an equivalent state [8], the next query can simply proceed by only one search. This gives us the instinct to use a WFSA to solve this problem. Figure 1 at the right side shows the query method in a WFSA based LM. We can see the WFSA will also speed up the back-off queries by the introduction of roll-back pointer. Thus both of the two query problems in LM can be successfully resolved with the concept of WFSA.

4   *N*-gram Language Model Based on WFSA

4.1   WFSA

A WFSA is conceived as an abstract automaton with a finite number of states. The state it is in at any given time is called the current state. It can change from one state to another when initiated by a triggering event or condition which is called the transition, and carry out weights for each transition.

Normally, a typical WFSA can be assigned by a 5-turple $M = (Q, \Sigma, I, F, \delta)$, where Q is a set of states, $I \subseteq Q$ is a set of initial states, $F \subseteq Q$ is a set of final states, Σ is the alphabet which represents the input and output labels, and $\delta \subseteq Q \times (\Sigma \cup \varepsilon)$ is the transition relation. A transition is labeled with ε if it can be traversed without input symbol. The label w_i in a input string L is accepted by the automation M is defined to be

$$L(M) \equiv \{w_i \in \Sigma, q \in Q | \delta(q, w_i) \cap F \neq \emptyset\} \tag{3}$$

The state is traversed according to the input labels until it reaches one of the final states. For each transition step, there will be an output which represents the weighted element.

4.2   WFSA Based LM Structure

We use *trie* as the basic structure of our compact WFSA language model. The nodes in *trie* are the set of finite state Q, and the root of *trie* is the initial state I. Each node of *trie* except the root is the set of final state F. The input label Σ is the alphabet of input sentences, and the weights are the probabilities for n-gram and back-off. The transition relation δ is composed by forward transition T_f and roll-back transition T_b. The forward transition traverses along the path of *trie* which is corresponding to forward query and the roll-back transition traverses with the roll-back pointer which points to the equivalent position in *trie*. It should be noted that the roll-back transition triggers spontaneously without any input when it reaches to the leaves of *trie* or carries out back-off queries, which represents the ε transition in WFSA.

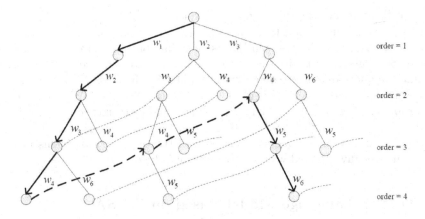

Fig. 2. The structure of a 4-gram WFSA based LM

Figure 2 shows an example of 4-gram LM based on the compact WFSA. Nodes in the *trie* are based on the sorted arrays [16] with probability, back-off, and an index (the solid line in Fig.2) into higher order of n-gram LM. Different with the previous work, the nodes of our WFSA based LM store a roll-back pointer (the dash line in Fig.2) for the m-order ($3 \leq m \leq n$). It is just because of these roll-back pointers that make our LM act as WFSA, which will be illustrated later in the next section. The 2-order omits roll-back pointer to 1-order as it can be easily queried by the vocabulary identifier. The nodes of w_5 at the 3-order and w_6 at the 4-order are pointing to the corresponding equivalents which is not shown in Fig.2. Notice the roll-back pointer in w_6 at the 4-order can safely point to the one at the 2-order, for the back-off probability is restricted to 1.0 if the direct back-off is not involved as described in Sect 2.1.

4.3   Query with WFSA Based LM

For a given input of word sequence w_1^L, the query process of LM can be seen as a series of state transitions based on WFSA. Take the 4-gram language model in Fig.2 as an example. The transition of query state is triggered by each input word $w_i(1 \leq i \leq 6)$ in w_1^6, and each state is corresponding to the node in *trie*. The state transition process is shown in Fig.3. The state s_i^j is represented by the node in LM, and i and j are the beginning and ending identifier of query fragments respectively.

It can be found that each transition triggered with the input of word (or *null*). The forward transition T_f is triggered for each of the input words. If the state is not involved in LM, the query process will continue traversing to the current state and trigger a roll-back transition T_b, until it successfully makes a forward transition. The roll-back transition T_b is just corresponding to the ε transition in WFSA.

The example of LM query process in Fig.3 is processed as follows: After initializing the query process, the current query state firstly traverses to the initial

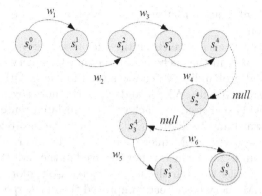

Fig. 3. N-gram LM query based on WFSA

state s_0^0. Then the state traverses forward to s_1^1, for the fragment w_1 exists in the language model. The same situation happens when w_2 and w_3 input, and the current state has reached s_1^3. Then the state transfers to s_1^4 and rolls back to s_2^4 spontaneously according to the roll-back pointer as it has reached the leaf node of *trie*. When word w_5 inputs, the state continues rolling back to s_3^4, as the state s_2^5 does not exist, until it traverses forward to the state s_3^5. At last, the current state gets to the final state s_3^6 and quits the query process after the last word w_6 inputs.

The pseudo code of query WFSA based LM is shown as follows:

Algorithm. Query WFSA based LM

Input: word string w_1^L
Output: $LMscore$ of w_1^L
for $i = 1$ to L **do**
   while(1)
      if $w_{i-n+1}^i \in LM$
         $LMscore * = \pi(w_{i-n+1}^i)$ and **break**
      else
         $LMscore * = \lambda(w_{i-n+1}^i)$
      end while
   end for
return $LMscore$

4.4   Hash Cache

To make further speed up of queries, we add a simple hash cache to our WFSA based LM to cache the repetitive queries when decoding a sentence in SMT system. Our cache uses an array of key-value pairs with the size fixed to 2^b for some integer b(we used 24). We choose the current state and input word as the key of our hash table. We use a b-bit hash function to compute the address in an array where we will place an output state and the carried out probability for each state transition.

For each query of the cache, we check the address of a key given by the b-bits hash. If the key located in the cache array matches the query key, then we get the output state and probability which are stored in cache. Otherwise, we fetch the probability from LM with WFSA and place the new key and value in the cache. The cache will be cleared for each of the translated sentences.

Both of the forward and back-off query speed can be improved by the cache as there are many repetitive LM queries in SMT. Moreover, when calculating the probability for an n-gram which is not involved in the LM, the back-off must perform multiple queries to fetch the necessary back-off information, although the WFSA based LM query has already improved the query speed substantially. Our cache retains the fully results of these calculations and thus saves additional computations in back-off queries.

5   Experiments and Results

5.1   Setup

We used the state-of-art hierarchical phrase-based translation system [17] as our baseline, and test the LM query efficiency on two Chinese-to-English translation tasks: IWSLT-07 (dialogue domain) and NIST-06 (news domain). The test sets of the two domains are IWSLT-07 test sets and NIST-06 test sets, which contain 489 sentences and 1664 sentences separately. We obtained the translation models (TM) following the same constraints as in Chiang [18]. We trained the 4-gram and 5-gram language models using SRILM and then converted them to our WFSA structure before decoding. The training corpora of the experiments are listed in Table 1.

Table 1. Training corpus for LM and TM

Tasks	Model	Parallel sentences	Chinese words	English words
IWSLT-07	TM[1]	0.38M	3.0M	3.1M
	LM[2]	1.3M	—	15.2M
NIST-06	TM[3]	3.4M	64M	70M
	LM[4]	143.M	—	377M

---

[1] The parallel corpus of BTEC (Basic Traveling Expression Corpus) and CJK (China-Japan-Korea corpus).

[2] The English corpus of BTEC+CJK+CWMT2008.

[3] LDC2002E18,   LDC2002T01,   LDC2003E07,   LDC2003T17,   LDC2004T07, LDC2004T08,   LDC2005T06,   LDC2005T10,   LDC2005T34,   LDC2006T04, LDC2007T09.

[4] LDC2007T07.

5.2   Results

Storage Space Experiments. We tested our implementation of WFSA based LM (**WFSA**) on the two tasks. Notice that there are no additional nodes in *trie* structure. For each node, there are only 5 additional bytes comparing with the **SRILM**. The bytes are composed by a 4 bytes integer and a 1 bytes character, which represent the roll-back pointer. Thus, the size of WFSA based LM is corresponding to the node number of *trie*, which makes it compact. The results are shown in Table 2.

Table 2. The comparison of LM size between SRILM and WFSA

Tasks	N-grams	**SRILM**(Mb)	**WFSA**(Mb)	$\Delta(\%)$
IWSLT-07	4	65.7	89.1	35.6
	5	89.8	119.5	33.1
NIST-06	4	860.3	1190.4	38.4
	5	998.5	1339.7	34.2

In Table 2, the storage sizes of WFSA based LM increase about 35% than the **SRILM** in the two domains. It is because of the extra bytes that keep the roll-back pointer in the *trie* node. However, the increment is acceptable as it is linearly dependent with the nodes of *trie*.

Query Speed Experiments. We used the 4-gram and 5-gram LM in IWSLT-07 and NIST-06 to test the query efficiency. We measured the time[5] required to perform each query in actual translation using the **SRILM** as our baseline. Then we measured the time of using WFSA based LM (**WFSA**) and introduced our cache to WFSA (**WFSA+cache**) to speed up the query. Times were averaged over 3 runs on the same machine. The results are shown in Table 3.

As expected, the use of **WFSA** speeds up the LM query substantially. The query speed in both domains has been improved by 57.1% and 59.5% in 4-gram LM, and 67.4% and 68.4% in 5-gram LM separately. The improvement of query speed in 5-gram LM is much better than 4-gram by about 10%. It suggests that our implementation of WFSA is suitable for higher n-grams. Although the WFSA has already improved the speed, it can be found our **WFSA+cache** queries more effectively. The query speed can be further improved by the introduction of cache in all of the translation tasks. The final implementation of our **WFSA+cache** can speed up the query by about 75%.

---

[5] All experiments were performed on a DELL server, with an Intel Xeon 5130 CPU running at 2.00 GHz and 8M of cache. The operation system is Ubuntu 7.10.

Table 3. The comparison of query time with different methods

N-grams	Methods	IWSLT-07(s)	NIST-06(s)
	SRILM	163	15433
4	**WFSA**	70	6251
	WFSA+cache	42	3907
	SRILM	261	25172
5	**WFSA**	85	7944
	WFSA+cache	59	6128

Analysis. We measured the probability of repetitive queries and back-off queries in 4-gram LM that occurred during decoding, which had a close relationship with our WFSA based LM. The results on the two tasks are shown in Table 4.

Table 4. The probability of back-off and repetitive query in 4-gram LM

Tasks	Back-off	Repetitive
IWSLT-07	60.5%	95.5%
NIST-06	60.3%	96.4%

It can be seen that back-off queries are widely existed in statistical machine translation and as many as about 60% in 4-gram queries are proceeding for back-off query. Notice that the probabilities of back-off queries are similar in both tasks, which are corresponding to the increment of query efficiency. It suggests that our model can effectively accelerate the back-off queries.

Although decoding a single sentence can trigger a huge number of LM queries, it can be found most of these queries are repetitive. Therefore, keeping the results of LM queries in a cache can be effective at reducing overall queries. This has been confirmed by our experimental results in the query speed experiments above.

6 Conclusions

We have presented a new method for faster LM implementation based on compact WFSA. We consider the LM query process as a series of state transitions with WFSA according to the context character of LM. This method improves the query speed effectively with a compact LM in size for SMT system. We have also described a simple caching technique which leads to performance improvements in over all decoding time. Our WFSA based language model can not only be used in the faster query of LM in SMT, but also be suitable in other nature language processing, such as speech recognition and information retrieval, etc.

References

1. Thorsten, B., Popat, A.C., Peng, X., Franz, J.O., Jeffrey, D.: Large Language Models in Machine Translation. In: Proceedings of EMNLP-CoNLL, pp. 858–867 (2007)
2. Goodman, J.: A Bit of Progress in Language Modeling. Technical report. Microsoft Research (2001)
3. Marcello, F., Mauro, C.: Efficient handling of n-gram language models for statistical machine translation. In: Proceedings of the 2nd Workshop on Statistical Machine Translation, pp. 88–95 (2007)
4. David, T., Miles, O.: Randomised language modelling for statistical machine translation. In: Proceedings of the ACL, pp. 512–519 (2007)
5. Kevin, K., Jonathan, G.: An overview of probabilistic tree transducers for na tural language processing. In: Proceedings of CICLing (2005)
6. David, C., Jonathan, G., Kevin, K., Adam, P., Sujith, R.: Bayesian inference for Finite-State transducers. In: Proceedings of the NAACL, pp. 447–455 (2010)
7. Adam, P., Dan, K.: Faster and Smaller N-Gram Language Models. In: Proceedings of the ACL, pp. 258–267 (2011)
8. Zhifei, L., Sanjeev, K.: A scalable decoder for parsing- based machine translation with equivalent language model state maintenance. In: Proceedings of the Second Workshop on Syntax and Structure in Statistical Translation, pp. 10–18 (2008)
9. Kenneth, H.: KenLM: Faster and Smaller Language Model Queries. In: Proceedings of the 6th Workshop on Statistical Machine Translation, pp. 187–197 (2011)
10. Lambert, M., William, B.: Statistical phrase-based speech translation. In: Proceedings of ICASSP (2006)
11. Okan, K., Willian, B., Philip, R.: A generative probabilistic OCR model for NLP applications. In: Proceedings of the HLT-NAACL (2003)
12. Alexis, N., Yannick, E., Frédéric, B., Thierry, S., de Renato, M.: A language model combining N-grams and stochastic finite state automata. In: Proceedings of Eurospeech (1999)
13. Reinhard, K., Hermann, N.: Improved backing-off for m-gram language modeling. In: Proceedings of the IEEE International Conference on Acoustics, Speech, and Signal Processing, pp. 181–184 (1995)
14. Slava, M.K.: Estimation of probabilities from sparse data for the language model component of a speech recognizer. IEEE Transactions on Acoustics, Speech and Signal Processing, 400–401 (1987)
15. Andreas, S.: SRILM: An extensible language modeling toolkit. In: Proceedings of Interspeech (2002)
16. Edward, W., Bhiksha, R.: Quantization based language model compression. In: Proceedings of Eurospeech (2001)
17. David, C.: A hierarchical phrase-based model for statistical machine translation. In: Proceedings of ACL, pp. 263–270 (2005)
18. David, C.: Hierarchical phrase-based translation. Computational Linguistics 33(2), 201–228 (2007)

A Comparative Study on Discontinuous Phrase Translation

Jiajun Zhang and Chenqqing Zong

NLPR, Institute of Automation Chinese Academy of Sciences, Beijing, China
{jjzhang,cqzong}@nlpr.ia.ac.cn

Abstract. Many research works have reported discontinuous phrase translation can significantly improve translation quality, but experiments are conducted in only one translation direction (e.g. Chinese-to-English) with only one language pair. Thus, two questions remain that whether the discontinuous rules are always much helpful in different language pairs? Furthermore, what kind of discontinuous rules (e.g. source-side discontinuity or target-side discontinuity) contributes most to the performance improvement? To answer these two questions, this paper conducts a comparative study on the contribution of different kinds of discontinuous rules in both translation directions with various language pairs. Then, with this comparative study, this paper proposes a role-based rule filtering strategy to filter the large amount of discontinuous rules that contribute very little to translation quality.

Keywords: statistical machine translation, discontinuous phrases, role-based rule filtering.

1   Introduction

On one hand, many research works[1,2,4,7,10,11] reported discontinuous phrase translation significantly improves the translation quality in statistical machine translation (SMT). However, nearly all the experiments are conducted only in one translation direction (e.g. Chinese-to-English) with only one language pair. Thus, it remains an interesting question whether the discontinuous rules always have a big contribution in different language pairs. This paper plans to answer this question using extensive experiments.

On the other hand, several researchers found that different kinds of discontinuous rules (e.g. source-side discontinuity or target-side discontinuity, Figure 1 for example) contribute to the translation quality quite differently and they reported the finding that source-side discontinuity plays a much more important role than target-side discontinuity in Chinese-to-English translation. This finding is reported at least by two related studies, i.e. [4] and [11]. Specifically, [11] used a syntax-based statistical machine translation system that aims at better translating non-continuous phrases. [4] extended a traditional phrase-based system for discontinuous phrase translation. They made great efforts to translate target-side discontinuity but they disappointedly found that

M. Zhou et al. (Eds.): NLPCC 2012, CCIS 333, pp. 164–175, 2012.

target-side discontinuity is much less useful in Chinese-to-English translation. They also reported the same finding using a hierarchical phrase-based system Joshua[6]. It seems that the finding is independent of translation models. Thus, there is another interesting question whether source-side discontinuity is much more useful than target-side discontinuity in the inverse direction English-to-Chinese translation and in other language pairs? This paper is going to give the answer with comprehensive experiments.

Source-side discontinuity:

在_zài X 中_zhōng → in X

Target-side discontinuity:
考虑_kǎolǜ X → take X into account

Fig. 1. Examples for source-side discontinuity and target-side discontinuity

In statistical machine translation (SMT), translation rules increase dramatically if discontinuity is allowed. Therefore, if we know some kinds of discontinuous rules are useless, we can remove large amount of such redundant rules without performance loss. Correspondingly, we propose a role-based rule filtering strategy.

2   Related Work

Our work described in this paper includes three parts: the first one and also the most important one is to study the relationship between source discontinuity and target discontinuity; the second one is investigating the contribution of discontinuity translation in different language pairs; and the third one is designing a role-based rule filtering strategy.

Relationship between source discontinuity and target discontinuity [11] tried to model discontinuity translation in tree sequence based model and found that source discontinuity is much more effective than target discontinuity in Chinese-to-English translation. [4] also discovered this phenomenon in their extended phrase-based model for non-continuous phrase translation. They meanwhile pointed out the phenomenon exists in hierarchical phrase-based model too. The reason has not been clearly explained.

Contribution of discontinuity translation in different language pairs [8] and [2] suggested that the ability to translate discontinuous phrases is important to model translation. [4,7,11] empirically showed that discontinuity translation indeed leads to substantial improvements. However, they all tested the discontinuity translation in only one translation direction for one language pair. It is worth to study whether it is much useful in other language pairs.

Rule filtering strategy [12] proposed a count-based rule filtering approach which discards rules occurring less than a minimum count. [9] removed those rules whose target parts are not well-formed dependency trees. [5] presented a pattern-based rule filtering method which considers the possible 66 rule patterns.

3   Discontinuous Rule Classification

In order to deeply investigate the discontinuous rules, we first classify them into different kinds. Generally, the discontinuous rules are classified into source-side discontinuity and target-side discontinuity. We can see that these two classes are overlapped. To have a finer classification, we can divide discontinuous rules into three kinds: source-only discontinuity (target is contiguous), target-only discontinuity (source is contiguous), and both-side discontinuity. Table 1 gives the classification details of hierarchical rules[2].

Table 1. Three Categories of Discontinuities. SDR, TDR and BDR denote source-side, target-side, and both-side discontinuous rules respectively

Categories	Rule's source	Rule's target
SDR	uXv $uXvX$ $XuXv$ $uXvXw$	Contiguous ones
TDR	Contiguous ones	$u'Xv'$ $u'Xv'X$ $Xu'Xv'$ $u'Xv'Xw'$ $u'XXv'$
BDR	uXv $uXvX$ $XuXv$ $uXvXw$	$u'Xv'$ $u'Xv'X$ $Xu'Xv'$ $u'Xv'Xw'$ $u'XXv'$

However, we still think this classification is not sufficient because most of both-side discontinuities can be obtained by combining two contiguous rules. For example, the rule $X \rightarrow \langle uX_1 vX_2, u'X_1 v'X_2 \rangle$ [1] is the concatenation of $X \rightarrow \langle uX, u'X \rangle$ and $X \rightarrow \langle vX, v'X \rangle$ if u is aligned to u' and v is aligned to v'. In order to make a strict classification, we define the *strict both-side discontinuity* with word alignments:

Definition: Given a rule $X \rightarrow \langle \gamma, \alpha \rangle$ which is both-side discontinuity with word alignment between γ and α, if a terminal element in one side is aligned to two or

---

[1] u, v, u', v' are terminal strings, we consider them as terminal element.

more terminal elements in the other side, then the both-side discontinuity is a strict both-side discontinuity.

For example, for the rule $X \rightarrow \langle uX_1 \, vX_2, u'X_1v'X_2 \rangle$, if u is aligned to both u' and v', we consider this rule as a strict both-side discontinuous rule.

4   Comparison Study on Discontinuous Phrase Translation

4.1   Experimental Set-Up

The translation system we use in this paper is an open-source hierarchical phrase-based system Joshua[6]. We conduct our experiments on four language pairs: Chinese-English, Spanish-English, French-English, and German-English. For Chinese-English, the training data, extracted from LDC corpora, consists of about 1.92 million parallel pairs. For the direction Chinese-to-English, the tuning set is NIST2006 test data and the test sets include NIST2005 test data (test-1) and NIST2008 test data (test-2). For the direction English-to-Chinese, we split NIST2008 test data into two parts: the first 800 sentences are used as tuning set and the rest 1059 sentences are used as test set (test-1). Another test set (test-2) uses NIST2005 Chinese-to-English first reference as source, and original source as reference. A 5-gram language model is built on the target part in both directions.

For other three language pairs, all data are from the fourth workshop of machine translation[2] (WMT09). The translation model is trained with Europarl corpus: about 1.48M sentence pairs for French-English and German-English, and 1.47M for Spanish-English. We train the 5-gram language models on the large monolingual data: 227M words for German, 218M words for French, 94M for Spanish and 549M for English. The tuning set is *Devset2009-a* consisting of 1025 sentences, the first test set (test-1) is *Devset2009-b* with 1026 sentences, and the second test set (test-2) is the test data of WMT09 including 2525 sentences.

The word alignment is obtained with GIZA++ and case-insensitive BLEU-4 is employed to evaluate the performance of translation results.

To have a detailed comparison, we design six groups of experiments according to the rules that are applied in translation: 1) only with contiguous rules (CR); 2) CR plus source-only discontinuous rules (+SDR); 3) CR plus target-only discontinuous rules (+TDR); 4) CR plus both-side discontinuous rules (+BDR); 5) CR plus both-side discontinuous rules excluding strict both-side discontinuous rules (-SBDR) and 6) with all rules (ALL). The 5th configuration is designed to test the importance of strict both-side discontinuity.

Tables 2-5 report all the translation results in four language pairs. The **bold** figures in tables just show which one, of source discontinuity and target discontinuity, leads to bigger gains.

---

[2] http://www.statmt.org/wmt09/

Table 2. Results of Chinese-English translation

gaps	C→E			E→C		
	tuning	test-1	test-2	tuning	test-1	test-2
CR	28.76	28.07	21.78	30.44	30.21	25.44
+SDR	**29.46**	**28.65**	**22.24**	30.60	30.22	25.54
+TDR	28.86	28.26	21.90	**30.94**	**30.75**	**25.73**
+BDR	29.31	28.78	22.33	30.99	30.85	25.62
-SBDR	29.05	28.37	22.06	30.71	30.64	25.51
ALL	29.69	28.87	22.68	31.47	31.31	25.89

Table 3. Results of French-English translation

gaps	F→E			E→F		
	tuning	test-1	test-2	tuning	test-1	test-2
CR	22.37	22.58	21.94	21.95	22.05	21.36
+SDR	**22.54**	**22.70**	22.01	21.93	21.94	21.10
+TDR	22.51	22.53	**22.05**	**22.06**	**22.00**	**21.35**
+BDR	22.61	22.68	21.98	22.27	22.11	21.53
-SBDR	22.62	22.63	21.91	22.10	22.01	21.46
ALL	22.58	22.72	21.80	22.24	22.08	21.50

Table 4. Results of German-English translation

gaps	G→E			E→G		
	tuning	test-1	test-2	tuning	test-1	test-2
CR	18.25	19.05	15.83	12.78	13.02	10.82
+SDR	**18.50**	**19.44**	**15.85**	**12.97**	13.20	11.00
+TDR	18.41	19.15	15.70	12.91	**13.24**	**11.15**
+BDR	18.51	19.42	15.69	12.82	13.32	11.24
-SBDR	18.43	19.20	15.61	12.72	13.20	11.06
ALL	18.60	19.45	15.92	13.03	13.18	10.98

Table 5. Results of Spanish-English translation

gaps	S→E			E→S		
	tuning	test-1	test-2	tuning	test-1	test-2
CR	23.62	23.50	22.17	23.10	22.95	21.14
+SDR	23.56	23.47	22.07	**23.24**	**23.07**	**21.37**
+TDR	**23.81**	**23.62**	**22.20**	23.17	22.95	21.31
+BDR	23.78	23.55	22.40	23.63	23.15	21.38
-SBDR	23.67	23.38	22.15	23.38	23.12	21.29
ALL	23.59	23.46	22.03	23.50	23.13	21.44

4.2   Contribution of Discontinuous Rules in Different Language Pairs

From Table 2, we can easily see that translation with all discontinuous rules (in ALL lines) substantially outperforms translation with only contiguous rules (in CR lines) and the gains are up to absolute 1.1 BLEU score in English-to-Chinese test-1 set. It verifies that discontinuous rules are very important in Chinese-English translation. It is in line with the conclusions of previous works[4,7,11] in which they only tested on Chinese-to-English translation. However, when coming to European language pairs, the discontinuous rules are much less effective. The best improvement is only 0.4 BLEU point on German-to-English test-1 set. Furthermore, translation with discontinuous rules sometimes even decreases the translation quality (such as that on Spanish-to-English translation). We speculate that the systematic divergency between Chinese and English is much larger than that between these European language pairs; thus the complicated translation rules such as discontinuous rules are very helpful in Chinese-English translation while these rules are not much necessary in European language pairs. In sum, the experimental results show that discontinuous phrase translation does not always contributes much to translation quality in any language pair.

4.3   Source Discontinuity vs. Target Discontinuity

If we focus on the bold figures in Tables 2-5, we can easily see that source discontinuity is not always more helpful than target discontinuity. In Chinese-English translation, the interesting discovery is obvious that the source discontinuity wins in Chinese-to-English translation while the target discontinuity wins in the inverse English-to-Chinese translation. In other three language pairs (Tables 3-5), it also seems if source discontinuity is more helpful in one translation direction, the target discontinuity is more useful in the inverse translation direction (test-2 set in F→E and tuning set in E→G are two exceptions), although the contribution difference between source discontinuity and target discontinuity is not significant. We believe that it is because the discontinuous rules do not contribute much in these three language pairs essentially.

4.4   Contribution of Both-side Discontinuity

Both-side discontinuity does not affect the contribution difference between source and target discontinuity since it has the same effect on both of them. We can see from the tables that both-side discontinuity always improves translation quality (+BDR lines in tables). To figure out how much of the improvement does the strict both-side discontinuity contribute, we re-train and re-test without the strict both-side discontinuities (-SBDR lines in tables). The performance decreases for the lack of SBDR in all cases. This indicates that the strict both-side discontinuity is important though the rules of this kind only account for a small part (less than 1/10 of BDR). By contrast, BDR excluding SBDR occupy a quite large part of all rules but the contribution is relatively small; therefore, lots of such rules of the kind are incline to be filtered.

5   Role-Based Rule Filtering

Knowing the contribution of different kinds of discontinuities can give us a lot of inspiration. For example, since we have known the target discontinuity is more effective in English-to-Chinese translation, we can specially handle the target discontinuity with syntactic or semantic information to further improve the translation quality. On the contrary, there will be little value to deal with target discontinuity with great efforts in Chinese-to-English translation.

The most direct idea we may think of is to filter the rules which have nearly no contribution to translation quality. Just take a look at Table 5 for Spanish-to-English translation, we can use the +TDR configuration as the best setting which obtains nearly the best performance but only contains less than 30% of all the rules. In the rest of this paper, we will introduce a role-based rule filtering strategy.

5.1   Rule Classification by Role

The number of translation rules extracted by the hierarchical systems is usually extremely large. Even though we only keep those which are relevant to the test set, the number of rules is still several millions. For example, the initial rule set for English-to-French test data exceeds 6 million rules. Thus, it is still a challenge to reduce the rule set without decreasing translation quality in order to improve the memory efficiency and speed up the decoder. Each rule filtering method should first classify the translation rules and then throw the rules of some classes away with specific strategy. [12] classified the rules based on their counts and removed the rules which occur less than a minimum count (such as 3). [9] divided the rules into two kinds: one must be well-formed dependency tree in the target part, the other is the rest. They only retain the rules of the first kind. [5] proposed a pattern-based rule classification. A rule pattern is composed by source format (terminal elements, non-terminal elements, and their order) and target format. For example, $\langle uX_1vX_2, u'X_1v'X_2 \rangle$ and $\langle uX, u'X \rangle$ are two patterns. In total, there are 66 possible rule patterns. They discarded the rules of patterns which do not reduce translation quality.

In this paper, we propose a role-based rule classification. The role here means the function that the rules show in translation. In principle, the rules in each translation model can be divided into two functions: one is for phrase translation; and the other is for phrase reordering. For hierarchical phrase-based models and syntax-based models, the phrase translation rules can be further classified into continuous phrase rules and discontinuous rules. Additionally, the composed rules[3] are sometimes useful. Based on the analysis and our classification of discontinuous rules, we partition the hierarchical rules into seven categories: (1) Lexical phrase rules (LPR); (2) Reordering rules (RR); (3) Source discontinuous rules (SDR); (4) Target discontinuous rules (TDR); (5) Strict both-side discontinuous rules (SBDR); (6) One non-terminal composed rules (CR1NT); (7) Two non-terminal composed rules (CR2NT)

The lexical phrase rules are just the rules without non-terminals. The rules, such as $X \rightarrow \langle uX, Xu' \rangle$ and $X \rightarrow \langle uX_1vX_2, u'X_2v'X_1 \rangle$, are reordering rules. We have detailed the meaning of the three kinds of discontinuous rules in previous sections. One non-terminal composed rules are the rules with one non-terminal but do not represent reordering and discontinuity translation, i.e. the rule $X \rightarrow \langle uX, u'X \rangle$ which can be concatenated by lexical phrase rule $X \rightarrow \langle u, u' \rangle$ and the general glue rule. Two non-terminal composed rules are similar to CR1NT. It is worth noting that RR and SBDR maybe overlap, i.e. if source terminals and target terminals in $X \rightarrow \langle uX_1vX_2, u'X_2v'X_1 \rangle$ cross linked, the rule also belongs to SBDR. To enable the role-based rule classification to form a partition of the rules, we consider the rules of this kind as SBDR.

With the role-based rule classification, we have investigated which kind rules are essential and which ones can be removed safely. The premise of our filtering strategy is that some kinds of rules are useless to translation quality in certain language pairs.

5.2 Filtering Strategy

Because we have known the contribution of different kinds of discontinuous rules, we can design different rule filtering strategies according to the different language pairs. For example, in Spanish-to-English translation, the +TDR configuration can be used as our basis for filtering since it has nearly the same performance with that using all rules and meanwhile excludes more than 70% rules. However, in Chinese-to-English translation, the ALL configuration cannot be substituted. Thus, in this case, we adopt the leave-one-out (LOO) method to test the effectiveness of each kind rule. In this subsection, the Spanish-to-English and Chinese-to-English translations (test-1 data set used as the test set) are used as instances to introduce the filtering strategies.

Spanish-to-English: Since the CR configuration in Table 2-5 includes LPR, and part of RR, CR1NT and CR2NT[3], we first test the case of +TDR configuration with CR1NT, CR2NT, and RR, and then study whether they are necessary[4]. To have a better comparison, we also try the pattern-based rule filtering strategy[5]. Table 6 gives the patterns which occupy the most part but are proved to be useless in Arabic-to-English translation[5].

The experimental results are shown in Table 7 and Table 8. An interesting thing we can see from Table 7 that the role-based rule filter can further discard a large number of rules (Line 3 in Table 7) and keep approximately the same performance with that using all rules. The rules of this configuration only account for about 16% of all rules. We are much surprised that the reordering rules are not important and can be removed in

---

[3] The remaining RR are $\langle Xu, u'X \rangle$ and $\langle uX, Xu' \rangle$. The remaining CR1NT include $\langle uX, u'X \rangle$ and $\langle Xu, Xu' \rangle$. The rest CR2NT are $\langle X_1uX_2, X_1u'X_2 \rangle$, $\langle X_1uX_2, u'X_1X_2 \rangle$ and $\langle X_1uX_2, X_1X_2u' \rangle$.

[4] Lexical phrase rules are basis for every translation model, and they should be included always. However, they can partly filtered by other strategies such as count-based method.

Spanish-to-English translation. The reason will be further investigated in our future work. Line 4 of Table 7 shows the configuration that only keeps lexical phrase rules (LPR) and target discontinuous rules (TDR) leads to degradation in translation quality.

Although Table 8 tells us that the pattern-based rule filter decreases the rule set without harming the translation quality, the reduced size of rule set is not as big as that done by our strategy.

Table 6. The useless patterns in [5]

a	$\langle uX, u'X \rangle$, $\langle Xu, Xu' \rangle$
b	$\langle X_1 u X_2, * \rangle$
c	$\langle X_1 u X_2 v, X_1 u' X_2 v' \rangle$ $\langle u X_1 v X_2, u' X_1 v' X_2 \rangle$
d	$\langle u X_1 v X_2 w, * \rangle$

Table 7. Effect of role-based rule filters and number of rules (in millions) for Spanish-to-English translation

role	tuning		test-1	
	rules	BLEU	rules	BLEU
+TDR	1.27	23.81	1.28	23.62
-RR1NT	**0.70**	**23.70**	**0.71**	**23.53**
-RR1NT -RR	**0.66**	**23.86**	**0.67**	**23.61**
-RR1NT -RR2NT -RR	0.40	23.35	0.41	23.29
ALL	4.13	23.59	4.23	23.46

Table 8. Impact of pattern-based rule filters and number of rules for Spanish-to-English translation

pattern	tune		test-1	
	rules	BLEU	rules	BLEU
-(a~d)	1.15	23.84	1.31	23.60

Chinese-to-English: As we have no idea which kind rules could be excluded in Chinese-to-English translation (see Table 2), we just apply the LOO strategy to filter rules from the start. Similarly, we also apply the pattern-based rule filtering strategy for comparison. The statistics are reported in Table 9-10. Different from Spanish-to-English translation, the rules of most roles are indispensable. Even for the composed rules with one non-terminal (CR1NT), [5] argued these rules are redundant for translation from Arabic to English and it is also verified by us in Spanish-to-English translation. However, the rules of this role are much useful in Chinese-to-English translation. Fortunately, we can still discard a lot of useless rules (CR2NT) and reduce the rule set by 20%.

Using the pattern-based strategy, the rules belong to pattern (b) and (c) can be thrown away. But, less than 20% rules can be removed with safe. We find that the reason why the rules of pattern (d) cannot be taken away is that about half of the discarded rules are strict both-side discontinuous rules that we have proved to be useful.

It is worth noting that our remaining rules after filtering are possible to be further filtered by other strategies (such as count-based). To sum up, our role-based strategy can give a preview of the contribution of the rules belonging to different roles. Of course, our strategy is effective since a large number of rules can be discarded if the translation quality is not degraded without these rules.

Another important thing we should notice is that, compared to 66 possible patterns in pattern-based rule filtering strategy, our strategy only classifies the rules into 7 roles and it is much simpler for experimentation. Furthermore, this classification method is also valid for other translation models, such as string-to-tree model[3] in which rules are made up of minimal rules (like the first 5 roles we discussed in this paper) and composed rules (similar to our CR1NT and CR2NT). Therefore, our rule filtering strategy is more robust.

Through using our role-based strategy in different language pairs, we observe that translation between Chinese and English requires complicated translation rules, but simpler rules are demanded in Spanish-English translation. Therefore, we conclude that the larger divergent between two languages, i.e. Chinese and English, the more complicated rules needed for translation between them.

Table 9. Effect of role-based rule filters for Chinese-to-English, rules in millions

role	tune		test-1	
	rules	BLEU	rules	BLEU
ALL	0.6	29.69	0.69	**28.87**
-CR1NT	0.37	29.20	0.43	28.27
-CR2NT	0.48	**29.85**	0.56	28.86
-RR	0.58	29.24	0.67	28.34
-SDR	0.58	29.35	0.67	28.50
-TDR	0.59	29.64	0.68	28.72
-SBDR	0.58	29.40	0.69	28.58

Table 10. Impact of pattern-based rule filters for Chinese-to-English translation

pattern	tune		test-1	
	rules	BLEU	rules	BLEU
a	0.46	29.22	0.54	28.37
b	0.56	**29.84**	0.65	**28.88**
c	0.53	29.76	0.62	28.84
d	0.59	29.49	0.68	28.69

6   Conclusions

In this paper, we present an empirical study on the contribution of different kinds of discontinuities in bidirectional translations in various language pairs. First, a method of discontinuity classification is proposed. Then, we analyze the symmetry of linguistic phenomena and conduct large scale experiments in different language pairs to answer the question why source discontinuity performs much better than target discontinuity in Chinese-to-English translation. Our interesting finding is that once the source discontinuity is more effective in one translation direction, the target discontinuity usually be more effective in the inverse direction. This gives us clues to determine source discontinuity or target discontinuity should be specially dealt with in certain translation direction for specific language pair. Furthermore, we have shown that discontinuity translation in some main European language pairs is not as useful as in Chinese-English language pair.

Having known the contribution of discontinuity translation, we finally propose a role-based rule filtering approach, which shows efficiency and more robust compared with the pattern-based strategy. Through our rule filtering strategy, we have found that the more divergent between two languages, the more complicated rules needed for translation between them.

Although the experiments are conducted using a hierarchical phrase-based translation model, we believe our findings are also valid in other translation models.

Acknowledgements. We would like to thank the anonymous reviewers for their great comments. The research work has been partially funded by the Natural Science Foundation of China under Grant No. 60975053 and 61003160 and also supported by Hi-Tech Research and Development Program ("863" Program) of China under Grant No. 2011AA01A207.

References

1. Bod, R.: Unsupervised syntax-based machine translation: The contribution of discontiguous phrases. In: Proc. of MT Summit 2007, pp. 51–57 (2007)
2. Chiang, D.: Hierarchical phrase-based translation. Computational Linguistics 33(2), 201–228 (2007)
3. Gally, M., Graehl, J., Knight, K., Marcu, D., DeNeefe, S., Wang, W., Thayer, I.: Scalable inference and training of context-rich syntactic translation models. In: Proc. of ACL-COLING 2006 (2006)
4. Galley, M., Manning, C.D.: Accurate Non-Hierarchical Phrase-Based Translation. In: Proc. of NAACL 2010 (2010)
5. Iglesias, G., Gispert, A., Banga, E.R., Byrne, W.: Rule filtering by pattern for efficient hierarchical translation. In: Proc. of EACL 2009, pp. 380–388 (2009)
6. Li, Z., Callison-Burch, C., Dyer, C., Ganitkevitch, J., Khudanpur, S., Schwartz, L., Thornton, W.N.G., Weese, J., Zaidan, O.F.: Joshua: An open source toolkit for parsing-based machine translation. In: Proc. of ACL 2009, pp. 135–139 (2009)

7. Lopez, A.: Machine translation by pattern matching. Ph.D. Thesis, University of Maryland at College Park (2007)
8. Quirk, C., Menezes, A.: Do we need phrases? Challenging the conventional wisdom in statistical machine translation. In: Proc. of HLT-NAACL 2006, pp. 9–16 (2006)
9. Shen, L., Xu, J., Weischedel, R.: A new string-to-dependency machine translation algorithm with a target dependency language model. In: Proc. of ACL 2008: HLT, pp. 577–585 (2008)
10. Simard, M., Cancedda, N., Cavestro, B., Dymetman, M., Gaussier, E., Goutte, C., Yamada, K., Langlais, P., Mauser, A.: Translating with non-contiguous phrases. In: Proc. of HLT-EMNLP 2005 (2005)
11. Sun, J., Zhang, M., Tan, C.L.: A non-contiguous tree sequence alignment-based model for statistical machine translation. In: Proc. of ACL-IJCNLP 2009, pp. 914–922 (2009)
12. Zollmann, A., Venugopal, A., Och, F., Ponte, J.: A systematic comparison of phrase-based, hierarchical and syntax-augmented statistical MT. In: Proc. of COLING 2008, pp. 1145–1152 (2008)

Handling Unknown Words in Statistical Machine Translation from a New Perspective

Jiajun Zhang, Feifei Zhai, and Chengqing Zong

NLPR, Institute of Automation Chinese Academy of Sciences, Beijing, China
{jjzhang,ffzhai,cqzong}@nlpr.ia.ac.cn

Abstract. Unknown words are one of the key factors which drastically impact the translation quality. Traditionally, nearly all the related research work focus on obtaining the translation of the unknown words in different ways. In this paper, we propose a new perspective to handle unknown words in statistical machine translation. Instead of trying great effort to find the translation of unknown words, this paper focuses on determining the semantic function the unknown words serve as in the test sentence and keeping the semantic function unchanged in the translation process. In this way, unknown words will help the phrase reordering and lexical selection of their surrounding words even though they still remain untranslated. In order to determine the semantic function of each unknown word, this paper employs the distributional semantic model and the bidirectional language model. Extensive experiments on Chinese-to-English translation show that our methods can substantially improve the translation quality.

Keywords: statistical machine translation, unknown words, distributional semantics, bidirectional language model.

1 Introduction

In statistical machine translation (SMT), unknown words are the source language words that are not seen in the training data and thus have no corresponding target translations. The current SMT systems either discard the unknown words or copy them literally into the output. It is well known that unknown words are a big hindrance which greatly influences the translation quality. This problem could be especially severe when the available bilingual data becomes very scarce.

A question arises that what kinds of negative impacts would the unknown words cause? First and at least, we cannot get the meaning of the unknown words in the target language. For instance, using our small-scale training data for Chinese-to-English translation, the Chinese word 诉请 is unknown in the test sentence "... 向 (to) 法院(court) 诉请...", thus we have no idea about the meaning of this word in the English side. Second, the unknown words can negatively affect the lexical selection and reordering of their surrounding words. Take the same Chinese sentence as an example, if the Chinese verb 诉请 is kept untranslated in the output, we are likely to

M. Zhou et al. (Eds.): NLPCC 2012, CCIS 333, pp. 176–187, 2012.

obtain the wrong phrase reordering *to the court诉请* while the correct one is *诉请 to the court.*

The conventional solution of unknown words is to find their target correspondence with additional resources in different ways[3,5,6,13,16,18,19]. They use multilingual data, web data or linguistic resources such as WordNet[17] to induce the translation of unknown words. By doing this, they hope to solve the above two problems perfectly. However, most of these work only address some part of unknown words, such as Named Entities[7,15], abbreviations[6,13], compounds[6] and morphological variants[2,9]. Therefore, many unknown words still remain untouched. Furthermore, for the unknown words handled, their translation may not help the lexical selection and reordering of the surrounding words because the translation is obtained from other resources rather than the original bilingual training data from which translation rules and reordering models are acquired. For example, even if a translation of the Chinese word *诉请* is found (*appeal* for instance) with additional resources, SMT systems have no idea about the reordering between *to court* and *appeal* because reordering model is trained without any information about the source word *诉请* and its translation *appeal.*

From the above analysis, we know that finding translation of unknown words needs additional resources and only some part of them can be well handled. Moreover, the translations obtained from additional resources are not consistent with the original training data and fail to guide the lexical selection and reordering of surrounding words. As we can see that, it is very difficult to obtain the correct translation of unknown words and meantime well guide lexical selection and reordering of surrounding words.

In this paper, we take a step back and try to answer the question whether we can solve the second problem of the unknown words without translating them. In other words, rather than trying hard to get the target translation of unknown words, we aim to handle the lexical selection and reordering of their surrounding words quite well without any additional resources. Our main idea is based on the following assumption: the lexical selection and reordering of the surrounding words depend on the semantic function the unknown word servers as. The **semantic function** of a word means the syntactic and semantic role the word plays in the sentence, and thus the semantic function determines what context the word should take in source and target language. In turn, we can say that two words are similar in semantic function if they often take the similar context. With above assumption, to solve the lexical selection and reordering of the surrounding words, we just need to determine the semantic function of the unknown word. Using the context as a bridge, we can denote the semantic function of a word W by another word W' which shares the most similar context with W. Therefore, the central idea of this paper is to find a known word having the most similar semantic function with the unknown word. Our method consists of three steps as follows:

First, we use the distributional semantic model and bidirectional language model respectively to find an in-vocabulary word in original training data, which shares the most similar context with the unknown word.

Second, we replace the unknown word with the found in-vocabulary word and input the test sentence to the SMT system. Then, we obtain the translation output.

Third, we find the target language word in the output, which is translated by the in-vocabulary word, and replace it back with the unknown word. The unknown words in the final output can still be handled with other approaches which aim to get their translations.

For example, we have a Chinese sentence "... 为(is) 百分之六 左右(about) ..." in which百分之六is an unknown word that in fact means 6%. Using the proposed model, we find that 一半(50%) in the training data takes the most similar context with the unknown word百分之六. Then, we replace the unknown word with一半 (50%) and the example sentence yields the translation "... is about 50% ..." since there is an entry "一半 左右 ||| about 50%" in the translation phrase table. At last, we replace 50% back with the unknown word百分之六resulting "... is about 百分之六 ...." It is easy to see that we obtain the correct reordering of the surrounding words and it makes the translation more understandable.

We can see from the method that the first step is the most important. Thus, it is our focus in this paper. We propose two approaches in the framework: distributional semantic model and bidirectional language model. Experiments show that, with appropriate constraints, the two models can find the in-vocabulary words sharing similar semantic function with the unknown words and can much improve translation quality as well.

2   Related Work

In SMT community, several approaches have been proposed to deal with the unknown words. Nearly most of the related research work focus on finding the correct translation of the unknown words with external resources. To translate all kinds of unknown words, [5,20] adopted comparable corpora and web resources to extract translations for each unknown word; [16,18] applied paraphrase model and entailment rules to replace unknown words with in-vocabulary words using large set of additional bitexts or manually compiled synonym thesaurus WordNet. More research works address some specific kind of unknown words, such as Named Entities (NEs), compounds and abbreviations. [1,7,15] utilized transliteration and web mining techniques with external monolingual and bilingual corpus, comparable data and the web to find the translation of the NEs. [13] presented an unsupervised approach to find the full-form representations for the unknown abbreviations. [9] translated the compound unknown words by splitting them into in-vocabulary words or using translation templates. [6] proposed a sublexical translation method to translate Chinese abbreviations and compounds. For translating highly inflected languages, several methods[2,11] used morphological analysis and lexical approximation to translate unknown words. However, almost all of the above works did not consider the lexical selection and word reordering of the surrounding words when searching the correct translation of the unknown words.

[12] addressed the problem of translating numeral and temporal expressions. They used manually created rules to recognize the numeral/temporal expressions in the training data and replaced them with a special symbol. Consequently, both of the translation rule extraction and reordering model training consider the special symbol. In the decoding time, if numeral or temporal expression is found, it is substituted by the special symbol so that the surrounding words can be handled properly and finally the numeral/temporal expression is translated with the manually written rules. However, they only deal with numeral/temporal expressions rather than any kind of unknown words.

Totally different from all the previous methods, we do not focus on trying great effort to find translations for the unknown words with huge external resources. Instead, we address the problem of the lexical selection and word reordering of the surrounding words caused by unknown words. In this paper, we consider all kinds of the unknown words and apply the distributional semantic model and the bidirectional language model to fulfill this task without any additional resources.

3   Distributional Semantic Model

Distributional semantics[4] approximates semantic meaning of a word with vectors summarizing the contexts where the word occurs. Distributional semantic models (DSM), such as LSA[10] and HAL[14], have proven to be successful in tasks that aim at measuring semantic similarity between words, for example, synonym detection and concept clustering[21]. DSM is effective to synonym detection when the corpus is large enough. However, in our task, the training data is limited and the unknown words in the test set are not equipped with rich contexts. Therefore, instead of obtaining the synonym of the unknown words, we take a step back to find the most appropriate word which has the similar semantic function with the unknown word with DSM.

Next, we elaborate how to construct the DSM for our task and detail how to find the in-vocabulary word which has the most similar semantic function with the unknown word.

3.1   Model Construction

As it is summarized in [4], the construction of the DSM usually includes seven steps: 1) linguistic pre-processing, 2) use term-document or term-term matrix, 3) choose structured or unstructured context, 4) apply geometric or probabilistic interpretation, 5) feature scaling, 6) normalization, and 7) similarity calculation.

In the linguistic pre-processing, we first merge the source-side of training data *TD* and evaluation data *ED*, resulting the whole monolingual data *MD*. Then, we segment and POS (part-of-speech) tagging the monolingual data *MD*. In this paper, we just use the surface form *word* as the target term and the context unit. The POS will be adopted as a constraint when choosing the most appropriate in-vocabulary word for each unknown word.

After pre-processing, we construct a term-term matrix for our task. In the matrix, each row is a vector denoting the context distribution for a target term and each column represents a context term. It is easy to see that both the number of rows and columns equals to the size of the vocabulary of **MD**. Suppose the size of vocabulary is N, then the term-term matrix is $N \times N$.

Then, we need to choose the specific context. In our work, each context term is chosen if it occurs within a window of K words around the target term. We can distinguish left context from right context so as to make the context structured. Here, we just utilize the unstructured context in order to avoid data sparseness. We will try different window Ks in the experiments to find the best one.

To apply the simple similarity calculation, we adopt geometric interpretation and consider the vector for a target word as a point in the vector space. In the following two steps, we detail how to construct the vector V_{tw} for each target word tw.

For a vector V_{tw}, the *ith* element denotes the distribution probability of the *ith* vocabulary word as the context for the target word tw. Naturally, we can record the co-occurrence frequency for each context term and use it as the *ith* element. In order to take the frequency of target word and context word into account, we adopt the association measures mutual information to do feature scaling. Suppose the occurrence count of target word tw and context word cw is f_{tw} and f_{cw}, the co-occurrence count of tw and cw is f_{fcw}, and the total occurrence count of all words is f_{aw}. Thus, the Pointwise Mutual Information (PMI) between tw and cw is:

$$PMI(tw, cw) = \log \frac{p(tw, cw)}{p(tw)\, p(cw)}$$
$$= \log \frac{f_{aw} \times f_{tcw}}{f_{tw} \times f_{cw}} \tag{1}$$

Therefore, the distributional context vector V_{tw} be $V_{tw} = \left(PMI(tw, cw_1), \cdots, PMI(tw, cw_N)\right)$.

Then, we normalize each vector V_{tw} by its L_2-norm, yielding the normalized vector V_{tw}^n.

Finally, we apply the cosine measure to calculate the similarity between two target words tw and tw', whose distributional context vectors are V_{tw}^n and $V_{tw'}^n$ respectively:

$$Sim(tw, tw') = \cos(tw, tw')$$
$$= \frac{\left\langle V_{tw}^n, V_{tw'}^n \right\rangle}{\left\| V_{tw}^n \right\|_2 \times \left\| V_{tw'}^n \right\|_2}$$
$$= \left\langle V_{tw}^n, V_{tw'}^n \right\rangle \tag{2}$$

3.2 In-vocabulary Word Search for Unknown Words

According to the evaluation data and training data, we can easily distinguish unknown words from in-vocabulary words. Assume that the unknown words set is *UWS* and the in-vocabulary words set is *IWS*. For each unknown word *UW*, our goal is to find the most appropriate word *IW** from *IWS* so that *IW** has the most similar semantic function with *UW*. With the similarity function defined above, we can use the following formula to meet our goal:

$$IW^* = \arg\max_{IW} Sim(UW, IW) \tag{3}$$

However, we find that using this formula without any constraint usually cannot obtain good results. Therefore, we require that the resulting in-vocabulary word *IW** should have the consistent part-of-speech with the unknown word *UW*. Accordingly, the search formula will be:

$$IW^* = \arg\max_{IW \in \{IW' | POS(IW') \cap POS(UW) \neq \Phi\}} Sim(UW, IW) \tag{4}$$

It should be noted that our final purpose is to improve the translation quality, but not all of the found in-vocabulary words using formula (4) can guarantee good translation with the context of the unknown word since they usually lack the corresponding phrase entry in the translation phrase table. Thus, if the found in-vocabulary word combining the context of the unknown word matches an entry in phrase table, it will facilitate the lexical selection and word reordering of the surrounding words. For instance, in the example sentence "... 为(is) 百分之六 左右(about) ...", an in-vocabulary word 一半 is found using (4) for the unknown word百分之六, and after replacement the sentence becomes "... 为(is) 一半 左右(about) ...". If there exists a substring一半 左右 has an entry "一半 左右 ‖ about 50%" in the phrase table, it leads to the correct reordering and word selection of the context. Therefore, in order to guarantee good word reordering and lexical selection, we can further require that any found in-vocabulary word, which combines the context of the unknown word, should have an entry in phrase table.

4 Bidirectional Language Model

In distributional semantic models, the context modeling does not address the word order of the context and the conditional dependence between them. For example, if the context and target word is $cw_{l\_4}\ cw_{l\_3}\ cw_{l\_2}\ cw_{l\_1}\ tw\ cw_{r\_1}\ cw_{r\_2}\ cw_{r\_3}\ cw_{r\_4}$ with window *K*=4, any word appearing in the window of the target word will be treated equally without considering the word position. As a result, this model misses a lot of important information.

A question arises that how to use the context more effectively? In theory, the goal of our task is to find the most appropriate in-vocabulary word for the unknown word given the left and right context of the unknown word. It can be formulized as follows:

$$IW^* = \arg\max_{IW} P\left(IW \mid cw_{left}, cw_{right}\right) \tag{5}$$

Now, let us focus on $P\left(IW \mid cw_{left}, cw_{right}\right)$ which models the probability distribution of generating a word given the left and right context. However, this probability is difficult to estimate because the condition is too strict. Following the n-gram probability estimation, we have two backoff ways for probability estimation: 1) back off to concerning only the left context $P\left(IW \mid cw_{left}\right)$; 2) back off to concerning only the right context $P\left(IW \mid cw_{right}\right)$. Then, we can take a step back and search the in-vocabulary word with the constraint combining the two backoff probabilities:

$$IW^* = \arg\max_{IW} P\left(IW \mid cw_{left}\right) P\left(IW \mid cw_{right}\right) \tag{6}$$

It is easy to see that the first backoff probability $P\left(IW \mid cw_{left}\right)$ can be modeled using a forward n-gram probability where n equals to the context window K plus one. Thus, we can just use the conventional n-gram probability estimation method to estimate the backoff probability of generating each in-vocabulary word given the left context. We name this backoff model the *forward language model*.

However, it is not intuitive to see how to estimate the second backoff probability $P\left(IW \mid cw_{right}\right)$. In contrast to the forward language model $P\left(IW \mid cw_{left}\right)$, $P\left(IW \mid cw_{right}\right)$ can be regarded as a *backward language model*. The difficulty lies in how to estimate the backward language model. In practice, the backward language model can be easily estimated through the reversion of the training sentence[22]. Take the following sentence for example:

$$w_1 \; w_2 \cdots w_{i-2} w_{i-1} w_i w_{i+1} w_{i+2} \cdots w_{m-1} \; w_m \tag{7}$$

After reversion, the sentence will be:

$$w_m \; w_{m-1} \cdots w_{i+2} w_{i+1} w_i w_{i-1} w_{i-2} \cdots w_2 \; w_1 \tag{8}$$

If we consider trigram language model, the forward trigram language model $p\left(w_i \mid w_{i-1} w_{i-2}\right)$ can be estimated using the original sentence (7) and the backward trigram language model $p\left(w_i \mid w_{i+2} w_{i+1}\right)$ can be estimated with the reversed sentence (8). During the backward n-gram language probability calculation, we can apply the same way to first reverse the test string.

Therefore, we call the formula (6) using the forward and backward n-gram language model the *bidirectional language model*. Like the distributional semantic model, we can impose the same part-of-speech constraints on the objective searching function (6) resulting the following formula:

$$IW^* = \underset{IW \in \{IW' | POS(IW') \cap POS(UW) \neq \Phi\}}{\arg\max} P\left(IW \mid cw_{left}\right) P\left(IW \mid cw_{right}\right) \tag{9}$$

Likewise, we can further require the obtained in-vocabulary word from (9) combing the context of unknown word must have a corresponding entry in phrase table.

Compared with distributional semantic model, the bidirectional language model can well model the word order and dependence among context words. In the following section, we first analyze how often we can find the correct in-vocabulary word sharing the same semantic function with the unknown word. Then, we substitute the found in-vocabulary words for the unknown words in test set and evaluate the effectiveness of these two models in SMT.

5   Experiments

5.1   Set-Up

Since the application environment of our model supposes the training data is relatively scarce[1], we use the relatively small data set to test our proposed models. In this experiment, we used the Chinese-English FBIS bilingual corpus consisting of 236K sentence pairs with 7.1M Chinese words and 9.1M English words. We employed GIZA++ and grow-diag-final-and balance strategy to generate the final symmetric word alignment. We trained a 5-gram language model with the target part of the bilingual data and the Xinhua portion of the English Gigaword corpus. NIST MT03 test data is adopted as the development set and NIST MT05 test data is employed as the test set. We used the open-source toolkit Urheen[2] for Chinese word segmentation and POS tagging. POS of unknown words are predicted by the MaxEnt model. The test set consists of 1082 sentences, and there are totally 796 distinct unknown words. According to the part-of-speech, the count distribution of the unknown words is: (NR, 273), (NN, 272), (CD, 122), (VV, 99), (NT, 14), (AD, 7), (JJ, 5), (OD, 2) and (M, 2).

5.2   Experimental Results

5.2.1   Accuracy of Semantic Functions
The proposed two models aim at finding the most appropriate in-vocabulary word that has the most similar semantic function with the unknown word. However, the models

---

[1] Our method can be applied in all the cases where there are unknown words in the test sentences. However, if the training data is relatively scarce and more unknown words exists, the proposed approach can achieve bigger improvements. Note that the training data cannot be too small so that most unknown words cannot find semantic similar in-vocabulary words.

[2] http://www.openpr.org.cn/index.php/NLP-Toolkit-for-Natural-Language-Processing/

cannot promise correct result for each unknown word. In this section, we investigate the accuracy of the two models respectively.

Since there is no automatic method to measure the accuracy of the semantic function between any two words, we ask two native speakers of Chinese to evaluate the accuracy manually. Table 1 and 2 give the statistics for the distributional semantic model (DSM) and the bidirectional language model (BLM). Table 1 shows the results of DSM model with different context window size and different constraints. Overall, the accuracy of DSM model is not high. We believe that it is because the context of the unknown word in test data is limited and the training data is not large enough. Specifically, we can see that requiring the found in-vocabulary word should have an entry in phrase table substantially outperforms the model only with POS constraint. Furthermore, among different context windows, the size of 6 performs best. In a deep analysis, we have found that the unknown words whose POS are NN and VV are the main reason for the low accuracy.

Table 2 shows the manual results for the BLM model (trigram in both directions) with different constraints. It is easy to see that the accuracy of the BLM model is much better than that of the DSM model. We think this is due to the modeling of context word order and dependence between them in the BLM model. We also notice that the model requiring the found in-vocabulary word should have an entry in phrase table performs best and achieves the accuracy 77.6%.

Table 1. Manual evaluation results for DSM model with different context window size and different constraints (only POS constrained and POS plus translation entry constrained)

window size	POS (accuracy %)	POS+Trans (accuracy%)
4	52.5	58.6
5	54.4	62.8
6	62.5	69.2
7	50.1	57.3

Table 2. Manual evaluation results for BLM model with different constraints

constraint	Accuracy (%)
without POS	68.5
with POS	73.9
POS+Trans	77.6

5.2.2 Translation Results

In this section, we evaluate the translation results of the DSM model and the BLM model. We use the open-source toolkit Moses to conduct all the experiments. We report all the results with case-insensitive BLEU-4 using shortest length penalty (main metric) and NIST. We employ re-sampling approach to perform statistical significance test [8].

Table 3 gives the translation results using the DSM model with different context window sizes and different constraints. The last line shows the performance of the baseline using default Moses. With only POS constraint, the DSM model with window 4 and 7 even degrades the translation quality. The reason is obvious since Table 1 shows that their accuracy of semantic function is only around 50%. When augmented with translation entry constraint, the model outperforms the baseline in all different window sizes. The model with window 6 performs best and obtains an improvement 0.42 BLEU score over the baseline.

Table 4 illustrates the translation results of the BLM model with different constraints. We can see that the bidirectional language model can always obtain better translation quality compared with the baseline. Specifically, the BLM model with the POS constraint significantly outperforms the baseline by 0.54 BLEU score. And when enhanced with translation entry constraint, the BLM model achieves the best performance and obtains an improvement of 0.64 BLEU score. The results have shown that the BLM model is very effective to handle unknown words in SMT even though the model is relatively simple.

Table 3. Translation results for DSM with different window sizes and constraints

window size	BLEU (%) POS	BLEU(%) POS+Trans	NIST POS	NIST POS+Trans
4	29.53	30.02	8.2254	8.3592
5	29.86	29.88	8.4487	8.3694
6	30.02	30.16	8.4296	8.3910
7	29.66	30.01	8.3724	8.4528
baseline	29.74		8.3139	

Table 4. Translation results for BLM with different constraints

constraint	BLEU (%)	NIST
without pos	29.89	8.3885
with pos	**30.28**	8.4108
pos+trans	**30.38**	8.4659
baseline	29.74	8.3139

To have a comprehensive comparison, we have also conducted the experiments with the forward language model and backward language model respectively. Table 5 and 6 give the translation results. The results in tables show that both forward language model and backward language model cannot outperform the bidirectional language model. The results also show that the forward language model performs better

Table 5. Translation results for forward language model with different constraints

constraint	BLEU (%)	NIST
without pos	29.65	8.2882
with pos	29.98	8.3900
pos+trans	30.21	8.4268

Table 6. Translation results for backward language model with different constraints

constraint	BLEU (%)	NIST
without pos	29.67	8.3189
with pos	29.82	8.4127
pos+trans	30.15	8.4602

than the backward language model. It is consistent with the conclusion drawn by [22] that forward language model is more effective than backward language model for Chinese.

6   Conclusion and Future Work

This paper presents a new idea to handle the unknown words in statistical machine translation from a new perspective. Instead of trying hard to obtain the translation of the unknown words, this paper have proposed two new models to find the in-vocabulary words that have the most similar semantic function with the unknown words and replace the unknown words with the found in-vocabulary words before translation. Thus, by doing this, we can well handle the lexical translation and word reordering for the context of the unknown words during decoding. The experimental results show that the proposed distributional semantic model and the bidirectional language model can both improve the translation quality. Compared with the distributional semantic model, the bidirectional language model performs much better. In the future, we plan to explore more features to handle unknown words in SMT even better. Furthermore, we are going to figure out what is the case if a source-side monolingual large corpus is used for the distributional semantic model.

Acknowledgement. We would like to thank the anonymous reviewers for their valuable comments. The research work has been partially funded by the Natural Science Foundation of China under Grant No. 60975053 and 61003160 and also supported by Hi-Tech Research and Development Program ("863" Program) of China under Grant No. 2011AA01A207.

References

1. Al-Onaizan, Y., Knight, K.: Translating named entities using monolingual and bilingual resources. In: Proc. of ACL 2002 (2002)
2. Arora, K., Paul, M., Sumita, E.: Translation of unknown words in phrase-based statistical machine translation for languages of rich morphology. In: Proceedings of the Workshop on Spoken Language Technologies for Under-Resourced Languages, SLTU 2008 (2008)
3. Eck, M., Vogel, S., Waibel, A.: Communicating unknown words in machine translation. In: Proc. of LREC 2008 (2008)
4. Evert. Distributional Semantic Models. In: Tutorial at NAACL-HLT 2010 (2010)

5. Fung, P.N., Cheung, P.: Mining very-non-parallel corpora: parallel sentence and lexicon extraction via bootstrapping and EM. In: Proc. of EMNLP 2004 (2004)
6. Huang, C., Yen, H., Yang, P., Huang, S., Chang, J.: Using sublexical translations to handle the OOV problem in machine translation. ACM Transaction on Asian Language Information Processing (2011)
7. Knight, K., Graehl, J.: Machine transliteration. In: Proc. of EACL 1997 (1997)
8. Koehn, P.: Statistical significance tests for machine translation evaluation. In: Proc. of EMNLP 2004 (2004)
9. Koehn, P., Knight, K.: Empirical methods for compound splitting. In: Proc. of EACL 2003 (2003)
10. Landauer, T., Dumais, S.: A solution to Plato's problem: The latent semantic analysis theory of acquisition, induction, and representation of knowledge. Psychological Review 104(2), 211–240 (1997)
11. Langlais, P., Patry, A.: Translating unknown words by analogical learning. In: Proc. of EMNLP 2007 (2007)
12. Li, H., Duan, N., Zhao, Y., Liu, S., Cui, L., Hwang, M., Axelrod, A., Gao, J., Zhang, Y., Deng, L.: The MSRA Machine Translation System for IWSLT-2010. In: Proc. of IWSLT 2010 (2010)
13. Li, Z., Yarowsky, D.: Unsupervised translation induction for Chinese abbreviations using monolingual corpora. In: Proc. of ACL 2008 (2008)
14. Lund, K., Burgess, C.: Producing high-dimensional semantic spaces from lexical cooccurrence. Behavior Research Methods 28, 203–208 (1996)
15. Jiang, L., Zhou, M., Chien, L., Niu, C.: Named entity translation with web mining and transliteration. In: Proc. of IJCAI 2007 (2007)
16. Marton, Y., Callison-Burch, C., Resnik, P.: Improved statistical machine translation using monolingually-derived paraphrases. In: Proc. of EMNLP 2009 (2009)
17. Miller, G.A.: WordNet: A lexical database for English. Comm. ACM 38, 11 (1995)
18. Mirkin, S., Specia, L., Cancedda, N., Dagan, I., Dymetman, M., Szpektor, I.: Source language entailment modeling for translating unknown terms. In: Proc. of ACL-IJCNLP 2009 (2009)
19. Nagata, M., Saito, T., Suzuki, K.: Using the Web as a bilingual dictionary. In: Proceedings of the ACL Workshop on Data-Driven Methods in Machine Translation (2001)
20. Shao, L., Ng, H.: Mining new word translations from comparable corpora. In: Proc. of COLING 2004 (2004)
21. Turney, P., Pantel, P.: From frequency to meaning: Vector space models of semantics. Journal of Artificial Intelligence Research 37, 141–188 (2010)
22. Xiong, D., Zhang, M., Li, H.: Enhancing Language Models in Statistical Machine Translation with Backward N-grams and Mutual Information Triggers. In: Proc. of ACL 2011 (2011)

Dependency Network Based Real-Time Query Expansion

Jiaqi Zou[1,*] and Xiaojie Wang[2]

School of Computer Science, Beijing University of Posts and Telecommunications
Beijing, 100876, China
jia7.zou@gmail.com, xjwang@bupt.edu.cn

Abstract. This paper presents a novel real-time query expansion method which offers expansion related to user query intention. A dependency relation network is first built by merging dependency trees of large numbers of sentences from a large-scale corpus. User queries are then expanded to verb-noun pairs or verb-attributes-noun multiple grams based on relations in the network, which is helpful to identify user intentions and to reduce search spaces. Experiments show that the proposed expansion method is not only effective in saving user inputs, but also brings significant improvement to retrieval performance.

Keywords: real-time query expansion, dependency relation, query intention.

1   Introduction

Real-time query expansion (RTQE) recommends a list of expanded query words when user types a query, which reduces user's keystrokes to complete information retrieval. Moreover, RTQE can help the user complete query intention, thus getting better retrieval performance. White and Marchionini [1] showed real-time and interactive query expansion is useful, it can reduce the time needed to perform a query and improve the query quality.

The most widely used way to RTQE is offering the most frequent query from the query log that includes the current input as a substring [2], [3]. With users inputting more letters or words, the expanded queries changes all along. So the more words inputted by users, the more precise the expanded words are. For example, in the RTQE method used by Microsoft Bing[1], when the inputted words are "olympic lo", the first expanded query is "olympic logo"; when the inputted words change to "olympic lon", the first expanded query changes to "olympic london 2012".

This kind of RTQE is based on the letters inputted. It expands words according to word frequency or word co-occurrence frequency. In the research of Ji et al. [2], they used enhanced string matching method to support interactive fuzzy keyword expansion.

An alternative method for RTQE uses user context information. Arias et al. [4] proposed a method using user context information on mobile platform. However, it lacks scalability due to the use of manually built rules collection. Bar-Yossef et al. [5]

---

[*] Corresponding author.
[1] www.bing.com

M. Zhou et al. (Eds.): NLPCC 2012, CCIS 333, pp. 188–198, 2012.

also used user context to recommend queries of the same search session that have current input as their prefix. Their method is effective when user input is short.

However, there is little work on RTQE concerning user's query intention. Strohmaier et al. [6] introduced an intentional query expansion method to make users' intentions more explicit during searching. By mapping implicit queries to explicit queries in the same search session from query logs, they suggested that explicit queries containing at least one verb word might reflect possible user intentions. Their results show that intentional query expansions can be used to diversify result sets and improve click-through ratio.

This paper proposes a RTQE method using a dependency network to get better query intentions. The dependency network is constructed using dependency relations from the parsing results of large-scale corpus. A dependency relation is either a verb-noun pair or a verb-attributes-noun multiple gram.

Experiments show that the proposed RTQE method improves the retrieval performance and reduces user input effort greatly. It is also suggested that dependency relations can be used to determine user's query intentions.

The rest of this paper is organized as follows. Section 2 describes the building of dependency network and the RTQE method based on this dependency network. The evaluation and experiments are detailed on section 3. Finally, section 4 gives the conclusion and future work.

2   Method

2.1   Representation of Query Intention

Border [1] proposed task-oriented classification of query intention, i.e. navigational, informational and transactional. He et al. [8] used search results to find query intention. They represented query intentions using verb-noun pairs. Duan et al. [9] pointed out that this kind of representation is suitable for both informational and transactional intention, but not good for navigational intention. Meanwhile, they showed that verb-noun pairs can be acquired from dependency relations in sentences.

But we found the verb-noun pairs are still not sufficient to express query intention clearly and completely. They can be used as the backbone of query intention. As an illustrating example, two queries "learn English language" and "learn programming language" are both represented by the verb-noun pair "learn language". But the intention difference between them is quite big. So other components needs to be added in verb-noun pair in order to describe query intention better.

In this research, we add modifiers of noun, namely attributes, to complete the query intention. We mainly consider pre-attributes here. Query intention can be represented by verb-attributes-noun. In English, the normal word order of attributes is determiner, adjective, participle, gerund and noun. Determiner contains article, possessive pronoun, substantive genitive, numeral and classifier which have little function in intention expression. So we only consider attributes of adjective, participle, gerund and noun words.

For the above example, after adding attribute to the verb-noun pair "learn language", the intention difference between them is clearly expressed.

2.2   Construction of Dependency Relation Network

First we collect dependency relations from large-scale sentences parsed according to dependency structures. Then we build dependency relation network by combining and relating these dependency relations.

Stanford Parser[2] is used here to do dependency parsing on the sentences. From the parsing result of each sentence, we extract dependency relations between verb and noun and relations between this noun word and its attributes.

For example, for the sentence "How to change a car tire", we get results as shown in Fig. 1 after dependency parsing using Stanford Parser.

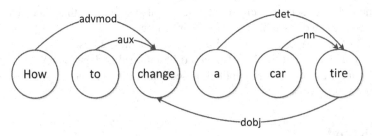

Fig. 1. Parsing result of sentence "How to change a car tire"

Each arrow in this figure means a binary dependency relation. We use vn[verb, noun] to represent dependency relation between verb and noun, and an[attribute, noun] to represent dependency relation between noun and its attributes. In this example, we get vn[change, tire] and an[car, tire].

We combine these two relations in a network to represent the query intention as shown in Fig. 2. Because user can input both verb and noun first when inputting queries, for the convenience of indexing during the RTQE process, we construct two networks for each query intention. One starts from verb as shown in the left of Fig. 2 and the other one in the right starts from noun. We attach the arrow that represents 'an' to that of 'vn' since 'vn' is the kernel relation in concern and 'an' is second level

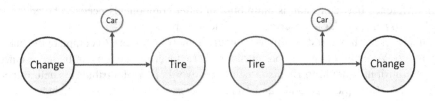

Fig. 2. The left network starts from verb, the right one starts from noun

2 http://nlp.stanford.edu/software/lex-parser.shtml

relation. Although the network is a little different from dependency network, we still call it dependency network in the following parts of the paper for simplification.

It should be noted here that in some sentences there are more than one attributes which have dependency relations with the head noun like "How to buy a used wedding dress". In this sentence, we extract vn[buy, dress] and an[used wedding, dress]. For this kind of sentence, we represent each attribute with a node. As concluded in linguistic analysis, the closer an attribute is to the noun, the closer relationship it has with the noun. So we first connect the attribute which is closet to noun, and then connect the second closet one, and so on.

In the above example, there is a verb node "buy", a noun node "dress", and two attribute nodes "used" and "wedding". In the network, verb node and noun node are connected first, that is vn[buy, dress]. Then the attribute node "wedding" is connected to the path between verb node and noun node. Finally the attribute node "used" is connected to attribute node "wedding". The network using verb node as starting node is shown in Fig. 3.

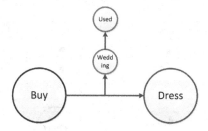

Fig. 3. Network with plural attributes

Moreover, for intransitive verbs, they are connected with noun word by a preposition word. So in the network between an intransitive verb node and a noun node, a preposition node is needed. We use vpn[prep, vn] to represent relation between intransitive verb and noun. For sentences such as "How to look up phone number", we extract vpn[up, vn], vn[look, number] and an[phone, number]. In the dependency network, the preposition node is attached to the path between verb node and noun node. The network of this example using noun node as starting node is shown in Fig. 4.

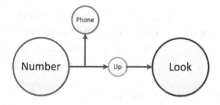

Fig. 4. Network with a prep node

After constructing network for each sentence, the next step is to combine all the networks. The combination is done separately for those starting from verb node and noun node. For networks start from verb node, if two of them share the same verb node, they will be combined into one network rooted with this verb. In this way, we can get all the dependency relations starting from the same verb in one network. Similar operation is done for networks starting from noun node. Finally, we have two dependency relation based networks. (Fig. 5)

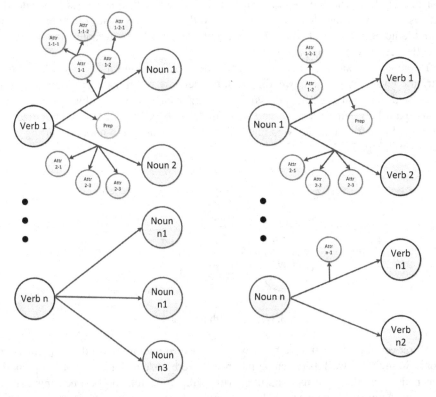

Fig. 5. A fragment of the combined network, attribute node is labeled by "Attr", preposition node is labeled by "Prep", the left one starts from verb, the right one starts from noun

2.3   RTQE Method

Based on this dependency relation network, we can expand noun for inputted verb and expand verb for inputted noun. Then we can expand attribute words for verb-noun pair to express query intention more complete and precise. Furthermore, by combining this kind of expansion with the string matching expansion technique, we construct a RTQE system.

Specifically this RTQE method works in the following process:

First, the user inputs some letters (prefix of a word, e.g., "ti") to the search box. According to the prefix, our system searches the starting nodes from the two dependency networks constructed in section 2.2 for words beginning with this prefix, and list matched words sorted by their frequency in the corpus (Fig. 6-a).

Second, when the user selects a word from the list, our system can locate the node in the network that stands for the selected word ("tire" in this example). Then our system can expand verbs or nouns connected to this node. (Fig. 6-b) The user can modify expanded words by inputting prefix (Fig. 6-c). After this step, the intention backbone (verb-noun) is built. If the verb is intransitive, we can get (verb-preposition-noun).

Third, when the user selects a verb or noun word shown in the expanded list, our system can locate this verb-noun relation in the network. If there are some attributes attached to this relation, our system will pop-up the attribute words as expanded words. The attributes that are closest to the nouns are expanded first, then the less closest ones (Fig. 6-d). Still user can reject one recommendation by typing letters he prefers (Fig. 6-e).

The procedure ends when there are no more words can be expanded or the user feels satisfied with the current query.

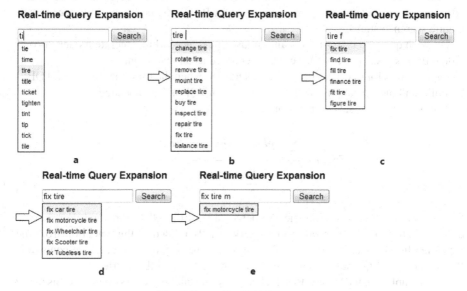

Fig. 6. Example of RTQE process

3   Experiments

We designed four experiments to test the performance of the RTQE method described in Section 2.

3.1   Experimental Corpus

We used corpus from www.ehow.com. This website is an online guide offering step-to-step instructions for how-to questions. According to Broder's query intention classification [7], how-to questions belong to informational intention. From Duan's research [9] we know that informational query intention can be represented by verb-noun pair. So we can represent the query intention of how-to questions by the improved method using verb-attributes-noun.

The corpus we used has articles of 20 categories from ehow, including Health, Cars, Computers, Food & Drink and so on. The total size of the corpus is 915,600 articles. Each article is a sequence of instructions about one how-to question, and each title represents this question. When building dependency relation network, we did dependency parsing for each title, like "How to fix motorcycle tire".

3.2   Experimental Evaluation Measurement

We invited 10 volunteers to participate in the experiments. All the volunteers have advanced engineering education background.

First we test how many keystrokes our RTQE method will save. Reducing users' efforts in generating queries is very important for RTQE method, especially for users of mobile search systems.

For each query, the keystrokes and mouse clicks needed to generate a query is recorded. Each keystroke or mouse click is recorded as an operation.

Suppose that for query x, the operations needed when the user does not use RTQE is $OPFull_x$, and the operations needed when using RTQE is $OPExpanded_x$.

The percentage of saved operations is:

$$Saved = \frac{\sum_{x=1}^{n}(OpFull_x - OpExpanded_x)}{\sum_{x=1}^{n}OpFull_x} \tag{1}$$

Second, we test the expansion success percentage of this RTQE method. For a given query intention, if the user can find a query exactly related to this intention from the expanded list, we call it a successful expansion. The expansion success percentage is the percentage of queries with a successful expansion in all the queries.

For example, the user wants to search a query "install windows system", if this query can be found in expanded list during RTQE process, then the expansion is successful, otherwise it is not.

Suppose that the number of all the queries is AllNum, the number of query with a successful expansion is SuccessNum. The expansion success percentage is:

$$SuccessPercentage = \frac{SuccessNum}{AllNum} \tag{2}$$

Moreover, in the queries with successful expansion, we compare the retrieval performance of the original query user typed in, the query after verb-noun expansion and the query after verb-attributes-noun expansion. The aim of this test is to know how much effect this RTQE method has for query intention completion.

We use precision and nDCG score for evaluation.

Precision means the percentage of retrieved correct answers of all the correct answers.

nDCG is a measure of effectiveness in information retrieval. We grade the relevance of a result from 0 to 3. 0 means this result is totally not related to the query while 3 means totally relevant. The rank of each result is done by the user who does this search.

Suppose that rel_x means the graded relevance of the result at position x in the search results. For a search result list, its DCG score is:

$$DCG_p = \sum_{x=1}^{p} \frac{2^{rel_x} - 1}{\log_2(1+x)}$$

(3)

And nDCG score is the DCG score divide the maximum possible DCG score from position 1 till position p.

$$nDCG_p = \frac{DCG_p}{IDCG_p}$$

(4)

Finally, we compare the RTQE result of our method with that of Microsoft Bing search engine.

According to the experiments described above, we assigned the following tasks for each test participant:

In accordance with the limit of the 20 categories, do search for a how-to question each time. Make sure that the tester is clear about the query intention before inputting. Use the RTQE method to expand the query.

Our system can get the amount of operations of the user for each query. The tester should record whether an expansion is successful or not.

After generating the query and doing search, the system will return the Top 10 search result of the three kind of queries. Rank the results by judging the relevance of each result with the query intention.

3.3   Experimental Results and Analysis

By the test of the volunteers, we get 200 queries and their test results as follows:

Table 1. Result of the operation number test

	Without RTQE	With RTQE
Average number of operations	15.0	5.437

Table 1 shows that the percentage of average saved operations is 63.75% after RTQE. It proves our RTQE method is very useful for saving user effort.

This is because the structure of the dependency relation network we built directly connects verb, noun and attributes which combine to be query intentions. So all the expanded words our system recommends are components of possible query intentions. And the expanded words are correct word collocations because we built the network using dependency parsing. Moreover, combining the dependency relation network with prefix string matching method makes our RTQE method more effective in reducing the operations needed.

We use the query in Fig. 6-e for example here. We use a letter "m" to find the word "motorcycle". Only in this step, eight operations are saved. We can see that this RTQE method really reduces the operations.

Table 2. Result of expansion success percentage test

Times	query expansion success	query expansion failed
	168	32

Table 2 shows the expansion success percentage is 84%. It means most of the queries in given categories can use our RTQE method to generate and the dependency relation network represents user query intention well.

Because we built the dependency relation network using a large-scale corpus, so nearly all the possible query intentions of selected categories are included in the network. Therefore, this RTQE method can get a high success percentage in this test.

Table 3. Result of retrieval performance

Query type	Precision	nDCG score
Original query word	0.73%	13.11%
Query after verb-noun expansion	9.47%	37.37%
Query after verb-attributes-noun expansion	79.2%	88.95%

The data of Table 3 is computed by the 168 queries in Table 2 which are successfully expanded. We found that the retrieval performance after verb-attributes-noun expansion is better than the performance after verb-noun expansion. And the performance of the latter is better than the performance of not expanded queries. Although the retrieval performance improves naturally with the increase of query words, but obviously importing words that do not relate to the query intention will make the retrieval performance drop. The significant difference in the performance of the three kinds of queries can prove our RTQE method is effective in representing query intention so that resulting in good retrieval performance.

We still use the query in Fig. 6-e as an example here. The search result of word "tire" are all things related with tire, but contains articles that do not deal with "fix tire", like "How to store a flat tire".

The result after verb-noun expansion is much better. All the results is related to "fix tire", like "How to fix a flat tire" and "DIY flat tire fix", which are not found by the first query method.

The result after verb-attributes-noun expansion is the best of the three. It clearly represents the query intention that we want to fix motorcycle tire. The articles found are like "the best way to fix a flat motorcycle tire". In contrast, the results of the second method cannot represent the feature "motorcycle".

However, sometimes the query result after verb-attributes-noun expansion is not the best. For example, the search result of "buy satellite phone" is not good as that of "buy phone". The reason is that the attribute "satellite" imports some articles that do not deal with "buy phone", like "How to call a satellite phone". But this kind of result is quite few so the overall result is influenced very little.

After this test, we compare our method with the widely used search engine Microsoft Bing. Bing has two query expansion functions. One is the RTQE function "Search suggestion", the other is "Related search" which offers possible useful queries after the users do searches. To get English expanded queries, the location option in Bing is set to United Kingdom. We try the 200 queries contributed by the volunteers in Bing.

After a preliminary investigation, we found that the RTQE result of Bing differs a lot if the word order of a query changes. For example, if we type words in the order of "learn street dance", Bing can offer the correct recommendations. However, if we change the order, Bing cannot recommend the words we want.

So we categories the RTQE result of Bing into three groups: cannot get correct recommendations (NOT); get correct recommendations only in normal word order(NORMAL); can get correct recommendations both in normal order and other word orders(ALL). Table 4 shows the test result of Bing RTQE method (do not contain "Related search" result.)

Table 4. Result of Bing RTQE test

Group	NOT	NORMAL	ALL
Percentage	49%	33%	18%

As shows in Table 4, half of the queries cannot get correct recommendations while 84% of the queries are successfully expanded in our method. Moreover, only 18% of the queries can get correct recommendations when the query words are not inputted in accordance with the normal word order in Bing, while both verb and noun words are allowed to be inputted first in our method.

For those queries that are not in the ALL group, we do search when the RTQE fails and judge the recommendation results of the 'Related Search' function. We find that only 13.3% of these queries can get useful query recommendations.

This test shows that our RTQE method has advantages when compared with industrial search engine.

After testing, we did survey of the testers on their experience of the RTQE method. We got the following message after summarizing their feedback.

This RTQE method is quick, and is able to meet the speed requirement of RTQE methods. And it is quite new and different from other RTQE methods. Most of the how-to questions in the 20 categories can be successfully expanded and the search results are satisfying.

But sometimes the testers feel inconvenience when doing search because currently the RTQE method can only handle verb, noun and attributes. And this method is category sensitive. When searching a query which is not in the given category, the expansion result is not good.

4   Conclusion

This paper proposed a novel RTQE method concerning user query intention. We used a large corpus from www.ehow.com to build a dependency relation network of verb, noun and attributes, then designed a RTQE method using this network. The proposed RTQE method is proved to be effective in representing user query intention and hence improve retrieval performance.

In the future, we will work on reducing the limit on the types of part of speech and do more research on offering personalized expanded results to represent the user intention better.

References

1. White, R.W., Marchionini, G.: Examining the effectiveness of real-time query expansion. Inf. Process. Manage. 43(3), 685–704 (2007)
2. Ji, S., Li, G., Li, C., Feng, J.: Efficient interactive fuzzy keyword search. In: WWW, pp. 371–380 (2009)
3. Barouni-Ebrahimi, M., Ghorbani, A.A.: On Query Completion in Web Search Engines Based on Query Stream Mining. In: Web Intelligence, pp. 317–320 (2007)
4. Arias, M., Cantera, J.M., Vegas, J., Fuente, P.D.L., Alonso, J.C., Bernardo, G.G., Llamas, C., Zubizarreta, Á.: Context-Based Personalization for Mobile Web Search. In: PersDB, pp. 33–39 (2008)
5. Bar-Yossef, Z., Kraus, N.: Context-sensitive query auto-completion. In: WWW, pp. 107–116 (2011)
6. Strohmaier, M., Kroll, M., Korner, C.: Intentional Query Suggestion: Making User Goals More Explicit During Search. In: WSCD, pp. 68–74 (2009)
7. Broder, A.Z.: A taxonomy of web search. SIGIR Forum, 3–10 (2002)
8. He, K., Chang, Y., Lu, W.: Improving Identification of Latent User Goals through Search-Result Snippet Classification. In: Web Intelligence, pp. 683–686 (2007)
9. Duan, R., Wang, X., Hu, R., Tian, J.: Dependency Relation Based Detection of Lexicalized User Goals. In: Yu, Z., Liscano, R., Chen, G., Zhang, D., Zhou, X. (eds.) UIC 2010. LNCS, vol. 6406, pp. 167–178. Springer, Heidelberg (2010)

Divided Pretreatment to Targets and Intentions for Query Recommendation

Yangyang Kang, Yu Hong[*], Li Yu, Jianmin Yao, and Qiaoming Zhu

School of Computer Science & Technology, Soochow University
No.1 Shizi Street, Canglang District, Suzhou City, Jiangsu Province, 215006
tianxianer@gmail.com

Abstract. We propose a query recommendation method called "Divided Pretreatment to Targets and Intentions for Query Recommendation", which concentrates on the structure, elements and composition of a query. Based on the recognition of query targets and query intentions by a classifying method, the clusters of query intentions are built following the clue of consistent and similar query targets. After that, query recommendations are generated by simple substitution of peer intentions. This method aims to explore a simple and efficient mechanism, which only analyzes and processes query itself and its internal attributes. The experiment demonstrates that, accuracy of "query targets" and "query intentions" recognition is 73.11%, while that of intention clustering reaches 55.67%. The p@1 value of query recommendation gets 57.83%.

Keywords: query recommendation, query target, query intention.

1 Introduction

Query Recommendation is an information retrieval technology to recommend identical or related queries for a particular query. Its core mission is to understand user's query intention through machine learning, mine the expressional forms of query with similar intentions, and finally realize mutual recommendation of the synonymous or associated queries. The ultimate purpose is to use the synonymous or associated queries as medium to share and mutually recommend better search results.

Currently, the main research form of query recommendation is to express user's potential query intention with the correlation information within the framework of information retrieval and outside the query such as relevant or pseudo-relevant text content or click and browsing retrieval behaviors, then measure query semantic consistency and intention association, and recommend approximate or related queries finally. However, we ignore to analyze or understand the intention from query itself because of sparse information, fuzzy structural relations and optional component forms.It is often used as a medium to auxiliarily mine external reference resources which contain richer and potential intention informations. Therefore, query itself was long considered "be unrefined" for intention analysis and query recommendation.

---

[*] Corresponding author.

M. Zhou et al. (Eds.): NLPCC 2012, CCIS 333, pp. 199–212, 2012.
© Springer-Verlag Berlin Heidelberg 2012

However, query is a direct intention expression of user, which describes real and appropriate meaning of intention. At the same time, query itself contains less noisy informations when semantic ambiguity and misspelling is ignored. In contrast, using external resources associated with the query for intention analysis will introduce a lot of noise which will mislead intention analysis and calculation. So, if there is an effective measure of expansion and disambiguation, the direct use of query itself can achieve the mining of correlation intention and query recommendation from the perspective most closed to user as well as intention expressed in behavior. Therefore, we propose a query recommendation method based on divided pretreatment to query targets and query intentions. This method includes three basic steps.

— Classifying and recognizing the words of query which describe the target and the intention.
— Clustering the words of query intention to mine consistent or similar intention.
— Using intention cluster to realize a simple substitution of peer intentions to form query recommendation.

Query target refers to the target entity, behavior or status which user retrieves. Query intention refers to the operations of intention or the motivations of retrieval which impose on the query target. For Example 1, there is a query *"Where is the No. 18 bus station?"*..Its query target is *"No. 18 bus station"* and query intention is *"where"*.

We can effectively overcome the sparsity and ambiguity of the query informations, through classifying and recognizing the targets and intentions of query with large-scale query samples. As the sparsity of the information which describes the intention, we can expand by different intention words with common target. There are queries such as "How to get to the 18 bus station?", "Where is the location of the 18 bus station" and "Where is the position of the 18 bus station" with common target "18 bus station" in large-scale query samples. We expand the intention *"where"* in example 1 to {*"where"*, *"how to get to"*, *"location"*, *"position"*} to enrich the description of original query intention. As description of target can cause ambiguity possibility, we can take different targets pointed to by same intention to disambiguate. For example 2, there is a query *"Apple Quote"* which query target is *"Apple"* and query intention is *"Quote"*. The target *"Apple"* is ambiguous because it may refers to the electronic product or fruit. So, we gather the queries with consistent intention words such as *"Iphone Quote"*, *"Ipod Quote"*, *"Computer Quote"*, *"Mainboard Quote"*. By extracting the description of targets, the lexical meanings {*"Iphone"*, *"Ipod"*, *"Computer"*, *"Mainboard"*} of target *"Apple"* in original query are formed to disambiguate effectively. While, *"Fruit"* is often gone with the word "Price", such as *"Banana Price"* rather than *"Banana Quote"*.

In the rest of the paper, we will first introduce the related work in Section 2. Then, we give the framework of a new query recommendation method based on divided pretreatment to targets and intentions in Section 3. Section 4 will show the modeling process of classifying and recognizing the targets and intentions of query. The method of intention cluster will be given in Section 5. We present and discuss the experimental results in Section 6. Finally, we conclude the paper in Section 7.

2   Related Work

According to the source of corpus, the methods of query recommendation are divided into two categories: *document-based* approaches and *log-based* approaches.

Document-based approaches exploit the words or phrases related to the query to constitute candidate recommended queries. Yanan Li et al. [1] proposed a division of *document-based* approaches into three categories. The first approach based on global documents is to find the words closed to the query through analyzing the relations between words in all documents, then construct the recommended queries. But it is difficult to be realized in real large-scale data. The second approach based on local document is to find the words or phrases related to the query in relevant documents. But it is difficult to get the relevant documents. The solution is to select *top-n* pseudo-relevant documents from search engine but it will introduce the noise of irrelevant documents. Nick et al. [2] proposed a hidden markov random walk model based on large-scale click logs to obtain the relevant documents that have not been clicked.The last approach based on manual editing corpus will have accurate results but deal with the new word in the network difficultly.

Currently, *log-based* approach is the main direction of research on query recommendation. Cao et al. [3] divided log-based approaches into two categories as *session-based* approach and *click-based* approach after summary of previous work. For *session-based* approach, Huang et al. [4] recommended mutually between queries through mining the queries co-occurred in the same session. For *click-based* approach, the similar queries were recommended through bipattite graph model which was built up with the user's click and history information. Jimin Wang et al. [5] proposed a method based on the numbers of common URLs clicked between queries. The basic assumption is that the more same clicked URLs two queries share, the more similar they are. Yanan Li et al. [6] proposed a method based on weighted SimRank to mine the indirect correction and semantic relation between queries. Mei et al. [7] apply Hitting Time to large-scale bipattite graph to rank the queries and obtain the consistent semantic queries. As the sparse of user clicks in query logs, the solution is to compute iteratively by transferring similarity with improved SimRank algorithm or reduce dimensions. But the calculation is complex which is difficult to be applied to the general search engine with high real-time demand.

The purpose of *document-based* approach and *log-based* approach is to better understand user query intention and recommend more high-quality queries. But the understanding of query intention is difficult because the sparsity and ambiguity of queries will cause the fuzziness and diversity of intentions and the deviation of retrieval results. Therefore, research on recognition of query intention has become popular in recent years.

3   Framework of Query Recommendation

The main framework is shown in figure 1 which contains two main parts: *offline-sys* and *online-sys*. For *offline-sys*, we first extract queries from query logs and utilize *"Targets*

& *Intention Recognition Model*" to extract target or intention words in each query. Then, we utilize "*Intention Cluster Model*" to build intention clusters. For *online-sys*, if there is a query under test, we first extract the target and intention of the query. Then, we determine the similarity of query intention and priori intention clusters with intention similarity matching. The most similar intention cluster is chosen as a candidate. Finally, we measure similarity on each word in candidate intention cluster with query intention test and rank intentions according to similarity. At last, the most similar intention word and query target will be combined to form recommended queries.

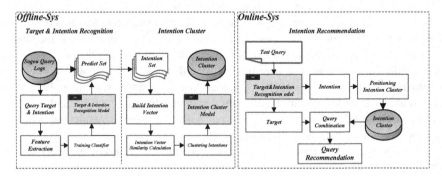

Fig. 1. Framework of Query Recommendation

4   Target and Intention Recognition Model

4.1   Query Preprocessing

Based on the rules of classification proposed by Broder et al. [8], *Beaze-Yates* divided query into three categories: informational, not informational and ambiguous. In this paper, we only focus on the informational queries because not informational queries doesn't contain target word (Such as query "*Quote*") and ambiguous queries only give target or intention word(such as query "*Apple*") with amiguous.

Thus, we propose three filtering rules to recognize and filter the not informational and ambiguous queries in preprocessing. 1)Filtering the queries which contain letter, numeral, punctuation or URL. Because considering the internal structure and the componential role information of queries from a semantic perspective, the noise brought about by above symbols should be avoided. 2)Filtering "short queries". In experiment, we extract the queries with more than two words to form query sets. 3)Filtering queries like title, news and notice. Such queries belong to navigational queries in nature. Search engine can identify and recommend a consistent navigation-al link with maximum string matching.

By taking the refined filter rules and remove the reduplicate queries, we collect *1.9* million queries from the query logs of *Sogou2008* to auxiliary query analysis and recommendation research. As the query resources coming from Chinese retrieval system *Sogou(Sogou 2008)* and the advantages of *ICTCLAS* dealing with query seg-mentation, we use *ICTCLAS* to realize the basic division of query features words.

4.2   Feature Selection

We should consider from multiple perspectives such as *lexical-based* perspective and *context-based* perspective to identify a word. Following, feature extraction method will be introduced separately.

- **Lexical-Based Perspective**

We choose four empirical classification features (shown in Table 1) from the *lexical-based* perspective. First, the word itself is an effective feature. The words such as "*免费*", "*在线*" and "*下载*" have obvious intention performance, while these words like "*大学*", "*计算机*", and "*单位*" express lower probability of intention than probability of target. Secondly, the head or tail character of word can be used as classification feature. For example, the character "*最*" among the words as "*最新*", "*最好*", "*最贵*" with a strong emotional color, can better transfer user's query intention. In contrast, another group of words "*在线*", "*热线*" and "*路线*" etc. reflect intention by the tail character "*线*". Finally, part of speech is an effective classification feature. The main grammatical structure of Chinese is *Subject-Verb-Object*, which Subject and Object consist of noun phrase and Verb consist of verbal phrase. Nouns and noun phrases often reflect the targets, while Verbs and verbal phrases often reflect the specific intention. Similarly, adjectives and adverbs appeared in the short text chapter (such as query) often express an emphasis on target state of query which can also reflect user's intention.

Table 1. Features of Classification

Feature	Description
Lexical-based	Word itself
	The head character of word
	The tail character of word
	Part of speech
Context-based	Word Frequency
	Word Position

- **Context-Based Perspective**

From the *context-based* perspective, we proposed two features as frequency and position. Frequency was considered as feature on the basis of an assumption that intention word cannot be used as independent query. It can combine with a large number of different types of target words to form a complete query description. For example, user does not often use "*下载*" as query independently because its description of itention is fuzzy. By using a combination of large different targets such as "*电影*", "*视频*", and "*软件*" etc, we can form a complete query semantics. So, the intention words are widely distributed, high frequency, and able to combine with various categories of words. In contrast, the target words have a single combination with other words, and the frequency of occurrence is much lower than intention words. For instance, target word "电影《黑衣人》" can only collocate a limited number of intention words such as "在线", "观看", "下载", and "光盘" or used as query directly and independently. Its probability of occurrence in the large-scale samples is much lower than intention words like "在线" and so on.

The position of word in the query used as classification feature comes from the phenomenon when user build query, they are used to put some words with purpose in the head or tail of the query, for example "在线观看电影黑衣人III" or "Facebook的上市时间是几号". So, the position of word in query is an effect feature. In this paper, the position feature is relative position after normalizing with calculating process as follows. Given a specific query w, $Ord(w)$ represents the order of w in the query and $Seq(Q)$ represents the number of words in the query. So the position feature of w is calculated as formula (1).

$$P_w = Ord(w) / Seq(Q), \qquad\qquad 公式(1)$$

5   Intention Cluster and Recommend

The purpose of intention cluster is to cluster the query words with consistent or related query motivation, so as to realize the reorganization and recommendation of query description by taking advantage of intention relation between internal clusters.

Intention cluster can be divided into two categories: 1) *Consistency-based* query intention cluster. It aims at cluster the words that are same with user's query intention; 2) *Preference-based* query intention cluster. It aims at cluster the words that meet user preference. The former is similar to the phenomenon which identify the expression of intention in different words but synonymous. The latter focus on mining associated intention words which point to similar goals.

5.1   Intention Vector

Intention set is a collection of intention words. If intention words matched and compared alone without considering whole query, it is difficult to identify consistent or associated intentions from semantic . We can only match the consistency of word type that cannot help reach the core purpose of intention cluster. Therefore, we propose the concept of intention vector to build the associated network of intentions.

The construction of intention vector comes from the rules that query can be conceptualized as the form of "<Target + Intention>". Intention should be combined with the specific target that makes sense. For example, the intention word "治疗" is unable to transfer any description of intention in the absence of target. Only together with explicit "治疗对象" such as "胃病", "失眠" and "产后综合症", the whole query has a complete semantic. On the basis on the rule, we propose a "skillfully deflected" description of intention vector. The description itself is not the lexical meaning of intention words or such as WordNet hyponymy lexical semantic relations features, but through large-scale query samples to describe the targets indirectly which high-frequencily co-occurred with intention words. For example, given a query intention word "治疗" or "症状", the form of vector constructed is shown in Table 2.

By building the intention vectors, we convert the correction intention measure into the similarity measure between vectors. The contact with intention is more closely if the intersection of intention vector is larger between different intention words.

Table 2. Intention Vector

Intention Word	Intention Vector
治疗	[癌症　骨刺　神经　胃病　胆固醇　……　手足口病]
症状	[妊娠　胃病　忧郁　癌症　手足口病　……　胃溃疡]

5.2　Intention Similarity Calculation

From the description of intention above, we attempt to use the correlation matching of intention based on VSM and Language Model. And such correlation is used as reference standard of cluster. The VSM[9] calculate with cosine similarity, and the Language Model[10] calculate with Kullback Leibler Divergence[11].

Through calculating similarity of intention with vector space model and measuring similarity of probability distribution between intentions with *KL* divergence, we realize the numerical measure of the correlation between intentions. With this measure, we use Apcluster clustering algorithm to cluster the intention words so as to form intention clusters and provide reference data for query recommendation.

- **Vector Space Model + Cosine Similarity**

Using VSM to describe intention, we need to estimate the numerical weight which gives to each dimensional target in the model. In this paper, we use *TF-IDF* to calculate the weight values. Assuming that intention word I_j co-occurred with n target words and each target presented by O_i, then the intention vector of I_j presents $V(I)=\{I_1, I_2, \dots I_j\dots I_m\}$. All different queries in the query sets can be represented as a vector $V(I)=\{I_1, I_2, \dots I_j\dots I_m\}$. The weight values of vector use the idea of *TF-IDF* for reference, which considers the target words to make a contribution to the intention words. As shown in formula (2), $w(O_i, I_j)$ represents the weight values that O_i co-occurs with I_j and $C(O_i, I_j)$ represents the times of O_i co-occurs with I_j in the large-scale query samples. $N(I)$ shows the number of all intention vectors. $N(O_i, I_j)$ represents the number of intention vectors that O_i and I_j co-occurs.

$$w(O_i, I_j) = \frac{C(O_i, I_j)}{\sum_{O_i \in V(I_j)} C(O_i, I_j)} \log \frac{N(I)}{\sum_{I_j \in V(I)} N(O_i, I_j)} \qquad \text{公式(2)}$$

TF value reflects the contribution that target word O_i makes to the intention word I_j. The larger the value is, the stronger the features of target are. But, *IDF* value reflects the contribution that target word O_i makes to the global intention. The larger the value is, the weaker the features of target are. Through *TF-IDF* calculating, we obtain each feature weight of intention vector. For two different query intention words, we can calculate its cosine similarity. The larger the value is, the more similar the intentions are.

- **Language Model + *KL* Divergence**

Besides, we introduce the language model to calculate the probability that intention words generate the targets words. *KL* divergence is used to measure whether the probability of intention vectors distributed is approximate.If two intention vector $V(I_i)=\{O_{i1}, O_{i2}, \dots , O_{in}\}$ and $V(I_j)=\{O_{j1}, O_{j2}, \dots ,O_{jm}\}$ is given, their *KL* divergence is calculated with the formula(3). In the equation, $p(o|I_i)$ represents the probability of target word o co-occurs with intention word I_i.

$$D(I_i \parallel I_j) = \sum_{o \in (V(Ii))} p(o \mid I_i) \log \frac{p(o \mid I_i)}{p(o \mid I_j)} \qquad 公式(3)$$

As the zero problem caused by sparse date for language model, we carry on further smoothing after normalizing probability in experiment. When the molecule is zero, we set $0*\log(0/p) = 0$. And when $p(w|I_j)$ is zero, we set $p(o|I_j) = 1/C_j$ which is the reciprocal of C_j. The C_j is the total number of all targets occur in the $V(I_j)$.In order to balance the deviation brought about by each sub-directions, we add two-way values $D(I_i\|I_j) + D(I_j\|I_i)$ as *KL* balanced index. The smaller the value is, the closer the probability distribution of intention vector is and the more similar they are.

5.3   Intention Recommendation

Based on the intention cluster above, we adopt a simple transductive approach for query recombination and recommendation. Given a query, we identify the intention words and targets, mine the targets co-occurred in the global query samples firstly. By building the description of intention vectors, we use VSM and language model to describe intention separately with cosine similarity and *KL* divergence to measure the similarity between intention words and prior intention clusters. The most similar cluster is chosen as candidate recommended set according to the similarity ranking. Finally, we combine the candidate intention words with the query target unorderedly to form new queries and recommend as related queries.

However, not all the intention words in the cluster are suitable for recombination and recommendation. The reason is the similarity measure cannot avoid focusing on the local property of cluster. In other words, the correction can only represent part of the intentions with the query intention under test. This phenomenon is a common problem that most clustering application technologies are difficult to avoid. For details, if clustering cohesion is too strong, the similarity reaches consistently in fact, which contributes to detect the queries with different words but synonymous for recommending synonymous queries. But at the same time, the detection of relevant intention will be ignored. That is, the kind of intentions have relevant preference such as *"Apple Mobile"* and *"Apple Computer"* but not consistent intention. In contrast, if clustering cohesion is weak, then the intention words in cluster must have a more fine-grained division. At the moment, the relevance always comes from one point or locality of cluster internal, and the rest parts are weak associated or unrelated intention words. As a result, we take the following steps to select the intention words of cluster and use for query recombination and recommendation. 1) Adjust cluster parameters until the number of intention words in cluster reaches 10, and then the cohesion is not strong. Apcluster should iterate over 200 times. 2) Match the most prior cluster and the similarity between query intention under test and each intention word of the cluster, and then to rank according to the similarity. 3) Select the top n intention words of sort for query recombination and recommendation. The value of n will be introduced in experiment part.

6   Experiment Setting and Result Analysis

In this section, we will introduce the experimental corpus and evaluating methods firstly; Then, give the main systems include Target and Intention Recognition System, Intention Cluster System and Query Recommendation System which participate in the test; Finally, we give the test results of each system and the corresponding analysis.

6.1   Corpus

The experimental data is *Sogou2008* query logs which contains user query information within a month. After filtering queries, we obtain *1,902,402* no-repeat informational queries and group the queries with same clicked URLs.

For the classification experiment, we take *968* groups queries for manually label with an average of 5. The queries in the same group must have at least one common click. On this basis, we invite three volunteers to label targets and intentions. These volunteers do research on query recommendation more than one year.

For the intention cluster experiment, *1,981* intention words are selected randomly and clustered. The form of labeling is to compare the intention words in cluster which provided by the automatic intention clustering system to intention words under test by human-labeling (three volunteers + cross-validation).

For query recommendation experiment, we extract *2,000* queries randomly and divide equally to six sample space for query recommendation test. The recommended results of each sample space are tested by a volunteer and taking *macro-average* representation of overall performance.

6.2   Evaluation Method

In the experiment of classification, we use the *precision, recall, F-value* and *global accuracy* for evaluation. Through statistical, the percentage of target words to intention words in query samples is close to 2:1. The distribution is reasonable because targets words are often more than intention words in the queries. Therefore, *baseline1* is the accuracy of target reaching 66.7%, which assumes that all query words are target words with the recall of targets is 100%. Correspondingly, *baseline2* is the accuracy of intention reaching 33.3% , which assumes that all query words are intentions for the prior probability with the recall of intention is also 100%.

For the evaluation of intention cluster, we take the proportion of correct intention words in clusters as *precision* and obtain the global performance by taking *macro-average* of all clustering performance. For query recommendation, we use *global precision(G-P), consistent precision(C-P), relevant precision(R-P)* and $P@n(1{\leq}n{\leq}10)$ to evaluate. Consistent precision refers to the recommended queries have the consistent semantics with original query(such as "位置" and "地点"), that is different words but synonymous. Relevant refers to the recommended queries is relevant with original query(such as "诊断" and "治疗"). The consistency and relevance is judged by human. *P@n* refers to the precision of query recombination and recommendation which use the most similar *top-n* intention words in cluster.

6.3   Experiment Results and Analysis

In this section, we give the experimental results of target and intention classification system, intention cluster system and query recommendation system as well as the analysis.

- **The Performance of   Target and Intention Recognition**

Table 3 shows the experimental results of target and intention classification system. *Sys-1* is *lexical-based* approach used only and *Sys-2* uses *Context-base* approach only. *Sys-3* combines two approaches above. We use *NaiveBayes* classifier and 10 *cross-validations* of the data set. Results display the similarity of global accuracy between *sys-1*and *sys-2*. But combined two kinds of features, the results improve about 3%~4%. The reason benefits from the advantage of indentifying intention words based on lexical meaning and target words based on context property.

Table 3. Targets and Intention Identify Results

System	Targets			Intention			Gobal Accuracy
	P(%)	R(%)	F(%)	P(%)	R(%)	F(%)	P(%)
Sys-1	77.8	74.7	76.2	55.7	59.8	57.7	69.55
Sys-2	69.0	95.2	80.0	68.0	19.2	30.0	68.86
Sys-3	77.2	83.4	80.2	63.2	53.7	58.1	73.11
Baseline1	66.7	100	80.0	0	0	0	66.7
Baseline2	0	0	0	33.3	100	49.9	33.3

Besides, the recall of target words in *sys-2* is highest reaching 95.2%. Correspondingly, its recall of intention words is lowest only 19.2%. Because of the *context-based* approach have poor effect on identifying the impact intention words. For example, for query "北京电信", the target word is "电信" and intention word is "北京". Its overall meaning is to find the telecom located in Beijing but not the telecom in other place. Here, "北京" is an implicit intention word different from the explicit intention words such as "下载", "浏览" and "报价". The frequency of implicit words is low and the position in the query is limited that makes no obvious distinction with target words. So using the feature alone will cause the misjudgment of implicit intention words. Especially, the numbers and frequency of implicit intention words are more than the explicit intention words. As a result, *sys-2* loses a lot of intention words because of the misjudgment. In contrast, *sys-1* can improve the recall of intention words but not lose the recall of target. So the lexical-based approach is effect for intention identification and part of speech and morphology is the most effective feature.

Considering the distribution of target and intention in real, the measure of comprehensive system performance should take F-value and global accuracy into consideration. As shown in table 3, *sys-3* has a more performance than above two. Moreover, the classifier mixed with features performs better than baseline1 and baseline2. Especially, the ability of identifying the intentions has improved 9.8 percent while that of target improve litter. As the target words distribute high is queries priori, the performance of baseline itself is already high. So the ability of identifying target words of *sys-3* has reached the condition for further treatment.

- **The Performance of Intention Cluster**

We construct *1,981* intention vectors to realize two kinds of intention cluster systems. The Apcluster algorithm was chosen because of the advantage without setting the numbers of clustering categories in advance. *Sys-VSM* refers to use Vector Space Model and *Sys-KL* uses Language Model to calculate KL Divergence. The experimental results of query intention cluster are verified by three volunteers. As shown in table 4, #1#2#3 represents three experimental samples. Obviously, the performance of *Sys-VSM* is better than *Sys-KL*.

Table 4. Intention Cluster Results

Volunteer	Sys-VSM			Sys-KL		
	P(%)	P(%)	P(%)	P(%)	P(%)	P(%)
	#1	#2	#3	#1	#2	#3
VolunteerA	48.63	57.98	51.11	24.05	37.08	32.52
VolunteerB	45.28	53.83	54.52	27.67	35.42	37.34
VolunteerC	44.18	55.19	49.95	28.32	34.19	35.55
Average	46.03	55.67	51.86	26.68	35.56	35.14

From the data of table 4, we can find the results of manual judgment swing greatly, and the most optimal performance is 55.67%. It demonstrates that the diversity of intentions have brought uncertainties to volunteers. At the same time, the *VSM-based* approach has smaller granularity of clustering so that the ability of distinguish the clustering intention clusters is stronger. But the global precision of *KL* Divergence based on language model is lower. And at the same experimental samples, the number of *KL* cluster is less than the VSM approach. It indicates the loose of semantic relation between queries and a more diverse form of combination between queries.

Besides, the results illustrate that not all intention words of cluster can be recommended equally, but ranking according to the similarity of intentions and recommend the prior.

- **The Performance of Query Recommendation**

The performance of query recombination and recommendation according to similarity is illustrated in Fig.2, whose horizontal axis P@n represents top n($1{\leq}n{\leq}10$) intention words and vertical axis represents mean precision(average of all P@n). The label "Eva$i$" ($1{\leq}i{\leq}6$) indicates different volunteers' accessments. As shown in the graph, recommendation precision goes down with n increases, and it reaches overall highest at P@1,which is 57.8% on average. We attribute it to the recommendation mechanism, which always chose the center-closest intention word first. And these words are always most representative for the cluster, which covers a wide range of meanings and is easily accepted by users. For example, an intention cluster contains words as follows: Example3: "看病(see a doctor)", "挂号(register)", "诊断(diagnose)", "开药(prescribe)" and "住院(hospitalization)". (cluster center is "看病(see a doctor)").

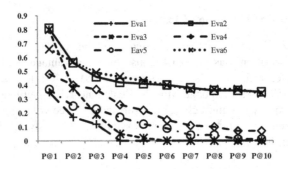

Fig. 2. Recommand System Performance

The cluster center *"see a doctor"* is most representative, thus has certain relations to all other words constitute queries, like *"how to register"*, *"who to diagnose"* or *"where for hospitalization"*. And it is reasonable to be a decent recommendation of highest probability.

However, Precisions drop quickly after *P@4*, which is caused by the relations between words outside the center, which were not absolutely consistent or related. As words outside center are related to the center in different aspects, and the candidate is only related to the center and a certain aspect, the results turn out to be other aspects are of little consistency. For example, a candidate intention is related to *"hospitalization"* in the above cluster, then *"where to register"*, which is constituted by *"register"*, is not a good recommendation for *"where for hospitalization"*. So, with the increasing n, words far from center and related aspects have higher probability of recommendation, which leads to lower precision.

Apart from that, table 5 lists the average precision of *P@n*($1{\leq}n{\leq}5$) in six sample spaces. The overall distribution is not gaussian distribution, which shows unbalance on two ends instead. The reason is, the different effects caused by different kinds of recommendations. Recommendations with high performance are words with obvious intentions, like "download", while those with low performance are words modifying the targets, like place names. Simple substitution of the latter ones may cause distortions of user intentions. Thus, a classification of queries according to user emphasis is needed to improve the system's performance.

| | | Table 5. P@N Values | | | | | | Table 6. Average Recommend Accuracy | | |

	P@1	P@2	P@3	P@4	P@5		G-P	C-P	R-P
Eva1	0.35	0.17	0.12	0	0	Eva1	0.028	0.011	0.018
Eva2	0.81	0.56	0.46	0.42	0.41	Eva2	0.336	0.013	0.324
Eva3	0.80	0.38	0.19	0.05	0.02	Eva3	0.065	0.015	0.050
Eva4	0.48	0.4	0.37	0.26	0.22	Eva4	0.123	0.113	0.010
Eva5	0.37	0.25	0.23	0.17	0.12	Eva5	0.065	0.016	0.048
Eva6	0.66	0.57	0.49	0.46	0.43	Eva6	0.331	0.004	0.327

Average precision of the system is shown in table 6. It shows a low overall precision, which is caused by not only the influences of different relations with cluster center (already discussed above), but also the irrational combination of target and intention words. Simple substitution of intention words in our method suffers from the problem of unsmooth semantics and unreasonable logics, which affects about 40% of all the intention words. For example, intention words "precious" and "expensive" are related, but when combined with target word "air", the situation is different. It is easy to understand "precious air", but not for "expensive air". Thus, the proper combination of intention words and target words are of vital importance to effective query generation, and is an essential part of our future work.

7   Conclusions

Our paper proposed a new query recommendation which concentrates on the analysis and application of query itself. It recognizes the target words and intention words by means of classification to describe their semantics based on massive query samples. After that, synonymous or related intention words are obtained by clustering for recommendation. Experiments show that our method can divided target and intention word effectively, and it gets 55.67% performance. P@1 reached 57.83% respectively.

However, there is still a large room for improvement. The experimental results show that the intention clustering performance influences queries recommendation a lot, and the clustering performance depends on the feature selection and matching algorithms. Therefore, future work will focus on feature selection method to enhance the intention description method and try to use semantic intention sample matching algorithm. For example, dividing the entity roles in the intention description, and employed into the similarity matching process. In addition, future work will also analyze the combination of target words and intention words, in order to form a fluent and logical query.

Acknowledgements. This research is supported by the National Natural Science Foundation of China (No. 60970056, 60970057, 61003152), Special fund project of the Ministry of Education Doctoral Program(2009321110006, 20103201110021) and Natural Science Foundation of Jiangsu Province, Suzhou City(SYG201030).

References

1. Li, Y., Wang, B., Li, J.: A survery of Query Suggestion in Search Engine. Journal of Chinese Information Processing 24(6), 75–84 (2010)
2. Craswell, N., Szummer, M.: Random Walks on the Click Graph. In: Proceedings of the 30th Annual International ACM SIGIR Conference on Research and Development in Information Retrieval (SIGIR 2007), Amsterdam, The Netherlands, pp. 239–246 (2007)
3. Cao, H., Jiang, D., Pei, J., et al.: Context-Aware Query Suggestion by Mining Click-Through and Session Data. In: Proceedings of the 14th ACM SIGKDD, pp. 875–883. ACM, New York (2008)
4. Huang, C.K., Chien, L.F., Oyang, Y.J.: Relevant term suggestion in interactive web search based on contextual information in query session logs. Journal of the American Society for Information Science and Technology 54(7), 638–649 (2003)
5. Wang, J., Peng, B.: User Behavior Analysis for a large-scale Search Engine. Journal of The China Society For Scientific and Technical Information 25(2), 154–162 (2006)
6. Li, Y., Xu, S., Wang, B.: Chinese Query Recommendation by Weighted SimRank. Journal of Chinese Information Processing 24(3), 3–10 (2010)
7. Mei, Q., Zhou, D., Church, K.: Query Suggestion Using Hitting Time. In: Proceedings of the 17th ACM Conference on Information and Knowledge Management (CIKM 2008), Napa Valley, California, pp. 469–478 (October 2008)
8. Broder, A.: A taxonomy of web search. SIGIR Forum, 3–10 (2002)
9. Wong, S.K.M., Ziarko, W., Wong Patrick, C.N.: Generalized Vector Spaces Model in Information Retrieval. In: Proceedings of the 8th Annual International ACM SIGIR Conference on Research and Development in Information Retrieval, New York, USA, pp. 18–25 (1985)
10. Song, F., Croft, W.B.: A General Language Model for Information Retrieval. In: Proceedings of the Eighth International Conference on Information and Knowledge Management, New York, USA, pp. 316–321 (1999)
11. Lavrenko, V., Allan, J., Deguzman, E., et al.: Proceedings of the Second International Conference on Human Language Technology Research, San Francisco, USA, pp. 115–121 (2002)

Exploiting Lexical Semantic Resource
for Tree Kernel-Based Chinese Relation Extraction

Liu Dandan, Hu Yanan, and Qian Longhua[*]

Natural Language Processing Lab
School of Computer Science and Technology, Soochow University
Suzhou, China, 215006
qianlonghua@suda.edu.cn

Abstract. Lexical semantic resources play an important role in semantic relation extraction between named entities. This paper exploits lexical semantic information based on HowNet to convolution tree kernels via two methods: incorporating lexical semantic similarity and embedding lexical sememes, and systematically investigates its effects on Chinese relation extraction. The experimental results on the ACE 2005 Chinese corpus show that the incorporation of lexical semantic similarity can significantly improve the performance whether entity-related information is known or not, while embedding lexical sememes can also improve the performance, but only when entity types are unknown. This demonstrates the effectiveness of lexical resources for Chinese relation extraction. In addition, the experiments also suggest that lexical semantic similarity facilitates the relation extraction, particularly the fine-grained subtype extraction, more than that of relation detection.

Keywords: Relation Extraction, Convolution Tree Kernel, Lexical Semantic Similarity, Lexical Sememe, HowNet.

1   Introduction

Relation extraction (RE) is an important information extraction task in natural language processing (NLP), with many practical applications, including learning by reading, automatic question answering, text summarization and so on. The goal of relation extraction is to detect and characterize semantic relationships between pairs of named entities in text. For example, a typical relation extraction system needs to extract a Person-Social relationship between the person entities "他" and "妻子" in the Chinese phrase "他 的 妻子" (his wife).

Generally, machine learning-based methods are adopted in relation extraction due to their high accuracy. In terms of the expression of learning examples (i.e., relation instances) they can be divided into feature-based methods and kernel-based ones. The key issue of feature-based RE is how to extract various lexical, phrasal, syntactic, and semantic features [1-7], which are important for relation extraction, from the sentence

---

[*] Corresponding author.

M. Zhou et al. (Eds.): NLPCC 2012, CCIS 333, pp. 213–224, 2012.

involving two entities, while for kernel-based RE, the structured representation of relation instances, such as syntactic parse trees[8-10], dependency trees[11], and dependency paths [12-13] etc., becomes the central problem. In Chinese relation extraction, many studies focus on feature-based methods, such as [14-16] while kernel-based methods, such as edit distance kernel [17], string kernel[19], convolution tree kernels over parse trees [20-21], have gained wide popularity.

It is widely held that lexical semantic information plays an important role in relation extraction between named entities, since two words, different in surface but similar in semantic, may represent the same relationship. For example, the two phrases "他 的 妻子" (his wife) and "她 的 丈夫" (her husband) convey the same relationship "PER-SOC.Family" in the ACE terminology, though "他" (he) and "她" (she), "妻子" (wife) and "丈夫" (husband) are two distinctive, yet semantically similar words. Therefore, different approaches are proposed to exploit this lexical semantic similarity in relation extraction. Chan et al.[6] and Sun et al.[7]use the corpus-based clustering techniques [21] to obtain the semantic codes of entity headwords, and then embed them as semantic features into the framework of feature-based relation extraction. However, it is difficult to determine the level of generality for semantic codes as regards different levels of relation types to be extracted.

In Chinese relation extraction, Che et al.[17] and Liu et al.[18] embed lexical semantic similarity based on TongYiCi CiLin [22] or HowNet to an edit distance kernel or a sequence kernel respectively for relation extraction. However, as the convolution tree kernels[23] exhibits their potential for relation extraction and witness wide applications far beyond the RE domain, the unresolved issue is whether or not the widely adopted convolution tree kernel can benefit from such lexical semantic resources. Bloehdorn and Moschitti[24] propose a generalized framework for syntactic and semantic tree kernels for Question Classification, which incorporate semantic information when computing structural similarity between two parse trees. Following their work, we incorporate lexical semantic similarity based on HowNet (abbreviated as HN), into convolution tree kernels, and compare its effect on Chinese relation extraction with that of directly embedding lexical sememes in tree structures.

The rest of the paper is organized as follows. In Section 2, we review the related studies while Section 3 introduces the tree structure used for RE in this paper. Section 4 elaborates two methods of exploiting a lexical resource for Chinese relation extraction. Section 5 reports experimental results and analysis. Finally, Section 6 concludes the paper and points out future directions.

2   Related Work

Due to the focus in this paper, this section only reviews the previous studies on the applications of semantic information to relation extraction.

In English relation extraction, there are three previous studies considering some kind of semantic information all in feature-based methods. Zhou et al. [1] first extract a country name list and a personal relative trigger word list from WordNet. They demonstrate that these two lists are helpful to distinguish the relations of

"ROLE.Residence" in ACE 2003 and of "PER-SOC.Family" in ACE 2004. Chan et al. [6] combine various relational predictions and background knowledge, including word clusters automatically gathered from unlabeled texts, through a global inference procedure called ILP (Integer Linear Programming) for relation extraction. They demonstrate that these background knowledge significantly improves the RE performance, particularly when the training data are scarce. Sun et al.[7] present a simple semi-supervised relation extraction system with large-scale word clustering. What they mean by semi-supervised learning is that the additional features are induced through word clustering from large-scale unlabeled texts, similar to Chan et al.[6]. Nevertheless, the subtle semantic commonality between words seems inherently difficult to be captured by feature-based methods.

On the other hand in Chinese RE, Che et al. [17] employ the Improved-Edit-Distance (IED) to calculate the similarity between two Chinese strings, and further considering lexical semantic similarity between words based on TongYiCi CiLin, their experiments show that the lexical semantic-embedded IED kernel method performs well for the person-affiliation relation extraction. Liu et al.[18] acquire lexical semantic similarity scores based on HowNet, a widely used Chinese lexical resource, and incorporate them into a sequence string kernel. Experiments on some ACE-defined fine-grained relationships show promising results. Up till now, no attempt has been made to incorporate such semantic information into tree kernel-based relation extraction, which seems more natural than feature-based methods and is exactly the focus of this paper.

3   Structured Representation for RE

The two key issues of tree kernel-based relation extraction are the representation of tree structure and the similarity calculation between trees. This section deals with the former while the next section discusses the latter.

Since the focus of this paper is the exploitation of lexical semantic resources to tree kernel-based RE, we directly adopt a state-of-the-art tree structure--the Unified Parse and Semantic Tree (UPST-FPT)[10]as the tree structure, which incorporates entity-related semantic information, such as entity types and subtypes in the Feature-Paired Tree (FPT) manner, into the Dynamic Syntactic Parse Tree (DSPT).

Figure 1 illustrates such a tree structure derived from the phrase "银行 总裁" (bank president) for a relation instance between the "银行" ORG (organization) entity and the

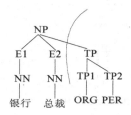

Fig. 1. Unified Parse and Semantic Tree with Feature-Paired Tree (UPST-FPT)

"总裁" PER (person) entity, where "TP1" denotes the entity type of the 1st entity and likewise "TP2" denotes that of the 2nd entity. The tree structure on the left of the dotted line is the DSPT while other entity-related semantic information, such as entity subtypes etc., is omitted for brevity.

4   Exploiting Semantic Resource in Tree kernels

This section first introduces convolution tree kernel for Chinese semantic relation extraction, then discusses two methods of using lexical semantic resource: incorporating into tree kernel computation and directly embedding into tree structures.

The first question for exploiting lexical semantic resource is, given too many words as leaf nodes in a parse tree, which of them are useful for relation extraction? Sun et al. [7] conduct a series of experiments using word clusters for different words in a relation instance, such as entity headwords, bag of headwords, the words before and after the entities etc., in a feature-based framework of RE and find that only entity headwords are important for RE. Therefore, we first consider the semantic information of lexical items corresponding to two entities involved in a relation instance. Moreover, we also consider the semantic information of the verb as Qian et al [10], if exists, between two entities, as some relation instances are clearly expressed in a verbal form.

4.1   Convolution Tree Kernel

The convolution tree kernel [23] counts the number of common sub-trees between two parse trees T1 and T2 as their similarity measure without explicitly considering the whole tree space.   It can be computed as follows:

$$K_{CTK}(T_1, T_2) = \sum_{n_1 \in N_1, n_2 \in N_2} \Delta(n_1, n_2)$$

(1)

where N_1 and N_2 are the sets of nodes for T_1 and T_2 respectively, and $\Delta(n_1, n_2)$ evaluates the number of two common sub-trees rooted at n_1 and n_2. It can be computed recursively as follows:

1. If the productions at n_1 and n_2 are different then $\Delta(n_1, n_2)=0$; otherwise go to Step 2;

2. If both n_1 and n_2 are part of speech (POS) tags, then $\Delta(n_1, n_2)=\lambda$; otherwise go to Step 3;

3. Calculate recursively as follows:

$$\Delta(n_1, n_2) = \lambda \prod_{k=1}^{\#ch(n_1)} (1 + \Delta(ch(n_1, k), ch(n_2, k))$$

(2)

where $\#ch(n)$ is the number of children of the node n, $ch(n,k)$ is the k-th child of the node n, and λ ($0<\lambda<1$) is a decay factor, which is used for preventing the similarity of sub-trees exceedingly depending on the size of sub-trees.

4.2   Semantic Convolution Tree Kernel: Incorporating Lexical Semantic Similarity

While convolution tree kernels exhibit promising results in the task of relation extraction [8-10, 25], they disregard lexical semantic similarity between words in parse trees, which is critical for relation extraction in some scenarios. Following the successful application of the syntactic and semantic convolution tree kernel [24] to the task of Question Classification (QC), we adopt a similar Semantic Convolution Tree Kernel (SCTK) to Chinese relation extraction with the lexical semantic similarity being calculated using Chinese lexical semantic resource.

The computation process of the SCTK is largely the same as that of the standard CTK except that in Step 1, one additional case should be considered as follows:

1. If the productions at n_1 and n_2 are the same, then go to Step 2; otherwise, if both n_1 and n_2 are the parents of entity headword nodes, then $\Delta(n_1, n_2) = \lambda *$ LexSim($HW1,HW2$); otherwise $\Delta(n_1, n_2)=0$;

where $HW1$ and $HW2$ denote the headwords corresponding to two entities immediately under n_1 and n_2 respectively and LexSim($HW1$, $HW2$) denotes the lexical semantic similarity between these two headwords which can be calculated using lexical resources such as HowNet.

HowNet[1], a commonly used Chinese lexical resource, is a lexical knowledge base with rich semantic information, where a word is described as a group of sememes in a complicated multi-dimensional knowledge description language, and the first sememe reflects the major feature of one concept. For example, the Chinese word "暗箱(camera obscura)" is described as: "part|部件, #TakePicture|拍摄, %tool|用具, body|身", "部件" is the first sememe of "暗箱". Due to its richness in lexical semantics, it has been widely exploited in various NLP researches [29, 30].

We adopt the software package by Liu and Li [31] to calculate lexical semantic similarity scores based on HowNet. The similarity score between content words (entity headwords or verbs) is a linear interpolation of four different similarity scores, i.e. similarity between primary sememes, that between other sememes, that between sets, and that between feature structures.

It is worth noting that in most cases, the entity headwords can be used directly to calculate their lexical similarity scores, e.g., in the Chinese relation instance "他 的 妻子" (his wife), both "他" (he) and "妻子" (wife) could be passed to the similarity calculation module since as common names they can be found in lexical resources. However, take the entity mention "大安森林公园" (DaAn Forest Park) as an example, since this headword is not a well-known proper noun and can not be found in HowNet, any similarity score involving this entity calculated using HN will be zero. Our solution to this problem is to first segment the entity headword into sequential words using the segmentation package and then to take the rightmost word as the new headword. For example, the entity mention "大安森林公园" is segmented into "大安 森林 公园" and then the word "公园" is passed to the lexical similarity calculation module.

---

[1] http://www.keenage.com/

However, when the entity is a person, no segmentation is performed since it is meaningless to calculate the similarity between the Chinese characters in person names. This strategy of segmenting the entity headword also applies to the method of embedding lexical sememes in tree structures.

4.3   Incorporating Lexical Sememes into Tree Structures

The alternate method to exploit the lexical resource is to directly embed semantic information to tree structures for relation instances, thus avoiding the intensive computation cost brought about by semantic convolution tree kernel. For HowNet, since the first sememe of a lexical item reflects the major propery of one concept, we only extract its first sememe as the semantic information and embed it into the tree structures. For example, in the relation instance"*台北 大安森林公园*"(Taipei DaAn forest park), the first sememes of HowNet corresponding to "台北"(Taipei) and "公园"(park, the head word) are "地方"(place) and "设施"(facility) respectively. After the sememes are extracted from HowNet, namely, "地方"(place) and "设施"(facility), they are attached to the root of the parse tree as shown in Figure 2, where "SHN1" and "SHN2" denote semantic information (the first sememes) based on HowNet corresponding to the 1st entity and the 2nd entity.

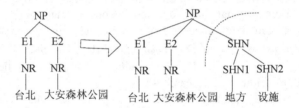

Fig. 2. Parse tree embedded with the first sememes of two entities

In addition, if there is a verb nearest to the 2nd entity along the path connecting two entities, a node "SHNV" followed by the verb's first sememe is also attached to the root node.

The first sememes of two entities or the verb are extracted from HowNet as follows:

1) find the lexical HW1、HW2 corresponding to the 1st and 2nd entity, and find the verb VLEX which near the 2nd entity;
2) search HowNet for the first sememes of HW1, HW2 and VLEX;
3) if the first sememe of a word does not exist, then the word will be further segmented, and again search the first sememe of the rightmost word after segmentation. Suppose that the first sememes are HCODE1、HCODE2 and HVCODE separately;
4) attach HCODE1、HCODE2 and HVCODE to the nodes SHN1、SHN2 and SHNV, which are further attached to the root of the parse tree.

5   Experimentation

This section experimentally investigates the effect of lexical semantic resources on Chinese relation extraction.

5.1   Experimental Setting

The ACE RDC 2005 Chinese corpus is used as the experimental datasets for Chinese semantic relation extraction. The corpus contains 633 documents, which were collected from newswires, broadcasts and weblogs. It defines 7 entity major types, 45 entity subtypes, 6 major relations types and 18 relation subtypes.

The corpus is first word-segmented using the ICTCLAS package, and then the corpus is parsed using the state-of-the-art Charniak's parser [32] with the boundaries of all the entity mentions kept. Finally, relation instances are generated by iterating over all pairs of entity mentions occurring in the same sentence, extracting corresponding tree structures and incorporating optional entity-related information (e.g., entity types, subtypes). In total, we obtain 9,147 positives and 97,540 negatives for Chinese relation instances.

In our experimentations, SVMLight-TK toolkit is adopted as our classifier since we usually treat RE as a classification problem. The package is modified to incorporate the lexical similarity calculation module. We apply the one vs. others strategy, which builds K classifiers so as to separate one class from the others. Particularly, the SubSet Tree (SST) kernel is used since it yields the best performance, while the decay factor λ (tree kernel) is set to the default value (0.4).

We adopt the five-fold cross validation strategy for training and testing, and the averages of 5 runs are taken as the final performance scores. The commonly used evaluation metrics are Precise, Recall, F-measure, which can be abbreviated as P/R/F1 respectively. Finally, in order to determine whether an improvement of performance is statistically significant or not, we perform approximate randomization tests similar to [33] using a Perl script adapted from Randomized Parsing Evaluation Comparator[2]. Conventionally, the performance difference is considered significant or very significant if $p \leq 0.01$ or $0.01 < p \leq 0.05$ respectively.

5.2   Experimental Results and Analysis

We first investigate the impacts of two different methods of using HowNet on the task of relation extraction. Then we compare our system with other state-of-the-art Chinese relation extraction systems.

Impact of Incorporating Lexical Semantic Similarity

Table 1 compares the performance of P/R/F1 for relation detection (2 types) and major type extraction (6 types) and subtype extraction (18 types) respectively on the ACE

---

[2] http://www.cis.uppen.edu/~dbikel/software/html#comparator

2005 Chinese corpus when lexical semantic similarity is incorporated in tree kernels for Chinese relation extraction. The DSPT (Dynamic Syntactic Parse Tree) [7] structure is used as the baseline (BL) without any semantic information. "ET" denotes that entity types (namely, major types and subtypes) are augmented into DSPT in the FPT (Feature-Paired Tree) [10] fashion while "HN" or "HNV" means either entity lexical similarity or verb lexical similarity based on HowNet is considered in the kernel computation. The 2nd column represents systems which incorporate various features or lexical similarity. For example, "(1)+HN" denotes considering the entity similarity on System 1, while "(3)+HN+HNV" considers both entity and verb similarity on System 3. The significance tests are conducted between a certain system (e.g., "(1)+HN") with its base system (i.e., System 1) and the performance increase, which is significant or very significant, is underlined or double-underlined respectively. Additionally, the best scores of P/R/F1 for each subtask are also highlighted respectively.

Table 1. Contributions of lexical semantic similarity for relation detection and extraction on the ACE 2005 Chinese corpus

No	Systems	Detection			Major types			Subtypes		
		P	R	F1	P	R	F1	P	R	F1
1	Baseline	**86.8**	54.5	67.0	72.6	46.2	56.5	70.1	43.1	53.4
2	(1)+HN	81.0	57.3	67.1	70.0	50.0	58.3	68.4	47.8	56.3
3	(1)+ET	85.9	62.5	72.3	80.1	58.9	67.9	76.7	56.1	64.8
4	(3)+HN	86.5	62.7	72.7	81.1	59.5	68.7	78.7	57.4	66.4
5	(3)+HN+HNV	86.4	63.2	73.0	81.1	60.0	69.0	79.1	57.5	66.6

The table shows that, in general, with the incorporation of lexical similarity, the Chinese RE systems achieve better performance no matter whether the entity type information is considered, though in different degrees. Specifically, the table also shows that:

- when the entity similarity is incorporated into the baseline, the R/F1 scores for relation extraction on major types and subtypes obtain very significant improvements (3.8/1.8 for major types, 4.7/2.9 for subtypes), while their P scores decrease moderately(-2.6 for major types, -1.7 for subtypes). This means more positive instances are recalled when considering the entity similarity, but at the expense of precision.
- when the entity types are provided, the incorporation of entity similarity significantly improves all the P/R/F1 scores for relation extraction on both major types and subtypes(1.0/0.6/0.8 for major types, 2.0/1.3/1.6 for subtypes). This suggests that entity similarity assisted by entity types is very helpful for Chinese relation extraction.

● when both the entity and verb similarity are considered on System 3, System 5 achieves very significant improvements for all the P/R/F1 scores on the three relation extraction subtasks, furthermore, all the P/R/F1 scores except P in relation detection, reach their peaks. This implies the verbs do help for relation extraction in a certain degree.

One important trend for these three subtasks, exposed in the table, is that, although the absolute performance scores decrease with the increase of the number of relations types to be extracted (e.g., F1 scores range from 73.0, 69.0 to 66.6 on System 5), the improvements brought about by lexical similarity increase progressively (i.e., the F1 improvements are 0.7, 1.1 and 1.8 units respectively). This demonstrates that lexical similarity can do better in discerning fine-grained relation types than just binary relation types, and thus more helpful for subtype relation extraction. This can be intuitively explained by the example "他 的 妻子" (his wife), where a relationship "PER-SOC.Family" exists between the entities "他" and "妻子". The phrasal structure determines that certain relationship exists, while the lexical semantics of two entities determines the specific type of their relationship.

Impact of Embedding Lexical Sememes

Table 2 compares the P/R/F1 performance scores for relation detection and relation extraction on the ACE 2005 corpus when the first sememes are embedded in tree structures like in Figure 2. Different from Table 1, "+HN" denotes embedding the first sememes of two entities, rather than considering lexical similarity in kernel computation. Likewise "+HNV" denotes embedding the first sememe of the verb, all the other notations are the same as those in Table 1. Table 2 shows that:

Table 2. Contributions of the first sememes for relation detection and extraction on the ACE 2005 Chinese corpus

No	Systems	Detection			Major types			Subtypes		
		P	R	F1	P	R	F1	P	R	F1
1	Baseline	86.8	54.5	67.0	72.6	46.2	56.5	70.1	43.1	53.4
2	(1)+HN	**87.0**	<u>56.7</u>	<u>68.7</u>	<u>77.3</u>	<u>51.4</u>	<u>61.8</u>	<u>74.5</u>	<u>48.6</u>	<u>58.8</u>
3	(1)+ET	85.9	<u>**62.5**</u>	<u>**72.3**</u>	<u>80.1</u>	<u>**58.9**</u>	<u>**67.9**</u>	<u>76.7</u>	<u>**56.1**</u>	<u>**64.8**</u>
4	(3)+HN	<u>86.6</u>	61.8	72.1	80.5	58.2	67.6	<u>77.2</u>	55.5	64.6
5	(3)+HN+HNV	<u>86.9</u>	61.2	71.8	**80.7**	57.6	67.2	<u>77.3</u>	55.1	64.3

● Similar to Table 1, when entity types are unknown, after the first sememes of two entities are embedded, the F1 scores achieve very significant improvements (1.7/5.3/5.4 units for detection, major types, and subtypes respectively), Moreover, the boost degree of performance is higher than that of lexical similarity incorporation, this implies that embedding the first sememes is likely better than lexical similarity incorporation when the entity types are unknown. Particularly, the performance boost comes from both precision and recall, rather than lexical similarity incorporation boosts the recall performance at the cost of precision decrease.

- Different from Table 1, when the entity types are known, embedding the first sememes of entities or verb does not yield any F1 improvements, though the precision is increased in most cases. This shows that when the entity types are known, embedding the first sememes makes the structured information more accurate but at the great expense of recall decrease.

Comparison with Other RE Systems

Table 3 compares the performance of major type relation extraction of our SCTK method with other state-of-the-art systems for Chinese relation extraction on the ACE 2005 corpus. However, the comparison is only for reference as different parts of the corpus or evaluation strategies are adopted by different systems. For example, Li at el. [16] adopt a feature-based method using two-fold training/testing strategies while Yu et al. [20] experiment on a subset of the ACE 2005 corpus, though using the same 5-fold cross-validation evaluation strategy. Nevertheless, this table shows that our single-kernel method achieves promising results and has the potential to combine with other feature-based methods for better performance improvement.

Table 3. Comparison of different systems on the ACE 2005 Chinese corpus

Systems	P(%)	R(%)	F1
Qian et al[10]: Composite kernel (linear+tree)	**80.9**	**61.8**	**71.1**
Li et al[16]: Feature-based	81.7	61.7	70.3
Qian et al[10]: CTK with USST	79.8	61.0	69.2
Ours: SCTK with UPST	81.1	60.0	69.0
Yu et al[20]: CTK with UPST	75.3	60.4	67.0
Zhang et al.[34]: Composite kernel	81.83	49.79	61.91

6   Conclusion and Future Work

In this paper, we empirically demonstrate the impact of lexical semantic resources of HowNet on Chinese relation extraction. We explore two methods of exploiting lexical semantic resources, i.e., incorporating HowNet-based lexical semantic similarity into tree kernels and directly embedding lexical sememes into tree structures. A series of experiments on the ACE 2005 benchmark corpus indicate that HowNet can significantly improve the performance of Chinese relation extraction via incorporating lexical similarity with or without entity-related information. On the other hand, embedding lexical sememes directly into tree structures, though as an intuitive method, improve the performance only when entity types are unknown. We also find that lexical similarity is better at extracting fine-grained relation types than just binary relationships. This suggests that when extracting more specific semantic relationships, lexical semantic resources are preferable.

For future work, different ways of calculating similarity based on lexical resources could be investigated to find the best one, and we will explore the corpus-based word similarity for Chinese relation extraction when lexical resources are not available in some domains other than the general domain.

Acknowledgement. This work is funded by China Jiangsu NSF Grants BK2010219 and 11KJA520003.

References

1. Zhou, G.D., Su, J., Zhang, J., Zhang, M.: Exploring Various Knowledge in Relation Extraction. In: ACL 2005, pp. 427–434 (2005)
2. Zhou, G.D., Su, J., et al.: Modeling Commonality among Related Classes in Relation Extraction. In: COLING-ACL 2006, pp. 121–128 (2006)
3. Zhou, G.D., Zhang, M.: Extracting Relation Information from Text Documents by Exploring Various Types of Knowledge. Information Processing and Management 43, 969–982 (2007)
4. Zhou, G.D., Qian, L.H., Fan, J.X.: Tree kernel-based Semantic Relation Extraction with Rich Syntactic and Semantic Information. Information Sciences 18(8), 1313–1325 (2010)
5. Jiang, J., Zhai, C.X.: A Systematic Exploration of the Feature Space for Relation Extraction. In: NAACL-HLT 2007, Rochester, NY, USA, pp. 113–120 (2007)
6. Chan, Y.S., Roth, D.: Exploiting Background Knowledge for Relation Extraction. In: COLING 2010, pp. 152–160 (2010)
7. Sun, A., Grishman, R., Sekine, S.: Semi-supervised Relation Extraction with Large-scale Word Clustering. In: ACL 2011, pp. 521–529 (2011)
8. Zhang, M., Zhang, J., Su, J., Zhou, G.D.: A Composite Kernel to Extract Relations between Entities with both Flat and Structured Features. In: COLING-ACL 2006, pp. 825–832 (2006)
9. Zhou, G.D., Zhang, M., Ji, D.H., Zhu, Q.M.: Tree Kernel-based Relation Extraction with Context-Sensitive Structured Parse Tree Information. In: EMNLP/CoNLL 2007, pp. 728–736 (2007)
10. Qian, L.H., Zhou, G.D., Kong, F., Zhu, Q.M., Qian, P.D.: Exploiting Constituent Dependencies for Tree Kernel-based Semantic Relation Extraction. In: COLING 2008, Manchester, pp. 697–704 (2008)
11. Culotta, A., Sorensen, J.: Dependency tree kernels for relation extraction. In: Proceedings of the 42nd Annual Meeting of the Association of Computational Linguistics, ACL 2004, pp. 423–439 (2004)
12. Bunescu, R.C., Mooney, R.J.: A Shortest Path Dependency Kernel for Relation Extraction. In: EMNLP 2005, pp. 724–731 (2005)
13. Nguyen, T., Moschitti, A., Riccardi, G.: Convolution Kernels on Constituent, Dependency and Sequential Structures for Relation Extraction. In: EMNLP 2009, pp. 1378–1387 (2009)
14. Che, W.X., Liu, T., Li, S.: Automatic Entity Relation Extraction 19(2), 1–6 (2005)
15. Dong, J., Sun, L., Feng, Y.Y., Huang, R.H.: Chinese Automatic Entity Relation Extraction. Journal of Chinese Information 21(4), 80–85, 91 (2007) (in Chinese)

16. Li, W.J., Zhang, P., Wei, F.R., Hou, Y.X., Lu, Q.: A Novel Feature-based Approach to Chinese Entity Relation Extraction. In: ACL 2008, pp. 89–92 (2008)
17. Che, W.X., Jiang, J., Su, Z., Pan, Y., Liu, T.: Improved-Edit-Distance Kernel for Chinese Relation Extraction. In: IJCNLP 2005, pp. 132–137 (2005)
18. Liu, K.B., Li, F., Liu, L., Han, Y.: Implementation of a Kernel-Based Chinese Relation Extraction System. Computer Research and Development 44(8), 1406–1411 (2007) (in Chinese)
19. Huang, R.H., Sun, L., Feng, Y.Y., Huang, Y.P.: A Study on Kernel-based Chinese Relation Extraction. Journal of Chinese Information 22(5), 102–108 (2008) (in Chinese)
20. Yu, H.H., Qian, L.H., Zhou, G.D., Zhu, Q.M.: Chinese Semantic Relation Extraction Based on Unified Syntactic and Entity Semantic Tree. Journal of Chinese Information 24(5), 17–23 (2010) (in Chinese)
21. Brown, P.F., Vincent, J.: Class-based n-gram models of natural language. Computational Linguistics 18(4), 467–479 (1992)
22. Mei, J.J., Zhu, Y.M., Gao, Y.Q., Yin, H.X.: TongYiCi CiLin, 2nd edn. Shanghai Lexicographic Publishing House, Shanghai (1996) (in Chinese)
23. Collins, M., Duffy, N.: Covolution Tree Kernels for Natural Language. In: NIPS 2001, pp. 625–632 (2001)
24. Bloehdorn, S., Moschitti, A.: Exploiting Structure and Semantics for Expressive Text Kernels. In: Proceedings of the Sixteenth ACM Conference on Information and Knowledge Management, Lisbon, Portugal (2007)
25. Qian, L.H., Zhou, G.D., Zhu, Q.M.: Employing Constituent Dependency Information for Tree Kernel-based Semantic Relation Extraction between Named Entities. ACM Transaction on Asian Language Information Processing 10(3), Article 15, 24 pages (2011)
26. Jiang, J., Conrath, D.: Semantic Similarity Based on Corpus Statistics and Lexical Taxonomy. In: Proceedings of International Conference on Research in Computational Linguistics, Taiwan (1997)
27. Resnik, P.: Semantic Similarity in a Taxonomy: An Information- Based Measure and its Applications to Problems of Ambiguity in Natural Language. Journal of Artificial Intelligence Research 11, 95–130 (1999)
28. Lin, D.: An Information-theoretic Definition of Similarity. In: Proceedings of the 15th International Conference on Machine Learning, Madison, WI (1998)
29. Suo, H.G., Liu, Y.S., Cao, S.Y.: A Keyword Selection Method Based on Lexical Chains. Journal of Chinese Information 20(6) (2006) (in Chinese)
30. Li, D., Ma, Y.T., Guo, J.L.: Words Semantic Orientation Classification Based on HowNet. The Journal of China Universities of Posts and Telecommunications 16, 106–110 (2009)
31. Liu, Q., Li, S.J.: Word Similarity Computing Based on How-net. Computational Linguistics, Chinese Information Processing, 59–76 (2002)
32. Charniak, E.: Immediate-head Parsing for Language Models. In: ACL 2001 (2001)
33. Chinchor, N.: The statistical significance of the MUC-4 results. In: MUC-4, pp. 30–50 (1992)
34. Zhang, J., Ouyang, Y., Li, W., Hou, Y.: A Novel Composite Kernel Approach to Chinese Entity Relation Extraction. In: Li, W., Mollá-Aliod, D. (eds.) ICCPOL 2009. LNCS, vol. 5459, pp. 236–247. Springer, Heidelberg (2009)

Research on Tree Kernel-Based Personal Relation Extraction

Cheng Peng[1,2], Jinghang Gu[1,2], and Longhua Qian[1,2,*]

[1] School of Computer Science & Technology, Soochow University
[2] Natural Language Processing Lab, Soochow University, Suzhou,
Jiangsu, 215006
qianlonghua@suda.edu.cn

Abstract. In this paper, a kernel-based personal relation extraction method is presented. First, a personal relation corpus is built through filtering and expansion from the ACE2005 Chinese corpus. Then, the structured information, which is appropriate for personal relation extraction, is constructed by applying pruning rules on the basis of the shortest path-enclosed tree. After that, *TongYiCi CiLin* semantic information is embedded into the structured information. Finally, re-sampling techniques are employed to alleviate the data imbalance problem inherent in the corpus distribution. Experimental results show that, the pruning rules, the embedding of semantic information and the application of re-sampling techniques can improve the F1 score by 3.5, 3.0 and approximate 3.0 units respectively compared with the baseline system. It suggests that the method we propose is effective for personal relation extraction.

Keywords: personal relation extraction, tree kernel, *tongyici cilin*, re-sampling, social network.

1 Introduction

In recent years, the application and popularity of WWW provides a huge repository of information for constructing social networks with the rapid development of Internet technology, which embodies a large number of persons of interest and the mutual relations among them. These mutual relations between persons of interest can be extracted from the information repository, and then social networks can be constructed consequently. The study of personal relation extraction attracts wide attention currently. According to the different information sources and extraction methods, these methods can be divided into two categories: from the Web pages and from plain texts.

Several representative studies of extracting social relationships from the Web pages are mainly as follows. Kautz et al. [1] and Mika et al. [2] employ the statistics of name co-occurrence in Web pages to extract the personal relationships. Chang et al. [3] adopt the Bayesian probability model to analyze the relationship between the personal entities for obtaining rich binary social relationships. Camp and Bosch [4]

---

* Corresponding author.

M. Zhou et al. (Eds.): NLPCC 2012, CCIS 333, pp. 225–236, 2012.

divide the personal relationships into positive, neutral, and negative according to emotional polarity, and then consider some lexical features, finally employing the SVM classifier to classify the relationships.

The methods of personal relation mining from Web pages mainly have two problems. First, the type of relationships is not sufficient, which only determines whether there is a relationship between personal entities, rather than considering the specific type of relationships. Second, the methods of processing ambiguous person's names are usually naive, lacking a fundamental solution to the problem of personal name disambiguation. With the maturity of natural language processing technology, mining the personal social relations from plain texts has gradually become practicable. This method can capture rich semantic relationships between personal entities in the natural language text, and solve the problem of ambiguous person names through coreference resolution within single document as well as cross documents.

Jing et al. [5] extract the relationships between personal entities and corresponding events from a specific domain of oral transcripts via named entity recognition, relation extraction and event extraction for building a corresponding social network. Due to the poor quality of transcribed texts, the F1 score of relation extraction is only about 30%. Elson et al. [6] proposes a method for extracting social networks from literature works. They find the two roles in a conversation by role name recognition and dialogue testing, then determine the relationships between the two roles and build social networks accordingly. However, the method they apply is only appropriate to dialog texts, and its domain adaptation is limited. In light of this, we consider employing the existing techniques for extracting rich personal relationships from natural language texts in the general domain, which mitigates the current problem of personal relationship extraction.

Relation extraction aims to identifying the semantic relation between entities from natural language text (MUC 1987-1998; ACE 2002-2005) [7]. At present, relation extraction methods are mainly feature-based [8-9] and tree kernel-based [10-15]. Feature-based methods map relation instance into a vector in a highly dimensional feature space and calculate vector similarity for machine learning approaches. The features usually include words, chunks, constituent and dependency parse trees as well as semantic information and other kinds of information. Tree kernel-based methods compare the similarity of two relation instances rendered as syntactic trees by calculating the common sub-tree of them. It can effectively capture the structured information of relation instances, and therefore tree kernel-based methods achieve better performance in the semantic relation extraction task.

In this paper, we also employ the tree kernel-based method for personal relation extraction. Owing to the specialties of personal relation extraction, the existing relation extraction technique is not fully applicable to it. In order to fully investigate personal relation extraction, we build a personal relation extraction corpus by expanding the ACE RDC 2005 Chinese corpus, and take SPT as the fundamental representation of relation instances. First, the SPT further trimmed through new pruning rules. Second, the semantic information of two current entities is incorporated into the structured information. Finally, re-sampling techniques are adopted to re-screen the training instances. All of these methods lead to the performance improvement of personal relation extraction.

In the rest of this paper, we first introduce the personal relation corpus in Section 2. We then describe our personal relation extraction method based on tree kernels in Section 3. In Section 4, we present our experimental results and analysis. The last section is a summary of this paper and some directions for future work.

2   Construction of a Personal Relation Corpus

In this paper, we employ the ACE2005 Chinese corpus as the experimental data for Chinese semantic relation extraction. Since the focus of this paper is to explore the relation between two personal entities, we retain the relation instances whose major types of two entities are both PER, resulting in a corpus which contains 651 instances of PER-SOC, 8 instances of EMP-ORG, and 12 instances of GEN-AFF.

All the existing relations are static in that they represent a relatively static state between persons, such as family relations. Moreover, we are also interested in the implicit description of social relations induced by dynamic events, such as interaction relationships between two persons. In the ACE 2005 corpus, there is a large amount of annotated event information, of which the events of CONTACT are closely associated with personal relationships. In order to enrich the types of personal relationships, we convert the events of CONTACT to interaction relationships between the entity participants in the event. For example, in the sentence "朱镕基昨天致电加拿大总理克雷蒂安(Yesterday Zhu Rongji called the Canadian Prime Minister Jean Chretien)", there is an event of the type "Contact. Phone-Write", and an interaction relationship between the two participants of "朱镕基(Zhu Rongji)" and "克雷蒂安(Jean Chretien)" can be induced.

According to the annotation format of the ACE 2005 documents, first, we pick up the events whose major type is CONTACT. Second, we obtain the event participants, whose event-argument is "Person-Entity". According to the combinatorial rule, if the number of person participants is greater than or equal to 2, we give each combination of any two persons a unique relationship ID, and finally generate one or more new CONTACT relationship. If the two involved entities already belong to another type of relationship, we retain the original relationship.

Eventually, there are 209 CONTACT relation instances obtained from the corresponding events, which includes two subtypes: Phone-Write and Meet. In total, we got 880 positive relation instances and 18,599 negative relation instances. Because personal relationships mainly contain the PER-SOC type and CONTACT type, the experimental results in this paper only list these two types as well as the overall performance.

3   Tree Kernel-Based Personal Relation Extraction

3.1   Structured Information for Personal Relation Instances

In tree kernel-based methods, a relation instance between two entities is encapsulated in a parse tree. Thus, it is critical to determine which portion of a parse tree is important. Zhang et al. [10] systematically explore five kinds of structured information, and their experimental results illustrate that Shortest Path-enclosed Tree (SPT) obtains the best performance. The SPT is part of a parse tree which is enclosed by the shortest path linking the two entities. Zhou et al. [11] proposed a Context-Sensitive Shortest Path-enclosed Tree (CS-SPT), which includes necessary context information beside the SPT. Qian et al. [15] generate a more concise and accurate Dynamic Relation Tree (DRT) using a series of heuristic rules based on the principle of constituent dependency. The preliminary experimental results show that the relation extraction performance of directly using these structured information is not satisfactory, which caused by the sentences of personal relation corpus are quite long. Therefore, in this paper, we eliminate redundant information from the SPT and recover the verb of right side entity to improve the personal relation extraction performance. Three pruning rules are listed as follows.

- Removing the entity coordination structure (RMV_ENTITY_CC): When a coordination structure appears in the path connecting the two entities, we can remove most of the coordinates to simplify the SPT structure. Since the semantic relations for all coordinates are the same, in order to highlight the involved entity, we only retain the coordinate in the path connecting the two entities while removing all other coordinates. As Fig. 1(a) shows, in the phrase "德仁和雅子的女儿" (the daughter of Naruhito and Masako), there is a coordination structure. When we consider the semantic relation between "德仁" (Naruhito) and "女儿" (daughter), the coordinate "雅子" (Masako) will interfere the SVM classifier. In order to accurately describe the relation between the entity "德仁" (Naruhito) and "女儿" (daughter), we only retain the coordinate of "德仁" (Naruhito), thus the phrase "德仁的女儿" (Naruhito's daughter) can accurately reflect the essence of personal relationship.

- Removing the NP coordination structure (RMV_NP_CC_NP): As removing the entity coordination structure, this also helps to reduce noise. We can use the same method to eliminate the redundant information of the coordination structure of noun phrases, leaving only the coordinate in the path connecting two entities. As Fig. 1(b) shows, in the sentence, "巴特列，以及玻利维亚总统班塞尔、智利总统拉戈斯出席了会议" (Batlle, and Bolivian President Banzer, Chilean President Ricardo Lagos attended the meeting), in order to identify the interaction relation between "巴特列" (Batlle) and "拉戈斯" (Ricardo Lagos), we just need to retain the noun phrase "巴特列 智利总统拉戈斯" (Batlle Chilean President Ricardo Lagos). The redundant part of "，以及玻利维亚总统班塞尔、" (, and Bolivian President Banzer,) contributes little role in determining the semantic relationships between two entities "巴特列" (Batlle) and "拉戈斯" (Ricardo Lagos). Removing this part of redundant information can improve the similarity of structured information and mitigate the problem of data sparseness, thus improve the performance of personal relation extraction. It is worthy to note that there are a large number of person names connecting with conjunction, comma and pause punctuations in relation instances of the CONTACT type, so we also take comma and pause punctuations as special types of coordination structures.

- Extending the verb right to the 2nd entity (EXT_RIGHT_VERB): According to linguistic knowledge, we know that the verb phrase reflects the semantic relationship. Verbs describe events, actions, states, change of states, and experiences, all of which are likely related to semantic relationships. According to corpus statistics, we find that only about 1/3 of the predicates is included in the shortest path tree while most predicates are pruned. Therefore, we attempt to recover the verb to enrich the context information of relation instances. In order to avoid noisy verbs being recovered, this paper only extends the verb phrase structure from the second entity to the lowest common node in SPT. As in Fig. 1(c), in the sentence"小学四年级学生给姑妈写信" (A fourth-grade student wrote a letter to aunt), the event participants "学生" (student) and "姑妈" (aunt) have a CONTACT type relation. SPT only contains the path connecting the two entities, thus unable to capture the corresponding relationship between them. Through the restoration of the verb "写信" (wrote), the new structured information can reflect the interaction nature between the entities "学生" (student) and "姑妈" (aunt).

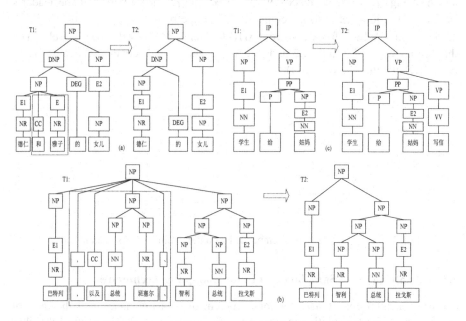

Fig. 1. The structured information of employing three pruning rules

3.2   Embedding *TongYiCi CiLin* Semantic Information

It is well known that semantic properties of entities are closely related to semantic , relationships, and thus play an important role in extracting semantic relations between entities. In Chinese relation extraction, Che et al. [16] calculate the similarity of instances using the edit-distance kernel-based method, considering the lexical semantic similarity in TongYiCi CiLin, and attain good performance in the person-affiliation relation. Liu et al. [17] perform Chinese relation extraction on three major types of ACE2005 corpus using string kernel-based method, considering the lexical semantic similarity in HowNet. Their experiments show that semantic similarity can improve the relation extraction performance.

TongYiCi CiLin (hereafter referred to as CiLin) is a Chinese thesaurus, in which each word has a code to represent its semantic category. It contains 77,492 words, among which the number of polysemous words is 8,860. It defines 12 major classes, 94 middle classes, 1,428 small classes, which are further divided into word groups and atomic word groups.

Semantic information can be embedded into the structured information: First, adding the semantic code to the parse tree; second, realizing a tree kernel function based on lexical semantic similarity. For simplicity, this paper employs the first method, which means adding the CiLin semantic information of two entities to structured information. The decay factor (the default is 0.4) makes the deeper level nodes have smaller contribution to the overall similarity for calculating the tree-kernel similarity, thus we add the semantic code information to the root of the parse tree. As shown in Fig. 2, in the sentence "领导人的家属联名写信给委员会" (The leader's families sent a joint letter to the council), the atomic word group codes of "领导人" (leader) and "家属" (families) are "Af10a02" and "Ah01B01" respectively. The children nodes of SC1 and SC2 nodes represent the lexical semantic codes of the 1st entity (E1) and the 2nd entity (E2).

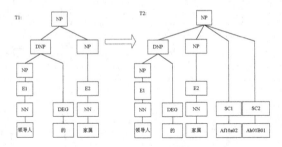

Fig. 2. Structured information embedded with the CiLin lexical semantic codes

3.3   Applying Over-Sampling and Under-Sampling Techniques

Our experimental corpus has a serious problem of data imbalance that the ratio of positive instances to negative instances is approximately 1:12. The skewed distribution of instances makes the SVM classifier heavily biased towards the majority-class instances, leading to classification performance deterioration. Therefore, it is considered as a serious problem needing an urgent solution.

Generally, re-sampling is an effective strategy to deal with the imbalanced data problem. Re-sampling refers to repeating collecting samples from a large number of samples under certain preconditions, and estimates the probability of occurrence of an event using the collected samples. Re-sampling has two variants: over-sampling and under-sampling. Over-sampling repeats minority-class samples to reach data balance, while under-sampling randomly select majority-class samples to reach data balance.

There are a large number of unnecessary repetitive minority-class samples in over-sampling, while many majority-class samples have not been fully utilized. In personal relation extraction, the structured information of negative samples is overwhelmingly large and diverse, so that their structured information has far more diversity than positive instances. The experimental results would not be satisfactory by making the balance between positive and negative samples. Therefore, we made several experiments under different proportions of positive and negative instances to obtain an optimal balance point. Specifically, in the process of under-sampling, we increase the ratio of negative instances to balance the structured information diversity of positive and negative instances while for over-sampling, we increase the ratio of positive instance gradually to make it more reasonable. In order to compare with the full sampling, the test sets for all experimental combinations are the same.

4   Experimental Setting and Results

This section first introduces the experimental setting, and then gives the experimental results and corresponding analysis.

4.1   Experimental Setting

In our experiments, we formalize personal relation extraction as a multi-class classification problem. SVM is selected as our classifier. In our implementation, we use open source tools SVMLight that supports the convolution tree-kernel function [18]. For efficiency, we apply the one vs. others strategy, which builds K classifiers so as to separate one class from all others and select the one with the largest margin as the final answer. To take full advantage of corpus resources and reduce the variation of the experimental results, we apply five-fold cross-validation strategy on the corpus. This strategy is widely used in the relation extraction research due to absence of large-scale corpus [10-15]. The evaluation metrics are commonly used precision (P), recall (R) and F1 score (F1). For comparison, our relation extraction task is focused on major relation types.

The corpus is parsed using the Charniak parser [20] with the boundaries of all the entity mentions kept. We iterate over all pairs of entity mentions occurring in the same sentence to generate potential relation instance. Then we insert a tag node on the parent of the entity POS node in the parse tree, marking the node as E1 or E2 respectively, or E if the entity is not involved.

In addition, for the purpose of determining whether the difference of two experimental results is statistically significant or not, we employ approximate random technology [19] for significant testing. Double underlines, single underlines and no underline are respectively used to stand for $p \leqslant 0.01$, $0.01 < p \leqslant 0.05$ and $p > 0.05$, that is, the difference is very significant, significant and not significant.

4.2   Experimental Results and Analysis

Effect of the Pruning Rules for Structure Information

Table 1 shows that, on the basis of SPT (baseline system), the P/R/F1 performance for personal relation extraction applying the three pruning rules. Outside the brackets are the results of the overlapping mode (that is, three different pruning rules were consecutively applied in a certain order), while inside the brackets are the results of the standalone mode (that is, each pruning rule is applied alone). All the significance tests are conducted between the total experimental results of the current system and the baseline system. The performance scores are underlined or not in terms of their p values. The experimental results show that, compared with SPT, three new pruning rules generally improve the performance of the personal relation extraction very significantly, with the overall F1 score increased by 3.5 units. We also find from Table 1:

— Both in the standalone and in overlapping modes, the improvement degree of three kinds of pruning rules are different. The RMV_NP_CC_NP rule improves the most; the RMV_ENITTY_CC rule affects less; the EXT_RIGHT_VERB rule contributes the least. The reason is that the number of NP coordination structures for RMV_NP_CC_NP is bigger than that of entity coordination structures for RMV_ENITTY_CC, thus the former rule removes much more redundant information than the latter, while the EXT_RIGHT_VERB rule only recovers a small number of verbs and these verbs are quite diverse.

— The F1 scores of the CONTACT type are significantly lower than those of the PER-SOC type, mainly caused by the low recall (about 10%-20%). The main reason is that PER-SOC instances are usually reflected in local range, while CONTACT relation instances have long distance between the two entities; the long distance increases the difficulty of extraction. What's more, the parsing performance for long sentences is worse, thus leading to decrease in the performance of relation extraction.

— The contribution of three pruning rules to the CONTACT type is far greater than to the PER-SOC type. Particularly, the recall of CONTACT increases over 11 units, making the F1 scores significantly increased. This attributes to the syntactic structure of CONTACT instances is more complex. Hence, the removal of noise information helps more.

In summary, the appropriate pruning rules can significantly reduce the noisy information of relation instances; thereby acquire concise and accurate structured information. This method can significantly improve the performance of personal relation extraction.

Table 1. The effect of pruning rules on personal relation extraction

Pruning Rules	PER-SOC			Contact			Total		
	P	R	F1	P	R	F1	P	R	F1
SPT	80.7	38.9	52.3	75.8	10.5	18.4	78.8	31.8	45.3
+RMV_ENTITY_CC	80.9	39.5	52.9	79.6	11.5	19.9	79.9	32.5	46.1
	(80.9)	(39.5)	(52.9)	(79.6)	(11.5)	(19.9)	(79.9)	(32.5)	(46.1)
+RMV_NP_CC_NP	82.4	39.8	53.5	81.7	18.2	29.6	81.6	34.3	48.3
	(81.5)	(38.4)	(52.0)	(83.3)	(21.0)	(33.5)	(81.3)	(34.0)	(47.8)
+EXT_RIGHT_VERB	81.8	39.6	53.3	81.2	21.5	33.9	81.0	35.0	48.8
	(80.9)	(38.3)	(52.8)	(62.0)	(11.0)	(18.6)	(75.9)	(32.6)	(45.5)

Effect of CiLin Semantic Information

Table 2 compares the effect of different levels of CiLin semantic information ("big class", "middle class", "small class", "word group" and "atomic word group") for personal relation extraction. The baseline system is the best one in Table 1 (SPT-OPT is a short name for the baseline system). We add a certain level of semantic information in each system. Among them, CL_B, CL_M, CL_S, CL_WG and CL_AWG stand for "big class", "middle class", "small class", "word group" and "atomic word group" respectively. Significant tests were conducted between the baseline system (SPT_OPT) and each system of adding semantic codes. The experimental results show that adding appropriate semantic information can significantly improve the performance of personal relation extraction.

— With the granularity of CiLin semantic information increasing gradually, the F1 overall performance rises progressively. When adding the "atomic word group" semantic code information, we get the best performance of F1 score with 3 units compares to the baseline system. The results indicate that the more detailed semantic information, the better for helping the personal relation extraction.
— For both PER-SOC and CONTACT types, the improvements of F1 scores come from a substantial increase in recall, while the precision remains almost unchanged, indicating that adding semantic information is helpful to recognize more positive instances.

Table 2. The effect of *CiLin* semantic information on personal relation extraction

Cilin Class	PER-SOC			Contact			Total		
	P	R	F1	P	R	F1	P	R	F1
SPT-OPT	81.8	39.6	53.3	81.2	21.5	33.9	81.0	35.0	48.8
+CL_B	81.9	38.1	51.8	81.8	23.5	36.2	81.2	34.3	48.1
+CL_M	78.7	41.6	54.3	79.4	22.5	34.9	78.2	36.7	49.9
+CL_S	81.4	41.0	54.4	81.1	22.9	35.6	80.5	36.4	50.1
+CL_WG	81.9	42.7	55.9	82.4	23.5	36.4	81.3	37.7	51.4
+CL_AWG	81.5	42.9	56.3	81.7	24.4	37.5	81.5	38.1	51.8

Effect of Re-sampling Techniques

In order to obtain the optimal ratio of the number of positive to negative instances, this paper investigates the effect of under-sampling and over-sampling for personal relation extraction in different ratios of positive to negative samples. Table 3 lists the experimental results of under-sampling and Table 4 lists those of over-sampling. POS: NEG in the first column of tables indicates that the proportion of positive and negative. Specifically, in under-sampling experiments, we add all the positive instances to the training set, and randomly select negative instances according to the ratio. In over-sampling experiments, we add all the negative samples to the training set, and randomly select positive instances according to the ratio. The baseline system is the best one in Table 2. For comparison, the testing set of every system is the same as the baseline.

Because the training data is selected randomly, the performances may differ. Therefore, each system of experiments is repeated five times, taking their average as the final results. We can demonstrate that in the tables, under-sampling and over-sampling can improve the performance.

Table 3. The effect of under-sampling for personal relation extraction

POS:NEG	PER-SOC			Contact			Total		
	P	R	F1	P	R	F1	P	R	F1
1:1	27.9	67.4	39.5	28.2	52.6	36.6	28.8	63.3	39.5
1:2	41.8	59.0	48.8	39.4	46.4	42.6	41.4	55.4	47.4
1:3	49.6	56.7	52.8	48.2	44.0	45.9	49.2	53.2	51.1
1:4	57.0	53.1	54.8	58.4	42.1	48.9	57.2	50.1	53.3
1:5	61.8	51.5	55.9	54.6	38.2	44.7	59.8	48.0	53.1
1:6	63.5	50.5	56.1	61.0	37.3	46.2	62.6	46.9	53.5
1:7	67.7	49.0	56.7	65.8	32.0	43.0	66.7	44.5	53.3
1:8	72.4	47.9	57.5	68.4	31.7	43.3	70.7	44.2	54.4
1:9	71.6	46.4	56.2	66.8	32.0	43.2	70.0	41.7	52.4
1:10	71.9	46.7	56.5	68.5	27.3	38.9	70.7	41.7	52.4
1:11	74.2	45.9	56.6	70.4	29.7	41.5	72.7	41.6	52.8
1:12	81.5	42.9	56.3	81.7	24.4	37.5	81.5	38.1	51.8

— Under-sampling and over-sampling in different ratios, in most cases, the performance is higher than the baseline system (with all positive and negative instances: 1:12). Under-sampling and over-sampling method balance the ratio of positive and negative instances; thus increase the weight of positive instances in the SVM classifier, leading to significant recall improvements. Although the precision declines a lot, overall, the F1 score increases significantly.

— Over-sampling performance scores are generally better than those of under-sampling, and they almost unchanged in a wide range. The main reason is that Under-sampling greatly reduces the number of negative instances in the training set, thus the structured information of negative instance is not fully utilized. On the contrary, Over-sampling just enhances the weight of positive instances; and keeps all the negative instances.

— For both under-sampling and over-sampling, the improvement of the CONTACT type is significantly higher than the PER-SOC type. The number of CONTACT instances is much less than that of PER-SOC ones, i.e., the ratio of positive and negative instance is even more unbalanced than that if the PER-SOC type, thus re-sampling technique has a greater impact on CONTACT type than on PER-SOC type.

Table 4. The effect of over-sampling for personal relation extraction

POS:NEG	PER-SOC			Contact			Total		
	P	R	F1	P	R	F1	P	R	F1
1:12	81.5	42.9	56.3	81.7	24.4	37.5	81.5	38.1	51.8
2:12	78.6	43.2	55.5	71.0	29.7	41.8	76.3	39.8	52.2
3:12	77.9	45.3	57.2	72.0	34.0	46.1	75.8	42.3	54.3
4:12	75.0	46.1	56.9	64.8	36.3	46.4	72.1	43.6	54.2
5:12	74.6	46.1	56.8	65.9	36.3	46.8	71.9	43.5	54.1
6:12	74.7	46.5	57.2	64.0	35.9	45.8	71.7	43.8	54.3
7:12	74.8	46.5	57.2	64.4	35.9	46.3	71.9	43.8	54.4
8:12	74.8	46.8	57.7	64.6	36.8	46.8	71.9	44.3	54.7
9:12	74.7	46.8	57.7	64.6	36.8	46.8	71.9	44.3	54.7
10:12	74.7	46.8	57.7	64.6	36.8	46.8	71.9	44.3	54.7
11:12	74.7	46.8	57.7	64.6	36.8	46.8	71.9	44.3	54.7
12:12	74.7	46.8	57.7	64.6	36.8	46.8	71.9	44.3	54.7

In summary, the re-sampling techniques, especially the over-sampling, can significantly improve the performance of personal relation extraction. However, this improvement of performance is at the cost of precision, while the tree pruning rules and semantic information addition significantly improve the recall as well as the precision. Therefore, the first two language-based methods are better than re-sampling techniques.

5   Conclusions

In this paper, we redefine the relation between person entities and build a personal relation corpus based on use the ACE 2005 corpus. In order to solve the problem of complex syntax trees of personal relation instances, we propose three pruning rules to remove the redundant information on the basis of SPT. Then we utilize the Chinese semantic resource, TongYiCi CiLin, to enrich the structured information of relation instances. Finally, for alleviating the data imbalance problem, we employ re-sampling techniques to reshuffle the training set. The experimental results shows that pruning rules, semantic information and re-sampling techniques can effectively improve the performance of personal relation extraction.

Although the proposed methods can effectively improve the performance of personal relation extraction, the overall F1 score is only 55%, still far away from the practical application. The future work is focused on building a large-scale personal relation corpus, generating more accurate and concise structured information, so as to further improve the performance.

Acknowledgement. This work is funded by China Jiangsu NSF Grants BK2010219 and 11KJA520003.

References

1. Kautz, H., Selman, B., Shah, M.: The hidden Web. AI Magazine 18(2), 27–35 (1997)
2. Mika, P.: Flink: Semantic Web Technology for the Extraction and Analysis of Social Networks. Journal of Web Semantics 3(2), 1–20 (2005)
3. van de Camp, M., van den Bosch, A.: A Link to the Past: Constructing Historical Social Networks. In: ACL-HLT, Portland, Oregon, USA, pp. 61–69 (2011)
4. Chang, J., Boyd-Graber, J., Blei, D.M.: Connections between the Lines: Augmenting Social Networks with Text. In: KDD 2009, Paris, France, pp. 169–177 (2009)
5. Jing, H., Kambhatla, N., Roukos, S.: Extracting.: Social Networks and Biographical Facts From Conversational. In: ACL, Prague, Czech Republic, pp. 1040–1047 (2007)
6. Elson, D.K., Dames, N., KcKeown, K.R.: Extracting Social Networks from Literary Fiction. In: ACL, Uppsala, Sweden, pp. 138–147 (2010)
7. ACE. Automatic Content Extraction,
   http://www.ldc.upenn.edu/Projects/ACE/

8. Kambhatla, N.: Combining Lexical, Syntactic and Semantic Features with Maximum Entropy models for Extracting Relations. In: ACL (Poster), Barcelona, Spain, pp. 178–181 (2004)
9. Zhou, G., Su, J., Zhang, J.: Exploring Various Knowledge in Relation Extraction. In: ACL, pp. 427–434. Ann Arbor, Michigan (2005)
10. Zhang, M., Zhang, J., Su, J., Zhou, G.: A Composite Kernel to Extract Relations between Entities with both Flat and Structured Features. In: COLING-ACL, Sydney, Australia, pp. 825–832 (2006)
11. Zhou, G., Zhang, M., Ji, D., Zhu, Q.: Tree Kernel-based Relation Extraction with Context-Sensitive Structured Parse Tree Information. In: EMNLP-CoNLL, Prague, Czech, pp. 728–736 (2007)
12. Zhou, G., Su, J., et al.: Modeling Commonality Among Related Classes in Relation Extraction. In: COLING-ACL 2006, pp. 121–128 (2006)
13. Zhou, G., Zhang, M.: Extracting Relation Information from Text Documents by Exploring Various Types of Knowledge. Information Processing and Management 43, 969–982 (2007)
14. Zhou, G., Zhang, M., Ji, D., Zhu, Q.: Tree Kernel-based Relation Extraction with Context-Sensitive Structured Parse Tree Information. In: EMNLP/CoNLL 2007, pp. 728–736 (2007)
15. Qian, L., Zhou, G., Kong, F.: Exploiting Constituent Dependencies for Tree Kernel-based Semantic Relation Extraction. In: COLING, Manchester, pp. 697–704 (2008)
16. Che, W., Jiang, J., Su, Z.: Improved-Edit-Distance Kernel for Chinese Relation Extraction. In: IJCNLP, JejuIsland, R. of Korea, pp. 132–137 (2005)
17. Liu, K., Li, F., Liu, L., Han, Y.: Implementation of a Kernel-based Chinese Relation Extraction System. Computer Research and Development 44(8), 1406–1411 (2007) (in Chinese)
18. SVMLight TK,
    http://download.joachims.org/svm_light/current/
    svm_light.tar.gz
19. Edgington, E.S.: Approximate Randomization Tests. Journal of Psychology, 143–149 (1969)
20. Charniak, E.: Immediate-head Parsing for Language Models. In: ACL, Toulouse, France, pp. 129–137 (2001)

Adaptive Topic Tracking Based on Dirichlet Process Mixture Model

Chan Wang, Xiaojie Wang, and Caixia Yuan

Beijing University of Posts and Telecommunications, Beijing, China
{wchan,xjwang,yuancx}@bupt.edu.cn

Abstract. This paper proposes a Dirichlet Process Mixture Model (DPMM) considering relevant topical information for adaptive topic tracking. The method has two characters: 1) It uses DPMM to implement topic tracking. Prior knowledge of known topics is combined in Gibbs sampling for model inference, and correlation between a story and each known topics can be estimated. 2) To alleviate topic excursion problem and topic deviation problem brought by existing adaptive tracking methods, the paper presents a new adaptive learning mechanism, the basic idea of which is to introduce tracking feedback with a reliability metric into the topic tracking procedure and make tracking feedback influence tracing computation under the condition of the reliability metric. The empirical results on TDT3 evaluation data show that the model, without a large scale of in-domain data, can solve topic excursion problem of topic tracking task and topic deviation problem brought by existing adaptive learning mechanisms significantly even with a few on-topic stories.

Keywords: adaptive topic tracking, ATT; traditional topic tracking, TTT, DPMM, Gibbs sampling, known topics.

1 Introduction

With the rapid development of Internet, the real-time, high-volume data stream resources increase rapidly, such as newswires, news broadcast, TV news, IM records, chat room messages, emails, twitter posts, etc. How to discover and track topics across such real-time streams is an urgent and practical problem.

The research of Topic detection and tracking aims to automatically organize and locate relevant stories from a continuous feed of news stories. There are several subtasks defined for the TDT evaluation. Among them, topic tracking task aims to associate incoming stories with topics that are known in advance. A topic is "known" by its association with stories that describe it. Thus each known topic is defined by one or more on-topic sample training stories (i.e., sample stories) [1].

The typical process of tracking system is: 1) building models of known topics and stories; 2) estimating correlation between them; 3) getting the tracking result of the story according to the correlation. In traditional topic tracking (TTT) methods, the known topic is represented using 1-4 sample stories given in advance [1] and keeps unchanged during tracking process. It is well known that the contents of topic will be

M. Zhou et al. (Eds.): NLPCC 2012, CCIS 333, pp. 237–248, 2012.

enriched and the topic focuses transfer gradually with newly incoming data, which is called topic excursion. Thus, adaptive topic tracking (ATT) which has self-learning ability becomes a new research trend. ATT rich the topic model through considering the additional on-topic stories during tracking process, which can improve topic tracking performance.

This paper proposes an adaptive topic tracking method based on DPMM. The remainder of the paper is organized as follows: Section 2 discusses related work firstly. Section 3 proposes TTT and ATT based on DPMM. Section 4 presents experiments and result analysis, finally conclusions are given in Section 5.

2   Related Work

Researchers put forward many correlation estimation methods according to different representation of topics and stories. Most topic tracking methods based on vector space model use Hellinger distance [2], cosine similarity [3] to measure correlations. Topic tracking methods based on language model express correlations of story and topic as a probability model. Taking unigram model for example, the correlation of story S and topic Z_i can be calculated as:

$$P(Z_i \mid S) = \frac{P(S \mid Z_i)P(Z_i)}{P(S)} \approx \{\prod_{w_j \in S} \frac{P(w_j \mid Z_i)}{P(w_j)}\}P(Z_i) \tag{1}$$

Where w_j is the jth word in S, $P(Z_i)$ and $P(w_j)$ is prior probability of Z_i and w_j, $P(w_j \mid Z_i)$ is probability of w_j under Z_i. Yamron [4], Lo [5], Spitters [6] used unigram model to conduct topic tracking and obtained good performance.

However, topic tracking task only have 1-4 sample stories to describe per known topic, so serious data sparse problem exists in tracking task. To alleviate this problem, representation method based on language model uses data smoothing technique to reestimate parameters, which needs a large quantity of background corpus as training data [5]. Moreover, existing topic tracking methods always need pre-set some parameters [7], such as correlation threshold, which also need training process. If the scale of training data is not large enough, or training data don't have the same words distributions as stories on question, parameters reestimation may have errors and lead to poor tracking performance.

Latent Dirichlet Allocation [8] (LDA) and DPMM are most commonly used topic models. In LDA, the number of topics must be preassigned, while the attractive advantage of DPMM is the number of mixture components is determined by the model and the data. They open new possibilities for parameter estimation in topic tracking task and solution of data sparseness problem. So this paper uses DPMM to estimate the correlation of stories with known topic.

Besides above problem, because of data sparseness and topic excursion, the topic model built by TTT should be poor and not accurate enough [9]. To solve above problems, ATT methods update the topic model based on tracking feedback during tracking process and following topic tracking process starts from the updated topic models, which make ATT have self-learning ability of topic tracking. The common updating methods are: add new correlated features to topic model, or continually adjust feature weights of topic model [4], or use two above methods simultaneously. This kind of ATT can alleviate imperfection of topic model in TTT caused by data sparseness. However, the tracking feedbacks add plenty of off-topic information into known topic model, causing that the updated topic will deviate far from the original topic. The problem becomes more and more serious in the tracking process. In general, this kind of ATT cannot improve the tracking performance to a great degree. This paper presents a new adaptive learning mechanism, the basic idea of which is to endow tracking feedback with a reliability metric. In tracking process, initial topic model keep unchanged. The correlation between story and known topic is estimated both under initial topic model and tracking feedback with the reliability metric. In our method, initial topic model don't contain off-topic information, and always influence tracing computation through a bigger influence metric. Thus, this method can reduce errors brought by off-topic stories and alleviate topic deviation problem.

3   ATT Based on DPMM

3.1   Task Description

To facilitate describing, we assume a collection of k known topics, $\{Z_1, Z_2, ..., Z_k\}$, and every topic is described by 1-4 sample stories which compose prior knowledge of the known topics. Topic tracking task aims to associate incoming stories with known topics one by one and detect all on-topic stories from following news stories.

With the assumption that prior probabilities of every word are equal, formula (1) can be simplified as:

$$P(Z_i \mid S) \approx \{\prod_{w_j \in S} P(w_j \mid Z_i)\} P(Z_i) \tag{2}$$

Formula (2) contains two parameters: $P(Z_i)$ and $P(w_j \mid Z_i)$. As mentioned above, parameter estimation of existing methods is easy to be affected by selection of data. To solve the problems, our paper takes DPMM to estimate formula parameters. The attractive advantage of DPMM [10] is topic information can be determined by the model and the data directly.

3.2   DPMM

The proposed method regards news texts as being generated by a sequence of underlying topics inferred using DPMM. The generation process of a text can be described as: for each word w in the text, firstly choose a component (topic) Z from a distribution θ. Topic Z is then associated with a distribution over words, φ. Finally, the word is chosen from φ. Notice we do not need pre-set the number of topics. Fig. 1 shows the graphical model depiction of DPMM, where N refers to the total number of words in text. Assume that θ and φ have Dirichlet prior with concentration parameter α and β respectively.

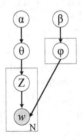

Fig. 1. Graphical model depiction of DPMM

In the paper, we use a Gibbs sampling procedure to infer parameters of the model [11]. Let w_j be the *jth* word of text. In Gibbs sampling, we need to sample Z_j, the topic of w_j. The relevant conditional distribution is:

$$P(Z_j \mid Z^-, W) \propto P(Z_j \mid Z^-)P(w_j \mid Z, W^-) \qquad (3)$$

Where W^- denotes the words except w_j. The prior for assigning w_j to either an existing topic or to a new one conditioned on other topic assignments (Z^-) is:

$$P(Z_j = z \mid Z^-) \propto \begin{cases} \alpha, \; if \; z = z_{new} \\ n_{-,z}, otherwise \end{cases} \qquad (4)$$

Where $n_{-,z}$ is the number of words assigned to topic z excluding w_j.

$$P(w_j = w \mid Z, W^-) \propto n_{w,z} + \beta \qquad (5)$$

Where $n_{w,z}$ is the number of times we have seen w associated with topic index z in (Z, W^-).

3.3   Model Description of ATT Based on DPMM

As analyzed in section 2, in most existing ATT algorithms, integrating plenty of off-topic information into known topic model will likely lead to topic deviation. To solve the problem, we propose an ATT system based on DPMM with a "reliability" metric. Reliability is defined as the dependent degree of the tracking feedback. As TTT, our ATT system preserves the initial topic models unchanged. But the significant difference is that we update a tracking feedback with the reliability metric, denoted by M_reli, and simultaneously use initial topic model and tracking feedback to compute correlation between stories and known topics.

The graphical model depiction of ATT based on DPMM is shown as fig. 2. Assume that S_t is the story at time t. ATT model introduces a new parameter: guidance information. Use GI_t to denote guidance information of model at time t, and guidance information at time 0 means prior knowledge of known topics.

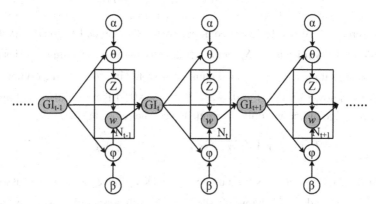

Fig. 2. Graphical model depiction of ATT

The generation process of S_t is determined by DPMM as described in section 3.2, but parameters θ and φ are jointly affected by GI_t, GI_t and tracing result of S_t decide guidance information at time $t+1$. Thus, guidance information consists of two parts: prior knowledge composed of sample stories and tracking feedback. In ATT model, they guide topic tracking process by different ways respectively.

3.4   Algorithm Flow

We first create a corresponding topic Z_i^+ for every topic. $col\_Z_i^+$ refers to set of on-topic stories which belong to topic Z_i in tracking feedback. Obviously, at the start of ATT, $col\_Z_i^+$ is an empty set.

At time t, the implementation process can be described as:

1. Implement Gibbs sampling, and combine prior knowledge of known topics during sampling, which can be detailed as follows.
   (a) Random Initialization:

   Assign a known topic to every word of story S_t randomly.

   (b) Gibbs sampling combining with prior knowledge of known topics:

   Use Gibbs sampling on every word of S_t. Based on procedure described in section 3.2, we can use formula (3) to obtain parameters of the model. Improved Gibbs sampling procedure not only take account of current texts, but also consider the effect of prior knowledge of known topics on current word. Based on this thought, formula (4) can be rewritten as:

$$P(Z_j = z | Z^-) \propto \begin{cases} \alpha, & \text{if } z = z_{new} \\ n_{-,z} + n_{col\_z}, & \text{otherwise} \end{cases} \qquad (6)$$

Where $n_{-,z}$ also refer to the number of words assigned to topic z excluding w_j in the word sets of S_t. col_z denotes word set of sample stories which belong to topic z. n_{col_z} is the number of words in col_z. If z do not belong to the known topic set, $col\_z = \Phi, n_{col\_z} = 0$. Likewise, after adding prior knowledge of known topics, formula (5) can be revised as:

$$P(w_j = w | Z, W^-) \propto n_{w,z} + n_{w,col\_z} + \beta \qquad (7)$$

In the formula, $n_{w,z}$ is the number of times we have seen word w associated with topic index z in the words sets of S_t excluding current word w. n_{w,col_z} refers to the number of w in word set col_z.

(c) Reach a steady state, end sampling procedure.

The improved Gibbs sampling shows that every sampling step is affected by prior knowledge of known topics. This step obtains word-topic distribution of S_t and realizes guiding role of prior knowledge of known topics in topic tracking.

2. This step add corresponding topic Z_i^+ to known topics set. There are $2k$ known topics, $\{Z_1, ..., Z_k, Z_1^+, ..., Z_k^+\}$. S_t-topic information can be obtained by:

(a) Based on sampling results of step 1, estimate parameters in formula (2), get the correlation of S_t and every known topics. Using formula (7) for reference, estimation formula of $P(w_j | Z_i)$ can be rewritten as:

$$P(w_j | Z_i) \propto N_{w_j, Z_i} + n_{w_j.col\_Z_i} + \beta \qquad (8)$$

Where, N_{w_j, Z_i} denotes the number of w_j associated with topic index Z_i in the word sets of S_t after sampling procedure.

Likewise, estimation formula of $P(Z_i)$ is:

$$P(Z_i) \propto N_{Z_i} + n_{col\_Z_i} \qquad (9)$$

Where, N_{Z_i} denotes the number of words with topic index Z_i in the word sets of S_t after sampling procedure.

(b) Combine formula (2), (8) and (9) to compute correlation between S_t and every known topic. Estimation formula of correlation between S_t and known topic Z_i, $P\_Adaptive(Z_i \mid S_t)$, can be rewritten as:

$$P\_Adaptive(Z_i \mid S_t) = (1 - M\_reli) * P(Z_i \mid S_t) + M\_reli * P(Z_i^+ \mid S_t) \quad (10)$$

Initial known topic models are built according to prior knowledge, but tracking feedback contains off-topic stories, thus M_reli is always less than 0.5. Based on formula (10), this step realizes guiding role of tracking feedback in topic tracking.

3. Assign the topic corresponding to the maximum correlation to S_t. Finally, add S_t to the corresponding stories set. Based on formula (6), sampling procedure allows the appearance of new topic and S_t may be assigned to a new topic. Under this situation, S_t is not associated with whichever known topic.

Repeat above steps for incoming news stories. Fig. 3 shows the flow chart.

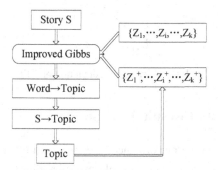

Fig. 3. Flow chart of DPMM based ATT

The characters of ATT based on DPMM:

1. In ATT model, guidance information consists of two parts: prior knowledge composed of sample stories and tracking feedback. In the implementation process, Gibbs sampling of step 1 realizes guiding role of prior knowledge, and formula (10) of step 2 realizes guiding role of tracking feedback.
2. From step 2, DPMM can compute relevant information of topics from the model and the data. Therefore, compared with existing topic tracking methods, ATT based on DPMM can directly estimate the correlations between story and every known topic, not requiring the correlation threshold comparison which needs to be trained via a large scale of in-domain data.
3. Because initial known topic models are reliable, our system ensures that initial known topic models always have bigger influence on correlation calculation than tracking feedback through setting M_reli. Thus, this method can reduce errors

brought by off-topic stories and alleviate topic deviation problem effectively brought by existing adaptive learning mechanisms.

3.5   TTT Based on DPMM

According to graphical model depiction of ATT described in section 3.3, this section cancels guiding role of tracking feedback in topic tracking and obtains graphical model depiction of TTT based on DPMM. In this model, guidance information only contains prior knowledge composed of sample stories, which keep invariant. TTT based on DPMM is similar to ATT, the difference is TTT based on DPMM don't need create a corresponding topic for every topic Z_i. The method computes correlation between story and every known topic via formula (2), (8) and (9) directly.

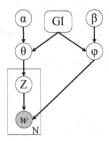

Fig. 4. Graphical model depiction of TTT

4   Experiments and Result Analysis

In TDT bakeoff [12], tracking performances are measured by error cost, C_{Det}, which is a weighted sum of the miss and false alarm probabilities. C_{Det} is usually transformed to the interval [0,1], $(C_{Det})_{Norm}$. The paper use $(C_{Det})_{Norm}$ to examine the tracking performances.

4.1   Results

We use TDT3 Chinese data as experiments test set. The premise of all experiments is that every known topic only has one sample story. The experiments examine the effectiveness of TTT and ATT based on DPMM separately.

4.1.1   Experiments of TTT

This part is a comparison between performances of TTT based on unigram model (B_TTT) and DPMM (D_TTT), which investigates influence of text feature selection simultaneously. B_TTT applies add-one smoothing to topic tracking task.

Our experiment designs four features to represent a known topic: feature set composed of content words, nouns and verbs, nouns, verbs are denoted by term_c, term_n+v, term_n, term_v respectively.

Firstly, we investigate the influence of model parameters of DPMM and different feature selection methods on topic tracking performances. In all experiments, parameter β is set at 0.01. Fig. 5 shows the relationship of tracking performance of D_TTT against influencing factors above.

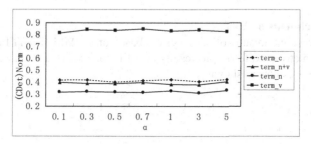

Fig. 5. Results of D_TTT

From fig. 5, we can find out:

1. When changing parameter α, $(C_{Det})_{Norm}$ values of term_v, term_c, term_n+v, term_n systems scatter in the range [0.81, 0.85], [0.40,0.43], [0.37,0.40], [0.30,0.34] respectively. The results verify that parameter α has little influence on tracking performance of D_TTT under a fixed feature sets.
2. Among different features, term_n contribute most to the performance, while term_v least. One likely reason is that verbs cannot represent the topic of stories. Among the results, when α is 3.0, and system choose nouns as feature, system obtain the best performance and smallest $(C_{Det})_{Norm}$, 0.3095.

Likewise, fig. 6 shows performance comparison between B_TTT and D_TTT.

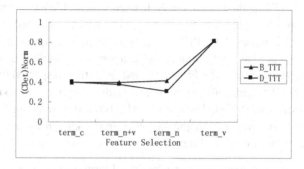

Fig. 6. Results of D_TTT and B_TTT

From fig. 6, we can find out:

1. Both B_TTT and D_TTT obtain poorest performance when choosing verbs as feature, which verify importance of feature selection in topic tracking task.
2. Under four feature selection conditions, all $(C_{Det})_{Norm}$ s of D_TTT are smaller than that of B_TTT system. Compared with B_TTT, the smallest $(C_{Det})_{Norm}$ of D_TTT reduces to 0.3095 from 0.3989. Therefore, using DPMM to implement topic tracking can improve the performance of topic tracking.

4.1.2   Experiments of ATT

Firstly, we investigate results of ATT system based on DPMM (D_ATT) with different reliability metrics. Referring to results of TTT, the experiment chooses nouns as system feature. Results are shown as fig.7.

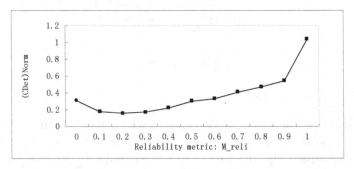

Fig. 7. Results of D_ATT

4.1.1 shows that best tracking performance of D_TTT is 0.3095, which is expressed by dot (the first point) in fig.7. Fig.7 shows that:

1. When $M\_reli < 0.5$, all $(C_{Det})_{Norm}$ s of D_ATT are smaller than that of D_TTT system. When $M\_reli = 0.2$, system obtains the best tracking performance. Compared with D_TTT, $(C_{Det})_{Norm}$ of D_ATT reduces to 0.1599 from 0.3095. Therefore, our ATT method can solve topic excursion problem to some extent.
2. When $M\_reli > 0.5$, the $(C_{Det})_{Norm}$ s of D_ATT increase obviously, and even are much bigger than those of D_TTT. Based on formula (10), initial known topic models and tracking feedback influence tracking results simultaneously, the influence degrees of them are $(1 - M\_reli)$ and M_reli respectively. The initial known topic models are built via prior knowledge. Inversely, tracking feedback may contain off-topic stories. Thus, when $M\_reli > 0.5$, tracking feedback have bigger influence on tracking computation than initial known topic models, which lead to bigger error of final tracking results.

Likewise, to assess the effectiveness of adaptive algorithm, this part uses a classical adaptive algorithm as a baseline: adding new correlated features to topic model, expressed by B_ATT. B_ATT system still uses DPMM for topic tracking.

Table 1. Best results of B_ATT and D_ATT

System type	B_ATT	D_ATT
$Min\{(C_{Det})_{Norm}\}$	0.2260	0.1599

Table 1 shows D_ATT has the much better performance than B_ATT. Compared with B_ATT, $(C_{Det})_{Norm}$ of D_ATT reduces to 0.1599 from 0.2260. The results verify effectiveness of adaptive algorithm proposed in our paper, and our adaptive algorithm can alleviate topic deviation problem effectively brought by existing adaptive learning mechanisms.

4.2   Result Analysis

Via experimental results, it can be concluded that:

1. DPMM is suitable for topic tracking task, and improves the tracking performance significantly compared with commonly used language model.
2. Results verify the importance of topic representation, and optimization of text feature selection algorithm can improve the tracking performance effectively.
3. Results show the influence of parameter of DPMM, α, on tracking computation can be neglectable. Based on this conclusion, topic tracking models (TTT and ATT) based on DPMM proposed in this paper don't contain any unknown system parameters, thus avoiding optimizing model parameters using additional data. The empirical results show that just with a few on-topic sample stories, TTT and ATT based on DPMM can achieve high topic tracking performance.
4. Results shown in section 4.1.2 verify the two characters of ATT based on DPMM: 1) D_ATT has the much better performance than D_TTT, which prove that our ATT method can solve topic excursion problem to a satisfactory extent. 2) D_ATT has much better performance than B_ATT, which verify our adaptive algorithm can alleviate topic deviation problem effectively brought by existing adaptive learning mechanisms.

5   Conclusion

Dirichlet Process Mixture Model (DPMM) considering relevant information of known topics is proposed for adaptive topic tracking. The method has two characters: 1) it uses DPMM to implement topic tracking and the basic idea is to implement Gibbs sampling to estimate correlation between a story and each known topic. Prior knowledge of known topics is exploited in Gibbs sampling procedure. Experimental results prove DPMM can improve tracking performance significantly. Results also verify importance of text feature selection in topic tracking task. Moreover, topic tracking methods based on DPMM can determine topic information via the model and the data directly, which can avoid parameter training process, reduce the errors and process times, and implement topic tracking task with a few on-topic sample stories effectively. 2) The paper presents a new adaptive learning mechanism, which can alleviate topic excursion and topic deviation problems simultaneously. The basic idea of our adaptive learning mechanism is to endow tracking feedback with a reliability metric. Our method makes initial topic model and tracking feedback influence computation of correlation between story and known topic under the condition of the reliability metric. Initial topic model which keep unchanged don't contain off-topic information, and always influence tracing computation through a bigger influence metric via influence metric setting. Thus, the method can reduce errors brought by off-topic stories and alleviate topic deviation problem. Results verify that our adaptive method can not only solve topic excursion problem to some extent, but also alleviate topic deviation problem effectively brought by existing adaptive learning mechanisms.

However, one major criticism of original DPMM is "Bag-of-Words" assumption by ignoring dependencies between words and neglecting word order, while in real data, each word is mutually related with other words and word order is also extremely important in text modeling applications. Thus, we will investigate how the dependencies between words and word order have impact on the model performance in the future work.

References

1. Allan, J., Carbonell, J., Doddington, G., et al.: Topic detection and tracking pilot study: final report. In: Proceedings of DARPA BNTU Workshop, pp. 194–218. DARPA, Lansdowne (1998)
2. Makkonen, J., Anonen-Myka, H., Salmenkivi, M.: Simple semantics in topic detection and tracking. Information Retrieval 7(3/4), 347–368 (2004)
3. Chen, F., Farahat, A., Brants, T.: Multiple similarity measures and source-pair information in story link detection. In: HLT-NAACL, Boston, pp. 313–320 (2004)
4. Yamron, J.P., Knecht, S., van Mulbregt, P.: Dragon's Tracking and Detection Systems for the TDT 2000 Evaluation. In: The Topic Detection and Tracking Workshop (2000)
5. Lo, Y., Gauvain, J.: The limsi topic tracking system for TDT 2001. In: The TDT Workshop. DARPA, Gaithersburg (2001)
6. Spitters, M., Kraaij, W.: Using language models for tracking events of interest over time. In: Proceedings of LMIR 2001, Pittsburgh, pp. 60–65 (2001)
7. Qiu, J., Liao, L.: Add Temporal Information to Dependency Structure Language Model for Topic Detection and Tracking. In: Proceedings of the International Conference on Machine Learning and Cybernetics, pp. 1575–1580. IEEE Press, Kunming (2008)
8. Blei, D.M., Ng, A.Y., Jordan, M.I.: Latent dirichlet allocation. Journal of Machine Learning Research 3(5), 993–1022 (2003)
9. Hong, Y., Zhang, Y., Liu, T., et al.: Topic detection and tracking review. Journal of Chinese Information Processing 21(6), 71–87 (2007)
10. Ferguson, T.S.: A Bayesian analysis of some nonparametric problems. Annals of Statistics 1(2), 209–230 (1973)
11. Neal, R.M.: Markov chain sampling methods for dirichlet process mixture models. Journal of Computational and Graphical Statistics 9(2), 249–265 (2000)
12. Luo, W., Liu, Q.: Development and Analysis of Technology of Topic Detection and Tracking. In: JSCL, Beijing, pp. 560–566 (2003)

Answer Generating Methods for Community Question and Answering Portals

Haoxiong Tao[1], Yu Hao[2], and Xiaoyan Zhu[3]

Department of Computer Science and Technology, Tsinghua University, China
taohaoxiong@gmail.com,
haoyu@mail.tsinghua.edu.cn,
zxy-dcs@tsinghua.edu.cn

Abstract. Community question answering (cQA) portals have accumulated numerous questions and their answers over time. Community users can search questions in cQA portals, but the returning answers often contain information which is redundant or irrelevant to the questions. Relying on the similar questions and their answers from the cQA portals, we propose appropriate answer generating methods for List-type and Solution-type questions (almost half of all questions). The results show that the answer generating methods can improve the answer quality significantly.

Keywords: community question answering, answer generating.

1 Introduction and Related Works

Nowadays, online community question answering (cQA) portals have become a popular way to acquire information. The workflow of online cQA portals is as following. The asker firstly posts a question in the cQA portals, and then other users can answer this question. When there are some answers to the question, the asker can select one answer as "Best Answer" from all the answers. In some cQA portals, the "Best Answer" also can be voted by other users. In recent years, questions and their corresponding answers of cQA portals have become an online knowledge base. Two of the main Chinese online cQA portals are Soso Wenwen (http://wenwen.soso.com) and Baidu Zhidao (http://zhidao.baidu.com). By May 2012, there have been more than 200 million solved questions on Soso Wenwen.

The online cQA portals have following limitations. Firstly, because of the workflow mentioned above, the asker can't get answers in real-time. According to Yang Tang's statistics on Baidu Zhidao[1], it takes about 14 hours for the asker to get the first answer in average. Secondly, the answers are provided by users on Internet. Due to the limitations of single user's knowledge, the quality of many answers is not high, some answers are even wrong. According to the analysis of English cQA portals by Liu et al. [2], about 25% "Best Answers" are not the best among all answers and at least 52% "Best Answers" are not the unique best answers.

Many cQA portals also support search service like search engine to overcome the unreal-time limitation. Users can search queries in cQA, and cQA will return some

M. Zhou et al. (Eds.): NLPCC 2012, CCIS 333, pp. 249–259, 2012.

similar questions and their links to users. But it also has two limitations. Firstly, after searching the queries, users need to click the similar questions' links in order to see the whole answers. Secondly, users always have to spend long time to find useful information because similar questions' answers always contain information which is redundant or irrelevant to the queries.

In order to return high-quality answers to users, previous research mainly focused on two aspects: (1) Trying to predict the quality of cQA answers, and then return the answers with high predicted quality to users [3-4]. To achieve good prediction performance, user profile information is generally needed. (2) Using multi-document summarization (MDS) techniques to summarize answers from different similar questions, and then return the summarized answer to users [5]. Answer generated by MDS techniques is always more comprehensive, but also is less readable.

To improve the answer quality, almost all well-perform systems introduce a question taxonomy [6-9]. The question taxonomy proposed by Fan Bu et al. [10] contains six question types, i.e., List-type, Solution-type, Fact-type, Definition-type, Navigation-type and Reason-type. For List-type questions, each answer will be a single phrase or a list of phrases. For example, "Idioms containing the word horse?" and "List Nobel prize winners in 1990s." are both List-type questions. For Solution-type questions, people ask these questions for solutions, so the sentences in an answer usually have logical orders. For example, "How to treat chronic pharyngitis?" and "How to make pizzas?" are both Solution-type questions. According to the statistics of Fan Bu et al. [10] of the questions of Baidu Zhidao, there are 23.8% questions are List-type questions and 19.7% questions are Solution-type questions. These two types of questions almost consist half of all questions.

Relying on the similar questions and their answers from the cQA portals, we propose appropriate answer generating methods for both List-type and Solution-type questions to generate high quality answers for users. The research framework of this paper is shown in Fig 1, and this paper's work is mainly focusing on the "Answer Generating Module".

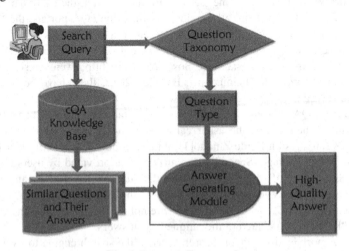

Fig. 1. Research Framework

The remainder of this paper is organized as follows: Section 2 introduces a clustering based answer generating method for List-type questions. Section 3 introduces a visible list based answer generating method for Solution-type questions. In the last section we conclude this work.

2   List-Type Questions

2.1   Answer Generating Method

According to the definition of List-type questions, each answer will be a single phrase or a list of phrases [10]. Table 1 shows an example of List-type question, "Idioms containing the word horse?" Many answers are a single phrase or a list of phrases. For example, the answer "Sensual pleasures: Describe the life is very extravagant" in the "Other Answers" is a single phrase which can answer the question. In this paper, such single phrase which can answer the List-type question is denoted as answer point.

By analysis of the answers of List-type questions, we find there are two characteristics as follows: (1) "Best Answer" often don't contain all answer points, which means "Other Answers" contain some additional answer points which are not in "Best Answer". But it takes long time for users to find the additional answer points in "Other Answers" because "Other Answers" often contain lot of information, among which some is redundant or irrelevant to the question. Take the question in Table 1 as an example, in the "Other Answers", "Sensual pleasures" is redundant because we have "Sensual pleasures : Describe the life is very extravagant" already. (2) Answer points which are high-quality or relevant to the question are often appear in more than one answers.

Base on the above two characteristics, we propose an answer generating method for List-type questions which is based on the clustering of answer points. Firstly, each answer is split into one or several answer points. Secondly, similar answer points are clustered into one category. Then for each category, a representative answer point is selected from each category for output. The answer generating method is shown in Table 2.

2.2   Method Result and Analysis

For the question shown in Table 1, the method shown in Table 2 is used to generate answer. The method output is shown in Table 3. The number at the end of each output means the number of answer points the corresponding category has after clustering. Take the first output as an example, its corresponding category has 3 answer points, two same answer points "Sensual pleasures: Describe the life is very extravagant" and another answer point "Sensual pleasures" with the same idiom.

From the above example, we find that compared to "Best Answer", the answer generated by the method in Table 3 contains more answer points, or more information. Furthermore, the outputs are ranked by answer point number each category has. The top ranking outputs have more similar answer points, therefore with high probability they have high quality and credibility. Because the outputs are ranked, we can also control the length of answer. Therefore, the answer generating method we proposed can improve the answer quality for List-type questions.

On the other hand, we also want to point out two points for the above answer generating method, for which further research is needed. (1) For the step 1 shown in Table 2, each answer should be split into answer points at first. For this paper, the answer is

Table 1. Example of List-type Questions

Question: 含有马字的成语(Idioms containing the word horse?)[1]
Best Answer:
马不停蹄，马齿徒增，马到功成，马翻人仰，马革裹尸，马工枚速，马首是瞻
Other Answers[2]:
【一马当先】作战或做事时，不畏艰难，勇敢地走在他人前面。
【千军万马】形容士兵众多，声势壮大。
【天马行空】喻才思豪放飘逸。
【声色犬马】形容生活非常糜烂。(Sensual pleasures: Describe the life is very extravagant)
声色犬马(Sensual pleasures)
一马当先
千军万马
寒蝉仗马
声色犬马 声：歌舞；色：女色；犬：养狗；马：骑马。形容剥削阶级荒淫无耻的生活方式。
走马观花
走马：骑着马跑。骑在奔跑的马上看花。原形容事情如意，心境愉快。后多指大略地观察一下。
马放南山：比喻不再作战，天下太平。
马马虎虎：草草率率，随随便便。形容办事草率。
......

[1] People ask this Chinese question for a list of idioms which containing the Chinese character "马" (means "horse" in English). Among the "Best Answer" and "Other Answers", we can see almost each phrase contains the Chinese character "马". If translate the Chinese answers into English, the answers will not contain character "马" or "horse" any more, which will make this example confusing. So we just list the Chinese answers in Table 1.

[2] Because there are too many answers to this question, we only list some representative answers instead of all answers. The URL of this question is http://zhidao.baidu.com/question/100494388.html

Table 2. Answer Generating Method for List-type Questions

Question q is a List-type Question, its similar questions have n answers, denoted as $A_1, A_2, ..., A_n$.

1.   Split each answer A_i into a set of answer points $S^{(i)} = \{s_1^{(i)}, s_2^{(i)}, ..., s_{n_i}^{(i)}\}$ by line or by sentence. Initially, each answer point $s_j^{(i)}$ is an independent category, denoted as $t_j^{(i)} = \{s_j^{(i)}\}$. The set of all categories is denoted as T.

2.   The similarity between two categories t_1 and t_2 is defined as:

$$sim(t_1, t_2) = \max_{s_i \in t_1, s_j \in t_2} sim(s_i, s_j) \qquad (1)$$

in which $sim(s_i, s_j)$ is defined as the cosine similarity of S_i and S_j based on words.

3.   Set a threshold τ. If there exist two categories in T with the similarity larger than τ, then cluster these two categories. Repeat this process until no categories can be clustered.

4.   After step 3, suppose there are k categories in T, i.e., $T = \{t_1, t_2, ..., t_k\}$. Then for each category t_i, select an representative answer point S_i, so that:

$$s_i = \max_{s_j} (\sum_{s \in t_i} sim(s, s_j)) \qquad (2)$$

5.   For each category t_i, the output is S_i and m_i, in which m_i is the number of answer points t_i has. Rank all the outputs by the answer point number from largest to smallest.

---

split by line or sentence, which works for most situations. But in some situations, the answer is not well formatted, which makes it hard to split answer into answer points. (2) For the step 3 shown in Table 2, the threshold is set to be a constant value by author for this paper. But different List-type questions vary a lot, so another research work is to find appropriate threshold for different List-type questions.

3   Solution-Type Questions

3.1   Visible List

Solution-type questions concentrate on solution, and the sentences in answers always have logical orders. The answer generating method based on clustering for List-type questions is not suitable for Solution-type questions, because the logical orders between sentences will be disrupted. Usually, the answer for a Solution-type question

Table 3. Example of the Method Result

Question: 含有马字的成语(Idioms containing the word horse?)

Best Answer:

马不停蹄，马齿徒增，马到功成，马翻人仰，马革裹尸，马工枚速，马首是瞻

Method Output[3]:

【声色犬马】形容生活非常糜烂(Sensual pleasures: Describe the life is very extravagant)(3)

兵强马壮 形容军队实力强，富有战斗力(3)

【驷马难追】话一说出口，难以收回(3)

走马观花（2）

后多指大略地观察一下(2)

【原班人马】同一批人员(2)

......

---

describes a solution to the question, so it often contains visible list. Visible list is a list explicitly indicates the sequence of all steps using mark numbers. Table 4 gives an example question from Baidu Zhidao, its answer contains several visible lists.

We choose 1179 solved Solution-type questions from Baidu Zhidao, and acquire similar questions and their answers from cQA. As the questions are solved, there is "Best Answer" for each question. According to the characteristics of visible list, we use mark number matching method to extract visible lists from all answers. Among all questions, there are 358(30%) questions' answers having visible lists, and the average length of their "Best Answer" is above 1400 words, which is definitely too long. In comparison, the average length of visible lists is around 600 words, which is much more concise. Take the question in Table 4 as an example. Compared to the "Best Answer", which contains more than 6500 words, List 3, List 4, List 5 can give a more brief answer to the question.

Table 4 shows that there could be more than one visible list in the answer. From the example, we can find some visible lists are good answers to the question, such as List 3, List 4, and List 5, while some are not good answers to the question, such as List 1 and List 2. The remainder of this section is organized as follows. We will propose a method to select the best list from all the visible lists in the second subsection. In the third subsection, we will evaluate this method and the quality of its result.

3.2   Select the Best List

In our dataset, there are 196 out of 358 (55%) questions have more than one visible list in their similar questions' answers. In this subsection, we will concentrate on how

---

[3] Here only list some top outputs, because the whole method output is too long.

Table 4. Example of Solution-type Question with Visible lists in Its Answers

---

Question: 慢性咽炎怎么治疗？（How to treat chronic pharyngitis?）[4]

Visible lists in answers:

List 1: Diagnostic criteria:

(1) Illness history: Repeated acute pharyngitis episode of excessive due to the long-term nasal to mouth breathing, alcohol and tobacco...

(2) Symptom: Throat discomfort or pain, or itching, dryness, burning, smoked a sense, foreign body sensation...

(3) Checking: Chronic throat congestion...List 2: Traditional Chinese Medicine cluster this disease into three types:

1. Yin Huo-yen type: Throat discomfort, pain, potential faint...

2. Phlegm and blood stasis type: Throat dryness, pain was stinging...

3. Yin-chun and dry type: Throat very itchy, burning, dryness and pain...

List 3: Treatment guide

1、The elimination of all risk factors...

2、Take different approaches to treatment based on different types of pharyngitis...

3、Not to make use of the Panda Hai blunt...

List 4: Three clever methods to treat chronic pharyngitis:

1、Massage: Thumb with the food, the middle finger to rub the sides of the throat 20 to 30 times...

2、Moxibustion: Mild moxibustion or acupressure, every 5 to 20 minutes...

3、Pricking blood therapy: Take the hard of hearing the upper vein...

List 5: Chronic pharyngitis diet modulating

1. Eat foods rich in collagen and elastin...

2. Intake of foods rich in B vitamins...

3. Eat less or not eat fried, spicy, spicy food...

---

[4] The answers to this question are too long, so we only list some visible lists by omitting detailed information.

to select the best list, namely, the most relevant list to the question. Firstly, we choose five features for every visible list as follows:

- First list

If the list is the first list of the answer, then this feature value is 1, otherwise its value is 0. Denote this feature as *FirstList*.

- The similarity between *guide words* and question

The visible list often contains *guide words*. In the example of Table 4, the first several words of List 1, "Diagnostic criteria", are the *guide words* of List 1. The *guide words* usually summarize the list, so the similarity between *guide words* and question can be used to help evaluate the relevant relationship between visible list and question. We calculate the cosine distance between the *guide words* and the words in question title as a feature, denoted as *GuideSimilarity*. For visible lists without *guide words*, *Guide-Similarity* is set to be a default value.

- Similarity between list content and question

Similar to *GuideSimilarity*, the cosine similarity between list content and question is also used as a feature, denoted as *ContentSimilarity*.

- The ratio of verbs and prepositions in list

The answer to a Solution-type question often gives a solution, so high-quality visible lists often contain much more verbs and prepositions. The word ratio of verbs and prepositions in the content of the list is used as another feature, denoted as *VpRatio*.

- Documents summarization based feature

In the first section, we mentioned that multi-document summarization (MDS) techniques can be used to summarize answers. For Solution-type questions, it's bad to return the summarized answer to users directly, because the logical orders between answers will be disrupted. But the summarized answer often has high information coverage, so we can use it to evaluate the information coverage of visible lists. In detail, suppose the summarized answer contains N sentences, for every visible list, if it contains k sentences out of the N sentences, then it will have a coverage score of k/N. This coverage score is used as a feature, which is denoted as *SummaryScore*.

For the above 5 features, each one is a [0, 1] value. For the 196 questions which had more than one visible lists, we manually label a score to all visible lists (the labeling standard will be introduced in the next subsection), and use them as the training set. For data training, we use Learning to Rank model to get the weight of every feature, and then select the visible list with the highest score as the best list. In this paper, we use the pairwise Ranking Perception model.

3.3   Experiment and Analysis

As mentioned above, we choose 1179 questions from Baidu Zhidao, and extract the visible lists from their similar questions' answers. There are 358 (30%) questions with visible lists in their similar questions' answers, and 196 (55%) of them with more than one visible list, and other 162 (45%) questions with only one visible list. This subsection can be divided into two parts: the first one part is to evaluate the method of selecting the best list; the second part is to evaluate the quality of best list as the answer.

To evaluate the method of selecting best list from all visible lists, at first we manually label a score to the 196 questions with more than one visible list, score 1 for high quality and score 0 for low quality. High quality means the visible list is relevant to the question, is complete and can answer the question, while low quality means the visible list is not relevant to the question, or is not complete enough to answer the question. After labeling all visible lists, there are 69 questions whose visible lists have the same score. As the goal of our experiment is to evaluate the method of selecting best list, these 69 questions have no meaning for this experiment, so we remove them and use remaining 127 questions for the experiment.

For the remaining 127 questions, if we randomly select a visible list for each question, the probability that the list is high-quality is 51.7%. If we always select the first list, the probability will increase to 63.8%. Use the method mentioned in the previous subsection, we combine different features to select best list. The result is as follows:

Table 5. Result of Selected Visible-lists

Features used to select	High quality probability
All	76. 4%
All-*VpRatio*	76. 4% (-0. 0%)
All-*SummaryScore*	75. 6% (-0. 8%)
All-*ContentSimilarity*	75. 6% (-0. 8%)
All-*FirstList*	74. 0% (-2. 4%)
All-*GuideSimilarity*	69. 3% (-7. 1%)

Table 5 shows, if we use all features, the probability to select a high-quality list is up to 76.4%, much higher than the method of random selection (51.7%) and selecting first list as the best list (63.8%). The most obvious decrease of high quality probability occurs when we delete *GuideSimilarity* from all features. This indicates that *GuideSimilarity* is a very important feature to select high-quality list.

Up to now, for 162 questions with only one visible list, the only one list could be the answer; for other 192 questions with more than one visible list, the selected best list could also be the answer. In order to evaluate the quality of using visible list as answer, we manually compare the quality of "Best Answer" and visible list for each question. We mainly focus on the relevance to question, completeness and whether containing redundant information. There are three cases, i.e., visible list is better than "Best Answer", "Best Answer" is better, or they are around the same. The evaluation result is as shown in Table 6:

Table 6. Evaluation Result

Result	Number of Question	Ratio
Visible list is better	91	25.4%
"Best Answer" is better	74	20.7%
Around the same	193	53.9%

From Table 6, we can conclude that using visible list as the answer is better than "Best Answer" on the whole. On the other side, for the questions above, the average length of visible list is 600 words, while the average length is more than 1400 words for "Best Answer", which is more than twice of visible list. Therefore, for Solution-type question, if the similar questions' answers contain visible lists, using the method we proposed to select visible list as the answer, can improve the quality of answer significantly.

4   Conclusion and Future Work

The research on answer generating methods for cQA portals is very important and meaningful. In this paper, relying on the similar questions and their answers from the cQA portals, we have proposed appropriate answer generating methods for List-type and Solution-type questions, which two types consists of almost half of all questions. For List-type questions, the answer generating method is based on the clustering of answer points. For Solution-type questions, the method is based on visible lists. The results show that the answer generating methods we propose can improve the answer quality significantly.

For the answer generating method for List-type questions, we plan to do further research to split the answer into answer points more robustly. For the answer generating method for Solution-type questions, we will introduce more semantic features to improve the semantic relevance between selected list and question. For other types of questions, we will also do further research to generate high-quality answers.

Acknowledgement. This work was carried out with the aid of a grant from the International Development Research Center, Ottawa, Canada, number:104519-006. This work was also supported by the Chinese Natural Science Foundation under grant No.60973104.

References

1. Yang, T.: Question Recommendation and Answer Summarization for cQA portals (Master Thesis), p. 3. DCST of Tsinghua University, Beijing (2010)
2. Liu, Y., Bian, J., Agichtein, E.: Predicting Information Seeker Satisfaction in Community Question Answering. In: SIGIR, pp. 483–490 (2008)
3. Jeon, J., Bruce Croft, W., Park, S.: A Framework to Predict the Quality of Answers with Non-Textual Features. In: SIGIR (2006)
4. Eugene, A., Carlos, C., Debora, D., et al.: Finding High-Quality Content in Social Media. In: WSDM (2008)
5. Liu, Y., Li, S.: Understanding and Summarizing Answers in Community-Based Question Answering Services. In: Proc. of ICCL (2008)
6. Jijkoun, V., Rijke, M.: Retrieving Answers from Frequently Asked Questions Pages on the Web. In: Proc. of CIKM (2005)
7. Hovy, E., Laurie, G., Ulf, H., et al.: Toward Semantics-Based Answer Pinpointing. In: Proc. of HLT (2001)
8. Moldovan, D., Harabagiu, S., et al.: The Structure and an Open-Domain Question Answering System. In: Proc. of ACL (2000)
9. Lytinen, S., Tomuro, N.: The Use of Question Types to Match Questions in FAQFinder. In: Proc. of AAAI (2002)
10. Bu, F., Zhu, X., Hao, Y., et al.: Function-based Question Classification for General QA. In: EMNLP 2010, pp. 1119–1128 (2010)

Summarizing Definition from Wikipedia Articles

Zhicheng Zheng and Xiaoyan Zhu

State Key Laboratory of Intelligent Technology and Systems, Tsinghua National
Laboratory for Information Science and Technology, Department of Computer
Science and Technology, Tsinghua University, Beijing 100084, China
zhengzc04@gmail.com, zxy-dcs@tsinghua.edu.cn

Abstract. Definitional questions are quite important, since users often
want to get a brief overview of a specific topic. It is a more challenging task to answer definitional questions than factoid questions. Since
Wikipedia provides a wealth of structural or semi-structural information which covers a large number of topics, such sources will benefit
the generation of definitions. In this paper, we propose a method to
summarize definition from multiple related Wikipedia articles. First, we
introduce the Wikipedia concepts model to represent the semantic elements in Wikipedia articles. Second, we further utilize multiple related
articles, rather than a single article, to generate definition. The experiment results on TREC-QA demonstrate the effectiveness of our proposed
method. The Wikipedia concept model outperforms the word model. Introducing multiple related articles helps find more essential nuggets.

Keywords: Definition, Summary, Wikipedia.

1 Introduction

In the daily life, people often want to know the definition of a specific topic.
As shown in Voorhees [1], the definitional questions occur relatively frequently
in logs of web search engines. Therefore, it is an important task to generate a
definition, which consists of the most important and interesting aspects for the
specific topic.

The task of definitional question answering, which aims to generate definitions
for given topics, was included in the past QA tracks of TREC [2], and the evaluation results showed that the task is much more difficult than the factoid and
list question answering [3]. Wikipedia, the largest online encyclopedia, contains a
large number of topics. Each topic corresponds to a Wikipedia article describing
it. For a given query, which represents exactly one topic, many search engines
(e.g., Google, Yahoo!, Bing) often rank the corresponding articles in Wikipedia
at top positions.

The first sentence or paragraph of a Wikipedia article may provide a brief and
concise description of the corresponding concept. However, only one sentence or
paragraph may be unable to cover enough important and interesting nuggets in
which the users are interested, while the full article in Wikipedia may be too long

M. Zhou et al. (Eds.): NLPCC 2012, CCIS 333, pp. 260–271, 2012.

to read. Thus, it is necessary to summarize the Wikipedia articles to generate definitions.

Some researchers have done a variety of work on using Wikipedia to solve the definition problem. Summarizing definition from a single Wikipedia article can achieve a quite good result [4]. Besides the single Wikipedia article, we find that the related articles can help generating a better definition for the topic, due to the following reasons: (1) If the information about a specific topic is mentioned frequently in its related Wikipedia articles, generally the information is more important or interesting than other information to the topic. Hence, the definition should include this information. (2) The motivation of using related articles is similar with the explanation as Wan [5]: From human's perception, users would better understand a topic if they read more related articles. Hence, by adopting the enlarged knowledge within the related articles, the quality of definitions will be improved.

In this paper, we propose to summarize definition from multiple Wikipedia articles. We first introduce a model to use Wikipedia concept to represent semantic elements in the articles. By observing the advantage of other related articles, we further propose to use the related articles to summarize definition. Based on the related articles, we can compute better weights for semantic elements corresponding to the topic. The main contributions of the paper lie in two aspects: (1) We introduce the Wikipedia concept model, by which the semantic elements in the article can be represented more precisely. (2) We utilize related Wikipedia articles, rather than a single article, to generate definitions. We also measure the impact of the related article sets to different topics. Extensive experiments show that our method performs well for definitional questions.

The paper is organized as follows. Section 2 discusses some related work. The method of definition generation is described in Section 3. Experiments in Section 4 show the novelty and advantages of our work. Conclusions and future work are outlined in Section 5.

2   Related Work

Definitional Question Answering was firstly introduced into the TREC-QA Track in 2003. The definitional question answering is usually recognized as a difficult task. Some researchers attempt to retrieve definitional sentences using some hand-crafted patterns [6,7,8]. Knowledge intensive approaches can retrieve sentences of high quality; however, it requires experts to define all possible lexical or syntactic patterns. The method is not scalable as it is time and labor intensive. To overcome the deficiency, Cui et al. [9] propose to adopt soft pattern matching. Their method outperforms significantly those approaches with manually constructed patterns on the data set of TREC-QA 2004.

The pattern matching based methods are topic dependent, so even the soft pattern methods require that the topics in the training set are not biased. Another way to answer the definition question is to explore words or terms related to topics, then to use the words or terms to select the definitional sentences. In

TREC 2006, Kaisser et al. [10] collected signature words from snippets returned by search engine, and then selected the sentences containing most weight of the terms. In this way, their system outperformed all the other systems significantly. Since the centroid words or terms are quite important to such methods, Kor and Chua [11] proposed to build such centroid terms from Wikipedia, NewsLibrary, Google snippets and other resources like Wordnet.

Since each Wikipedia article is essentially an overview of a concept, Wikipedia is a good source of answering definitional questions. It is straightforward to extract definition for a topic from Wikipedia. The corresponding Wikipedia article is supposed to be highly focused on the topic, so each sentence in the article describes the topic no matter whether it contains the topic terms or not. Based on this assumption, Ye et al. [4] use EDCL to summarize the Wikipedia article as definition to the topic. EDCL is an extended document concept lattice model (DCL [12]) to combine Wikipedia concepts and non-textual features such as the outline and infobox.

However definitional question answering aims to find important and interesting nuggets for a topic, as mentioned by Kor and Chua [11], the important and interesting nuggets often come in the form of trivia, novel or rare facts about the topic that tend to strongly co-occur with direct mention of the topic keywords. Making use of related articles in Wikipedia will be helpful to generate the definition for the topic. On the other hand, it is challenging to summarize a single Wikipedia article. As analyzed in Ye et al. [4], the written style of Wikipedia articles is quite different from the free text used in traditional summarization tasks. In general, the guideline for composing Wikipedia articles is to avoid redundancy. Hence, there are low redundancies between the sentences within a Wikipedia article, compared to other types of documents. This is not compliant with the assumption that in traditional extractive summarization that the contents which are repeatedly emphasized should be included [13]. To overcome the problem, Ye et al. [4] try to group similar Wikipedia concepts and seek important contents by utilizing non-textual features such as outline and infobox. In addition, our proposal that incorporates other related articles is easier to identify key concepts with repeated mentions; hence, it will be more appropriate to use multiple document summarization methods.

The idea of generating a definition from related Wikipedia articles, as introduced above, to some extent is similar to single document summarization by expanding the single document to a small number of related documents [5,14,15]. Different from free-text documents, Wikipedia articles are organized structurally. Therefore, the categories of a Wikipedia article and the links between Wikipedia articles can be useful in finding related articles.

With related articles in hand, the definitional question answering can be approached as a multiple document summarization problem. Document summarization is a hot topic these years, and researchers have proposed many methods, such as Maximal Marginal Relevance (MMR [16]), document cluster centroid based [17] and some other graph-based methods (like LexRank [18] and TextRank [19]. Gillick and Favre [20] present an Integer Linear Program for exact inference under a maximum coverage model for summarization. In the summarization framework, it is important to investigate a good way to represent the content of text. Gabrilovich and Markovitch [21] explore Wikipedia articles to be semantic representation for text, which inspired researchers to explore encyclopedia knowledge to help summarization work. In this paper, we also propose a representation model making use of Wikipedia articles. Then, we use both the Maximal Marginal Relevance and Maximum Coverage methods to generate summary as definition, and analyze the effects of multiple related articles under different summarization algorithms.

3   Method

In the paper, we propose to summarize a definition from multiple related Wikipedia articles to a given topic. We firstly identify the corresponding Wikipedia article for a given topic. Then, we expand the Wikipedia article to a related Wikipedia article set, and we finally use multi-document summarization techniques to extract the definition for the topic. In this section, we will present the problem formulation, and then we will describe the article expansion methods and the multi-document summarizing methods in detail.

3.1   Representation Model

We first give some symbols of the representation model. Denote that d represents a Wikipedia article. For a given topic t, we aim to give a brief definition def_t to t. As mentioned, there is a Wikipedia article d_t, which focuses on describing the topic t. And with some article expansion methods, we get a Wikipedia article set D_t which contains the Wikipedia articles related to d_t. Here, Dt at least contains d_t. Each article d_i consists of n_i sentences, denoted as s_j^i ($j = 1$ to n). Each sentence is represented as a concept vector. Assuming that there are totally K concepts, denoted as c_k ($k = 1$ to K). For each s_j^i and c_k, we calculate a weight $w_j^i(k)$ according to the importance of c_k in s_j^i. Similarly, we calculate $W^t(k)$ representing the importance of c_k to specific topic t.

Next, we will give two different methods to construct the concept vector space and calculate the weights for each concept in a topic: (1) A simple way to represent concepts by words; and (2) A more precise method to represent the concept by Wikipedia concepts.

Words Model. It is an intuitive way to represent concept by each word. We can calculate $w_j^i(k)$ as TF-IDF weight:

$$w_j^i(k) = tf_j^i(k) * idf(k)$$

Here, $tf_j^i(k)$ is the term frequency of c_k in s_j^i, and $idf(k)$ is the inverse document frequency of c_k, which is calculated on the whole Wikipedia corpus.

We calculate $W^t(k)$ by summing up the weight of all the sentences in all related articles:

$$W^t(k) = \sum_{d_i \in D_t} \sum_{j=1}^{n_i} w_j^i(k)$$

Wikipedia Concept Model. The word model could not precisely represent the exact concept in a text. Consider a person's name: *'Jordan Hill'* with the other two different names: *'Jordan Farmer'* and *'Grant Hill'*. By word model, *Jordan Hill* overlaps with the other two names in the concept vector space. However, they should be distinguished as three different concepts. Inspired by Gabrilovich and Markovitch's work [21], we investigate to using Wikipedia articles to represent a text instead of word model. We define the Wikipedia concepts as the concepts that can be mapped to Wikipedia articles, and we construct the concept vector space by using Wikipedia concepts, in which way we expect that it is able to better represent the content of sentence.

There are many inner links in Wikipedia. Each link consists of an anchor text and a target Wikipedia concept that it links to. We collect the anchor text and target Wikipedia concepts of all the inner links. All the anchor text form a phrase set A, and according to the inner links each phrase a in the set is mapped to a set of Wikipedia concepts, which is denoted as $C(a) = \{c_k\}$. And by counting link pairs of a and c_k, which is denoted as $l_k(a)$, we could assign a prior probability $p_a(k)$ to each c_k in $C(a)$ as:

$$p_a(k) = \frac{l_k(a)}{\sum_{c_i \in C(a)} l_k^a}$$

For each sentence s_j^i in d_i, with the dictionary consisting of phrases in A, we detect a set of anchor phrases $A_j^i = \{a_z\}$ by applying forward maximum matching in s_j^i. And then we assign a Wikipedia concept to each a_z according to both the context of the Wikipedia article and the prior distribution of Wikipedia concept. We operate as follows:

1. Collect the inner links in d_i, and count the number of links with different target Wikipedia concepts (Denote the number of links with target Wikipedia concept c_k as l_k^i).
2. For each a_z in A_j^i, the probability of that c_k is assigned to a_z is calculated as:

$$p(c_k|a_z, d_i) = p_{a_z}(k) \cdot \frac{l_k^i + \alpha}{|C(a_z)| \cdot \alpha + \sum_{j=1}^{|C(a_z)|} l_j^i}$$

where α is a smooth factor to avoid zero probability when $l_k = 0$ (In experiments, we set $\alpha = 0.1$), and $|C(a_z)|$ is the size of the set of Wikipedia concepts that a_z is mapped to.

3. For each a_z, we assign the Wikipedia concept c_k with highest $p(c_k|a_z, d_i)$.

After assigning Wikipedia concepts to all anchor phrases in A_j^i, we calculate the concept frequency $cf_j^i(k)$ of c_k by counting the occurrence number of c_k in s_j^i.

On the other hand, for each c_k, we also count the number of links whose target Wikipedia concept is c_k. Denote the number as l_k, it can be obtained by $\sum_a l_k(a)$. And the original importance of c_k, denoted as $coi(k)$, is calculated as:

$$coi(k) = \log l_k$$

The weight of c_k in s_j^i can be calculated by multiplying $cf_j^i(k)$ and $coi(k)$:

$$w_j^i(k) = cf_j^i(k) \cdot coi(k)$$

We can get $W^t(k)$ by the same way as the words model.

Additionally, we add each attributes of infobox of d_i as pseudo concepts. We rank the sentences in d_i according to the similarity of the sentences and the attribute, and add the pseudo concept to the top 2 sentences. The original importance of the concept is manually assigned, and then we treat them as common Wikipedia concepts.

3.2   Wikipedia Article Expansion

The motivation to summarize definition from multiple related Wikipedia articles is as follows: (1) The principle of typical extractive summarization approaches is that the contents which are repeatedly emphasized should be included. (2) As Wikipedia articles are human-written overview pages in which redundancy has been avoided, it is difficult to weight the importance of different concepts just using a single Wikipedia article. Therefore, it is more appropriate to summarize definition with multiple related articles. (3) A concept may be important and interesting when the concept mentioned in highly related Wikipedia articles.

In the paper, to make better use of Wikipedia's structural information, we retrieve the related Wikipedia articles to a specified Wikipedia article d_t using its inner links. However, even d_t contains an inner link links to another Wikipedia article $d_{t'}$, it does not always imply that d_t is related with $d_{t'}$. In fact many phrases in a Wikipedia article link to other articles just because there are entries for the corresponding Wikipedia concepts. To verify the relatedness, $d_{t'}$ is added into D_t if and only if $d_{t'}$ and d_t link with each other.

3.3   Multi Wikipedia Articles Summarization

Related articles also bring in more noises when generating definition by the extractive summarization approaches. To avoid the noises, we make a constraint that when generating definition for topic t, we only extract the sentences from d_t. As the purpose of the Wikipedia editors, the corresponding Wikipedia article d_t should always focus on the topic t. With the limitation, we miss some nuggets that exist in other related Wikipedia articles, but we ensure the relatedness between the extracted sentences and the topic t.

We utilize two multiple documents summarization algorithms: Maximal Marginal Relevance (MMR) and Maximum Coverage (MC). As we model the articles and make a constraint, we will describe the summarizing methods next.

Maximal Marginal Relevance. A good summary should meet the following two conditions: (1) The summary focus on the topic of the article set; (2) The summary need to avoid redundancy. The MMR algorithm considers both factors, and repeatedly select the sentence that can be more representative for the article set and has less redundancy with the sentences already selected.

As we assume that the content of the corresponding article d_t should focus on t, so the representativeness of a sentence s_j^t for article set D_t, denoted as $RP(s_j^t|D_t)$, is calculated as:

$$RP(s_j^t|D_t) = \sum_{c_k \in s_j^t} W_k^t$$

And the redundancy between two sentences s_j^t and $s_{j'}^t$, denoted as $RD(s_j^t|s_{j'}^t)$, is calculated as:

$$RD(s_j^t|s_{j'}^t) = \sum_{c_k \in s_j^t \cap s_{j'}^t} W_k^t$$

So under the condition of existing summary sentence set S_t, the maximal marginal relevance sentence s_{mmr} is calculated as:

$$s_{mmr} = \arg \max_{s \in d_i \setminus S_t} \{RP(s, D_t) + \max_{s' \in S_t}\{RD(s, s')\}\}$$

Maximum Coverage. Gillick and Favre proposed a summarization method based on maximum coverage. The method selects sentences with a globally optimal solution that also address redundancy globally. They choose to represent information at a finer granularity than sentences, with concepts, and assume that the value of a summary is the sum of the values of the unique concepts it contains. They also present the Integer Linear Program for exact inference under the model. We formulate our ILP problem as follows:

$$\text{Maximize:} \quad \sum_k W^t(k) \cdot SumC_k$$

$$\text{Subject to:} \quad \sum_j o_j^t \leq L$$

$$o_j^t \cdot Occ_j^t(k) \leq SumC_k, \forall k, j$$

$$\sum_j o_j^t \cdot Occ_j^t(k) \geq SumC_k, \forall k$$

$$SumC_k \in \{0,1\}, \forall k$$
$$o_j^t \in \{0,1\}, \forall j \qquad (1)$$

Here, $SumC_k$ represents whether c_k occurs in the summary or not, o_j^t means whether s_j^t is selected in the summary or not, and $Occ_j^t(k)$ equals 1 if and only if $cf_j^t(k) \geq 1$. Since the concept weight is always positive in the model we defined, (1) can be equally transformed to:

$$\text{Maximize:} \quad \sum_k W^t(k) \cdot SumC_k$$

$$\text{Subject to:} \quad \sum_j o_j^t \leq L$$

$$\sum_j o_j^t \cdot Occ_j^t(k) \geq SumC_k, \forall k$$

$$SumC_k \in \{0,1\}, \forall k$$
$$o_j^t \in \{0,1\}, \forall j \qquad (2)$$

(2) removes the second constraint in (1), and the complexity of (2) is reduced.

4   Experiment

4.1   Experiment Setting

We evaluate our method on the corpus of TREC-QA in 2004-2006 (TREC 13-15). For each topic, we retrieve the corresponding Wikipedia article. Because the focus of the paper is on summarization evaluation, we simply ignore the topics in TREC-QA where the corresponding articles do not exist in Wikipedia. We evaluate the summarization performance by pourpre [22]. Like prior studies [9,4], we also treat the answers of factoid/list questions as essential nuggets, and add them to the gold standard list of definition nuggets. To avoid the influence of those nuggets that do not exist in Wikipedia corpus, we only consider the nuggets that could be found in Wikipedia. So we first explore the available answers in Wikipedia Corpus, and the result is shown in Table 1. Among 215 topics in TREC 13-15, we could obtain 190 Wikipedia articles corresponding to the exact topics. As our corpus was downloaded in 2009, the available topic number and available nuggets number in the single article are both larger than those in 2007, which indicates that the Wikipedia not only covers more and more new topics, but also covers more old topics. So the idea of using Wikipedia as a resource to answer definitional questions is feasible. As mentioned in Section 3.3, we limit our algorithm to select sentences only from d_t. We observe that this constraint caused a lost of 25% essential nuggets could be found in related Wikipedia article set. It seems to be a huge loss in recall, but we can benefit the precision. We evaluate the precision of the two special ways of summarization, using the entire corresponding article as summary (S_{alls}) and using all the related articles in D as summary (S_{allm}). The precision of S_{alls} is 0.169 while the precision of S_{allm} is 0.029. Without the constraint on sentence selection, the number of the nuggets that can be retrieved will increase, but it introduces too many noises. With comprehensive consideration about recall and precision, the sentence selection constraint is reasonable.

Table 1. Availability Analysis

	Wikipedia 07	Wikipedia 09
Available Topics	180/215	190/215
Available Nuggets (single article)	47%	55%
Available Nuggets (multiple articles)		72%

We examine the quality of definition summary by nugget recall (NR, only consider the nuggets can be found in d_t) and an approximation to nugget precision (NP) on answer length. NR and NP are then combined using F1 and F3 measures. The evaluation is automatically conducted by Pourpre v1.1.

4.2 Performance Evaluation

To measure the performance of different models, we evaluate the quality of definition produced by MMR and MC algorithms combined with different representation models and article sets: Word model with a single article (Word), Wikipedia concept model with a single article (Concept), and Wikipedia concept model with related article set (C + M). The maximum number of sentences in a summary was set to 10. As the result shown in Table 2.

Table 2. Evaluated Result (sentences num = 10)

	NP	NR	F3	F1
Word (MMR)	0.576	0.574	0.561	0.545
Concept (MMR)	0.634	0.580	0.572	0.573
C+M (MMR)	0.649	0.609	0.601	0.599
Word (MC)	0.593	0.591	0.579	0.564
Concept (MC)	0.646	0.604	0.596	0.593
C+M (MC)	0.667	0.637	0.629	0.623

In both the summarization algorithms, the Wikipedia concept model outperforms the word model and the related article set helps improving the performance. We get following observations from the results:

1. Both the two algorithms benefit from the Wikipedia concept model. On all the evaluation metrics, the Wikipedia concept model outperforms the word model. For example, the Wikipedia concept model outperforms word model by about 5.1% on F1 score with both MMR algorithm and MC algorithm.

2. The related article set can help improving the performance in both the two algorithms. When using the related articles, all the evaluation metrics achieve improvements. For example, on F3 score, the MMR algorithm improves by 5.1% and the MC algorithm improves by 5.5%.
3. The Wikipedia concept model contributes more to precision than to recall. The Wikipedia concept weight can better represent the basic information elements in a sentence, and it helps to avoid selecting redundant sentences in a summary. Since we don't cluster the Wikipedia concepts, the redundancy in a Wikipedia article is too low to give guidance to get the essential nuggets. So when using Wikipedia concepts, the improvement on recall metric derives from that when more different nuggets are selected, more essential nuggets may be covered. The analysis can also explain why the recall of the Wikipedia concept model is even lower when the summary is short.
4. The related article set leads to more improvement in terms of nugget recall than the Wikipedia concept model. The more important the concepts are, the more frequent they occur in other related articles. The related article set will enhance the weight of these concepts, then the summarization algorithms will tend to choose the sentences containing these concepts. Hence, article expansion helps to extract more essential nuggets. For example, Table 3 lists most important concepts for topic *Manchester United Football Club* while using a single article and the related article set. Since in the main article about *Manchester United Football Club*, *win, season, player* are mentioned many times, they obtained a quite high weight in the single article although their original importance in Wikipedia is low. Related articles repeat the concepts of the relevant matches and main opponents, which are more important to the topic. Hence, while using related article set, the summarization algorithms will prefer to extracting the sentences containing these important concepts, which will improve the performance.

Table 3. Important Concepts for Manchester United Football Club

Rank	Single Article	related Articles
1	Manchester United F.C.	Manchester United F.C.
2	Association football	FA Cup
3	English language	Premier League
4	Win (baseball)	Liverpool F.C.
5	Season (sports)	UEFA Champions League
6	Player (game)	Arsenal F.C.

5   Conclusion

In the paper, we present a framework of summarizing definition from multiple Wikipedia articles. Experiments with different summarization algorithms demonstrate that the explicit semantic representation via Wikipedia concepts benefits the extraction of definition. The experiment results also show that the related articles can weight concepts more effectively than a single article, particularly for those general and popular topics. The framework proposed in the paper achieves excellent results on TREC-QA data, which demonstrates the feasibility of our methods.

However, using the extractive summary as definition still faces some problems, such as the discourse consistency between the extracted textual segments. In the future, we are considering using some generative summarization techniques (such as compression, reordering) to improve the consistency quality.

Acknowledgement. This work was carried out with the aid of a grant from the International Development Research Center, Ottawa, Canada, number:104519-006. This work was supported by the Chinese Natural Science Foundation under grant No.60973104.

References

1. Voorhees, E.M.: Overview of the trec 2001 question answering track. In: Text REtreival Conference (2001)
2. Voorhees, E.M.: Overview of the trec 2004 question answering track. In: Text REtreival Conference (2004)
3. Voorhees, E.M., Dang, H.T.: Overview of the trec 2005 question answering track. In: Text REtreival Conference (2005)
4. Ye, S., Chua, T.S., Lu, J.: Summarizing definition fromwikipedia. In: ACL 2009 (2009)
5. Wan, X., Yang, J.: Single document summarization with document expansion. In: AAAI 2007 (2007)
6. Blair-Goldensohn, S., McKeown, K.R., Schlaikjer, A.H.: A hybrid approach for qa track definitional questions. In: Text REtreival Conference (2003)
7. Xu, J., Licuanan, A., Weischedel, R.: Trec 2003 qa at bbn: Answering definitional questions. In: Text REtreival Conference (2003)
8. Harabagiu, S., Moldovan, D., Clark, C., Bowden, M., Hickl, A., Wang, P.: Employing two question answering systems at trec 2005. In: Text REtreival Conference (2005)
9. Cui, H., Kan, M.Y., Chua, T.S.: Generic soft pattern models for definitional question answering. In: SIGIR 2005 (2005)
10. Kaisser, M., Scheible, S.: BonnieWebber: Experiments at the university of edinburgh for the trec 2006 qa track. In: Text REtreival Conference (2006)
11. Kor, K.W., Chua, T.S.: Interesting nuggets and their impact on definitional question answering. In: SIGIR 2007 (2007)
12. Ye, S., Chua, T.S., Kan, M.Y., Qiu, L.: Document concept lattice for text understanding and summarization. Information Processing and Management 43(6), 1643–1662 (2007)
13. Silber, H.G., McCoy, K.F.: Efficiently computed lexical chains as an intermediate representation for automatic text summarization. Computational Linguistics 28(4), 487–496 (2002)

14. Wan, X., Yang, J., Xiao, J.: Incorporating Cross-Document Relationships Between Sentences for Single Document Summarizations. In: Gonzalo, J., Thanos, C., Verdejo, M.F., Carrasco, R.C. (eds.) ECDL 2006. LNCS, vol. 4172, pp. 403–414. Springer, Heidelberg (2006)
15. Wan, X., Yang, J.: Collabsum: exploiting multiple document clustering for collaborative single document summarizations. In: SIGIR 2007 (2007)
16. Carbonell, J., Goldstein, J.: The use of mmr, diversity-based reranking for reordering documents and producing summaries. In: SIGIR 1998 (1998)
17. Radev, D.R., Jing, H., Stys, M., Tam, D.: Centroid based summarization of multiple documents. Information Processing and Management 40, 919–938 (2004)
18. Erkan, G., Radev, D.R.: Lexpagerank: Prestige in multi-document text summarization. In: EMNLP 2004 (2004)
19. Mihalcea, R., Tarau, P.: Textrank - bring order into texts. In: EMNLP 2004 (2004)
20. Gillick, D., Favre, B.: A scalable global model for summarization. In: ACL 2009 (2009)
21. Gabrilovich, E., Markovitch, S.: Computing semantic relatedness using wikipedia-based explicit semantic analysis. In: Proceedings of the 20th International Joint Conference on Artificial Intelligence, vol. 6, p. 12. Morgan Kaufmann Publishers Inc. (2007)
22. Lin, J.J., Demner-Fushman, D.: Methods for automatically evaluating answers to complex questions. Information Retrieval 9(5), 565–587 (2006)

Chinese Named Entity Recognition and Disambiguation Based on Wikipedia

Yu Miao, Lv Yajuan, Liu Qun, Su Jinsong, and Xiong Hao

Key Laboratory of Intelligent Information Processing, Institute of Computing Technology,
Chinese Academy of Sciences, Beijing, China 100190
{yumiao,lvyajuan,liuqun,sujinsong,xionghao}@ict.ac.cn

Abstract. This paper presents a method for named entity recognition and disambiguation based on Wikipedia. First, we establish Wikipedia database using open source tools named JWPL. Second, we extract the definition term from the first sentence of Wikipedia page and use it as external knowledge in named entity recognition. Finally, we achieve named entity disambiguation using Wikipedia disambiguation pages and contextual information. The experiments show that the use of Wikipedia features can improve the accuracy of named entity recognition.

Keywords: swikipedia, named entity recognition, named entity disambiguation.

1 Introduction

A large of new information emerged and formed information explosion with the rapid development of information technology and Internet. Many emerging information processing technologies such as information retrieval, information extraction, data mining and machine translation appeared in this background. Named entity is the main carrier of information and it expresses the main content of the text. It is the very import part of these researches. The research on named entity recognition has strategic significance to language understanding and information processing.

At present, there are a lot of researches on named entity. The methods can be divided into three types. One is rule-based method. Its effect is good, but writing rules is time-consuming and labor-intensive and it lacks field adaptive capacity. The second is statistics-based method. Although statistics-based method has a good ability of model learning without human intervention, it is limited by the limited scale of the training corpus. As a result the last work emerged which combine rule-based method and statistics-based method. It aimed to reduce the complexity and blindness of the rule-based method. In recent years, a large number of new words are emerging and most of them are named entity including person names, location names and organization names. Traditional rule-based or statistics-based method can't satisfy the named entity recognition and translation tasks, because of the accelerated update speed and expanding scale. In this work, we research on named entity recognition based on network resources in order to improve the performance of the tasks.

M. Zhou et al. (Eds.): NLPCC 2012, CCIS 333, pp. 272–283, 2012.

This article studies basic page, disambiguation page, redirection page, structured categories, hyperlinks and information box. First, we establish Wikipedia database using open source tools named JWPL. Second, we extract the definition term from the first sentence of Wikipedia page and use it as external knowledge in named entity recognition. Finally, we achieve named entity disambiguation using Wikipedia disambiguation pages and contextual information. The experiments show that the use of Wikipedia features can improve the accuracy of named entity recognition.

2   Wikipedia

Wikipedia is a multilingual, web-based, free-content encyclopedia. Since its creation in2001,Wikipedia has grown rapidly into one of the largest online encyclopedia attracting the majority of Internet users to contribute their knowledge to achieve a huge amount of data sharing .There were 441,405 articles in Chinese and 3,917,431 articles in English. Next we will describe basic page, disambiguation page, redirection page, structured categories, hyperlinks and information box of wikipedia in detail.

2.1   Basic Page

A basic page is also known as an entry which describes a real world entity or concept corresponding to a subject. Basic page has a simple title which usually corresponds to the standard name of the entity. Alternative name and abbreviation are defined on redirection page and linked to this page. The first few paragraphs of the basic page especially the first sentence give us the definition and basic description of the entity concept. The following paragraphs expand the detailed description of the entity from all angles on the topic.

2.2   Redirection Page

Entities in the real world usually have two or more names. These different names describing entities of the real world are synonyms. Redirection page in the wikipedia is to solve the synonym problem. Only one of the most representative words in synonyms in Wikipedia is the title of the basic page and the others are titles of redirection pages. When the word matches to the redirection page it will be automatically re-link to the basic page which have the real description of the entity. For example, we entered a word named CAS in the search box. CAS is a redirection page ,so it is directly redirected to the basic page named Chinese Academy of Sciences.

2.3   Disambiguation Page

Disambiguation page is used to deal with the ambiguous name. The so-called ambiguity means the same name may refer to different entities. For example, Washington may refer to President George Washington, it may also refer to Washington State。

Disambiguation page in wikipedia lists the entries which may refer to different entities and contains links to the basic page. It does a brief introduction of every entry in a sentence. For example, we input Washington in the search box. Its disambiguation page lists wikipedia entry named George Washington(first President of the United States of America). Click it and you can enter the corresponding basic page. It also list the entry named Washington State(a state on the Pacific coast of the United States of America) and many other entries related with Washington.

2.4   Categories

Wikipedia provide a grid-like classification system which is edited by the public. An entry belongs to one or more categories in the classification system. A Category is usually constituted by a noun phrase which describe the entity attributes or type information. For example, entity Li Ning belongs to the category "1963 births", "living people", "Chinese male artistic gymnasts", "Chinese businesspeople" and so on. In addition, each category has its own parent categories and subcategories. For example, category" Chinese business people" has four parent categories such as "Businesspeople by nationality" and "Chinese people by occupation" and six subcategories such as "Chinese real estate businesspeople" and " Hong Kong business people". In this way, Wikipedia's classification system constitutes a hierarchical structure which is not a tree in strict sense, but a directed acyclic graph.

3   Named Entity Recognition based on Wikipedia

3.1   Extract Wikipedia features

We do a summary introduction of wikipedia in the second quarter. The first few paragraphs of the basic page especially the first sentence give us the definition and basic description of the entity concept. We can understand the properties of the entity according to the first sentence without reading the full text. The following lists a few examples of the first sentence of the Wikipedia:

（ 1 ） The **Chinese Academy of Sciences** **(CAS)**, formerly known as **Academia Sinica**, is the national academy for the natural sciences of the People's Republic of China.

(2) **Li Ning** (Simplified Chinese: 李宁; Traditional Chinese: 李寧; Pinyin: Lǐ Níng; born March 10, 1963 in Laibin, Guangxi) is a well-known Chinese gymnast and entrepreneur.

(3) **Beijing** is the capital of the People's Republic of China and one of the most populous cities inthe world

---

It can be seen from the example, the core term in the noun phrase after the defining verb is a very good knowledge which reflects the attributes of the entry. We extract the core terms to observe, "The Chinese Academy of Sciences is a academy" , "Li Ning is a entrepreneur", "Beijing is a city". We can see that this definition term "agency", "entrepreneur", "city" help us to judge an entry is a name, a local name or a organization name. Therefore, we want to extract the core terms used in the first sentence from the Wikipedia article as an additional source of knowledge added to the process of named entity recognition. The specific steps to extract the wikipedia features are as follows:

(1) Do word segmentation and part of speech tagging in the first paragraph of wikipedia

(2) Extract the core term after the defining verb in the first sentence of the first paragraph

(3) Extract the core term in the last sentence of the first paragraph if there is no defining verb

(4) The wikipedia features extracted by the above steps are shown in Table 1

Table 1. Examples of wikipedia features

wikipedia entry	wikipedia feature	wikipedia entry	wikipedia feature
Donald Ervin Knuth	Professor	Li Ning	Entrepreneur
Euskara	Language	Yunnan	Province
Young learn ourselves	Reading book	Zhangguorong	Entertainer
Soft-WorldInternational Corporation	corporation	Wenjiabao	Premier

3.2 Add Wikipedia Features to Named Entity Recognition

We usually annotate corpus using IOB2 tags as we represent named entities. InIOB2 tagging, we use "B-X", "I-X", and "O" tags, where "B", "I", and "O" means the

Recently	O
Stefanie	B-singer
Sun	I-singer
' s	O
album	O
sold	O
well	O

Fig. 1. the marked results with wikipedia features

beginning of an entity, the inside of an entity, and the outside of entities respectively. Suffix X represents the wikipedia feature of an entity. In the process we apply the knowledge of Wikipedia, the suffix "X" represents the wikipedia features. For example, given a sentence "Recently, Stefanie Sun's album sold well". For example, if we search for "Stefanie Sun" is a Wikipedia entry and extract its wikipedia feature"singer", the marked results of this sentence with wikipedia feature are shown in Figure 1.

4   Experiments and Analysis

4.1   Experiments of Extracting Wikipedia Feature

The test set used in this article are randomly selected from the 372,969 Wikipedia page in wikipedia feature extraction module. It contains a total of 1000 pages. We extract Wikipedia features on the 1000 pages and get the correct rate of 91.5%. Because some sentences are too long, there exists extraction errors .For example, "Information science(or information studies) is an interdisciplinary field primarily concerned with the analysis, collection, classification, manipulation, storage, retrieval and dissemination of information" . For example, "Information science (or information studies) is an interdisciplinary field primarily concerned with the analysis, collection, classification, manipulation, storage, retrieval and dissemination of information." The wikipedia feature extracted by our method is object which is obviously wrong. The correct result should be subject. Because it is relatively long, the final properties fell on the core term of the last clause other than the first clause. First sentence is the defining sentence, it is usually relatively short, entity attribute is in the first sub-sentence in most of the situations. To solve this kind of error, we can do syntax analysis specially on long sentences to find the core words of the parsing results. This article does not introduce a complex syntactic analysis by taking into account the good correct rate of this method coupled with the high cost of parsing.

4.2   Experiments in Named Entities Coverage of Wikipedia

This article use 863 named entity evaluation corpus in 2004 which contain 367 documents and 19,102 sentences. There are 30,955named entities in this 19,102 sentences(named entity in this article specially refers to person name, location name and organization name). LDC dictionary contains a large number of named entities and proper nouns. This article compares wikipediaentry with LDC dictionary. We respectively use them to math 863 named entity evaluation corpus to test the named entity coverage of wikipedia. Test results are shown in Table 2.

As can be seen from Table 4.5, The named entity coverage of Wikipedia is 12.18% higher than that of the LDC dictionary. Although the scale of wikipedia entries are far smaller than the LDC dictionary(788, 745 less),the matched entries with wikipedia have only 4,374 less than that with LDC dictionary in 863 named entity evaluation corpus. So we can see that the named entity coverage of wikipedia is high.

Table 2. Test results in named entity coverage of wikipedia

	The scale of entry	The number of matched entries	The number of matched NE	NEproportion
LDC dictionary	1,161,714	32,611	13,151	53.74%
Wikipedia	372,969	19,951	17,525	65.92%

4.3   Experiments of Named Entity Recognition Based on Wikipedia

In this section, we demonstrate the usefulness of the wikipedia feature for NER. We divide the 863 named entity evaluation corpus into two sets. One is the training set including 17, 102 sentences and the other is the test set including 2000 sentences. We use CRF as the classifier of named entity recognition and do three tests. We carry out the first test with the common features such as word and POS, the second test with LDC dictionary in additional to the common features and the third test with wikipedia feature in additional to the common features.

We annotate the 863 named entity evaluation corpus in a word sequence. "Sheng Huaren" in the example have appeared both in the LDC dictionary and wikipedia and its wikipedia feature is "economist". The annotated corpus is shown in Figure 2.

Word	pos	type
the	n	O
director	j	O
of	prep	O
state	n	O
economic	n	O
Sheng	nr	B-PER
Huaren	nr	I-PER
spoke	m	O
in	p	O
public	a	O

Word	pos	LDC	type
the	n	O	O
director	j	O	O
of	prep	O	O
state	n	O	O
economic	n	O	O
Sheng	nr	B	B-PER
Huaren	nr	I	I-PER
spoke	m	O	O
in	p	O	O
public	a	O	O

Word	pos	LDC	type
the	n	O	O
director	j	O	O
of	prep	O	O
state	n	O	O
economic	n	O	O
Sheng	nr	B-economist	B-PER
Huaren	nr	I-economist	I-PER
spoke	m	O	O
in	p	O	O
public	a	O	O

common features   LDC feature and common features   wikipedia feature and common features

Fig. 2. Annotated 863 named entity corpus

This article uses CRF++ tool, the above defined three feature templates and corresponding three annotated corpus to test the performance of the named entity recognition. The test results are shown in Table 3 and 4 :

Table 3. Test results of named entity recognition （in word sequence）

	P	R	F
Common features	83.13	87.57	85.35
LDC feature	83.52	87.84	85.68
Wiki feature	84.46	88.81	86.64

Table 4. Test results of named entity recognition （in character sequence）

	P	R	F
Common features	82.24	84.89	83.56
LDC feature	82.51	85.27	83.89
Wiki feature	82.77	85.75	84.26

As is seen from experimental results, the Wikipedia features improved the accuracy in F-measure by 1.29 points(in word sequence) and 0.7 points(in character sequence) compared with common features. Compared with LDC dictionary, the Wikipedia features improved the accuracy in F-measure by 0.96 points and 0.37 points respectively. The wikipedia feature can play a good role in named entity recognition.

The simple method that extracting defining feature from the Wikipedia page can effectively improve the correct rate of named entity recognition. The results show that the structured features of Wikipedia is conducive to extraction of knowledge. Our method is simple but effective because of the following reasons: (1) If a Wikipedia page is a disambiguation page, we will not extract the defining feature of its corresponding Wikipedia, so we will not bring the wrong noise where it might be existed. (2) If a Wikipedia page is non-ambiguous pages, it will describe the main meaning of most editors agreeing on this entity. The reason that the extracting Wikipedia definition features is helped to improve the correct rate of   named entity recognition is the main meaning of the entities are frequently used in the corpus. In our method, there is still room for improving , for example, the disambiguation of ambiguous entities. If the Wikipedia pages make continuous rapid growth at the current rate, perhaps all of the Wikipedia entity will become ambiguous entity in the latest future. We need a disambiguation method to find the most appropriate page from the multiple pages listed in the disambiguation pages.

5   Named Entity Disambiguation Based on Wikipedia

Entity ambiguities refers to an entity alleged corresponding to the problem of real-world entities. For example , the following three entities alleged "Washington" :

U.S. founding fathers of Washington ;

Washington, DC, the capital of the United States.

Washington, located in the northwestern United States.

They separately refer to the three real-world entity : "America's first president"、 "the U.S. capital " and "the U.S. state of Washington". In the task of Named entity recognition, the alleged "Washington" may be a person name (George Washington), or a local name (Washington, DC, or Washington), and we need to determine which the true type of the alleged entity are belonged to , and this is named entity disambiguation.

5.1   The Processes of Named Entity Disambiguation Based on Wikipedia

Wikipedia disambiguation page lists the entity alleged ambiguities. And it provides us with a good disambiguation information. If there is "Washington" in a sentence, and "Washington" is an ambiguous entity, it may be a person name or a local name. The original model of random condition is not very accurate in classifying. And the "American President" entry which "George Washington" entry at, where the Wikipedia disambiguation page list , can help us determine to decide "George Washington" is a name. Besides another cited "Washington State" entry where it has the "American states" entry, can also let us be certain about the "Washington State" is the local name. Through the Classification and Labeling of Wikipedia entries we can properly mark the category of the named entities they belong to in 80% of Wikipedia coverage rate、 95% of correct rate. Intuitively, we can determine the "Washington" should be which entity through the current context of a sentence, so we think about a method : we calculate the similarity of all the pages listed in the sentence of the documentation and Wikipedia disambiguation page, then find out the most similar Wikipeia page to the current sentence, finally give a more accurate label of the current entity   through the entity identified by the Wikipedia. Therefore, we propose to build the double-layer CRF for named entity disambiguation based on context information , the specific process is shown in Figure 3:

5.2   Training Wikipedia Corpus with CRF

All of the existing Wikipedia entries in Wikipedia page are marked with   the symbols of "[[]]", so we use the classification label ,from Wikipedia named entity dictionary (including names dictionary, gazetteer and agencies name a total of 135,504 data dictionary) , to match the entry in the "[[]]" , if the entry exists in the named entity dictionary, we marked the entry with the type of the named entity , otherwise the entry does not exist in the named entity dictionary, the symbol of "[[]]" will be stripped, and ultimately we will convert the Wikipedia corpus   with a training data of named entity label. The original Wikipedia corpus and the named entity annotation corpus after converting are shown in Figure 4 and 5, in which person name, place name, organization names marked separately with PER、 LOC、 ORG .

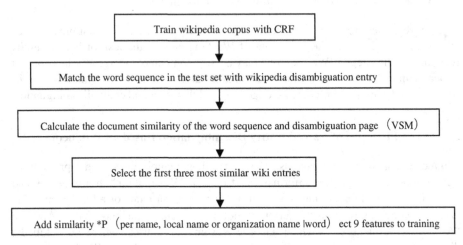

Fig. 3. Named entity disambiguation processes based on Wikipedia

[[Steven Paul "Steve" Jobs]](/ˈdʒɒbz/; February 24, 1955 – October 5, 2011)[6][7] was an American businessman and technology visionary. He is best known as the co-founder, chairman, and chief executive officer of [[Apple Inc.]]

Fig. 4. The original corpus of Wikipedia

[[Steven Paul "Steve" Jobs]]PER (/ˈdʒɒbz/; February 24, 1955 – October 5, 2011)[6][7] was an American businessman and technology visionary. He is best known as the co-founder, chairman, and chief executive officer of [[Apple Inc.]]ORG

Fig. 5. Wikipedia named entity annotation corpus

The correct marked rate of Wikipedia marked corpus named entities after converting is about 95% ,and the recall rate is about 80%. CRF are maked use of to go on training and self re-marking on the label corpus to achieve a higher recall rate.

5.3   The Examples of the Disambiguation of Wikipedia

A simple example can show us the process of the disambiguation. For example, there is a sentence which is "Bloomberg flew to Washington to promote his own ideas" in our testing collection ,then we find the word "washington" is a disambiguaion page on wikipedia through the maximum matching wikipedia entry, and in this disambiguation page lists all the possible ambiguity entry, a total of seven, such as "Washington. DC", "Washington State", "Denzel Washington", these entries have been marked as entity type in the first step a CRF-based training and we have retained the probability of each entity type. We calculate the similarity of the document of the given sentence and the nine Wikipedia page, then find the top three highest similarity of the wiki page which are "Washington State", "Washington DC" and "Washington Town" ,and add nine characteristics of the Similarity (Washington State) * P (person's name | Washington State), similarity (Washington State) * P (local names | Washington State), similarity (Washington State) * P (agency name | Washington State). . similarity ("Washington Township") * P (organization name | Washington town) and so on to the CRF training and testing. It is more intuitive to see Figure 6.

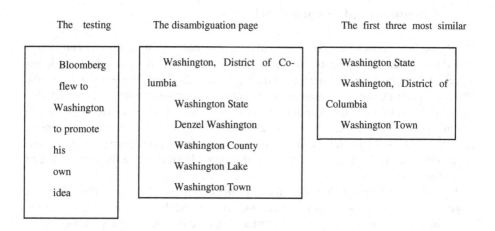

Fig. 6. Example of named entity recognition based wikipedia

6   The Analysis of Named Entity Disambiguation Based on Wikipedia

The corpus used in this study is the same as the terms in section 4th, and we add 9 disambiguation characteristics on the basis of the original wiki features, and the results of the study are shown in Table 5.

The F value is improved by 0.43 in the experimental results, after combining the Wikipedia disambiguation feature,and the effect is significant opposed to the limited corpus number of ambiguous entities .The example of correcting based on the Disambiguation method: "The ITTF has announced the latest world rankings, and the men's singles aspects of German Boer continued in the first place", there are ambiguities of " Boer " in this sentence, "boer" can be place names (refer to South Sudan city)

Table 5. Experimenal results of named entity disambiguation based on wikipedia

	P	R	F
wikipedia feature	84.46	88.81	86.64
named entity disambiguation	84.73	89.42	87.07

or names (refer to table tennis players of Germany).At first "boer" is mislabeled as local name, after combining the Wikipedia disambiguation features, some contextual features, such as Germany, table tennis, men's singles " are used to help the system correcting the category into the right type person name.

7   Summary and Future Work

Firstly we introduces of the defining feature of Wikipedia as an additional knowledge added to the based named entity recognition in the CRF, and the method is simple but effective in improving the rate of correcting th named entity recognition. Then the Wikipedia corpus converted into a named entity annotation corpus is illustrated, this huge label corpus helps us to further improve the performance of named entity recognition, and we make full use of Wikipedia's disambiguation pages and context information to build a double-layer CRF system for carrying out named entity disambiguation. The study shows that the method proposed can improve the correct rate of named entity disambiguation.

In named entity recognition, we only make use of the first sentence of the Wikipedia page, so we can consider that making full use of the Wikipedia category labels, hyperlinks, and other rich resources to further improve the correct rate of named entity recognition.

References

[1] Shun, Z., Wang, H.: Named Entity Recognition Research. Modern Library and Information Technology (6), 42–47 (2010)
[2] Zhou, K.: Rule-based named entity recognition. Hefei University of Technology, Anhui (2010)
[3] Li, J., Wang, D., Wang, X.: Chinese organization name recognition based on template matching. Information Technology (6), 97–99 (2008)
[4] Huang, D., Yue, G., Yang, Y.: Chinese local name recognition based on statistics. Journal of Chinese Information 17(2), 36–41 (2003)
[5] Huang, D., Yang, Y., et al.: Identification of Chinese Name Based on Statistics. Journal of Chinese Information Processing (2001)
[6] Wan, R.: Chinese organization name recognition. Dalian University of Technology, Liaoning (2008)
[7] Qiao, Y.: Chinese named entity recognition with the combination of rules and statistics. Shandong University, Shandong (2007)

[8] Kazamaand, J., Torisawa, K.: Exploiting Wikipedia as external knowledge for named entity recognition. In: Proceedings of the Joint Conference on Empirical Methods in Natural Language Processing and Computational Natural Language Learning, pp. 698–707 (2007)

[9] Nothman, J., Curran, J.R., Murphy, T.: Transforming Wikipedia into named entity training data. In: Proceedings of the Australasian Language Technology Association Workshop, pp. 124–132 (2011)

[10] Cucerzan, S.: Large-scale named entity disambiguation based on Wikipedia data. In: Proceedings of the Joint Conference on Empirical Methods in Natural Language Processing and Computational Natural Language Learning, pp. 708–716 (2007)

The Recommendation Click Graph: Properties and Applications*

Yufei Xue, Yiqun Liu, Min Zhang, Shaoping Ma, and Liyun Ru

State Key Laboratory of Intelligent Technology and Systems,
Tsinghua National Laboratory for Information Science and Technology,
Department of Computer Science and Technology, Tsinghua University,
Beijing, 100084, China
yufei.xue@gmail.com

Abstract. Query recommendations help users to formulate better queries and to obtain the desired search results. Users' clicks on query recommendations contain a great deal of information about search intent, query ambiguity and search performance. We use query recommendation click information contained in search logs to construct a recommendation click graph. A directed edge in the graph connects the prior query and the clicked recommended query. By analyzing the graph, we develop methods for finding ambiguous queries and improving the search results. The experimental results show that our method for finding ambiguous queries is effective, and using recommendation click information can improve the search performance of ambiguous queries.

Keywords: query recommendation, user behavior, search intent.

1 Introduction

Query recommendation technology is widely used by commercial search engines. A search engine provides related queries in a search result page. If the query does not present useful search results, users can click on any related query to find more web resources. Our analysis shows that users click recommended related queries in approximately 15% of search sessions.

The query recommendation click log contains a large volume of information about users' search intents and their perspectives on search results. A user's click on a recommended query implies that the recommended query describes what he wants, whereas the search results of previous do not satisfy his information needs well enough. Because search engine users usually click recommended queries after reviewing the result page, the clicked recommendation should be a direct and precise reflection of the user's intent. The query recommendation click logs contain less noise than the logs of query reformulation because all clicked queries

---

* This work was supported by Natural Science Foundation (60903107, 61073071) and National High Technology Research and Development (863) Program (2011AA01A205) of China.

M. Zhou et al. (Eds.): NLPCC 2012, CCIS 333, pp. 284–295, 2012.

are selected by both the search engine and the user. In this sense, the data in query recommendation click log is very reliable.

In this paper, we introduce the concept and properties of a query clicking graph, which is a graph that depicts all of the query recommendation clicking information contained in user logs. This graph aggregates all users' query recommendation click actions during a specific period. In the graph, each node represents a query. A directed edge (q_i, q_j) indicates that a user clicked the recommended query, q_j, when he searched q_i. We do both global and local analysis on the graph. These efforts can help us to learn the properties of queries and user intents. We introduce the following applications for the recommendation click graph:

Optimizing search results. Exploring users' click actions on query recommendations can help us to understand users' search intents. Thus, the recommendation click graph can help the search engine to improve the search performance.

Recognizing ambiguous queries. If users click disparate recommended queries, the previous query might be highly ambiguous. The ambiguity might be caused by the ambiguity of the query expression or the users' uncertain search intent. Graph analysis algorithms can help us to find ambiguous queries in a recommendation click graph.

The remainder of this paper is organized as follows. Section 2 introduces related work. Basic concepts and assumptions of our work are given in Section 3. In Section 4, we discuss the properties of recommendation click graphs. Section 5 discusses our local analyzing methods for recommendation click graphs to improve search performance. Section 6 shows our approach to identifying ambiguous queries. In Section 7, we summarize our work and discuss query recommendation and the recommendation click graph.

2   Related Work

The Web is naturally presented as a graph. Often, the nodes of a web graph represent the web pages, and the edges represent links between pages. Web graphs are used to estimate the quality of web pages. Link analysis is a data-analysis technique that uses a link graph to estimate page quality. Examples of well-known link analysis algorithms are the HITS [1], PageRank [2] [3] and TrustRank [4] algorithms. These link analysis algorithms have common assumptions: (1) the links imply recommendation and (2) the page quality can spread through the hyperlinks. With these assumptions, link analysis algorithms are often applied to other types of graphs.

Search queries can also be presented by graphs. Baeza-Yates defined 5 types of query graphs [5]: word, session, URL cover, URL link and URL terms. Three types of information are used to construct query graphs: the query terms, the searching and clicking behaviors during the query session and the content of clicked URLs. Baeza-Yates et al. used some of the query graphs to mine query logs for semantic relations between queries [6]. The five types of graphs are useful for recommending related queries. A query-flow graph is a representative query graph [7] and performs well in query recommendation applications [8] [9].

Unlike present methods, the recommendation click graph is based on existing query recommendations and the click log. This graph is used to detect ambiguity in queries and to learn users' intents.

Query recommendation is an important are of study. The query recommendation algorithms focus on finding similar queries. Zaiane et al. used query terms, search result snippets and other simple text information to find similar queries [10]. Because the semantic information from query and search results is limited and hard to analyze, most recent studies on query recommendation use user behavior data to detect related queries [11] [12] [13]. Some studies [14] [15] use a bipartite graph of search query and clicked URL to determine and recommend related queries. These studies assume that two queries are similar if they lead users to click on the same URLs. Kelly et al. studied the usage of query recommendation [16]. Their research showed that query recommendations are frequently used by users and can be very helpful.

For a search engine to understand a user's search intent, it must be able to identify an ambiguous query. Some queries are ambiguous in nature. The search intent of such queries can be detected by analyzing related documents and user behavior. Song et al. summarized three types of queries: ambiguous, broad and clear. They used a supervised learning approach to classify queries by analyzing the text of the search results [17]. He and Jhala developed a method to understand a user query based on a graph of connected related queries [18]. Veilumuthu and Ramachandran developed a clustering algorithm that uses the user session information in the user log and query URL entries to identify clusters of queries that have the same intention [19].

3   Preliminaries

3.1   Basic Concepts

Recommendation click log. A recommendation click log is a part of a search engine's user log. It records all clicks on query recommendations. Recommendation click pair. A user's click on a query recommendation is represented by an ordered query pair $\langle q_i, q_j \rangle$. This pair indicates that a user submitted query q_i to the search engine and clicked recommended query q_j on q_i's search result page. We call q_i the source query and q_j the destination query. Pairs with the same source and destination queries are recorded as a single recommendation click pair in our work.

Recommendation click graph. The recommendation click graph uses the previous two concepts.

Definition 1: The recommendation click graph is a directed graph $G_c = (V, E)$, where:

- the set of nodes, $V = \{q | q$ appear in the recommendation click log as a source or destination query$\}$, and
- $E = \{(q_i, q_j) | < q_i, q_j >$ is a recommendation click pair in the recommendation click log$\}$.

Like other web graphs, the recommendation click graph might have more than one weakly connected component. Because the recommendation click graph is based on recommendation click pairs, there are no isolated vertices in the graph, i.e., there are at least two queries in a connected component. More properties of the recommendation click graph are described in following sections.

3.2 Semantic Basis

Some basic assumptions on the semantics of query recommendation click actions are fundamental to the recommendation click graph developed here. When a user clicks a recommended query, this action expresses a relationship between the source and destination queries. Using the recommendation click pair $\langle q_i, q_j \rangle$ as an example, we assume that there are two possible latent meanings for a user's click on a query recommendation:

- *Assumption 1* q_j describes the user's information needs more precisely than q_i, or

- *Assumption 2* q_j does not describe the user's information needs more precisely than q_i, but the user is interested in q_j and wants more information.

Clicks described by assumption 1 usually make the user's search intent more precise. For example, the recommendation click pair $\langle$ Lady Gaga songs, Lady Gaga poker face$\rangle$ corresponds to a more precise intent description. Clicks described by assumption 2 appear frequently. The recommendation click pair $\langle$ Lady Gaga songs, top 100 songs$\rangle$ is an example of this type of click. In most cases, the source query and destination query are related. However, the query pair can be about different topics.

In our work, we are interested in recommendation click pairs that comprise related queries. The recommendation click graph can help researchers to view related queries from different perspectives.

4 Properties of the Recommendation Click Graph

We extracted a recommendation click log from an August 2010 user log of a Chinese commercial search engine. The log recorded 58,334,303 clicks on query recommendations. From these data, we constructed a recommendation click graph that contained 23,516,620 vertices and 31,569,262 directed edges. We obtained statistical distributions for the in-degree and out-degree of each vertex. The distributions are shown in Fig. 1. Both the in-degree and out-degree distributions approximately follow a power law distribution. This property is very similar to a hyperlink graph. Given this similarity, there are many effective and widely used analyzing algorithms developed for hyperlink graphs that might also be appropriate for recommendation click graphs.

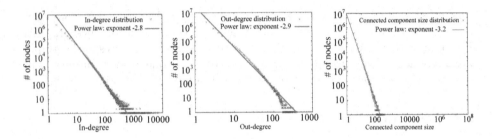

Fig. 1. Distribution of in-degree and out-degree

Fig. 2. Distribution of component size

4.1 Connected Components

We analyzed the connected components in the recommendation click graph without regard to the direction of the edges. Of the 2,668,331 components in the graph, 71% have only 2 vertices, i.e., most of the components are very small. Our statistics show that approximately 60 components have more than 100 vertices. The largest component has 16,298,916 vertices, which is approximately 70% of the vertices in the graph. This result indicates that many queries are connected in the recommendation click graph. These queries include most of the hot topics of the search engine during the period covered by the query log. As shown in Fig. 2, the distribution of the connected component sizes approximately follows a power law distribution.

4.2 Strongly Connected Components

A strongly connected component is a directed sub-graph in which there is a directed path between any ordered pair of vertices. In a recommendation click graph, queries that appear in the same strongly connected component can be strongly related.

In our recommendation click graph, there are 20,978,260 strongly connected components. The distribution of component sizes follows a power law distribution. Of the strongly connected components, there are 20,695,423 components that have only one vertex. These vertices account for approximately 88% of the vertex set. This result indicates that approximately 10% of the queries both recommend other queries and are recommended by other queries in the graph. This property is in accord with user behavior patterns and can be explained as follows. Because the user queries follow a power law distribution, most queries have a low frequency. Low frequency queries have no chance to be recommended. As mentioned in Section 3.2, for many recommendation click pairs, the destination query refined the intent of the source query. Therefore, few queries are both source and destination. In the recommendation click graph, the largest strongly connected component contains 1,816,759 vertices, approximately 7.7% of the vertices in the graph.

5   Local Analysis of a Recommendation Click Graph

In a recommendation click graph, an edge (q_i, q_j) denotes that a user has clicked the query recommendation q_j while he searched q_i. Because the recommendation click pair is selected by both the search engine and the user, we assume that adjacent queries in a recommendation click graph are semantically similar.

A user clicks a query recommendation when he finds the search result insufficient. He may try a recommended query that describes his needs more precisely or a query that appears to yield better results. The search result page of the related queries might provide what the user is seeking. The local analysis of a recommendation click graph can help us to improve the search result by including some search results of high-quality adjacent queries.

5.1   Local Subgraph

Definition 2: For query q_i in a recommendation click graph, we define a local subgraph of q_i as

$$G_{Sub(i)} = (V_{Sub(i)}, E_{Sub(i)}),$$

where

$$V_{Sub(i)} = q | distance(q, q_i) \leq 2 \cup q_i, E_{Sub(i)} = E \cap (V_{Sub(i)} \times V_{Sub(i)}).$$

The local subgraph of q_i contains the queries that are most related to q_i.

5.2   HITS applied to a Local Subgraph

HITS is a link analysis algorithm for evaluating web pages. The algorithm is applied to a subgraph of a hyperlink graph. The indicators for each web page are called hubs and authorities. The hub value indicates how efficiently users are led to other useful pages using the hyperlinks on the page. The authority value indicates how many good hub pages link to the page.

We apply the algorithm and concepts of HITS to a recommendation click graph. A query that has a high authority value is linked to several other queries. A query that has a high hub value leads users to other queries. In this work, we are interested in the queries that are frequently searched and do not lead to additional clicks of query recommendations. Queries that have a high authority value and a low hub value might satisfy more users' needs and be less ambiguous. We find such queries using the local graph of query q_i and use their search results to improve the search performance of q_i.

5.3   Experiments of Optimizing Search Results

We randomly selected 442 queries that had an out-degree 8 and extracted their local subgraphs. The local subgraphs of queries that have an out-degree less than 8 might not be large enough to support a HITS analysis.

We collected statistics on the numbers of nodes and edges in the 442 sub-graphs. Fig. 3 shows that the numbers of nodes and edges are linearly related. Table 1 lists the maximum, minimum and average numbers of nodes and edges. These statistics show that the sizes of the local subgraphs can vary widely.

Table 1. Properties of local subgraphs

	Maximum	Minimum	Average
# of nodes	18271	14	865.1
# of edges	78808	13	3009.4
(# of edges)/(# of nodes)	12.2	0.93	2.8

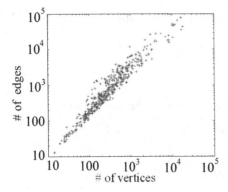

Fig. 3. Dimensions of local subgraphs

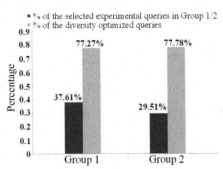

Fig. 4. Experiment Results on Algorithm 1

We used the query's local subgraph to optimize the search results. We randomly selected 117 queries (Group 1) that had an out-degree = 8 or 9. These queries were not the most frequent queries in the search engine, but their local subgraphs were large-enough to support the HITS algorithm. These queries might be a representation of a general user query. We examined Group 1 from the user's perspective. We identified 44 queries on which the search engine did not perform very well, but the user found related resources through a query recommendation. We performed Algorithm 1 on the 44 queries and obtained optimized search results. Three annotators were asked to compare the optimized search results with the original search results and vote for the list that contained results that are more diverse. For 34 of the 44 selected queries (approximately 77%) the search results optimized using Algorithm 1 were deemed to be more diverse.

Algorithm 1.

1: Select q_i as the query to be improved.
2: Extract q_i's local subgraph $G_{Sub(i)} = (V_{Sub(i)}, E_{Sub(i)})$ from the recommendation click graph.
3: Iteratively calculate the authority and hub values for all queries in the subgraph using the HITS algorithm.
4: Select a threshold hub value, h_t for hub value. Create a query set $Q = \{q|Hub(q) < h_t, (q_i, q) \in E_{Sub(i)}\}$.
5: Sort the queries in Q by authority values and take n largest queries.
6: Construct 2 search result sets: $R_i = \{r|r \in SearchResultsOf(q_i)\}$, $R = \{r|r = TopResultOf(q), q \in Q\}$
7: Sort the search results in $R_i \cap R$ according to the rank in q_i's search results and store in List L_1;
8: Sort the search results in $R \setminus R_i$ according to the order of the authority of the corresponding query, and store in List L_2;
9: Sort the search results in $R_i \setminus R$ according to its rank in q_i's search results and store in List L_3;
10: Output individual results from L_1, L_2, L_3 in turn, until there are 10 search results.

We repeated the above experiment on 61 randomly selected queries (Group 2) that had higher search frequencies and out-degrees. These queries might be more ambiguous than the queries in Group 1. We examined the queries and found 18 queries on which the search engine did not perform well. For 14 queries, the search results produced by our algorithm were more diverse. Because the queries in Group 2 are hotter than Group 1, the queries in Group 2 might perform better in the search engine. Note that the percentage of queries that do not perform well enough is lower for Group 2 (18/61) than for Group 1 (44/117). Approximately 77% of the queries selected in Groups 1 and 2 were optimized by Algorithm 1. The experimental results are shown in Fig. 4.

Our algorithm is naive and does not always yield better results than those obtained by the search engine, particularly when the search engine performs a query well. Nevertheless, our local subgraph method can improve the search results of queries.

6 Finding Ambiguous Queries

6.1 Inverse PageRank

Inverse PageRank is a link analysis algorithm used to determine the seed pages for the TrustRank algorithm [4].

For a directed graph $G = (V, E)$, inverse PageRank requires a related graph $G' = (V, E')$, where

$$(q_i, q_j) \in E' \iff (q_i, q_j) \in E.$$

We perform PageRank on the link-inverted graph G' to obtain the inverse PageRank for G.

The inverse PageRank can be explained using the concepts of PageRank as follows:

- In G, a vertex's inverse PageRank is higher if it has more out-links.
- In G, a vertex's inverse PageRank is higher if the vertices to which it points have high inverse PageRanks.

Some studies have shown that search engine users often issue short and ambiguous queries [20]. In this case, users might continue by clicking query recommendations. It is reasonable to assume that the level of ambiguity of a query is related to the dispersion of the query's recommendation clicks. Based on this assumption, the inverse PageRank values of a recommendation click graph show the level of query ambiguity.

6.2   Experiments

We applied the inverse PageRank algorithm on the recommendation click graph. We sorted the inverse PageRank values into descending order and divided them into 10 buckets. The sums of the inverse PageRank values in each bucket were equal. The sizes of buckets are shown in Fig. 5.

To verify if the inverse PageRank can be used to determine the ambiguity of queries, we asked 4 annotators to examine queries sampled from the 10 buckets. We randomly selected 1010 queries and asked the annotators to score each query: 3 indicated a clear query, 2 indicated an intent ambiguous or broad query, and 1 indicated a semantically ambiguous query. Through discussions, the annotators ensured that they had no serious disagreement on the semantics of any query. For 828 of the 1010 queries, at least three annotators give the same score. The kappa coefficient of their annotations was $\kappa = 0.466$ [21].

For each query, we calculated the average, maximum and minimum scores. In addition, we calculated the average of the 3 types of statistical scores in each bucket. The results are shown in Fig. 6. The scores in the first five buckets are higher than the scores in the last five buckets. Moreover, the scores increase from Bucket 1 to Bucket 5, whereas the scores of the last five buckets are not significantly different. Although the first 5 buckets contain approximately 30% of the queries, they contain most of the ambiguous queries.

We randomly selected 233 queries from the graph and sorted the queries into descending inverse PageRank order. We divided the queries into 10 buckets of approximately the same size. The annotators labeled the top 3 search results of the 233 queries in 5 levels, and we calculated the NDCG3 for all of the queries. For each bucket of queries, we computed the average and standard deviation of the NDCG3. Fig. 7 shows the statistical results. From Bucket 1 to 10, the average NDCG3 decreases, whereas the standard deviation increases. Although queries that have higher inverse PageRanks contain more ambiguity, these results indicate that they perform better than queries that have lower inverse PageRanks. This result seems counterintuitive, but it is reasonable. As mentioned above, the inverse PageRank algorithm gives higher values to the vertices that have more out-links.

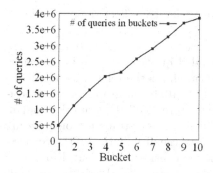

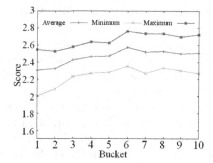

Fig. 5. Bucket size

Fig. 6. Ambiguity score statistics

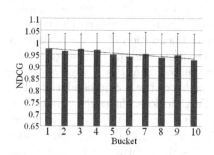

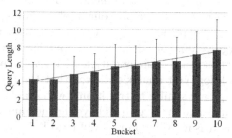

Fig. 7. Avg. and Stdev. of NDCG values

Fig. 8. Avg. and Stdev. of query lengths

In a recommendation click graph, the out-degree is related to the search frequency of the query. Therefore, hot queries are more likely to receive higher inverse PageRanks. The higher NDCG3 values obtained in the previous buckets are explained by the better performance of hot queries in commercial search engines. The average lengths of the queries increase from Bucket 1 to Bucket 10 (shown in Fig. 8). The work of Jansen et al. [20] showed that most queries in web search engines are short, and long queries are very infrequent. This work confirms that the queries in the preceding buckets are hotter in the search engine.

From the experimental results and analysis, applying the inverse PageRank algorithm on a recommendation click graph is an effective tool to evaluate query ambiguity.

7   Discussions and Conclusions

According to the definition and construction of recommendation click graphs, the graph is strongly related to user behaviors and the search engine's query recommendation algorithms. Because the user behaviors on query recommendations is the object of our research, the behaviors and algorithms do not affect our methods of constructing and analyzing the recommendation click graph.

However, changes in the recommendation algorithm can affect the properties of the graph.

In the commercial search engine that we used to build the recommendation click graph, there are at most 10 recommended queries for each input query. However, the query recommendation algorithm allows the related queries to be updated, and the out-degree may be greater than 10. In the graph for our experiment, the largest out-degree was 391, and there were 254,639 queries that had an out-degree greater than 10. In other search engines, the strategies for updating query recommendations might be different; thus, the distribution of the vertices' out-degrees might be different. In our work, we considered the out-degree as a representation of query ambiguity, and the recommendation algorithm can affect our judgment of query ambiguity. However, it is reasonable to believe that frequent changes in recommended queries imply that the source query is complex and unclear. Therefore, our methods are applicable in different search engines.

In this paper, we noted that the query recommendation click log contains a large volume of information about user search intent and query ambiguity. We proposed a recommendation click graph constructed from the recommendation click log. Our analysis showed that the properties of the recommendation click graph are similar to traditional web graphs. Furthermore, the edges in both web graphs and query graphs have the meaning of "like" or "recommend". Therefore, it is reasonable to apply well-used link analysis algorithms to the recommendation click graph. In this way, we can improve search performance by mining the recommendation click graph to learn more about users' behaviors and intents. We have applied the HITS algorithm on a query's local subgraph to select reliable recommended queries. These related queries can be used to improve the diversity and performance of the query. We have applied the inverse PageRank algorithm to a recommendation click graph to evaluate query ambiguity. The results showed that the inverse PageRank values reflect the query ambiguity. This result was confirmed by both annotation and query length statistics.

An important direction for future work is to analyze the recommendation click graph to learn users' search intents. Furthermore, an advanced ranking algorithm can be developed to improve search results using query recommendations.

References

1. Kleinberg, J.M.: Authoritative sources in a hyperlinked environment. J. ACM 46, 604–632 (1999)
2. Brin, S., Page, L.: The anatomy of a large-scale hypertextual web search engine. Computer Networks and ISDN Systems 30(1-7), 107–117 (1998); Proceedings of the Seventh International World Wide Web Conference
3. Page, L., Brin, S., Motwani, R., Winograd, T.: The pagerank citation ranking: Bringing order to the web (1998)
4. Gyöngyi, Z., Garcia-Molina, H., Pedersen, J.: Combating web spam with trustrank. In: Proceedings of the Thirtieth International Conference on Very Large Data Bases, VLDB 2004, vol. 30, pp. 576–587. VLDB Endowment (2004)

5. Baeza-Yates, R.: Graphs from Search Engine Queries. In: van Leeuwen, J., Italiano, G.F., van der Hoek, W., Meinel, C., Sack, H., Plášil, F. (eds.) SOFSEM 2007. LNCS, vol. 4362, pp. 1–8. Springer, Heidelberg (2007), http://dx.doi.org/10.1007/978-3-540-69507-3_1
6. Baeza-Yates, R., Tiberi, A.: Extracting semantic relations from query logs. In: Proceedings of the 13th ACM SIGKDD International Conference on Knowledge Discovery and Data Mining, KDD 2007, pp. 76–85. ACM, New York (2007)
7. Boldi, P., Bonchi, F., Castillo, C., Donato, D., Gionis, A., Vigna, S.: The query-flow graph: model and applications. In: Proceedings of CIKM 2008 (2008)
8. Boldi, P., Bonchi, F., Castillo, C., Donato, D., Vigna, S.: Query suggestions using query-flow graphs. In: Proceedings of the 2009 Workshop on Web Search Click Data, WSCD 2009, pp. 56–63. ACM, New York (2009)
9. Bai, L., Guo, J., Cheng, X.: Query Recommendation by Modelling the Query-Flow Graph. In: Salem, M.V.M., Shaalan, K., Oroumchian, F., Shakery, A., Khelalfa, H. (eds.) AIRS 2011. LNCS, vol. 7097, pp. 137–146. Springer, Heidelberg (2011), http://dx.doi.org/10.1007/978-3-642-25631-8_13
10. Zaïane, O.R., Strilets, A.: Finding Similar Queries to Satisfy Searches Based on Query Traces. In: Bruel, J.-M., Bellahsène, Z. (eds.) OOIS 2002. LNCS, vol. 2426, pp. 207–216. Springer, Heidelberg (2002), http://dx.doi.org/10.1007/3-540-46105-1_24
11. Baeza-Yates, R., Hurtado, C., Mendoza, M.: Query Recommendation Using Query Logs in Search Engines. In: Lindner, W., Fischer, F., Türker, C., Tzitzikas, Y., Vakali, A.I. (eds.) EDBT 2004. LNCS, vol. 3268, pp. 588–596. Springer, Heidelberg (2004), http://dx.doi.org/10.1007/978-3-540-30192-9_58
12. Yan, X., Guo, J., Cheng, X.: Context-aware query recommendation by learning high-order relation in query logs. In: Proceedings of CIKM 2011 (2011)
13. Szpektor, I., Gionis, A., Maarek, Y.: Improving recommendation for long-tail queries via templates. In: Proceedings of the 20th International Conference on World Wide Web, WWW 2011, pp. 47–56. ACM, New York (2011)
14. Ma, H., Yang, H., King, I., Lyu, M.R.: Learning latent semantic relations from clickthrough data for query suggestion. In: Proceeding of CIKM 2008 (2008)
15. Mei, Q., Zhou, D., Church, K.: Query suggestion using hitting time. In: Proceeding of CIKM 2008 (2008)
16. Kelly, D., Cushing, A., Dostert, M., Niu, X., Gyllstrom, K.: Effects of popularity and quality on the usage of query suggestions during information search. In: Proceedings of the 28th International Conference on Human Factors in Computing Systems, CHI 2010, pp. 45–54. ACM, New York (2010)
17. Song, R., Luo, Z., Wen, J.R., Yu, Y., Hon, H.W.: Identifying ambiguous queries in web search. In: Proceedings of the 16th International Conference on World Wide Web, WWW 2007, pp. 1169–1170. ACM, New York (2007)
18. He, X., Jhala, P.: Regularized query classification using search click information. Pattern Recognition 41(7), 2283–2288 (2008)
19. Veilumuthu, A., Ramachandran, P.: Intent based clustering of search engine query log. In: Proceedings of the Fifth Annual IEEE International Conference on Automation Science and Engineering, CASE 2009, pp. 647–652. IEEE Press, Piscataway (2009)
20. Jansen, B.J., Spink, A., Bateman, J., Saracevic, T.: Real life information retrieval: a study of user queries on the web. SIGIR Forum 32, 5–17 (1998)
21. Fleiss, J.L.: Measuring nominal scale agreement among many raters. Psychological Bulletin 76(5), 378–382 (1971)

A Linked Data Generation Method for Academic Conference Websites

Peng Wang[1], Mingqi Zhou[1], Xiang Zhang[1], and Fengbo Zhou[2]

[1] School of Computer Science and Engineering, Southeast University, Nanjing, China
[2] Focus Technology Co., Ltd, Nanjing, China
{pwang,x.zhang}seu.edu.cn, zhoufengbo@made-in-china.com

Abstract. This paper proposes an automatic method for extracting information from academic conference Web pages, and organizes these information as ontologies, then matches these ontologies to the academic linked data. The main contributions include: (1) A page segmentation algorithm is proposed to divide conference Web pages into text blocks. (2) According to vision, key words and other text features, all text blocks are classified as 10 categories using bayes network model. The context information of text blocks are introduced to repair the initial classified results, which are improved to 96% precision and 98% recall. (3) An ontology is generated for each conference website, then all ontologies are matched as an academic linked data.

Keywords: Web information extraction, Ontology, Linked data.

1 Introduction

With the popularity of semantic Web technologies and the emergence of intelligent applications such as semantic search, more and more plain or semi-structured Web data is need to be reorganized as semantic data, which is the foundation of many intelligent applications. Linked data is such large scale semantic data. Recently, more and more linked data such as DBpedia [1], Freebase and Google knowledge graph is used in many fields including knowledge engineering, machine translation, social computing and information retrieval. Academic linked data is important for academic social network analysis and mining. However, current academic linked data is based on database like DBLP and mainly describe paper publication information. Therefore, academic activity knowledge are not included by current academic linked data. Academic conferences websites not only contain paper information, but also contain many academic activity information including research topic, conference time, location, participants, awards, and so on. Obtaining such information is not only useful for predicting research trends and analyzing academic social network, but also is the important supplement to current academic linked data. Since academic conferences Web pages are usually semi-structured and content are diversity, there is no effective way to automatically find, extract and organize these academic information to linked data.

To generate linked data from semi-structured pages, it usually needs three phases: Web information extraction, ontology generation and linked data construction. Web

M. Zhou et al. (Eds.): NLPCC 2012, CCIS 333, pp. 296–307, 2012.

information extraction is a classical problem [1-3], which aims at identifying interested information from unstructured or semi-structured data in Web pages, and translates it to into a semantic clearer structure such as XML and domain ontology. Although academic conference Web pages usually have strict layout and content description, there is no a fixed template for all conference Web pages to follow. An ontology formally represents knowledge as a set of concepts within a domain, and the relationships among those concepts [4]. However, generating ontology is a challenge [5-6]. Linked data is a way to employ ontology languages such as RDF to describe and share knowledge on the Web [7-9]. More and more linked data is generated in recent years, and it contains the knowledge about geographic information, life science, Wikipedia data, government information, images, and so on. Linked data is also the foundation of many intelligent applications such as semantic search and social network.

In summary, this paper has following contributors: (1) We propose a new page segmentation algorithm, which use DOM tree to compensate the information loss of classical vision-based segmentation algorithm VIPS; (2) We transform the conference Web information extraction problem into a classification problem, and classify text blocks as pre-defined categories according to vision, key words, text and content information; The initial classification results are improved by post-processing. Finally, academic information is extracted from the classified text blocks. (3) A global ontology is used to describe the background domain knowledge, and then the extracted academic information of each website is organized as local ontologies. Finally, academic linked data is generated by matching local ontologies. Our experimental results on the real world datasets show that the proposed method is highly effective and efficient for extracting academic information from conference Web pages and generating high quality academic linked data.

2   Page Segmentation

To extract the academic information, we first segment Web pages into blocks by VIPS[10], which is a popular vision-based page segmentation algorithm. VIPS can use Web page structures and some vision features, such as background color, text font, text size and distance between text blocks, to segment a Web page. These text blocks can be constructed as a vision tree, which assures that all leaf nodes only contain text information. VIPS can obtain good segmentation results for most Web pages, but we find it will lose important information when deal with some Web pages. It is caused by the reason that VIPS algorithm is only based on vision features of page elements, so it would ignore blocks whose display is inconsistent. Therefore, we introduce DOM-based analysis to improve VIPS segmentation results, especially finding missed text blocks.

First, we need to obtain the basic vision semantic blocks by analyzing DOM tree of Web pages. A vision semantic block is a text block with independent meaning. A lot of blank nodes are removed from HTML tags. Then we traverse DOM tree to extract vision semantic blocks. A vision semantic block is between two newline tags such as <br/> and only contains style tags and texts.

Algorithm 1 shows the detail of generating the VIPS complete tree. Let SB be vision semantic block, LN be layout node of vision tree generated by VIPS, and DN be data node. This algorithm includes three steps: (1) It finds a SB by traverse LN to search matched layout nodes; (2) If it finds a matched layout node, then this node is also a vision semantic block; (3) If it does not find a matched layout node, then add this SB into the vision tree. This algorithm not only assures that there is no information loss, but also preserves the structure of vision tree. Fig. 3 shows the part of VIPS complete tree for bottom part of AAAI2010 main page. As vision tree shows, VIPS only extracts the text with bold font. It is not the result we expect. After the processing of Algorithm 1, new semantic blocks are added to the vision tree, which is the complete tree with correct text blocks.

Algorithm 1. Generating VIPS complete tree algorithm
Input: \<LayoutNode,DataNode> LNDN[], VIPS result PN
Output: a VIPS complete tree T

1	**begin**
2	**for** (PN.children[i] in PN.children[])
3	**if** (LNDN[] has key PN.children[i])
4	add LNDN[PN.children[i]] to T
5	**else**
6	add new DataNode(PN.children[i]) to T
7	LN_saved[].add(PN.children[i])
8	**end**
9	**while** (LN_saved[] is not empty) {
10	currentLN = LN_saved[0]
11	LN_saved[].remove(0)
12	currentDN = LNDN[currentLN]
13	**for** (currentLN.children[i] in currentLN.children[])
14	**if** (LNDN[] has key currentLN.children[i])
15	add LNDN[currentLN.children[i]] to T
16	**else**
17	add new DataNode(currentLN.children[i]) to T
18	LN_saved[].push(currentLN.children[i])
19	**end**
20	**end**
21	**end**

Since some blocks such as navigation, copyright and advertisement do not contains the academic information. We regard these blocks as noise, which should be removed from VIPS complete tree. The noise removing process uses some vision features[11]. (1) **Position features** include block position in horizontal and vertical on page and ratio of block area to page area. (2) **Layout features** include alignment of blocks, whether neighbor blocks are overlapped or adjacent. (3) **Appearance features** include size font, image size, and font of link. (4) **Content features** include common words of blocks and special order of some words. According to these vision features, we can remove noise nodes from VIPS complete tree.

3   Text Blocks Classification

The academic information of a specific conference is distributed within a set of pages. For instance, the *Overview* page of the conference Web site usually contains the conference name, time, and location information, and a *Call for Papers* page usually contains topics of interest and submission information. In general, we are primarily concerned with five types of academic information on a conference website: (1) *Information about conference date*: conference begin and end date, submission deadline, notification date of accepted papers, and so on. (2) *Information about conference research topics*: call for papers(or workshops/research papers/ industrial papers), topics of interests, sessions, tracks and so on. (3) *Information about related people and institute*: organizers, program committee, authors, companies, universities, countries and so on. (4) *Information about location*: conference location, hotel, city and country.   (5) *Information about papers*: title, authors of papers.

We divide all text blocks into 10 categories as Table 1 shows: (1)**DI**: It describes date information; (2)**PI**: It describes location information; (3)**AR**: It refers to top level information such as research area; (4)**TO**: It refers to research topics, and a AR block may have some corresponding TO blocks; (5)**PO**: It describes the role of people in conference such as Speaker and Chair. (6)**PE**: It refers to information of a person; (7)**PA**: It is the information about papers; (8)**CO**: It refers the blocks which is combined by the above 7 categories blocks; (9)**R**: It refers to the interested blocks but not belong to any categories; (10)**N**: It refers to the blocks not only belong to any categories but also not related to academic information. Fig. 4 shows each category and corresponding examples.

Table 1. Categories of text blocks

	Category	Description
Date	DI(dateItem)	Dates about conference events
Location	PI(placeItem)	Location function and address
Research	AR(area)	Research area in high level
	TO(topic)	Research topic in each area
People	PO(position)	Positions of participants such as *Speaker*, *Chair* and *Co-Chair*
	PE(peopleItem)	People names and institutions
Paper	PA(paper)	Paper type, title and authors
Other	CO(collection)	Set of some above blocks, such as DI+PI means that it contains date and location. For example, a PI+DI in AAAI-11page: "AAAI is pleased to announce that the Twenty-Fifth Conference on Artificial Intelligence (AAAI-11) will be held in San Francisco, California at the Hyatt Regency San Francisco, from August 7–11, 2011."
	R(related)	Not belong to above 8 categories, but contains useful information, such as workshop information.
	N(notRelated)	Not belong to above 8 categories and does not contain useful information

According to these categories, we can select some features to measure a given text blocks. We use vectors as Table 2 shows to describe each blocks. For a text block, we construct its features according to vision, key words and text content information. For example, given a text block: "Paper Submission Due: **Friday, May 6, 2011 (23:59 UTC - 11)**" and its HTML source code: *<li> Paper Submission Due: Friday, May 6, 2011 (23:59 UTC - 11)</li>*, its feature can be constructed as:

(1) **Vision features**: isTitle=false, isHeader =false, startWithLi=true, left=(280-0)/950=0.3 (page width:950, left margin: 0, text left margin:280), with=640/950=0.7 (text width: 640);

(2) **Key word features**: nearestTitle=DI (its nearest and isTitle=true blocks is about date information), dateNum=2 (it contains 2 date words: Submission and Due), paperTypeNum=1 (it contains 1 key word about paper: Paper);

(3) **Text content features**: fontSize=0, fontWeight=0, textLength=58, textLink=0, wordNum=11, nameNum=5, wordToName=11/5=2.2.

There are many famous existing classification algorithms such as C4.5[8], K-Nearest Neighbors (kNN)[9] and Bayes Network[10]. C4.5 and Bayesian Network are the most widely used classifier models. After comparing the two classifier models, we choose bayesian network model to solve the text blocks classifier problem.

Table 2. Feature vectors of text blocks

Vector	Description	Value
isHeader	Whether the biggest font size	bool
isTitle	Whether the title font size	bool
nearestTitle	Type of the nearest title block	int
textLength	Length of text block	int
fontSizeToAverage	Average font size	int
fontWeightToAverage	Average font weight	int
startWithLi	Whether start with <li>	bool
dateTypeNum	Number of key words about date type, such as *deadline*	int
dateNum	Number of key words about date, such as *January*	int
placeTypeNum	Number of key words about location type, such as *Place*	int
placeNum	Number of key words about location, such as *Italy*	int
areaNum	Number of key words about research area	int
nameNum	Number of names	int
institutionNum	Number of institutions	int
positionNum	Number of positions	int
authorNum	Number of authors	int
abstractTypeNum	Number of key words about abstract	int
paperTypeNum	Number of key words about paper type	int
wordNum	Number of words of text blocks	int
wordToName	Ratio of number of words to number of names	double
linkTotext	Ratio of length of link to length of blocks	double
left	Ratio of left margin to page width	double
width	Ratio of block width to page width	double

The classified results can be improved by post-processing, which includes repairing wrong classified results and adding missed classified results. The text blocks with wrong classification can be determined by two sides:

(1) A block has special features but cannot be classified correctly. For example, given text block *"Camera Ready Papers Due: Thursday, August 11, 2011"*, which have typical DI features, namely, *dateNum=1, dateTypeNum=1, isDateArea*=true

and *isPreviousDate* = true. However, this block is classified as Related. For this situation, it can be repaired by identify some typical combination of features. This method is suitable for text blocks with clear features, such as DI, TO, PO and PE.

(2) A text block is classified as a category but it does not contain corresponding features. For example, text blocks about submission instruction would be classified as CO. Although it contains a lot of words, it usually does not contain any people name, date or location. Therefore, we can check its feature values *wordToName*, *dateNum*, *dateTypeNum* and *placeNum* to determine whether it is a CO category. According to this way, we can repair some wrong classifications.

Some text blocks are classified as R category, and they have useful information, but their categories are not clear. These blocks should be checked further. Therefore, we use context feature to determine the blocks with R category. The context feature consists of 11 boolean values: *isDateArea, isPlaceArea, isTopicArea, isPeopleArea, isPaperArea, isPreviousDate, isPreviousPlace, isPreviousTopic, isPreviousPeople, isPreviousPaper* and *isVisuallySame*. We propose some rules to add text blocks without clear classification.

Rule 1: DateItem complete rule: A DI text block usually appears as three situations: (1) It appears as page title with bold and big font size; (2) It appears with other DI text blocks; (3) It appears separately. Since a DI block is very dependent to key words, for any situation, key words and other features should be considered.

For situation (1), we can use a simple rule to detect: *dateNum*>0 && *wordNum*<=5 && *isTitle*=ture.

For situation (2), the corresponding rule is : (*isPreviousDate* ||*isDateArea*) && *isVisuallySame* && *isDateArea* && *index-areaIndex*==1 && *isPreviousDate* && *isNextDate* && *isDateArea* && *isPreviousDate* && (*dateNum*>0 || *dateTypeNum*>0).

For situation (3), the rule is *startWithLi* && (*dateNum*>0 || *dateTypeNum*>0) && *wordNum*<= DATE_ITEM_WORD_NUM.

Rule 2: PlaceItem complete rule: PI classification usually has high precision. Some key words and text content features can determine whether a R block is a missed PI block. The rule is: *placeNum*>1 && *wordNum*<PLACE_WORD_NUM.

Rule 3: Area complete rule: A AR text block usually has big font size. Therefore, its complete rule is *isHeader*=true.

Rule 4: Topic complete rule: A TO text block has typical context features. It begins with a <li> tag, and if its neighbor block is TO, it is possible TO block too. The complete rule is: (*isTopicArea* || *isPreviousTopic*) && (*isVisuallySame*) && (*isTopicArea*) && (*index-areaIndex*=1) && *startWithLi*.

Rule 5: Position complete rule: A PO text block usually has big font size and few words, and it is also has key words about position. The complete rule is *isTitle* && *wordNum* < POSITION_WORD_NUM && *positionNum* > 0.

Rule 6: PeopleItem complete rule: A PE block should consider its context. Usually, it follows PO blocks. Some PE blocks begin with <li> tag, and some PE blocks contain key words about universities or companies. Most PE blocks have capital letters and short content. The complete rule is: (*isPeopleArea*||*isPreviousPeople*) && *isVisuallySame* && *isPeopleArea* && *index-areaIndex*=1 && *startWithLi* && *isPreviousPeople* && *institutionNum*>0 && *wordToName*< PEOPLE_WORD_TO_NAME && *wordNum* < PEOPLE_WORD_NUM.

Rule 7: Paper complete rule: A PA block usually begins with <li>, and its list is similar to TO blocks. The corresponding complete rule is: (*isPaperArea*||*isPreviousPaper*) && *isVisuallySame* && *nameNum*> TITLE_UPPER_WORD_NUM && *startWithLi* &&

nameNum>TITLE_UPPER_WORD_NUM && *isPaperArea* && *index-areaIndex*=1 && *nameNum*> TITLE_UPPER_WORD_NUM.

After the post-processing, initial classification results will be improved greatly. For the reason that classified text blocks describe a special information, these blocks are the academic information we want to extract. Namely, this paper solves an information extraction problem by transforming it into a text block classification problem.

4   Ontology Generation

To obtain the academic linked data, we need to organize the extracted academic information. Therefore, we first manually build a global ontology as background knowledge of academic domain, then automatically construct local ontologies for each conference website.

After investigating a lot of conference websites and some ontologies related to academic domain, we manually construct a global ontology for describing the knowledge of academic conference. The global ontology contains 97 concepts and 27 properties. Fig. 1 shows part of global ontology. Besides the hierarchy, concepts can be related by properties. For example, property *hasAuthor* can link two concepts *Paper* and *Author*, which are domain and range of *hasAuthor*. Global ontology has not instances, and it is stored as an ontology language RDF file.

For a local ontology, its concepts and properties are contained in global ontology. We don't consider the new knowledge which is not described in global ontology. Therefore, for a extracted academic information, it is either a concept or an instance of local ontology. However, not all extracted information can be translated to concepts or instances directly. Therefore, the concepts and instances should be determined by the context of the academic information. For example, a paper information

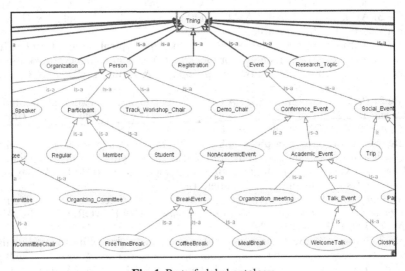

Fig. 1. Part of global ontology

usually appears in PA text blocks and contains title and authors, so it is an instance of concept *Paper*, all authors are instances of concept *Author*, titles will be the property values, and authors will be the values of *hasAuthor*. Through the above process, we can generate a local ontology for each conference website.

5   Linked Data Generation

In order to link all isolate local ontologies as the academic linked data, we need to match these ontologies. The linguistic-based method is a popular ontology matching techniques[12-13]. For the reason that text in ontology can describes some semantics, the linguistic-based matching method can discover matching results by calculating similarities between text documents For an academic conference local ontology, it contain regular and abundant text, therefore, the linguistic-based method is suitable. We use the ontology matching API provided by ontology matching system Lily [13] to discover matching results between local ontologies. Lily is an excellent matching system and can produce high quality matching results.

Our ontology matching strategy is calculating matches for each two ontologies, then associate all ontologies   into the linked data by these matches. This strategy has the benefit of handling a number of generated local ontologies, but its disadvantage is consuming a lot of time for matching many ontologies. Fig. 2 shows part of linked data for three conferences. If two instances are matched, they can be combined in the linked data graph.

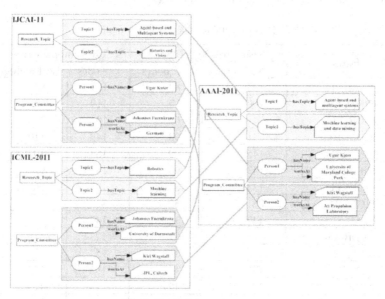

Fig. 2. Part of the linked data

6   Experiments

6.1   System Implementation and Dataset

The system is mainly implemented in Java, and the Web page segmentation module is implemented in C#. We also use Weka, an open-source machine learning library, to classify text blocks. Our experimental results are obtained on a PC with 2.40GHz CPU, 2GB RAM and Windows 7.

We collect 50 academic conference Web sites in computers science field, which has 283 different Web pages and 10028 labeled text blocks. In order to evaluate our approach, 10 students manually tag all the text blocks as reference results. The results are saved in CSV files.

We randomly select 10 sites which contain 62 pages as training dataset for constructing bayes network model. Other 40 conference Websites are used as test dataset. We use Precision, Recall and F1-Measure as criteria to measure the system performance.

6.2   Experimental Results and Analysis

First experiment is verifying the complete tree. Table 3 shows the vision tree results generated by VIPS and the complete tree results generated by our new algorithm on 15 conference websites. We can see that the complete trees have more leaf nodes than vision trees. It means our algorithm can find more text blocks than VIPS.

The experimental results of removing noise blocks are given in Table 4. We can observe some facts: (1) There are many noise blocks in the complete tree. In some websites, almost half of all blocks are noise blocks. (2) Our removing noise method can

Table 3. Experimental results of VIPS complete tree

Websites	Vision tree by VIPS		VIPS complete tree	
	Nodes	Leaf nodes	Nodes	Leaf nodes
AAAI-10	106	82	109	85
CIKM-11	109	80	119	90
ICDE-10	94	69	101	76
ICDM-10	131	98	143	110
ICSE-11	145	99	153	107
INFOCOM-10	143	93	143	93
SIGIR-11	133	86	133	86
SIGMOD-10	86	59	86	59
SOSP-11	147	101	147	101
VLDB-10	117	81	123	87
AAAI-11	153	108	157	112
ACL-11	178	137	193	152
AIDE-11	170	121	174	125
ASAP-10	50	31	59	40
ASPLOS-11	60	39	76	55

Table 4. Experimental results of removing noise from VIPS complete tree

Websites	Initial complete tree		Remove noise complete tree		Removed node /Before removed	
	Nodes	Leaf nodes	Nodes	Leaf nodes	Nodes	Leaf nodes
AAAI-10	109	85	45	30	0.59	0.65
CIKM-11	119	90	64	32	0.46	0.64
ICDE-10	101	76	46	22	0.54	0.71
ICDM-10	143	110	105	70	0.27	0.36
ICSE-11	153	107	80	37	0.48	0.65
INFOCOM-10	143	93	103	69	0.28	0.26
SIGIR-11	133	86	75	42	0.44	0.51
SIGMOD-10	86	59	49	27	0.43	0.54
SOSP-11	147	101	125	85	0.15	0.16
VLDB-10	123	87	42	17	0.66	0.80
AAAI-11	157	112	102	68	0.35	0.39
ACL-11	193	152	158	110	0.18	0.28
AIDE-11	174	125	108	71	0.38	0.43
ASAP-10	59	40	46	17	0.22	0.58
ASPLOS-11	76	55	39	17	0.49	0.69
Avg.					**0.39**	**0.51**

remove average 39% noise nodes and 51% noise leaf nodes. Therefore, it will reduce the number of nodes should be processed in extraction and improve the efficiency.

The second experiment is the comparison between initial classification results and the results after post-processing. The results are obtained on 20 randomly websites. Table 5 evaluates all the classification results. We have two conclusions: (1) The initial classification results only have average 0.75 precision, 0.67 recall and 0.68 F1-measure. After post-processing, the classification results are improved to average 0.96

Table 5. Experimental results of text blocks classification

Category	Initial classification			Post-processing		
	Precision	Recall	F1	Precision	Recall	F1
DI	0.95	0.75	0.84	0.96	0.99	0.98
AR	0.84	0.91	0.87	0.92	0.98	0.95
TO	0.90	0.41	0.57	0.99	0.99	0.99
PO	0.80	0.69	0.74	0.99	0.98	0.99
PE	0.85	0.60	0.71	0.99	0.99	0.99
PI	0.79	0.72	0.75	0.97	0.97	0.97
CO	0.35	0.80	0.49	0.91	0.95	0.93
PA	0.50	0.50	0.50	1.00	1.00	1.00
Avg.	0.75	0.67	0.68	**0.96**	**0.98**	**0.97**

precision, 0.98 recall and 0.97 F1-measure. Therefore, the post-processing key roles in academic information extraction. (2) Some text blocks like DI, PO, PE and TO, which have clear vision and text content features, have better classification results. The average F1-measure on these blocks is 0.99.

We selected 5 websites: AAAI-11, ASPLOS-11, NIPS-11, ICPR-11 and PKDD-11, then analyze the generated ontologies. Table 6 shows the statistics of some kinds of generated ontology information. We can see that these ontologies have average 0.97 precision, 0.99 recall and 0.98 F1-measure. Therefore, our method can generate high quality academic ontologies for conference websites.

Finally, we match the 3109 generated ontologies, then integrate them as a linked data.

Table 6. Statistics of generated academic ontologies for conferences

websites		AR	DI	PI	PE	TO	CO
AAAI-11	C	7	58	2	51	81	0
	R	0	0	1	1	0	0
	M	0	0	0	3	0	0
ASPLOS-11	C	2	23	7	15	11	2
	R	1	0	0	0	0	0
	M	0	1	0	0	0	0
ICPR-11	C	1	18	0	0	24	0
	R	0	0	0	0	0	0
	M	0	1	0	0	0	0
NIPS-11	C	1	16	0	58	10	0
	R	0	0	0	0	0	0
	M	0	0	0	4	0	0
PKDD-11	C	1	26	1	26	0	0
	R	0	0	0	0	0	0
	M	0	1	0	2	0	0
Total	C	12	141	10	150	126	2
	R	1	0	1	1	0	0
	M	0	3	0	9	0	0
	Precision	0.92	1.00	0.91	0.99	1.00	1.00
	Recall	1.00	0.98	1.00	0.94	1.00	1.00
	F-measure	0.96	0.99	0.95	0.97	1.00	1.00

7   Conclusions

This paper addresses the problem of extracting academic information from conference Web pages, then organizing academic information as ontologies and finally generating academic linked data by matching these ontologies. An new approach to extract academic information is proposed. A global ontology is used to describe the background domain knowledge, and then the extracted academic information of each website is organized as local ontologies. Finally, academic linked data is generated by matching local ontologies

Acknowledgments. This work is supported by the NSF of China (61003156 and 61003055) and the Natural Science Foundation of Jiangsu Province (BK2009136 and BK2011335).

References

1. Chang, C.-H., Kayed, M., Girgis, M.R., Shaalan, K.: A Survey of Web Information Extraction Systems. IEEE Transactions on Knowledge and Data Engineering 18(10), 1411–1428 (2006)
2. Hammer, J., Mchugh, J., Garcia-molina, H.: Semistructured data: the TSIMMIS experience. In: Proceedings of the 1st East-European Symposium on Advances in Databases and Information Systems (ADBIS 1997), St. Petersburg, Rusia (1997)
3. Arocena, G.O., Mendelzon, A.O.: WebOQL: Restructuring documents, databases, and Webs. In: Proceedings of the 14th IEEE International Conference on Data Engineering (ICDE 1998), Orlando, Florida, USA (1998)
4. Gruber, T.R.: Towards Principles for the Design of Ontologies Used for Knowledge Sharing. International Journal of Human Computer Studies (43), 907–928 (1995)
5. Maedche, A., Staab, S.: Ontology Learning for the Semantic Web. IEEE Intelligent Systems 16(2), 72–79 (2001)
6. Suryanto, H., Compton, P.: Discovery of Ontologies from Knowledge Bases. In: Proceedings of the First International Conference on Knowledge Capture (2001)
7. Bizer, C., Heath, T., Berners-Lee, T.: Linked Data-The Story So Far. International Journal Semantic Web and Information System 5(3), 1–22 (2009)
8. Bizer, C.: The Emerging Web of Linked Data. IEEE Intelligent Systems 24(5), 87–92 (2009)
9. Bizera, C., Lehmannb, J., Kobilarova, G., et al.: DBpedia - A crystallization point for the Web of Data. Journal of Web Semantics 7, 154–165 (2009)
10. Cai, D., Yu, S., Wen, J.-R., Ma, W.-Y.: VIPS: a Vision-based Page Segmentation Algorithm. Microsoft Technical Report (2003)
11. Liu, W., Meng, X., Meng, W.: ViDE: A Vision-Based Approach for Deep Web Data Extraction. IEEE Transactions on Knowledge and Data Engineering 22(3), 447–460 (2010)
12. Shvaiko, P., Euzenat, J.: A Survey of Schema-Based Matching Approaches. In: Spaccapietra, S. (ed.) Journal on Data Semantics IV. LNCS, vol. 3730, pp. 146–171. Springer, Heidelberg (2005)
13. Kalfoglou, Y., Schorlemmer, M.: Ontology mapping: the state of the art. The Knowledge Engineering Review 18(1), 1–31 (2003)
14. Wang, P., Xu, B.: Lily: ontology alignment results for OAEI 2009. In: The 4th International Workshop on Ontology Matching (OM 2009), Washington DC, USA (October 25, 2009)

Author Index

Printed in the United States
by Baker & Taylor Publisher Services